WINGS OF FAME™

Aerospace Publishing Ltd
AIRtime Publishing Inc.

Published quarterly by
Aerospace Publishing Ltd
179 Dalling Road
London W6 0ES
UK

ISSN 1361-2034
Aerospace ISBN 1 86184 041 1 (softback)
1 86184 042 X (hardback)
AIRtime ISBN 1-880588-23-4

Published under licence in USA and Canada by AIRtime Publishing Inc., 10 Bay Street, Westport, CT 06880, USA

Origination by
Chroma Graphics, Singapore
Printed by
Officine Grafiche DeAgostini, Novara, Italy

The *Wings of Fame* web site, containing details of every issue of *Wings of Fame*, subscription information and details of other products, can be found at:

http://www.wingsoffame.com

For their assistance in the preparation of this volume of *Wings of Fame*, the authors and publishers gratefully acknowledge the assistance of the following:

For their help with the F-102 article: Marty J. Isham, widely recognised as the leading authority on Air Defense Command and especially to Ray Wagner and A. J. Lutz of the San Diego Aerospace Museum and to Dr. Rob Young, historian of the National Air Intelligence Center, Wright-Patterson AFB, Ohio. Thanks also to Terry Panopalis, Norman Taylor, Bulent Yilmazer and these F-102 pilots: Robert Archibald, Harold Blackshear, Bill Krawski, Malcolm McDaniel, Roger Pile, Charles Quist, and to F-102 maintainer Clem Koselke

Ian Brodie and Ewan Fallow at the New Zealand Fighter Pilots' Museum/Alpine Fighter Collection for their help with I-153 pictures and data

Brigadier Chevallier, Comodoro Nogueira, Comodoro Quelett, Comodoro Pastrán, Mayor Britos, Capitan Bano, Suboficial Auxiliar Piazza and Horacio J. Clariá for their cooperation and assistance with the FAA Canberra article

The *Air Combat* article on No. 101 Sqn, IDF/AF has been reviewed and approved by the Israeli Censor for publication.

The editors of WINGS OF FAME™ welcome photographs for possible publication, but cannot accept any responsibility for loss or damage to unsolicited material.

Wings of Fame™ is a registered trademark in the United States of America of AIRtime Publishing Inc.

Wings of Fame™ is published quarterly and is available by subscription and from many fine book and hobby stores.

SUBSCRIPTION AND BACK NUMBERS:

UK and World (except USA and Canada) write to:
Aerospace Publishing Ltd
FREEPOST
PO Box 2822
London
W6 0BR
UK
(No stamp required if posted in the UK)

USA and Canada, write to:
AIRtime Publishing Inc.
Subscription Dept
10 Bay Street
Westport
CT 06880, USA
(203) 838-7979
Toll-free order number in USA:
1 800 359-3003

Prevailing subscription rates are as follows:
Softbound edition for 1 year: $59.95
Softbound edition for 2 years: $112.00
Softbound back numbers (subject to availability) are $16.00 each, plus shipping and handling. All rates are for delivery within mainland USA, Alaska and Hawaii. Canadian and overseas prices available upon request. American Express, Discover Card, MasterCard and Visa accepted. When ordering please include card number, expiration date and signature.

WINGS OF FAME™

CONTENTS

Volume 17

They Also Served

Blackburn Firebrand & Firecrest

'If an aircraft looks right, it will fly right,' runs the oft repeated adage. Firebrand pilots would often repeat this little homily, usually adding that the Blackburn Firebrand looked like a battleship – but didn't fly quite as well as one! Arguably one of the ugliest aircraft ever to see service with the Fleet Air Arm, the Firebrand was slow to develop and when it finally did enter service the aircraft enjoyed only the briefest of front-line careers.

EK601 (background) and EK617 are early production Firebrand Mk IVs from the batch of 102 completed from May 1945. Most were delivered into storage and later converted to Mk V (and in some cases Mk 5A) standard.

Although remembered (when remembered at all!) as a barely successful, short-lived and little-produced torpedo-armed strike fighter, the Blackburn Firebrand was originally developed to meet a rather different and more important requirement. The official Specification N.11/40 which resulted in the Firebrand called for a short-range, cannon-armed carrierborne interceptor to replace the Blackburn Skua and Fairey Fulmar.

In the lead-up to World War II, the Fleet Air Arm still believed that fighters should be two-seaters (preferably with a power-operated gun turret), and that their primary roles would be to escort carrierborne bombers and strike aircraft, and to intercept long-range reconnaissance aircraft. In the event of an enemy attack against the carrier, many believed that the best place for the fighters would be 'below decks' to protect them from any flying shell splinters! It was optimistically expected that the fleet would be able to defend itself against air attack with its own guns, and that air attacks would be suicidal for the attacker.

Even before the Japanese air attack on the US Navy's Pacific Fleet at Pearl Harbor in December 1941, and the same month's loss of the British capital ships HMS *Repulse* and HMS *Prince of Wales* to Japanese air power, these confident expectations were being brushed aside, while German bombers and reconnaissance aircraft (let alone fighters) proved they could simply open their throttles and outrun aircraft like the Skua. This, however, was not difficult to do: with a top speed of only 225 mph (362 km/h), the Skua was slower even than the Gloster Gladiator biplane!

Specification N.8/39 issued in March 1939 failed to address the fundamental problem, but did at least outline a carrierborne fighter with a fixed forward-firing armament of four 20-mm cannon. Blackburn began preliminary work on this two-seat fighter specification, which was reduced to a single-seater when rewritten as N.11/40. This latter specification finally started to recognise some of what was needed, and called for 400-mph (644-km/h) performance, 4-hour endurance, an armament of four 20-mm cannon, and a single-seat configuration. While the formal responses to the specification progressed at peacetime pace, the situation at sea in the opening phases of World War II demanded a more urgent response, and the Supermarine Seafire was rushed into service as a development of the Spitfire.

But while the Spitfire was undergoing urgent

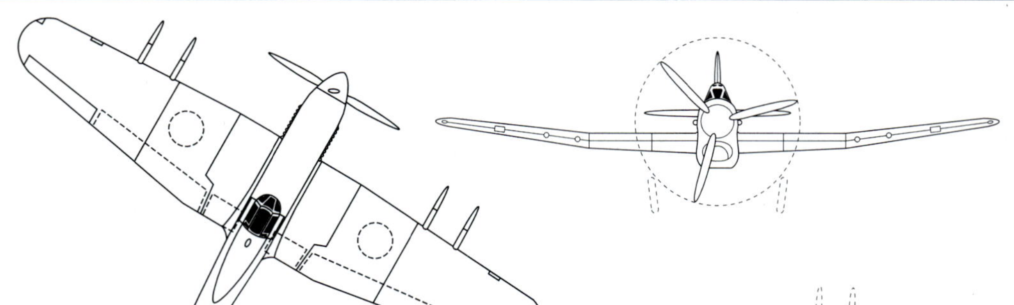

Hawker P.1009

Tendered in 1941, to Specification N.11/40, P.1009 was based on the Typhoon. For the carrier-based naval strike role the so-called 'Sea-phoon' would have carried additional fuel in long-span folding wings. If nothing else, the Typhoon would have allowed the pilot a better view than the Firebrand.

The Blackburn B-48, dubbed Firecrest by its manufacturer, was an attempt to improve the Firebrand's performance and, in particular, the view afforded the pilot. The latter was a major point of criticism in the Firebrand and was certainly considerably improved in the B-48. Unfortunately, overall performance was not.

modification for carrierborne operation, and while the Grumman F4F Wildcat (renamed by the British as the Martlet) was hurriedly acquired under the terms of the Lend-Lease Act, the Admiralty carefully examined Hawker's proposed P.1009 and Blackburn's B-37 to meet its specification, failing to realise that it had been rendered irrelevant. The P.1009 was a 'Fleet Fighter' variant of the Typhoon, sometimes referred to as the 'Sea-phoon', and would doubtless have made an equally poor fighter, whereas the B-37 was an all-new design, albeit one which also used the troubled Napier Sabre engine. Blackburn accordingly received a contract (Contract 156337/40) for three prototypes, the first of which (DD804) made its maiden flight on 27 February 1942. By this time the B-37 had already been named Firebrand. This maiden flight was made from Leconfield by Fight Lieutenant Arthur Thompson, since Blackburn's factory aerodrome at Brough was badly waterlogged, and since Leconfield offered better facilities and a longer runway. The aircraft was towed tail-first to Leconfield on its own mainwheels, just as the same company's Buccaneers would later be trucked from Brough to Holme on Spalding Moor for their first flights.

While never the 'handsome' or 'elegant' aircraft described by contemporary propaganda, the Firebrand did have a very purposeful aspect with its closely-cowled 2,305-hp (1719-kW) Napier Sabre III engine. This was an inline 'H' section 24-cylinder liquid-cooled monster of an engine, driving a massive de Havilland three-bladed propeller of the variable-pitch and constant-speed type, and relied for cooling on massive radiators housed behind huge intakes in the extended wing centre section. The forward fuselage was of circular section (this later making integration of the Centaurus easier) with a structure of tubular steel covered by enormous detachable panels. Behind the engine were the main and auxiliary self-sealing fuel tanks (with a total capacity of 239 Imp gal/1086.5 litres), after which came the cockpit and a transition to an oval-section stressed skin centre/rear fuselage of oval section.

The Firebrand's wing was built around a substantial two-spar centre section, to which were attached Botha-type outer panels, the latter being rigged with a dihedral of 5°. A heated, felt-lagged bay in the centre of each outer wing panel formed the gun bay, which was designed to accommodate a pair of 20-mm Hispano cannon with 200 rounds per gun. The wing was fitted with a combination of hydraulically operated Fowler and subsidiary flaps, which occupied the entire trailing edge from the end of the centre section out to the Frise ailerons. In planform, the wing had a straight, untapered centre section, with tapering outer panels and rounded tips. The main spars had forged steel fork-end fittings with heavy duty latch pins, whose removal allowed the outer wing panels to be manually swivelled, leading edge up, and then manually folded back to rest almost parallel to the fuselage sides. Removal or reinsertion of the locking pins was achieved by using a Skua-type crank and screwjack in each mainwheel well. This arrangement made the 'folded Firebrand' extremely narrow, without the height penalty that would have been imposed had the long-span outer wing panels folded conventionally upwards, and removed the need for a second fold.

'No Step'

The Firebrand had a conventional tail unit, although the singularly graceless fin and inset rudder were positioned well forward of the tailplane and elevators, to prevent blanking. The tailcone extended well aft, and housed the hydraulic gear for the arrester hook and for the

DD804, the Firebrand prototype, was to be the basis for a new fighter for the Fleet Air Arm when it took to the air in February 1942. It was a fast aircraft with excellent range, but agility was not a strongpoint and remained a source of weakness throughout the Firebrand's career.

Above: DD815, the third Firebrand, was delivered straight to A&AEE in September 1942 and was employed almost exclusively for armament trials.

Left: The second Firebrand, DD810, flew 4½ months after the first aircraft on 15 July 1942. Engaged in deck landing trials aboard* Illustrious *in early 1943, the aircraft was damaged in a force landing following engine failure on 20 February. The airframe was rebuilt as the TF.Mk II prototype and reserialled NV636, flying as such in March 1943. The first prototype had been unarmed; '810 had two 20-mm Hispano cannon installed, but a full complement of four cannon fairings!

fully retractable castoring tailwheel. The main landing gear units retracted inwards, and consisted of single wheels on conventional telescopic oleos, with cantilever axles. Fully enclosed when retracted, the main landing gear had angular doors with straight edges. One of these was virtually parallel to the ground when the aircraft was parked, and made a useful step for the ground crew. A junior stress engineer originally stressed the door accordingly, but was told to lighten it, in the expectation that the Royal Navy would simply paint 'No Step' on it instead. They never did, and generations of sailors used the door as a step without ill effect.

The second prototype (DD810) made its maiden flight on 15 July, and the third (DD815) followed on 15 September. Both were flown for these first flights by Thompson. Whereas the first aircraft had been a pure aerodynamic test aircraft, the later prototypes had some armament, DD810 having two of the planned four cannon installed (but with all four barrels!) together with racks for a 500-lb (227-kg) bomb below each wing. The second prototype was destined to become the first of the breed to land on a carrier, deploying to Macrahanish after hand-over to the Royal Navy on 11 October 1942, and deck landing trials were then undertaken aboard HMS *Illustrious*.

Despite its general air of clumsiness, the Firebrand did show some promise, and the engine installation was exceptionally clean and streamlined, though the bulky leading-edge radiators somewhat spoiled the aircraft's lines. The Firebrand did at least offer a range performance sufficient to open the possibility of intercepting enemy aircraft far out from the carrier. But this potential was overlaid by some serious problems – not least that the bulky Firebrand would never be able to cope with single-engined, land-based fighter opposition. The Firebrand was fast enough (though it would always fall far short of the 400 mph/644 km/h demanded) thanks to its powerful engine: the prototype demonstrated a speed of 330 mph (531 km/h) at 15,000 ft (4570 m) and achieved 344 mph (554 km/h) at 20,000 ft (6095 m). But it was a very heavy and large machine, with a weight almost twice that of the Martlet and a span of 50 ft (15.24 m) by comparison with the Spitfire's figure of slightly under 37 ft (11.28 m), and while its firepower was impressive its agility was decidedly lacking.

Catalogue of problems

The Firebrand prototype also demonstrated a veritable catalogue of 'minor' problems, including inadequate directional stability, over-balanced ailerons and severe distortion through the windscreen quarterlights. The aircraft swung markedly on take-off, and tended to float on landing, neither of these a characteristic promising for a machine intended for carrier use! The Firebrand was also difficult to service, with an engine change taking 24 man-hours, and folding the wings taking a six-man team some 10 minutes. US Navy contemporaries were beginning to feature powered wing-folding by this time. Despite its unsuitability for carrier use, the Firebrand was sent to sea, and the second prototype was briefly trialled aboard HMS *Illustrious*, as noted above. The aircraft subsequently flew into the overhead bucket system of a cement works when on a dead-stick approach to Brough and was virtually destroyed, though the pilot was uninjured.

By September 1942 the Seafire was in front-line service and the Martlet was an 'old hand', and it finally dawned on the Lords of the Admiralty that the Firebrand was an irrelevance. Having spent money on the Firebrand, however, their Lordships were unwilling simply to ditch the aircraft, and looked around for an alternative role in which the type could be gainfully employed. The answer they came up with was as a replacement for the Fairey Swordfish, many of which had actually been built under licence by Blackburn, and to supplement the Fairey Barracuda that was then entering service as a Swordfish replacement.

Traditional Fleet Air Arm TBR (Torpedo Bomber and Reconnaissance) or TSR (Torpedo Strike and Reconnaissance) aircraft were inevitably three-seaters, with the pilot augmented by a dedicated navigator/plotter and a radio-operator/gunner, but the Firebrand was seen as a fast torpedo dropper for use against the most heavily defended targets, perhaps operating in conjunction with the Barracuda, which would find the target and might itself attack to 'mop up' after the Firebrand. A fast torpedo delivery platform had become something of a 'holy grail' following the insane bravery of the Swordfish crews involved in the attack on the German ships KMS *Scharnhorst*, *Gneisenau* and *Prinz Eugen* as they made their 'Channel Dash' in February 1942.

Upper left: Production Firebrand F.Mk I DK367 was used by A&AEE Boscombe Down to test a rocket projectile installation.

Left: DK363, the first production F.Mk I, is seen here at Luton in 1944 during trials of a tropical intake and air cleaner. Note the intake under the aircraft's nose, which spoiled somewhat the lines of the closely-cowled Sabre powerplant.

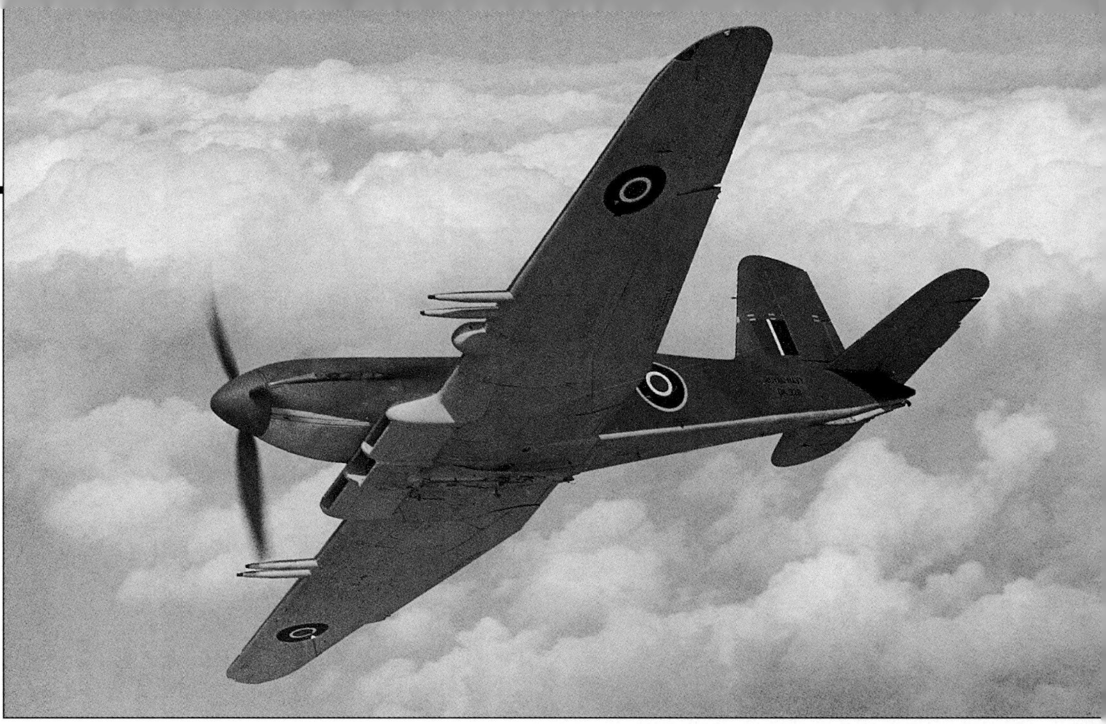

The first prototype was sent to Napier at Luton for various modifications, including a new 'power egg' type of powerplant installation, with the engine slung from forged light alloy engine bearers, though the switch of Sabre production to the Typhoon meant that only five of the new powerplants were completed. Meanwhile the wreckage of DD810 was rebuilt as NV636, the prototype Firebrand TF.Mk II, accommodating a single 18-in (457-mm) diameter torpedo below the centre section. The torpedo carrier had two positions, allowing the torpedo to adopt a nose-down, tail-up stance with the landing gear extended, then going 1o nose-up (the dropping position) with the landing gear retracted. The torpedo was fitted with a large Monoplane Air Tail Mk IV when carried by the Firebrand, this automatically being jettisoned as the torpedo hit the water. The centre section of NV636 was widened, increasing overall span from 50 ft (15.24 m) to 51 ft 3½ in (15.63 m). The aircraft first flew in its new guise on 31 March, 1943. The torpedo modifications had only a minor impact on performance, and NV636 was looped and rolled (a torpedo in place) in front of the Minister for Aircraft Production, Sir Stafford Cripps. By now the modified Firebrand was displaying much better handling characteristics, with little swing on take off, better stability and better ailerons. The aircraft still displayed an alarming trim change when the throttle was opened up after a simulated 'missed wire' and this was sufficient to render it potentially unacceptable for carrier use.

The Ministry steps in

It was then that the Ministry of Aircraft Production stepped in, insisting that the Sabre engine was more urgently required for the Typhoon (finding its feet as a fighter-bomber) than for what was clearly regarded outside the Admiralty as the 'hare-brained' Firebrand. But despite having been deprived of the Firebrand's planned role and intended powerplant, the Admiralty was not to be put off.

A new strike fighter requirement was formulated and Specification S.8/43 was issued to cover this. It was expected that this requirement would be met by a Firebrand powered by the 2,400-hp (1789-kW) Bristol Centaurus VII two-row, 18-cylinder radial engine driving a four-bladed propeller.

Fifty Sabre-engined Firebrand F.Mk I warplanes had already been ordered, however, and nine of these (DK363/371) were completed without provision for a torpedo and delivered for use as development aircraft for the planned production-standard, Centaurus-engined, torpedo-carrying variant. Five of the batch ended up with the Aircraft & Armament Experimental Establishment at Boscombe Down, and another was evaluated by the Royal Navy at Lee-on-Solent.

Above: The Firebrand was as imposing in the air as it was one the ground, though its streamlined appearance was spoiled somewhat by the large radiator and engine air intakes under its nose. This is DK378, the fifth production Mk II.

Right: NV636, the erstwhile DD815 and the first Mk II, is seen carrying an 18-in torpedo for its new role as a torpedo-fighter. Blackburn proposed a number of Sabre-engined Firebrand derivatives, including the B-41 single-seat fighter for the RAF, the B-42 with high-lift wing, and the B-43 twin-float seaplane fighter. All remained on the drawing board.

Even more astonishingly, 12 further aircraft (DK374/385) were built as Firebrand TF.Mk II machines to meet Specification S.8/43 with the Sabre engine and full torpedo-carrying capability. These aircraft had a neat torpedo camera fairing inboard of the innermost cannon on the port leading edge, a feature which would reappear on all subsequent aircraft, though surprisingly not on the prototype Firebrand TF.Mk III. Some of these Sabre-engined and torpedo-equipped aircraft went to the Torpedo Development Unit at Gosport and seven of the last eight eventually served with No. 708 Squadron at Lee-on-Solent. This formed on 2 October 1944 under the command of Lieutenant K. Lee-White as the Firebrand Tactical Trials Unit. No. 708 Squadron was derived from 'B' Flight of No. 764 Squadron, which actually had one or two Firebrands on charge for a few days before it was redesignated as No. 708 Squadron. Lee-White collected the unit's first Firebrand from Boscombe Down on 30 September, and the squadron's Firebrands flew with torpedoes and rockets, and engaged in mock combat with borrowed Seafires, from which it proved relatively easy to run away, but which were difficult for a Firebrand actually to fight. No. 708 Squadron was plagued by aircraft

From October 1944 until August 1945, No. 708 Sqn flew six Firebrand TF.Mk IIs (DK380-385) in its guise as the Firebrand Tactical Trials Unit. Combat practice sorties were flown but were plagued by unserviceability and the disruption caused by the constant modification to which the Firebrands were subjected. Based at RNAS Lee-on-Solent, No. 708 was to be the only FAA squadron to take Firebrands on charge before the end of the war in Europe, the Firebrand Mk II being the first single-seat torpedo-carrying aircraft to see FAA service for over 20 years. The aircraft were finished in the Extra Dark Sea Grey/Dark Slate Grey/Sky scheme of the period.

Left: The 10th Firebrand Mk I airframe (DK372) was completed as the first Centaurus-powered Firebrand – the Mk III prototype. The 2,400-hp (1790-kW) Centaurus VII drove a four-bladed Rotol airscrew, while the aircraft's rear fuselage was cut down and a redesigned cockpit canopy fitted.

Lower left: The second Mk III prototype, DK373, was completed with a clear-view, teardrop canopy (also later fitted to '372) and was later to receive an enlarged Mk IV-type tailfin.

unserviceability, and by the reluctance of the Sabre engine to start. The squadron also suffered constant interruptions by Blackburn and other agencies, which continually wanted to modify the aircraft. But the squadron did receive Firebrands before the war ended, and Lee-White and Lieutenant P. G. Lawrence carried out deck landing trials aboard HMS *Glory* on 6 May 1945, and later aboard HMS *Pretoria Castle*. These two men were destined to go on to play an increasingly important part in the Firebrand's operational career. No. 708 Squadron also gained the distinction of being the Royal Navy's first Firebrand unit.

These first in-service Firebrands wore standard FAA camouflage of the period, with extra dark sea grey and dark slate grey disruptive camouflage on the upper surfaces and with sky undersurfaces. Two letter codes (commencing OA) were applied in yellow aft of the roundel. Apart from its size, the Firebrand TF.Mk II looked every inch like a sleek operational fighter, which was perhaps somewhat misleading. In fact, the Firebrand TF.Mk II was generally judged to be well-engineered, but unreliable and with very poor control and stability characteristics.

Radial-engined trouble-maker

Several projects based on the Sabre-engined Firebrand TF.Mk II were drawn up, including the B-41 as a long-range escort fighter for the RAF, the B-42 with a high-lift wing, and the amazing B-43 floatplane fighter intended to be based near potential targets which had no conventional airfield. None of these progressed beyond the drawing board, and No. 708 Squadron relinquished its last Firebrand TF.Mk II late in 1945, having started to re-equip with the Centaurus-powered Firebrand TF.Mk III in August 1945.

The new Centaurus-engined Firebrand TF.Mk III made an appearance on 21 December 1943, with the maiden flight of the first (DK372) of two prototypes. The pilot was Squadron Leader J. R. Tobin, who later lost his life in a Firebrand. DK372 and DK373 had been laid down as the 10th and 11th Firebrand F.Mk I aircraft, but were never flown as such and were completed with Centaurus engines. The Firebrand TF.Mk III featured an enlarged rudder (with greater chord) and had spring tabs on all the primary flight control surfaces. The rear fuselage was cut down, and the Spitfire type three-piece canopy, with a fixed windscreen and rear section as well as a sliding central section, was replaced by a two-piece enclosure with a fixed windscreen and a sliding canopy section, initially with a solid rear fairing integral with the spine. This was soon replaced by a 'proper' bubble canopy. Although Blackburn had already had ample time to 'sort out' the Firebrand, the company continued to develop the aircraft and its systems. Gun firing trials at Brough caused some problems to local trawlermen: one machine was jacked up into a flying attitude to fire its cannon at a deep sandbank. This eventually eroded to the point at which 20-mm projectiles penetrated it completely, and went whizzing across the river, narrowly missing a fishing boat. Despite all of Blackburn's efforts, some problems remained.

As with previous Firebrand variants, service testing revealed a need to fine-tune the handling, and while agility and climb-rate had improved, view for the pilot and performance had suffered. But the Firebrand TF.Mk III, known to the manufacturer as the B-45, did have some good points too, even in prototype form, including a novel low airspeed indicator mounted outside the cockpit, in front of the port quarterlight, allowing the pilot to keep his head up out of the cockpit throughout the approach. The aircraft also had a well-thought out RATO (Rocket-Assisted Take-Off) installation, and handled well even when the rockets fired on one side only. The aircraft also featured powerful airbrakes above and below each wing. These were used in the final stage of a torpedo attack run, allowing the Firebrand to run in at 'full chat', and then suddenly to decelerate to an airspeed at which the torpedo could be released. If the torpedo were released too quickly, it would enter the water at the wrong angle, after which it might probably break up and would certainly not 'run true'.

Precipitous order

Before the Firebrand TF.Mk III's problems could be sorted out, the type was precipitously ordered into production, and the Royal Navy received another batch of aircraft (27 of them this time, serialled DK386/412, the last 17 with the Centaurus IX engine and vibration dampers in the engine mounts) which were of little use except for trials. A handful of the Firebrand TF.Mk III aircraft went to second-line squadrons (Nos 700, 703 and 778 Squadrons each receiving one or two, and No. 708 Squadron taking six). No. 700 Squadron was a Maintenance Test Pilot Training Unit, while No. 778 Squadron was a Carrier Trials Unit and No. 703 Squadron served as the naval flight of the RAF's ASW Development Unit. None of these units needed Centaurus-engined Firebrands, and arguably none needed Firebrands at all, but they did provide some useful work for otherwise unwanted aircraft. The majority of the Firebrand TF.Mk III machines went straight to No. 1 Receipt and Despatch Unit at Anthorn, though in the event they were destined to stay there until scrapped, and were never despatched to units.

The next Firebrand sub-variant did actually see operational front-line service, albeit briefly, and albeit without going to sea. Under the Blackburn designation B-46, the Firebrand TF.Mk IV had a larger rectangular vertical tail surface, offset 3° to port and carrying a massive horn-balanced rudder, and this could cope with a wider diversity of warloads, including 45-Imp gal (204.5-litre) underwing fuel tanks, or a 100-Imp gal (454.6-litre) centreline tank. The Firebrand TF.Mk Mk IV was still no fighter, with an inadequate all-round view, poor manoeuvrability (especially in roll) and a performance that remained unimpressive even by 1943 standards. Its sheer size also made it a huge target for 'proper fighters'. The aircraft,

The Firebrand Mk III proved unsuitable for FAA service and, in the Mk IV, Blackburn needed to address a number of problems. An enlarged tailfin, offset three degrees to port, countered a tendency to swing on take-off (thanks to the considerable torque generated by the four-bladed Rotol propeller), while a horn-balanced rudder improved control during carrier landings. With the declining importance of the torpedo as a naval strike weapon came a wider diversity of warloads, including a pair of 2,000-lb bombs, 16 60-lb R/Ps or drop tanks in place of the torpedo.

The Firebrand Mk IV was the first to enter front-line FAA service, with No. 813 Sqn in 1945. Based at RNAS Ford, the squadron flew Mk IVs for just over a year, though it never went to sea with the type. These views of an early production example, from a series by Charles E. Brown, show well the aircraft's purposeful lines.

however, was a good dive-bomber and promised to be a good torpedo and strike aircraft, and was also sufficiently solidly built to promise its pilots a good chance of walking away from an accident!

And finally to the frontline

The first Firebrand TF.Mk IV (EK601, the first of an order for an astonishing 102-aircraft production batch) made its maiden flight on 17 May 1945. No. 813 Squadron re-formed at RNAS Ford on 1 September 1945 under the newly promoted Lieutenant Commander Lee-White. No. 813 Squadron thereby became the first front-line Firebrand squadron. The type made the Firebrand's public debut on 29 September, on the occasion of the Air Transport Auxiliary's Farewell Display. This was perhaps appropriate, since the Firebrand had been one of the most challenging aircraft ever flown by the pilots of the ATA. The first time one of the ATA's young female pilots arrived at Brough to take delivery of a Firebrand, it caused quite a stir. The still-secret Firebrand was regarded as being 'a bit of a handful' and a 'real man's aeroplane' and some of the less forward-looking 'old salts' at Brough were surprised to see a 'mere slip of a girl' arriving to collect one. In the same year, the City of Bradford held a War Weapons Week, and the Yorkshire-built Firebrand was invited to participate. Special permission was gained for an ultra-low-level series of flypasts, but haze over the industrial West Riding saw the test pilot assigned the task select the wrong part of what was already becoming the Leeds-Bradford conurbation, and he gave Leeds a vigorous and unexpected 'beat-up' instead, for which permission had not been granted. There were a few complaints, but in those days no-one minded too much. Air power, after all, was perceived to have just saved the nation from the Nazi menace.

The new FAA front-line unit formed around a nucleus of highly experienced Firebrand operators from No. 708 Squadron. This unit led the nine-squadron victory flypast over London on 8 June 1946, and participated in a number of high-profile air displays. The aircraft were painted in the same colour scheme as contemporary Hawker Sea Furies, with extra dark sea grey topsides and fuselage sides, and with sky undersides. The aircraft originally wore the 'FD' code for Ford, with individual letters, sometimes prefixed by the number '1'. There was no doubt that the Centaurus-engined Firebrands looked the part, all brutal power and shark-like menace. However, all was not well with the ill-fated Firebrand, and No. 813 Squadron disbanded on 30 September 1946 as a result of the serviceability problems which plagued the aircraft. The squadron had never taken its aircraft anywhere near an aircraft carrier, much to the chagrin of its pilots. This failure was not enough to halt Firebrand production, and the original batch of 102 Firebrand TF.Mk IV aircraft built under Contract No. Ctts/Acft/931 (EK601/638, EK653/694 and EK719/741) was augmented by a further batch of 68 more (EK742/748, EK764/799 and EK827/850). It begins to seem remarkable that 80 more Firebrands (EK851/867, EK885/913 and EK934/967) had been cancelled at the end of the war. Production ended in March 1947, before another Firebrand squadron could form.

Virtually all of the last batch of 68 Firebrands were converted to B-46 standard (Firebrand TF.Mk V) before delivery to the fleet, while 63 of the first batch of 102 aircraft were also converted to Firebrand TF.Mk V standard. When No. 813 Squadron reformed under Lieutenant Commander A. W. R. Turney on 1 May 1947, it did so with the new variant, which was destined to prove more successful. Externally similar to the TF.Mk IV, the Firebrand TF.Mk V introduced longer-span aileron tabs and horn-balanced elevators, improvements which cured the flutter which had almost destroyed a Firebrand TF.Mk IV being operated by Blackburn, and which helped improve longitudinal stability in the climb. The aircraft remained a 'bit of a handful' in some parts of the envelope, and would still drop a wing alarmingly at the stall. It would also spin if provoked, and in the spin proved difficult to recover. Peter Lawrence, one of Blackburn's

This view of EK850, the last production Firebrand, shows the aircraft shortly after conversion from TF.Mk IV to TF.Mk V standard in 1947. The horn-balanced elevators which, with longer-span aileron tabs, were introduced to cure a flutter problem, are readily discernable.

As well as the imposing Rock of Gibraltar, an RAF Shackleton MR.Mk 1 and FAA Sea Fury are visible in the background of this view of Firebrand Mk 5 EK773, captured some time during 1951. At a time when FAA carrierborne types were transitioning from an Extra Dark Sea Grey colour scheme to a predominantly Sky finish, part of the Firebrand's cowling has apparently come from a repainted aircraft. Coded '183/CW', '773 is No. 738 Sqn aircraft, normally based at RNAS Culdrose.

Below left: A number of Firebrands, of various marks, served with Service Trials Unit No. 703 Sqn, including Mk 5 EK747/'T'. By April 1949 the aircraft had joined No. 813 Sqn, but on 23 July was ditched in Poole Harbour after a losing power on take-off from Lee-on-Solent.

test pilots, discovered this when he was forced to deploy the specially fitted anti-spin 'chute after his aircraft failed to recover in 11 turns of a fully developed spin. The Firebrand TF.Mk 5 also had modified dive brakes and an enlarged arrester hook. Quite soon after it entered service, the Firebrand TF.Mk V underwent a change of colour scheme, with the sky undersides extending up the fuselage sides and fin to leave only the top decking and the upper surfaces of the wing and tailplane in the darker colour. From some angles, this helped the Firebrand look more like a Sea Fury, though the massive rectangular after-thought of a fin was always a give-away, even if an onlooker failed to notice the aft location of the cockpit. While the ageing Sea Fury could not carry a torpedo, it was in every other respect a far superior aircraft to the Firebrand TF.Mk 5, as the type had been redesignated in mid-1948, in every role.

For some years it appeared that the 131 Firebrand TF.Mk 5 warplanes would equip only a single FAA front-line squadron. This remarkable state of affairs was the more amazing for drawing so little comment in the aviation and general press! In the end, a second 12-aircraft Firebrand unit did form, and because some Firebrands had fairly short lives, quite a high proportion of the production total did see brief service with the two units. A disgracefully large number of aircraft went straight from Blackburn to a series of holding units, and never put in a day of productive service. Quite a few were scrapped with only 'delivery mileage on the clock'.

By the time No. 827 Squadron finally re-formed with the Firebrand on 13 December 1950, the new colour scheme was applied to about half of the operational aircraft, but the old colour scheme soon began to disappear more rapidly. No. 827 Squadron had returned to RNAS Ford from the Far East, where it had flown the Fairey Firefly. It had been intended to re-equip with the Westland Wyvern, but the development of this type had been protracted, and the decision was taken to re-equip the squadron, under Lieutenant Commander R. Henderson, with the Firebrand pending availability of the Wyvern. A mere five months after its formation, No.827 Squadron flew its aircraft out to RNAS Hal Far to join HMS *Illustrious*, returning to the UK aboard the carrier before joining HMS *Eagle*.

On Malta, the squadron practised day and night attacks against RN and US Navy warships, and soon found that night torpedo attacks were extremely challenging, with a very high degree of navigational accuracy required to find a darkened ship target while flying at 150 ft (45 m). Tactics were refined and developed, and the squadron borrowed a two-seat Firefly and its observer for use as a navigation leader and to fire illuminating 'Glow-worm' rockets in the target area.

Aboard the *Eagle*, the Firebrands of No. 827 Squadron were partnered by the Vickers Supermarine Attackers of No. 800 Squadron, which must have made the Blackburn strike fighters look even more anachronistic.

"...to the end a disaster..."

The Firebrand TF.Mk 5 at last gave the Royal Navy a Firebrand variant capable of being operated safely and usefully in a front-line role, although it was said that the Firebrand TF.Mk 5 demanded greater finesse and airmanship from its pilots than did many of its contemporaries. However, the great Eric 'Winkle' Brown judged that the Firebrand, while a competent enough aircraft when operating from a conventional runway, remained "to the end a disaster as a deck-landing aircraft". The nose was too long

With its hook, landing gear and massive Fowler flaps extended, Mk V EK727/'120' prepares to land. The 'A' tailcode indicates deployment with No. 813 Sqn aboard HMS* Indomitable. *The aircraft carries racks for a torpedo, bombs and R/Ps.

Immaculately presented Mk 5A EK621 carries race number '81' applied for participation in the 1949 Air League Challenge Cup race at Elmdon. Blackburn P. G. Lawrence won the event on 30 June at an average speed of 302 mph (486 km/h).

Firebrand production

F.Mk I prototypes:
Three prototypes, comprising:
DD804, DD810, DD815

F.Mk I:
Nine production aircraft, comprising:
DK363-DK371

TF.Mk II:
One prototype* and 12 production aircraft, comprising:
NV636 (rebuilt from DD810*, see F.Mk I prototypes above), DK374-DK385

TF.Mk III:
Two prototypes and 27 production aircraft, comprising:
DK372, DK373, DK386-DK412

TF.Mk IV:
170 production aircraft, comprising:
EK601-EK638, EK653-EK694, EK719-EK741, EK742-EK748, EK764-EK799, and EK827-EK850.

TF.Mk V conversions:
131 conversions, comprising:
EK609, EK614, EK617, EK621, EK623, EK624, EK625, EK626, EK627, EK628, EK632, EK633, EK634, EK636, EK637, EK638, EK654, EK655, EK656, EK658, EK659, EK660, EK661, EK662, EK663, EK664, EK665, EK667, EK668, EK669, EK670, EK672, EK673, EK674, EK675, EK676, EK677, EK678, EK679, EK680, EK681, EK682, EK684, EK687, EK689, EK690, EK691, EK692, EK693, EK694, EK695, EK721, EK724, EK725, EK726, EK727, EK729, EK731, EK734, EK736, EK737, EK738, EK740, plus EK742-EK748, EK764-EK799, and EK827-EK850.

TF.Mk 5A conversions:
Seven conversions, comprising:
From TF.Mk. V: EK726, EK769 (prototype/TI),
From TF.Mk. IV: EK728, EK730, EK732, EK733, EK735.

EK601, the first of 170 TF.Mk IVs, flew on 17 May 1945. Issued to No. 778 Sqn for intensive deck landing trials aboard* Pretoria Castle *in September, it suffered a landing accident on the 19th.

Firebrand operators

A surprising number of Fleet Air Arm units operated the Firebrand at one time or other. A complete list of these units follows, giving examples (in *italics*) of aircraft known to have flown with a given squadron.

Second-line units

No. 700 Squadron:
A Maintenance Test Pilot training unit, No. 700 Squadron used the Firebrand TF.Mk III between June 1945 and March 1946, while based at Worthy Down then (from November 1945) Middle Wallop. Later versions were used after the squadron's April 1946 move to Yeovilton. The unit's Firebrands operated alongside a variety of other types.
TF.Mk III: DK396, DK412
TF.Mk 5: EK787

No. 703 Squadron:
Forming the Naval Flight of the RAF's Anti-Submarine Warfare Development Unit, No. 703 Squadron at Thorney Island used a succession of Firebrands, of various marks, between December 1945 and March 1952. From May 1948 the unit also functioned as a Service Trials Unit, and this became its sole function after April 1950, when it moved to Ford. The unit's Firebrands operated alongside a variety of other types.
TF.Mk III: DK407, DK409
TF.Mk IV: EK667
TF.Mk 5: EK628, EK741 '031/LP', EK767 'LP033', EK775, EK793

No. 708 Squadron:
No. 708 Squadron formed from 'B' Flight of No. 764 Squadron at Lee-on-Solent on 1 October 1944, taking over the mantle of the Firebrand Tactical Trials Unit. The squadron flew TF.Mk IIs until August 1945, and then TF.Mk IIIs. The squadron moved to Gosport in January 1945, then to Ford on 6 September 1945. The CO and several of the pilots formed the core of No. 813 Squadron when it formed, and the rump of the unit moved first to Fearn on 5 December 1945, and then on 8 January to Rattray, where the squadron disbanded on 26 February 1946. The Firebrands operated alongside a variety of early-Mark Seafires.
TF.Mk II: DK375 'OK', DK380, DK381, DK382 'OF', DK383 'OC', DK384, DK385
TF.Mk III: DK397, DK398, DK404 'FD-Z', DK405, DK406, DK409

No. 717 Squadron:
No. 717 Squadron at Rattray, primarily equipped with Barracudas and operating as a Torpedo Bomber Reconnaissance Training Squadron, seems to have taken charge of at least two of the disbanding No. 708 Squadron's Firebrand TF.Mk IIIs, though it disbanded on 22 March 1946, and one of the aircraft returned to Lee on Solent on 18 February, the other becoming an instructional airframe at HMS *Ariel*, Culcheth.
TF.Mk III: DK397, DK404 '3F-1'

No. 736 Squadron:
No. 736 Squadron at St. Merryn is quoted as having operated the Firebrand from March 1948, alongside Harvards, Fireflies, Martinets, Seafires, Sea Furies and Sea Hornets. The squadron moved to Culdrose on 1 February 1950 as the Naval Air Fighter School, equipped mainly with Sea Furies. Half of the unit (including all the Firebrands) split off to form No. 738 Squadron on 1 May 1950.

No. 738 Squadron:
Operating as part of the Naval Air Fighter School, No. 738 Squadron at Culdrose flew a mixed bag of Firebrand TF.MK IVs and TF.Mk 5s, Seafires, Sea Furies and Sea Hornets from 1 May 1950, when it formed out of No. 736 Squadron. The Seafires, Sea Hornets and Firebrand TF.Mk 5s broke off to form No. 759 Squadron on 16 August 1951.
TF.Mk 5: EK724, EK731 '151/CW', EK738, EK745 '183/CW', EK770 '180/CW', EK773

No. 759 Squadron:
No. 759 Squadron formed as the No. 1 Operational Flying School on 16 August 1951, from No. 738 Squadron. It was equipped with Seafires, Sea Hornets and Firebrand TF.Mk 5s, and gained both Sea Furies and a Jet Conversion Course (with two-seat Vampires and Meteors) in 1952. The Firebrands bowed out in February 1953.
TF.Mk 5: EK770, EK844 '182/CW'

No. 764 Squadron:
Operating as a User Trials Flight testing radio and other equipment, No. 764 Squadron also used Barracudas and Avengers for torpedo trials, and formed a 'B' Flight at Lee-on-Solent on 1 September 1944 for tactical trials of the Firebrand. The first aircraft arrived on 30 September, but the flight then became No. 708 Squadron on 2 October.
TF.Mk II: DK370

No. 767 Squadron:
No. 767 Squadron was a 'Clockwork Mouse' squadron, using a variety of aircraft types to give training to what were then called Deck Landing Control Officers (later LSOs). At least one Firebrand TF.MK 5 (EK733) appeared on the roll during July 1950, augmenting Seafires, Fireflies, Harvards, and Sea Furies.
TF.Mk 5: EK733

No. 778 Squadron:
The Firebrand was used by No. 778 Squadron during its time as a Service Trials Unit and Carrier Trials Unit. The F.Mk I was used from February 1943, while the TF.MK III was used from April until September 1945, and the TF.Mk IV from September 1945 until October 1946. The Firebrand was only one of a large number of types in use by the unit.
F.Mk I: DD815
TF.MK III: DK395
TF.Mk IV: EK657

No. 787 Squadron:
No. 787 Squadron had the Firebrand TF.Mk 5 briefly on its books between May and October 1947, when it served as the Air Support Development Section of the Naval Air Fighting Development Unit. The squadron's Firebrands operated alongside Sea Furies, Sea Hornets and Vampires.
TF.Mk V: EK792

No. 799 Squadron:
No. 799 Squadron's strength included a number of Firebrand TF.Mk 5s (some of which may possibly have been inherited from No. 767 Squadron) during its time as a Yeovilton-based Flying Check and Conversion Refresher training unit. The unit's Firebrands operated alongside Sea Furies and Harvards.
TF.Mk 5: EK773, EK777, EK798, EK829

Operational units

No. 813 Squadron:
No. 813 Squadron 'enjoyed' two incarnations as a Firebrand unit. Its first life began on 1 September 1945, at Ford, forming around a nucleus provided by No. 708 Squadron, and flying Firebrand TF.Mk IVs. It disbanded on 30 September 1946. In its next incarnation No. 813 Squadron was shore-based at RNAS Ford from April 1947, deploying aboard *Implacable* and *Indomitable*. The squadron's TF.Mk IVs wore the tailcode 'FD' when shore-based, after initially wearing four-digit fuselage codes commencing 'FD-1A'. With TF.Mk 5s the same tailcode was retained when shore-based, but the letter 'C' was used aboard *Implacable* and *Indomitable*.
TF.Mk IV: EK613 'FD-1H' and 'M', EK624 'FD-1P', EK628 'FD-1N', EK633, EK665 'FD-1L', EK667, EK672 'FD-1C', EK729 'FD-1A' and 'FD-1N',
TF.Mk 5: Known serials and codes too numerous to list

No. 827 Squadron:
The second front-line Firebrand unit, No. 827 Squadron was shore-based at RNAS Ford from December 1950 until December 1952, and deployed aboard *Illustrious* and *Eagle*. The squadron's aircraft (TF.Mk 5s only) wore the tailcode 'J' when deployed aboard *Eagle* or 'FD' when shore-based.
TF.Mk 5: Known serials and codes too numerous to list.

Blackburn's engineers employed a wing-fold design similar to that used by the Firebrand's contemporary, the Fairey Firefly, with a break between the undercarriage and cannon bay. The folding and spreading operations were manual and required the assistance of a sizeable deck party.

and the pilot sat too far aft to be ideal, while rudder trim was too "fussy", requiring too much adjustment with relatively minor changes in throttle setting. At carrier approach speeds (80 kt; 92 mph;148 km/h) the aileron response was sluggish, and the aircraft was getting uncomfortably close to the stall (77 kt; 87 mph; 143 km/h with flaps and gear down, and with the engine off). The external ASI was more than a luxury in the Firebrand, it was a life-saver! Finally, the aircraft could float over the wires and into the barrier all too easily, and even if the wires were engaged, the aircraft was heavy, and required a relatively long landing run. Deck accidents were unsurprisingly commonplace.

The final variant, the Firebrand TF.Mk 5A, was fitted with hydraulically boosted ailerons. This finally cured the Firebrand's remaining

Blackburn Firebrand TF.Mk IV

1 Handhold, ground handling
2 Starboard navigation light
3 Starboard aileron
4 Spring tab
5 Aileron hinge control
6 Starboard Fowler flap
7 Auxiliary flap
8 Flap rail
9 Flap control mechanism
10 Starboard gun bay
11 Starboard outer ammunition magazine
12 Upper surface dive brake
13 Dive brake hinge mechanism
14 Lower surface dive brake
15 Starboard cannon muzzles
16 Drop tank, 45-Imp gal (205-litre) capacity
17 Rotol four-bladed propeller
18 Spinner
19 Propeller hub mechanism
20 Engine cowling intake ring
21 Cooling air fan
22 Engine cowling fasteners
23 Bristol Centaurus IX air-cooled 18-cylinder, sleeve valve, two-row radial engine
24 Exhaust pipes
25 Ram air intake
26 Carburettor air intake duct
27 Carburettor air heater
28 Fireproof bulkhead
29 Engine mounting struts
30 Cooling air outlet louvres
31 Oil tank, 24½ Imp gal (111-litre) capacity
32 Oil tank filler cap
33 Forward fuselage tubular girder construction
34 Front spar attachment
35 Main fuel tank, 168-Imp gal (764-litre) capacity
36 Fuel tank bracing strut
37 Fuel tank cradle attachments
38 Forward fuselage bottom longeron
39 Rear spar attachment
40 Cockpit bulkhead
41 Windscreen de-icing fluid filler cap
42 Instrument panel
43 Control column
44 Engine control runs
45 Rudder cables
46 Auxiliary fuel tank, 71-Imp gal (323-litre) capacity
47 Cockpit port control console
48 Engine throttle and propeller controls
49 Pilot's seat
50 Safety harness
51 Deck landing ('head-up') air speed indicator
52 Combined torpedo and gunsight
53 Bullet proof windscreen
54 Sliding cockpit canopy cover
55 Headrest
56 Head armour
57 Armoured rear cockpit bulkhead
58 Rear fuselage attachment joint
59 Canopy jettison unit
60 Torpedo director
61 Cockpit canopy rail
62 Starboard wing folded position
63 Aerial mast
64 Access panel
65 Fuselage top decking construction
66 Rear fuselage upper main longeron
67 Fin root fairing
68 Tailfin construction
69 Starboard tailplane
70 Aerial cable
71 Rudder horn balance
72 Rudder construction
73 Rudder trim tab
74 Trim tab hinge control
75 Spring tab
76 One-piece elevator
77 Port spring tab
78 Port trim tab
79 Tailplane construction
80 Tail navigation light
81 Elevator hinge controls
82 Elevator mass balance weight
83 Arrester hook
84 Arrester hook damper
85 Rudder mass balance weight
86 Rudder hinge control
87 Catapult 'hold back'
88 Fin attaching double frame
89 Tailwheel shock absorber strut
90 Tailwheel
91 Tailwheel doors
92 Rear fuselage frame and stringer construction
93 Trim control push rods
94 Fuselage bottom longeron
95 Fuselage double frame
96 Jacking point
97 Radio equipment bay
98 Retractable boarding step
99 'MAT 4' torpedo director vanes
100 Wing fold joint
101 Centre-section split flap
102 Wing fold hinge
103 Port Fowler flap
104 Inboard flap rail
105 Flap construction
106 Auxiliary flap hinge control
107 Flap control rod
108 Synchronising drive shaft
109 Outboard flap rail
110 Aileron hinge control
111 Port aileron
112 Aileron tab
113 Wingtip construction
114 Handhold, ground handling

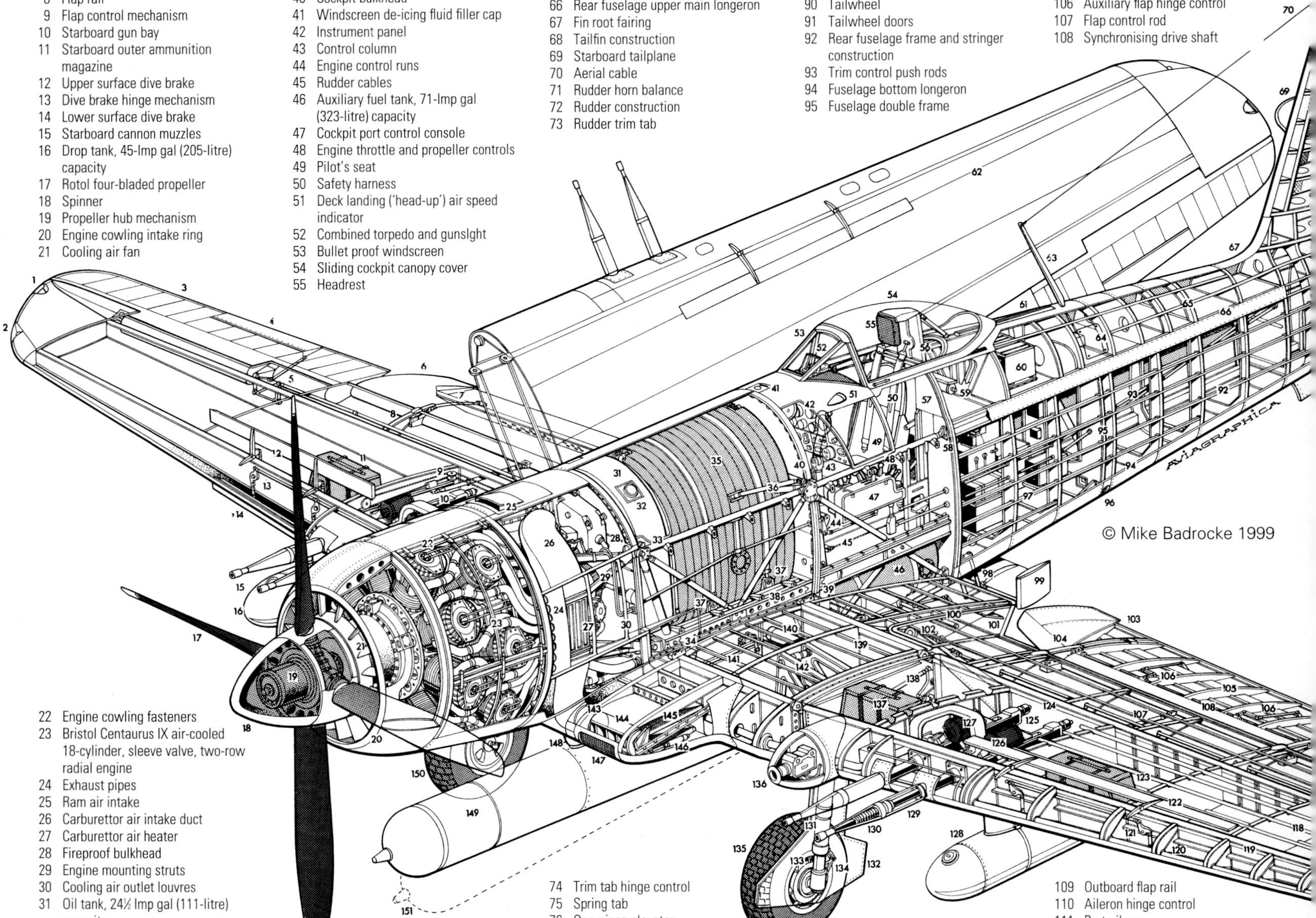

© Mike Badrocke 1999

This fine view of No. 813 Sqn's Mk V EK628, flying from HMS Indomitable *in 1951, shows well the 18-in torpedo installation and the Monoplane Air Tail Mk IV fitted to the weapon to aid its flight.*

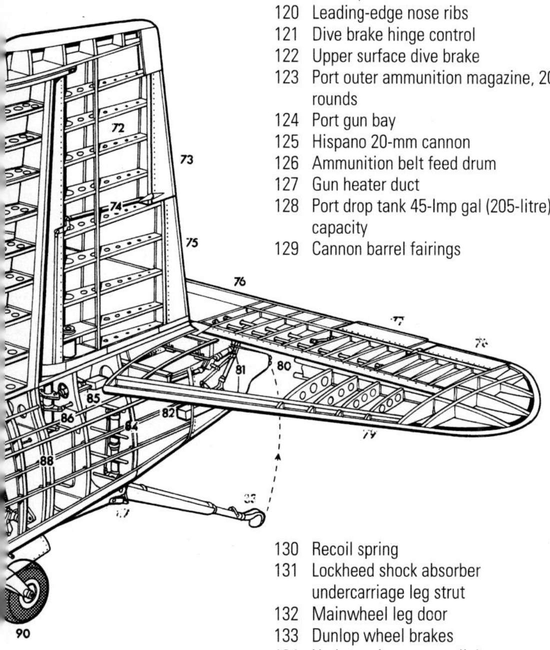

115 Port navigation light
116 Rear spar
117 Wing rib construction
118 Tubular wing stringers
119 Front spar
120 Leading-edge nose ribs
121 Dive brake hinge control
122 Upper surface dive brake
123 Port outer ammunition magazine, 200 rounds
124 Port gun bay
125 Hispano 20-mm cannon
126 Ammunition belt feed drum
127 Gun heater duct
128 Port drop tank 45-Imp gal (205-litre) capacity
129 Cannon barrel fairings
130 Recoil spring
131 Lockheed shock absorber undercarriage leg strut
132 Mainwheel leg door
133 Dunlop wheel brakes
134 Undercarriage torque links
135 Port mainwheel
136 Torpedo camera
137 Port inner ammunition magazine, 200 rounds
138 Wing fold latching mechanism
139 Wing centre-section construction
140 Hydraulic accumulator
141 Mainwheel well
142 Undercarriage hydraulic retraction mechanism
143 Engine air intake
144 Air intake shutter
145 Intake filters
146 Shutter control jack
147 Intake screen, oil cooler to starboard
148 Two-position torpedo carrler
149 1,850-lb (840-kg) torpedo
150 Starboard mainwheel
151 Torpedo in 'undercarriage down' position

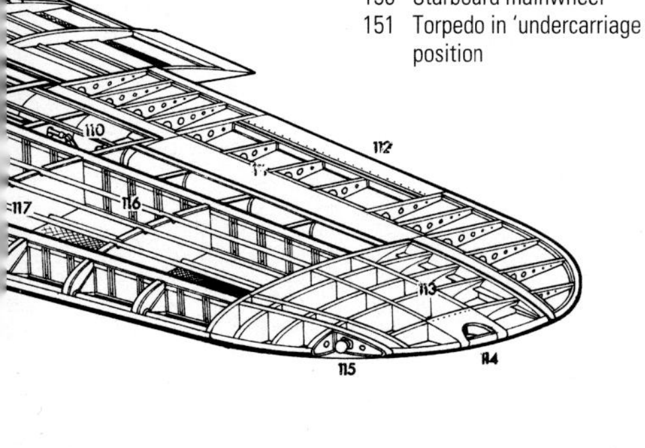

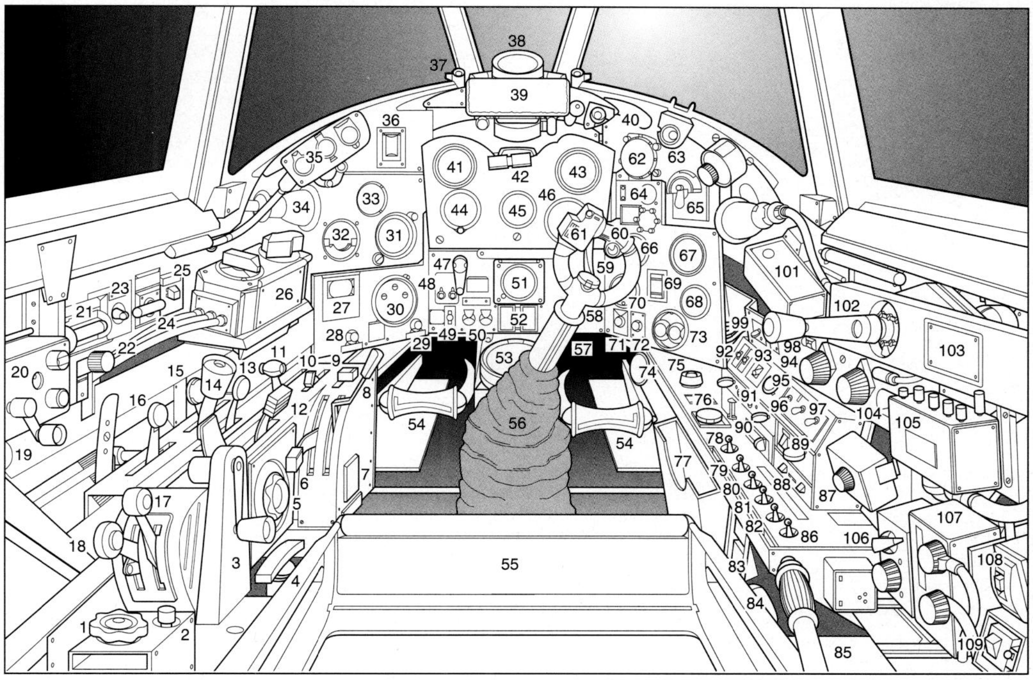

Blackburn Firebrand TF.Mk 5 cockpit instrumentation key

1 Rudder trimmer control
2 Deck arrester hook indicator light
3 Elevator trimmer control
4 Engine priming pump
5 Throttle and RPM control levers damper
6 Undercarriage control lever
7 Undercarriage safety lock acces patch
8 Flap control lever
9 Supercharger control
10 Air-intake filter control
11 Fuel cut-off control lever
12 RPM control lever
13 Engine cooling shutters control lever
14 Throttle control lever
15 Master engine fuel cock
16 Air intake heat control lever
17 Tailwheel strut centralising control lever
18 Deck arrester hook control lever
19 Safety harness stowage
20 ZBX control unit
21 RP/bombs master selector three-way switch
22 Auxiliary light switch
23 RP pairs/salvo switch
24 RATOG master switch
25 Torpedo director switch
26 Torpedo director control unit
27 Rudder and elevator trimmers indicator
28 Supercharger warning light
29 Undercarriage warning light
30 Undercarriage position indicator
31 Altimeter
32 Altitude limit switch
33 Torpedo depth indicator
34 Cockpit light
35 Altitude warning lights
36 Torpedo depth setting three-way switch
37 Gunsight skid indicator lights (two)
38 Gunsight
39 Gunsight padded mounting
40 Windscreen de-icing handpump and regulator
41 Airspeed indicator
42 Hood jettison release handle
43 Artificial horizon
44 Rate of climb and descent indicator
45 Direction indicator
46 Turn and bank indicator
47 Dive brakes control lever
48 Ignition switches
49 Fuel booster pump switch
50 Oil dilution (left)/engine starter and booster-coil (right) pushbuttons
51 RI compass indicator
52 Correction card holders
53 Magnetic compass
54 Rudder pedals
55 Pilot's seat
56 Control column
57 Compass light switch
58 Cockpit and windscreen heating control finger plates (obscured by control grip)
59 Wheel brakes lever
60 Radio 'press-to-talk' switch
61 Combined guns/bombs/RP/torpedo cine camera 'wobble' switch
62 Pneumatic supply and brakes pressure gauge
63 ASV warning light
64 Oxygen supply/regulator control panel
65 Fuel transfer cock
66 Boost gauge (partially obscured by control grip)
67 RPM indicator
68 Engine temperature gauge
69 Oil pressure gauge
70 Oil temperature gauge (partially obscured by control grip)
71 Fuel pressure warning light
72 Fire warning light
73 Fuel contents gauge
74 Cartridge starter re-indexing control
75 Fuel transfer warning light
76 Wing drop tanks/SCI jettison switch
77 Map case
78 Bomb fuzing (nose) switch
79 Bomb fuzing (tail) switch
80 Bomb (port) selector switch
81 Bomb (centre/or torpedo) selector switch
82 Bomb (starboard) selector switch
83 Signal pistol stowage clip
84 Seat-raising handle
85 Hydraulic handpump
86 Bomb distributor switch
87 IFF auxiliary control unit
88 Recognition lights control panel
89 Identification/resin lights control panel
90 Navigation lights control panel
91 Formation lights control panel
92 Camera 'sunny/cloudy' selector switch
93 Camera ON/OFF master switch
94 Torpedo camera/camera gun selector switch
95 Power failure warning light
96 RI compass switch
97 Pressure head heater switch
98 Emergency lighting master switch
99 RP salvo switches
100 Cockpit light
101 RP auto selector
102 Cockpit canopy operating handle
103 Data plate
104 IFF demolition switches
105 Radio control unit
106 IFF control unit
107 IFF supply socket
108 Ground/flight switch
109 ARI.5748 DC and AC control switches

Four carriers played host to the two front-line Firebrand squadrons. No. 813 Sqn Mk Vs (above) enjoyed short periods aboard HMS* Implacable *(deck letter/tailcode 'C') between 1947 and 1950. No. 827 Sqn received Firebrand Mk Vs in late 1950 and took these aboard* Illustrious *the following year, before joining* Eagle *('J') on four occasions during 1952 (left and below).

Below: If nothing else the Firebrand was a robust aircraft. Though it did little to inspire the affections of the pilots who flew it, aircrew knew that in the event of an accident they had a better chance of walking away from a wrecked Firebrand than from most other contemporary types. These landing mishaps were recorded during No. 813 Sqn operations aboard* Indomitable *in 1951. EK748 (below), carries a centreline 45-Imp gal (205-litre) drop tank.

handling faults and resulted in an acceptable aircraft, although still not a good one. This sub-type was the first Firebrand variant not to use a Roman numeral in its original designation, since designations officially switched from Roman to Arabic numbers in June 1948. A prototype conversion (EK769) was made from a Firebrand TF.Mk 5, and was followed by another former TF.Mk 5 (EK726) and by five aircraft (EK728, EK730, EK732, EK733 and EK735) converted from TF.Mk IV standard. There is no evidence that any of the Firebrand TF.Mk 5A machines ever served with a FAA squadron, and as far as can be ascertained the bulk of these aircraft went straight from conversion by Blackburn to the RDU at Anthorn, where they remained until struck off charge and scrapped – another expensive waste of time and effort.

However badly suited the Firebrand was to carrier operation, the two front-line squadrons eventually made more than 15 carrier deployments during their five-year existence, operating from HMS *Eagle*, *Illustrious*, *Implacable* and *Indomitable*. No. 813 Squadron settled in with the 1st Carrier Air Group, forming the strike element while No. 801 Squadron (with de Havilland Sea Hornet F.Mk 20 machines) provided the fighter element. The 1st CAG initially deployed aboard the *Implacable*, switching to the *Indomitable* from November 1950, making cruises in Home, Mediterranean and Norwegian/Arctic waters. While shore-based, No. 813 Squadron participated in the King's Birthday Review flypast at Gosport on 10 June 1948, and at an air display at RNAS Bramcote two days later.

Eventually, though, the Firebrand was replaced by the new, turboprop-powered Wyvern, with No. 827 Squadron disbanding on 3 December 1952 and No. 813 Squadron soldiering on until May 1953, when conversion to the Wyvern began. The squadron flew its last Firebrand sorties in August. By then, the air-dropped torpedo was not considered to be a particularly viable weapon, and most naval strike aircraft used rockets or bombs as their primary weapons, while propeller-driven combat aircraft were beginning to look increasingly anachronistic. The Vietnam War would later show that propeller-driven carrier-borne attack aircraft had not quite had their day, although no one should ever make the mistake of believing that the Firebrand could ever have been a British counterpart to the great Douglas Skyraider.

B-48 Firecrest

Nor was the stillborn B-48 Firecrest much better. The B-48 began life in early 1944, as a response to Specification S.28/43 issued on 26 February. This called for a 'Firebrand Torpedo Fighter with a redesigned wing and improved view for the pilot'. The aircraft was a derivative of the Firebrand TF.Mk 5, powered by a 2,475-hp (1845-kW) Centaurus 59 engine driving a five-bladed propeller, with electrically operated gills on the cowling and with a multi-bladed cooling fan behind the propeller. The cockpit was raised and moved forward over the wing, while the fin was heightened and reduced

RT651, the first B-48 prototype (above), flew on 1 April 1947. Though derived from the Firebrand Mk 5, the B-48 (unofficially named Firecrest by its manufacturers) was a quite different machine. Its inverted gull wing was among a number of new features and imparted good STOL characteristics – a take-off run of 430 ft (130 m) in a 25-kt (46-km/h) wind – and much improved low speed handling. While maximum speed was some 35 kt (65 km/h) better than that of the Firebrand Mk IV, at 330 kt (611 km/h) at 19,000 ft (5790 m), climb rate was little better. Manoeuvrability, in the view of renowned test pilot Eric 'Winkle' Brown, was the crucial test and one that the B-48 failed, being less nimble, in Brown's opinion, than even the Firebrand TF.Mk 5A. One improvement over the Firebrand was the type's hydraulically folding wings (below left) which used a double fold and made for a very compact airframe. The second B-48 prototype was not completed, but a third aircraft (VF172, below) was flown in 1948 and employed by Blackburn as a test aircraft for the power-boosted ailerons intended for the Firebrand Mk 5A. It also differed from the first machine in having a mainplane with reduced dihedral on the outer wing panels – three degrees, compared to nine degrees.

in chord, producing a more pleasing profile.

The Firecrest's wing was even more dramatically redesigned. With a straight trailing edge and sharp taper on the leading edge, the wing was of thin, laminar-flow section, and was of inverted gull-wing configuration in a manner reminiscent of the Vought F4U Corsair, with hydraulic wing folding upwards immediately outboard of the main landing gear units at about one-third span and back downwards/ inwards at about two-thirds span. The aircraft lacked the prominent leading-edge extensions which housed the radiator and oil cooler on the Firebrand. The trailing edge of the Firecrests wing was fitted with four Fowler-type high-lift flaps, with auxiliary flaps on the outer pair only. These gave the aircraft good STOL characteristics, and excellent low-speed handling. Firebrand-type dive brakes were fitted above and below each wing, and all control surfaces were fitted with electrically actuated trim tabs.

Two Firecrest prototypes were ordered, and the first (RT651) of these was rolled out at Brough in February 1947. It was then towed to Leconfield, where it made its maiden flight on 1 April, before returning to Brough to complete its flight trials. The aircraft was unarmed, but did have provision for two 500-lb (227-kg) bombs, rockets or podded 0.5-in (12.7-mm) machine-guns. The second prototype (RT656) was not completed, but a third Firecrest (VF172) was completed for experimental work, with Firebrand TF.Mk 5A type boosted ailerons and with reduced dihedral on the outer wings.

The Firecrest enjoyed better performance than the late Firebrand, and gave its pilot a much better all-round view of his surroundings. But manoeuvrability was not really any better, the aircraft's advantages did not justify production investment, and the type was abandoned to become little more than a footnote in Blackburn's history.

Lack of versatility

Quite apart from its failings as an aeroplane, the Firebrand was simply too specialised an aircraft for the post-war, peacetime Fleet Air Arm. Even the Wyvern which replaced it was considerably more versatile, although what the Royal Navy really needed were versatile multi-role aircraft such as the Sea Fury and, later, the Sea Hawk. And these fine aircraft rendered the Firebrands and their like an interesting irrelevance. This was why the Firebrand was never embarked on carriers deploying for operations over Korea during the Korean War. The Fireflies and Sea Furies actually used could fly fighter, fighter-bomber and reconnaissance missions with equal facility, and while the Firebrand's ruggedness may have given it a useful tolerance to battle damage, there was simply too much likelihood that it would have been unsuitable for many of the missions demanded of the allied carrier air wings in the conflict. In the final analysis, the aircraft was better than some of its critics might have us believe, though it never had the opportunity to show what it could do 'for real', and after the briefest of operational careers, vanished from the scene. Scrapped with almost indecent haste, or used for fire-fighting or as 'catapult dummies', the Firebrand was soon extinct, and not one example survives today. This is perhaps a shame, and it is interesting to speculate as to how the aircraft might have performed as an unlimited racer. Blackburn test pilot P. G. Lawrence flew a modified Firebrand TF.Mk 5 (EK621) to win the Air League Challenge Cup at Elmdon in June 1949, clocking up an average speed of 302 mph (486 km/h). The aircraft was powered by a water/methanol-boosted Centaurus 57 engine, and had its wing-root air intakes faired over and replaced by a smaller cooler intake atop the cowling.

After the failure that was the Firebrand, the company nonetheless persisted with the development of naval aircraft. The B-54/ YA-5/YB-1 was probably superior to the Fairey Gannet (though Fairey needed the work, and got the contract), while the next Blackburn naval aircraft to enter service with the Royal Navy was the hugely successful Buccaneer. The Brough-based aircraft manufacturer certainly knew how to make amends!

Jon Lake

Shahaks over the Sinai

101 Squadron, IDF/AF in the Six Day War

Part Two: The Mirages prove their worth

In the five days that followed 5 June 1967, the air forces of the Arab nations surrounding Israel continued their attacks, but were met with swift resistance from the IDF/AF's fighter units. 101 Squadron's aircraft were not only at the forefront of these defensive operations, but also undertook offensive raids, strafing airfields and bombing SAM sites with their hard-working Shahaks.

Above: Adorned with the 101 squadron fin stripes and squadron badge, a Shahak approaches the end of the runway carrying the standard pair of under-wing fuel tanks. This aircraft – 57 – was flown by Capt Guri Palter on an interdiction mission to the Mitle area on 6 June 1967.

6 June: D-Day plus one

In the early morning hours of 6 June both the EAF and IrAF attempted to retaliate but only presented the IDF/AF Shahaks with the opportunity to demonstrate their value as defensive weapons. At 04.22 a pair of 101 Squadron Shahaks led by Captain Itshak Barzilai in Shahak 73 was scrambled to the area of El-Arish to engage EAF Su-7s, and the leader shot down one Su-7. In the following 50 minutes, another two 101 Squadron pairs were scrambled to that area. The second pair was Major Amos Lapidot and Lieutenant Giora Epstein in Shahak 56, the latter scoring the first of his eventual total of 17 kills. The third 101 Squadron pair, Major Baruch Buff Friedman in Shahak 06 and Lieutenant Avshalom Ran in Shahak 77, was also successful and both the leader and his wingman claimed one Su-7 each.

At 09.53 a pair, Captain Guri Palter in Shahak 73 and Major Giora Furman in Shahak 81, was scrambled to engage EAF MiG-21s in the area of El-Arish. Guri Palter recalls: "I was leading but just prior to the engagement I had a communication failure. The controller ordered, 'On the right and above, break right,' but I did not hear him so I did not turn. (Major) Furman broke right and engaged them. Then I understood that I could not hear, and I also broke. I saw (Major) Furman shoot down a MiG-21 and as I got into position on the other MiG-21 I got a low fuel state warning. I had to shut down the afterburner and I radioed, 'There is a MiG over here, guys, get him.' I headed east to disengage and the MiG was about 2500 m behind me. A [119 Squadron] formation came to

Capt Yochai Richter claimed his first kill – an Egyptian MiG-19 – in Shahak 34 on 6 June 1967.

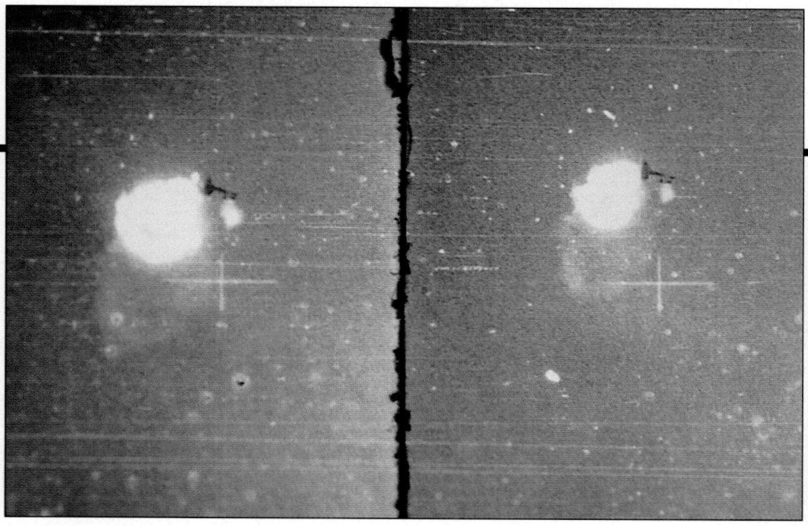

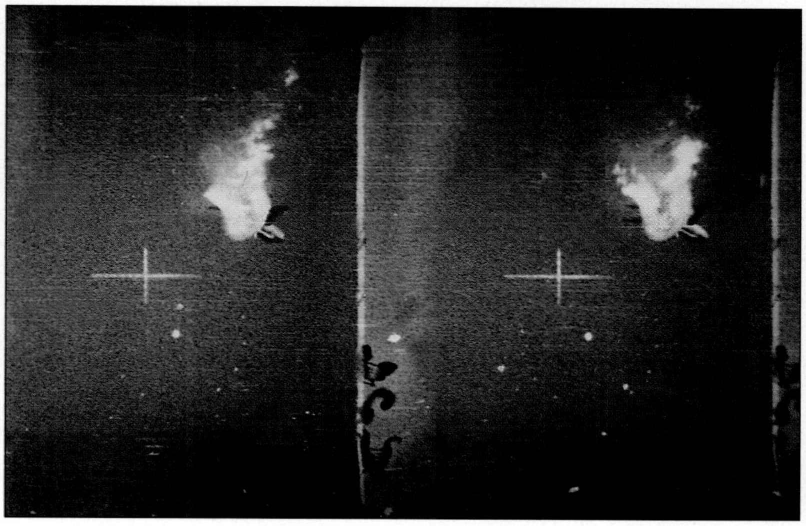

Egyptian fighters were generally at the receiving end in battles with 101 Squadron Shahaks. The aircraft above (most likely a MiG-17) has suffered a secondary explosion of ordnance or a fuel tank under the starboard wing, while the MiG-21 (right) is trailing a spectacular fireball. The MiG-21 was renowned for the way it exploded, due to the proximity of an oxygen bottle and a high-octane fuel tank.

support us and (Captain) Uri Ye'ari shot down the MiG. It was an all-weather MiG-21 with a large radome."

Giora Furman adds his own view of the same air combat: "On the second day I came to fly with 101 Squadron and my first flight was a CAP. I flew with Guri Palter whom I had instructed while he was an air cadet, still on Stearmans and Harvards. I told him, 'You lead, I am a visitor,' and we patrolled for a long time over Tel-Nof. Finally, we were vectored towards Port Said where we met the MiGs. When you do not fly regularly on a type of aircraft you worry about the fuel state. In the area of Port Said it was the end of the fuel tanks in the wings.

"Palter turned the other way. I shot down the first and then I got worried about the fuel but (Captain) Uri Ye'ari came in and he shot down the other MiG. It turned out that my instincts were right, I arrived at Hatzor with about 200 litres while Palter landed at Hatzerim.

"It was from 300 m without the radar. What I remember from that kill is that immediately after he got hit he just stopped in the air and I had to evade him. By then he was hanging from his parachute and I had to worry about my fuel state."

Ending the successful series of air engagements on 6 June was a pair of 101 Squadron Shahaks, Major Oded Marom in Shahak 15 and Captain Uri Shachar in Shahak 59, which engaged two EAF MiG-19s over Jabel Mara during the hot noon hours. Each Shahak pilot shot down one MiG-19.

Air-to-ground successes

The success in the air-to-air combats did not overshadow the effectiveness of the IDF/AF Shahaks in the air-to-ground role. A four-ship formation which was led by Lieutenant Colonel David Ivry in Shahak 52 also included Captain Avner Slapak, Lieutenant Ilan Gonen and Lieutenant Eldad Ran. The mission was to attack Syrian forces in the area of Bnot Ya'acov bridge but en route to the target area the pilots saw something that eventually changed their mission, as Avner Slapak recalls.

"We flew towards Bnot Ya'acov bridge at about 7,000-10,000 ft over the West Bank when I saw down below, at Dotan Valley near Jenin, tanks advancing west and shooting. I looked and I saw that they were shooting at half-tracks which were retreating west. Half-tracks were our guys, west was toward Israel. I said to Ivry, 'Look down.' Ivry asked the controller, 'Do we have Patton tanks in this area?' and the controller replied, 'No, we do not have Pattons on the Jordanian front, attack them.'

"We bombed and they stopped. We then strafed and the Pattons, which had external fuel tanks, began to catch fire. We then saw an amazing sight: the Pattons turned east and started to retreat, the half-tracks saw it, stopped, turned and started to chase the Pattons!"

The day ended with an attack mission led by Major Dan Sever in Shahak 75. The target was Egyptian armour at Wadi Kouriya in Sinai, just west of Bir Tmada; the tactic was a high-altitude attack with Tadmor bombs. The Tadmor was an electromagnetic proximity detonator designed to explode the bomb above the surface. Obviously, it was not thought that the Shahaks could knock out a tank with a direct hit, and to use a regular bomb with the usual seven- to 15-second delay detonator would have been useless in the Sinai desert. The compromise was to use the Tadmor, which exploded the bomb above the surface. Though not able to destroy a tank, the explosion above the surface would maximise the blast and fragment damage.

7 June: New Egyptian tactics

Failing to obtain any positive results in air engagements against the IDF/AF Shahaks, the EAF employed a new tactic in the early morning hours of 7 June. EAF MiG-21s were sent to lure the intercepting Shahaks into the launch envelope of the Egyptian SA-2 batteries in the area of the Suez Canal. These attempts failed, and later that morning the Shahaks attacked the Egyptian SA-2 batteries, not only because of the aforementioned tactic but also because IDF troops were approaching the canal and the SA-2 threat had to be eliminated so that proper close air support could be maintained. However,

Second-line bases were attacked by 101 Squadron in the second attack wave. Victims included this pair of undispersed Egyptian Ilyushin Il-14s.

Two Super Mystères, each loaded with two fuel tanks and a pair of bombs, await the landing of 101 Squadron Shahak 52. On 7 June 1967 Guri Palter flew this aircraft on a combat air patrol.

the 101 Squadron formation which attacked an Egyptian SA-2 battery on the morning of 7 June, led by Lieutenant Colonel Arlozor Lev, did so only as a target of opportunity during an interdiction mission to the Mitle area in Sinai. The 101 Squadron pre-planned attacks on the Egyptian SA-2 batteries would only follow on the next day, 8 June.

Most of the air-to-air activity over Sinai on 7 June was concentrated in the areas of Ras Sudar and Sharm El-Sheikh. In the area of A-Tur, four 101 Squadron Shahaks led by Major Amos Amir in Shahak 09 engaged four EAF MiG-19s during the noon hours and claimed two MiG-19 kills, while a third MiG-19 was seen to crash due to a spin, as Amos Amir recalls.

"At first we were planned to attack Cairo West. There was intelligence information that two Algerian MiG squadrons had arrived in Egypt and were based in Cairo West, so we were ordered to attack Cairo West. I did not like that order, but an order is an order. We briefed and at the last moment we were given a change of mission, to do an interdiction between A-Tur and Sharm El-Sheikh. When we got near to the Gulf of Suez the controller told us that there were MiGs in the area, and we intercepted them. By then we were quite concerned because everybody had shot down MiGs and we had not even seen one in the air. It was very frustrating. It was a four-ship formation of MiG-19s. I do not know what they were doing there, maybe they came to attack or to patrol. It was a very simple combat. The MiG-19 was an inferior aircraft, a bad fighter. We just came in on their tails and shot them down, two of them. Another one, for an unknown reason, maybe he panicked, entered a spin and crashed."

Columns of smoke rise from an Egyptian Air Force air base after an IDF/AF attack. Considerable damage was done, not only to the bases themselves, but also to any aircraft caught on the ground.

The second MiG-19 kill was credited to Captain Yochai Richter in Shahak 34. The MiG-19s probably came from Ardaka, so in the afternoon four 101 Squadron Shahaks attacked both Ardaka air base – where two Mi-6s were destroyed – and the nearby radar station. The pilots were Major Ezra Aharon, Lieutenant Itshak Peer, Captain David Baruch and Captain Yosef Arazi. Yossi Arazi recalls: "We flew along the coasts of Sinai to Sharm El-Sheikh and south over the Red Sea for the first time. It was such an impressive landscape that for a moment you forgot about the war. We did not find anything at Ardaka. There were two helicopters which were set on fire, while I, with another Shahak, tried to set on fire the huge fuel tanks. We strafed and we observed hits but the tanks did not catch fire, maybe they were empty. We did not feel that we saved Israel in that strike, but the view was amazing. It was a beautiful flight because of the amazing southern Sinai landscape, which we saw for the first time."

Later that evening Major Ezra Aharon in Shahak 08 was involved in a search for a ship. "There were reports about a target at sea about 10-20 km from Gaza. The first aircraft on alert, Guri Palter, was scrambled with flares. He located the ship but each time he entered a pass to drop flares his screen was covered with a lot of blips. We did not understand, we knew nothing about electronic warfare. I was next and I was scrambled with two heavy bombs; it was thought that it was an Egyptian destroyer. Both me and Guri were ex-119 Squadron night-fighter pilots. In that squadron we developed night bombing techniques. It was not accurate, but a destroyer is a large target and there was a chance, but the same thing happened again. There were two types of screens, long range and short range. I located the ship but each time I got nearer and switched to short-range screen, the screen was covered with millions of blips. I did a few futile passes and then we thought that he would drop flares and I would bomb, but it was the same story. I thought the blips were a lot of fishing boats escaping from Gaza. The next morning the ship was attacked and when I returned from an attack sortie at Sinai I saw it smoking. It was the [USS] *Liberty*."

A second 101 Squadron Shahak was lost around midnight when Captain David Baruch in the ex-119 Squadron Shahak 84 was scrambled to intercept an EAF Il-28 over western Sinai. It was probably an SA-2 ambush, for the last words heard from Baruch were, "Oh god, an SA-2 is locked on me".

8 June: *Liberty* attacked

Day four, 8 June, was the third consecutive day in which the EAF launched its combat aircraft at first light to attack IDF forces in northern Sinai. A 101 Squadron formation engaged EAF MiG-17s near Romani and Lieutenant Colonel Zorik Lev in Shahak 33 was credited with a MiG-17 kill.

The US Navy 6th Fleet spy ship, the USS *Liberty* (AGTR-5), was targeted at noon after the nocturnal attempt to attack the ship by 101 Squadron Shahaks was frustrated by EW. In the morning the *Liberty* was spotted by a pair of 101 Squadron Shahaks, and this was followed by an attack by Super Mystères, a pair of 101 Squadron Shahaks and torpedo boats of the Israeli navy. When 101 Squadron learned that Israel had mistakenly attacked a US Navy ship, the pilots were shocked, since they were sure they had attacked an Egyptian navy ship. Another formation of 101 Squadron Shahaks was also vectored to the area, as Giora Furman recalls.

"They started to call formations which were returning from attack missions to an unidentified ship. It had already been attacked. We came overhead and were prepared to come in but the pilots who had attacked talked with the controller about whether or not they had seen a flag, and they decided to stop the attack immediately. We were at 12,000-14,000 ft and we did not come in, but we saw our boats coming in and the smoke."

Above and right: A 101 Squadron pilot jumps into the cockpit of Shahak 52 with a groundcrewman close behind to help secure him into his cockpit. A QRA aircraft, the Shahak carries a single R.530 Yahalom AAM. Notably, the aircraft displays a single kill marking in these photographs, signifying victory over a Syrian MiG-21 on 7 April 1967 while flown by Iftach Spector. On the 20 July 1967 the same pilot and aircraft destroyed an Egyptian MiG-21 – dating these photographs between these two dates.

Targeting SAM sites

Attacking Egyptian SAM batteries is, today, mainly connected with the Attrition War and the IDF/AF McDonnell Douglas F-4E Phantoms, but the Shahaks also engaged Egyptian SA-2 batteries during the Six Day War. Prior to the war the IDF/AF had identified 12 SA-2 sites along the Suez Canal, and as the IDF ground troops approached the Suez Canal area the IDF/AF turned its attention to this threat. The SA-2 strikes commenced on 7 June and the effort continued on 8 June. At 11.47 a three-ship formation took off to attack, by strafing, an SA-2 battery at El-Hafir, west of Suez City. The leader was Major Amos Amir in Shahak 81, No. 2 was Captain Binyamin Beni Romach and No. 3 was Lieutenant Giora Epstein in Shahak 51.

Amos Amir recalls: "There was something very strange. When we crossed the Gulf of Suez we heard on the radio, crystal clear, a message with our callsign to break. When you are told to break, you break, you do not ask questions. We all broke. I looked to the right, I looked to the left – nothing. We were heading back and had already reached the coast of Sinai, but I could see nothing. Who had called us to break?

"We turned back, attacked and destroyed the battery with cannon fire. There was another call on the radio but I decided to ignore it. My aircraft was damaged by AA fire but I discovered this only after I landed, when I saw two big holes in the fuselage. To this day, I do not know who called us. It might have been an Egyptian intelligence aircraft, it might have been our EW aircraft which saw something, maybe an indication of the launch of missiles. We were flying at low altitude so it might not have been from the local area, rather from an aircraft at high altitude. It had to be somebody who knew we were there, who knew our callsign, who knew that timing was critical. I really do not know."

101 Squadron launched two Shahak formations at 15.42 and 15.43, each subsequently losing one aircraft. The first formation was led by Major Ezra Aharon in Shahak 06 with Major Giora Furman as his wingman, Captain Binyamin Romach and Lieutenant Ilan Gonen. The mission of the formation was to attack an Egyptian SA-2 battery and it was accomplished successfully, but Captain Binyamin Beni Romach was lost, possibly a victim of AA fire which protected another SA-2 battery, as Ilan Gonen recalls.

"We were to strafe, not bomb, an SA-2 battery near Bilbeis because we had to fly low. We flew at a very low altitude very deep into Egypt: we crossed Sinai, we crossed the Suez Canal and then we flew deep into the Nile Delta. When we crossed the Suez Canal at low altitude we accidentally passed over an SA-2 battery which was defended with a lot of AA fire. They simply raised the barrels of their weapons and fired at us.

"Beni Romach was No. 3 and he got hit. I suppose that he was hit in his body and he pulled-up. I

Above: Three Tupolev Tu-16 'Badgers' caught on the gun camera film of a 101 Sqn Shahak. The nearest aircraft is armed with a pair of AS-1 'Kennel' ASMs.

Below: Another Tu-16 drifts into a Shahak's gunsight. The far example (coded '08') is thought to be the aircraft shown in the foreground of the previous photograph.

instinctively climbed with him. I informed the leader that No. 3 had been hit. He looked backward, saw us and shouted, 'Descend immediately!' I automatically escorted him because it is an instinct of a wingman whose leader got hit: you escort him in order to help. I did not obey and I stayed with Beni Romach despite the heavy AA fire. Then Beni Romach rolled over and crashed. I levelled, and with a lot of a heartache we simply carried on. It was very difficult for me. We could not help. If he had ejected then we would have had a dilemma, but he did not eject.

"We proceeded at a very low altitude and then we pulled up as far as was safe and strafed the command post of the battery, not the missiles. The leader pulled up and did not hit, but I was behind so I recognised the centre of the battery quite quickly and my strafing pass was very accurate. Not only did the command post of the battery catch fire, it also fell on its side. When we pulled out there was a terrific AA fire. Real hell. I reported to the leader that I hit the command post, that I completed the mission, that there was no need to return, but the leader said, 'We are coming in for another pass to make sure.'

"I said, 'There is a terrifying AA fire and I hit it, there is no need,' but he repeated, 'We are coming in!' so we came in. They saw us turning and they shot at us all the time. It was the heaviest AA fire that I can recall from such a short distance. Luckily, we did not get hit and when we came out the leader said, 'No. 4, you were right! The command post is burning on its side.' I admired his courage and determination - after such an experience en route, to come in for a second pass just to make sure. Despite the horrifying AA fire and the mental pressure, we did it."

The second 101 Squadron formation engaged EAF MiG-21s which reportedly were escorting dark-painted Algerian MiG-17s. Captain Yosef Arazi in Shahak 15 was leading Captain (reserve) Maoz Poraz, as Yossi Arazi recalls.

"At first we ironed the skies west of Be'er Sheva. Suddenly, we heard Captain Avraham Shalmon from 119 Squadron informing that Il-28s were crossing the Sinai coast near Bardavil. We rushed to that area but found nothing. We climbed and when we had no more than one-third of our fuel left, the controller, Igal Ziv who had graduated the same Flying Course as I did, called to me, 'MiGs are attacking our troops at Kantara, go there.' We flew to Kantara and started to patrol at low altitude. With 1200 litres of fuel left, the minimum for a safe return to base from that area, I was about to order Maoz to return to base when I saw explosions on the ground, with a MiG-21 emerging from these explosions. I looked around and I saw four Egyptian MiG-21s and four dark-painted MiG-17s which I think were Algerian aircraft. We had intelligence information that Algeria was sending MiG-17s to Egypt and these aircraft were painted differently.

"Two things crossed my mind. The first was what the hell was going on? In this war we attacked, so why did they attack our troops? These were not the rules of the game! Then I thought about Avner Slapak. Avner Slapak was the best pilot in the squadron. I thought to myself, how can I return to the squadron and tell Avner Slapak that I saw eight MiGs in the air and I did not shoot down even one, no matter what my fuel state was?

"We were still flying with empty 1300-litre external fuel tanks so I ordered the jettison of the tanks. It was at low altitude and high speed, over 500 kt, and the jettisoning of the tanks rocked the aircraft so violently that the parachute on which I was seating moved forward between my knees. I sank in the seat, my knees were in such a position that I could not reach the pedals and I could not see anything behind me!

Combat with a MiG-21

"That was how I entered combat. I caught a MiG-21 but then I saw another MiG on my tail, launching his air-to-ground rockets at me. I broke and I ordered Maoz to take him, and Maoz chased him further south toward Ismailiya. I was left alone with seven MiGs. I tried to follow a MiG-17 but suddenly I passed a MiG-21 and I entered scissors with him. We were so low that I looked at the shadow of my aircraft on the ground. If I did not see another shadow, I continued; if I saw another shadow, I broke. I broke two or three times until a MiG-21 simply flew into my sight, asking for a cannon burst. I fired but I was probably a bit excited and my aiming was not good. I then remembered Major Aryeh Ben-Or. He had engaged MiGs before the war but failed to shoot them down, and when he returned he said, 'To shoot down a MiG you have to be super

An Egyptian MiG-17 passes through the stream of 30-mm shells from a Shahak's pair of DEFA 552 cannon. Almost all air-to-air kills by Shahaks were made with this weapon.

persistent, they do not fall by themselves,' and so I organised my gunsight and pushed the trigger until the MiG-21 exploded in the air. It was so low that the pilot had no chance, there was no parachute and it simply exploded. The MiG-21 had its oxygen bottle very close to a high-octane fuel tank, making for an interesting pyrotechnic phenomenon and a very impressive explosion. I then saw another MiG, at 600 m but in a pretty high deflection angle. It was far from ideal but I had no more fuel, so I fired. I exhausted my ammunition but I did not hit it.

Fuel starvation

"When we entered the combat it was clear to me that I would not be able to return to Hatzor, but I ordered Poraz to disengage at 600 litres and go for an emergency landing at El-Arish. After I shot at the second MiG I escaped at low altitude; I had no ammunition and no fuel, and there were still six MiGs out there. While flying at low altitude I saw an Israeli helicopter flying toward that area. I tried to warn him that there were MiGs out there but I could not contact him, though later I learned that all those MiGs left the area after I shot down my MiG. I flew for a minute at low altitude and then I climbed to plan my landing at El-Arish. It was then when I heard Maoz Poraz informing that he had no fuel left and that he was planning to land on the Kantara-El-Arish road. The asphalt of these roads was merely a black colour on the sand, so I ordered him to eject, which he did. When we entered combat I ordered not to use the afterburner but apparently he did not save fuel, for there was no reason he should have less fuel than I did.

"I was at high altitude and I saw both El-Arish and Hatzerim. I had 200 litres left and I thought that if I landed at El-Arish it would take three days to recover the aircraft, so I opted for Hatzerim. I landed with barely 70 litres of fuel. Who did I meet there but my good friend Major Aryeh Ben-Or? I told him about the air combat, my aircraft was refuelled and I returned to Hatzor. Colonel Binyamin Beni Peled was the base commander, and when I arrived he met me and said, 'Well done, but f...'; 'well done' for the kill, 'f...' because my wingman ejected."

Above: Iraqi pilot Capt Monir Radfa defected to Israel in August 1966 in this MiG-21F (Iraqi air force serial 534) after a well planned Mossad operation. The aircraft was evaluated by the IDF/AF Chief Test Pilot, Lt Col Daniel 'Danny' Shapira in late 1966, providing much useful data for the Six Day War.

Below: 101 Squadron Shahak 42 is the aircraft in which Maj Ezra Aharon flew escort missions alongside Lt Col Danny Shapira in eleven anti-MiG-21 sorties between September and November 1966. The aircraft was also used to accompany the MiG-21 during its test evaluation in Israeli skies.

9 June: Comparative calm

Day 5 was a relatively uneventful day for the 101 Squadron Shahaks. A defence suppression action in support of a heliborne assault at Ras Sudar was unplanned: Lieutenant Colonel David Ivry and Captain Guri Palter flew a CAP mission to protect the IDF/AF Sud Aviation Super Frelon helicopters which were about to land IDF troops at Ras Sudar. The fighters which were to act as defence suppression in support of the helicopters did not arrive, so the Shahaks were switched to this mission, as Guri Palter recalls: "Mystères or Super Mystères had to attack the area before the arrival of the helicopters. Suddenly, the controller ordered us to rush to Ras Sudar because the helicopters were about to land and the defence suppression (aircraft) had not arrived, there was no one to cover the helicopters. We did two passes and then we saw a truck full of soldiers stopping at the centre of the runway and the men disperse to fight the helicopters which were some five minutes away. We did three or four strafing passes and we wiped them out. The troops landed and said, 'It's all quiet, go home, thank you.'"

On 9 June Major Dan Sever and Lieutenant Giora Epstein flew the first of two search flights to find the remains of Captain David Baruch's Shahak. The 9 June flight was flown in Piper Super Cub 03 and the second flight was on 11 June in Piper Super Cub 64. Dan Sever recalls: "The idea was to search from Jabel Mara, which we

Above: 101 Squadron targeted a number of SA-2 batteries towards the end of the war. The missile complexes had the disadvantage of being fixed, and once located pilots could choose to avoid known batteries. Later the IDF/AF could attack them at their convenience.

Right: Shahak 77 is seen armed with eight bombs for the air-to-ground mission. Piloted by Lt Giora Epstein, this aircraft attacked an Egyptian SA-2 battery at El-Hafir on the 8 June 1967. Gioria Epstein had shot down a Sukhoi Su-7 two days earlier.

101 Squadron attacked a range of targets including airfields (above, note the MiG-21 exploding beyond the column of smoke) as well as more traditional battlefield interdiction targets (below, Egyptian vehicles in the Sinai).

were sure he had overflown. We located a lot of wreckage. It was very easy to identify a wreckage of an aircraft in the sands of Sinai since there was a large, black mark of fire on the sand. We flew very low so we simply overflew a wreckage until we could identify it, whether it was Egyptian or Israeli. We found a lot, even the wreckage of the aircraft which I shot down on 5 June. We did not find David Baruch's Shahak. Eventually, it was found closer to the Suez Canal in an area which we were not allowed to overfly in the Piper."

Unpleasant surprise

An unpleasant surprise awaited Major Dan Sever when he returned to Hatzor. During the search the two 101 Squadron pilots landed at the former EAF El-Arish and Jabel Libni air bases, which were being operated by special IDF/AF forward runway teams. The commander of one of those teams called over Major Dan Sever and gave him six completely new captured Soviet AK-47 automatic rifles, a gift to the Hatzor wing squadron commanders.

Dan Sever continues: "We returned to Hatzor and I took the squadron's vehicle to give each squadron commander his AK-47. I came to 105 Squadron and I said, 'I have a present for Bet-On,' and the answer I got was, 'Bet-On is dead, his aircraft was shot down over the Golan Heights four hours ago.'"

Lieutenant Colonel Shlomo Bet-On was the commander of the Hatzor wing Flying Squadron. He was a former commander of 105 Squadron so he flew as a Hatzach with that squadron until he was killed on 9 June when his Super Mystère was shot down by Syrian AA fire. Lieutenant Colonel David Ivry in Shahak 08 was scrambled to the Golan Heights to search for Lieutenant Colonel Bet-On, but with no positive results. The loss of Lieutenant Colonel Bet-On also directly affected 101 Squadron, since Major Giora Furman, who was planned to succeed Major Amos Lapidot as 101 Squadron CO, took over the command of the Hatzor wing Flying Squadron. As a result, Major Dan Sever became acting CO when Major Amos Lapidot left the squadron immediately after the end of the war until the new 101 Squadron CO, Lieutenant Colonel Oded Marom, arrived in November 1967. (Prior to the Six Day War the rank of an IDF/AF squadron commander was a major, but after the war it was changed to a lieutenant colonel.)

In his second scramble on that day Lieutenant Colonel David Ivry in Shahak 33 led Captain Yochai Richter on a dusk patrol over the Suez Canal in the area of Kantara. They chased an EAF MiG-21 but Lieutenant Colonel Ivry was only able to bring back excellent photos of the Egyptian fighter.

101 Squadron Shahaks of the Six Day War

04 (no information)

06 at least one kill: an EAF Su-7 on 6 June 1967 (Baruch Friedman)

08 (no information)

09 at least 1 kill: an EAF MiG-19 on 7 June 1967 (Amos Amir)

12 (no information)

15 at least 4 kills: an EAF MiG-19 on 6 June 1967 (Oded Marom), an EAF MiG-21 on 8 June 1968 (Yosef Arazi), an EAF MiG-21 on 25 March 1970 (Oded Marom) and an EAF MiG-21 on 10 July 1970 (Moshe Hertz)

33 at least three kills: an EAF MiG-17 kill on 8 June 1967 (Arlozor Lev), an EAF MiG-21 on 26 June 1969 (Iftach Spector) and an SAF MiG-21 on 8 July 1969 (Eitan Ben-Eliyahu), exported to Argentina in 1982

34 at least 3 kills: an EAF MiG-19 on 7 June 1967 (Yochai Richter) and two EAF MiG-21s 27 July 1970 (Iftach Spector)

42 flown by Major Ezra Aharon, Head of Flight Test Section in IDF/AF AHQ, as escort to the ex-Iraqi MiG-21 during its test in comparison flights in Israel in September-November 1966; flown by Major Dan Sever in Runway Piercing Bomb (RPB) tests in November 1966

51 at least 1.5 kills: an SAF MiG-21 on 9 November 1972 (Ilan Gonen) and shared an EAF MiG-21 kill on 24 October 1973 (Dan Sever)

52 at least 5.5 kills: an SAF MiG-21 on 7 April 1967 (Iftach Spector), an EAF MiG-21 on 20 July 1967 (Iftach Spector), two EAF MiG-21s on 27 March 1970 (Israel Baharav), an EAF MiG-21 on 10 July 1970 (Iftach Spector) and half a kill of a Soviet-flown MiG-21 on 30 July 1970 (Iftach Spector)

56 at least 4 kills: an EAF Su-7 on 6 June 1967 (Giora Epstein), an SAF MiG-21 on 24 February 1969 (Amnon Shamir) and two SAF MiG-21s on 8 July 1969 (Giora Furman). "The best aircraft we had. Regrettably, it was lost. Better than the 59, better than the 82. The best aircraft we had." Giora Epstein, 3 September 1997

57 at least 1 kill: an EAF MiG-21 on 9 February 1970 (Avinoam Keldes), shot down by an EAF MiG-21 on 9 February 1970 (Avinoam Keldes POW in Egypt)

59 13 kills: an SAF MiG-21 on 14 July 1966 (Yoram Agmon), an EAF Il-14 on 5 June 1967 (Ilan Gonen), an EAF MiG-19 on 6 June 1967 (Uri Shachar), an EAF MiG-21 on 7 July 1969 (Oded Marom), an EAF MiG-21 on 20 July 1969 (Giora Yoeli), an EAF Su-7 on 11 September 1969 (Giora Epstein), an EAF MiG-21 on 11 November 1969 (Yair Sela), an EAF MiG-21 on 4 January 1970 (Oded Marom), an EAF MiG-21 on 6 March 1970 (Iftach Spector), two EAF MiG-21s on 10 July 1970 (Israel Baharav), an SAF MiG-21 on 13 September 1973 (Avraham Shalmon) and an EAF AS-5 on 6 October 1973 (Eitan Karmi). Damaged in a take-off accident on 7 October 1973 (Israel Baharav injured), rebuilt by IAI and returned to service in October 1974, converted to a reconnaissance aircraft, exported to Argentina in 1982. Believed to have crashed in Argentina; now publically displayed in Rosario, Santa Fe.

62 (no information)

73 at least 1 kill: an EAF Su-7 on 6 June 1967 (Itshak Barzilai)

75 (no information)

77 at least 5 kills: an EAF MiG-21 on 5 June 1967 (Dan Sever), an EAF Su-7 on 6 June 1967 (Avshalom Ran), two EAF MiG-21s on 25 March 1970 (Giora Epstein) and an EAF MiG-21 kill on 16 March 1970 (Menachem Sharon)

81 at least 6 kills including an EAF MiG-21 on 6 June 1967 (Giora Furman), an EAF Su-7 on 15 July 1967 (Yoram Agmon), an EAF MiG-17 on 10 December 1968 (Oded Marom), an EAF MiG-21 on 6 October 1969 (Oded Marom) and an EAF MiG-21 on 25 March 1970 (Israel Baharav), lost in an accident in October 1970 (Captain (reserve) Avner Slapak ejected)

82 at least 6 kills including an EAF MiG-21 kill on 20 July 1969 (Giora Epstein), an EAF Su-7 on 24 July 1969 (Shamuel Gordon), an EAF Su-7 on 11 September 1969 (Ilan Gonen), an EAF MiG-21 on 6 October 1969 (Israel Baharav) and an EAF MiG-21 on 11 November 1969 (Menachem Sharon)

83 a 119 Sqn aircraft, damaged on 5 June 1967, made an emergency landing at Hatzor and was taken over by 101 Sqn. It was flown by Captain Guri Palter on 7 June 1967, by Major Ezra Aharon on 8 June 1967 and by Major Amos Amir on 9 June 1967. Returned to 119 Sqn after the war, transferred to 101 Sqn in October 1970. At least 11 kills including an EAF MiG-21 kill on 15 July 1967 (Ran Ronen), an SAF MiG-17 on 11 December 1969 (Yitzhak Nir), an EAF MiG-21 on 26 February 1970 (Avraham Shalmon), an EAF MiG-21 on 27 March 1970 (Arnon Lapidot), an EAF MiG-21 on 2 April 1970 (Avraham Gilad), an EAF Su-7 on 28 April 1970 (Dror Harish) and an EAF MiG-21 on 14 May 1970 (Amos Amir). Lost in the 1970s

84 a 119 Sqn aircraft, an RJAF Hunter kill on 29 November 1966 (Ran Ronen), transferred to 101 Sqn just prior to the Six Day War, crashed on 7/8 June 1967 (Captain David Baruch killed)

86 a two-seat Mirage IIIBJ, ferried to Israel as 4X-FUX (Marignian-Gioia del Colle on 10 March 1966 and Gioia del Colle-Tel-Nof on 11 March 1966) by Daniel Shapira and Guri Palter, 4.5 kills including 3 EAF MiG-21s on 24 October 1973 (Giora Epstien). Exported to Argentina in 1982.

Devoid of drop-tanks, Shahak 15 comes in for a landing. The aircraft displays the 101 badge on the tail but has yet to receave the fin stripes. The aircraft wears none of the kill-markings that would later adorn it.

Above: Shahak 52 is seen on QRA at Hatzor. The aircraft is armed with a single Matra R.530 Yahalom semi-active radar homing AAMs and a pair of small supersonic external fuel tanks.

Seen in flight over Israel in March 1967 are 101 Squadron Shahaks (4)09, (9)42 and (9)51. The aircraft in the foreground is believed to be Shahak 52, though its serial been censored.

10 June: Final Shahak loss

By the last day of the war, 10 June, the fighting in Sinai was virtually over and the IDF/AF was concentrating on supporting the capture of the Golan Heights from the Syrians. The Shahaks flew both CAP and attack missions. Just before 12.00 a 119 Squadron Shahak flown by Lieutenant Colonel Shamuel Shefer, the Tel-Nof air base CO, was shot down by either Syrian AA fire or fragments from the explosion of an ammunition truck which he strafed. The pilot ejected and was retrieved from enemy territory by a Sikorsky S-58 helicopter. Until the arrival of the helicopter, Lieutenant Colonel David Ivry in Shahak 75 and Lieutenant Giora Epstein in Shahak 51 had covered their endangered colleague.

Shlomo Aloni

The cockpit layout of the Shahak, typical of a late 1950s/early 1960s jet fighter, was cramped (especially for the larger pilot) and had a somewhat restricted view.

The IDF/AF destroyed in Operation Moked not only the fighting elements of the EAF but also the support elements. In this 101 Squadron Shahak gun camera film an EAF Ilyushin Il-14 is being strafed.

Shahak 59 – Veteran Mirage

Above: The top-scoring Shahak was 59, which was credited with 13 kills in the hands of a number of different pilots during its Israeli service career. During the Six Day War the aircraft downed an Egyptian Il-14 on 5 June and a MiG-19 the next day. It's finest hour was on 10 July 1970 when, piloted by Israel Baharav, it downed a pair of Egyptian MiG-21s.

Inset: The Shahak fleet saw a lot of combat during its service life, many aircraft carrying kill markings. Here a groundcrewman applies the ninth kill to what is belived to be Shahak 59. The 'two-star' roundels represent UAR (Egyptian) kills, while the 'three-star' markings are Syrian.

Shahak 59 was among a batch of Mirages sold to the Argentine air force as attrition replacements after the Falklands War, becoming C-715. After retirement (possibly due to accident damage) it was placed on display at the Liceo Aeronautico, a high school in Rosario, Santa Fe. The IDF/AF has reportedly taken steps to secure this historic aircraft's return to Israel, though to date (mid-1999) it remains in Argentina.

101 Squadron in the Six Day War – the final analysis

Analysing the results of an IDF/AF Shahak squadron in the Six Day War is not an easy task. The three IDF/AF Shahak squadrons were not only the spearhead of the IDF/AF but they were virtually multi-role units which performed almost any mission: battlefield air interdiction, close air support, suppression of enemy air defences (a more recent term, but this is exactly what the IDF/AF Shahaks did in 1967), quick-reaction alert and, of course, the much sought-after air combats. 101 Squadron flew a total of 337 sorties in the Six Day War, an average of slightly more than 56 sorties per day and slightly more than 11 sorties per pilot, or almost two sorties per pilot per day. There is no marked difference between the number of sorties flown by the more experienced leaders and by the younger, inexperienced pilots: Lieutenant Colonel David Ivry flew 14 sorties totalling 16 hours and 10 minutes in the air, including 90 minutes of night flying (an average of one hour and nine minutes flying time per sortie); Major Ezra Aharon flew 13 sorties, Major Amos Amir flew 12 sorties, Major Dan Sever flew 14 sorties, Captain Guri Palter flew 13 sorties, Lieutenant Giora Epstein flew 12 sorties and Lieutenant Eldad Palter flew 13 sorties totalling 12 hours and 20 minutes in the air for an average of 57 minutes flying time per sortie (daytime only).

Operation Moked on 5 June focused the attention of 101 Squadron on the offensive attack of enemy air bases on the one hand, and on defensive CAPs and QRA scrambles on the other. The squadron flew a total of 85 sorties, of which 40 were attacks on enemy air bases, 42 were either QRA scrambles or CAPs, and only three were committed to attack. However, many of the CAPs and QRA scrambles ended in ground attacks, namely strafing, in response to the immediate and urgent requirements of the ground controller. The first day of the war was the only day in which 101 Squadron pilots flew four sorties per day. Six pilots (David Baruch, Oded Marom, Guri Palter, Itshak Peer, Amnon Shamir and Avner Slapak) achieved such a number, while 13 pilots flew three sorties each and the remaining 11 (including Captain Yair Nueman who was killed on his second mission) flew two sorties each. None of the pilots, however, made more than two attacks on enemy air bases during that day.

The focus on 6 June shifted dramatically. The squadron flew 39 CAPs and QRA scrambles, very similar to the previous day, but Operation Moked was over and the 101 Squadron Shahaks flew a total of 33 BAI and CAS sorties on all three fronts – Egypt, Jordan and Syria – though the vast majority of these missions were flown over Sinai. Another two sorties that day were a photo reconnaissance escort mission by two Shahaks flown by Major Amos Amir in Shahak 12 and Lieutenant Itshak Peer. The maximum number of sorties per pilot on this day was three, performed by 16 pilots, while the other 13 pilots flew two sorties each.

Beginning on 7 June, the number of CAPs and QRA scrambles began to decline, with 29 such sorties on that day. The number of attack sorties was also declining, to 25, of which four developed into air combat. Another four sorties on 7 June were flown to attack Ardaka air base, while that evening the squadron was busy searching for a ship (the aforementioned US Navy spy ship *Liberty*) with three sorties. Naturally, the number of sorties per pilot was also declining, only eight pilots flying three sorties each on 7 June. Two sorties were flown by 17 pilots (including Captain David Baruch who was killed on his second flight), one sortie was flown by three pilots and one pilot did not fly at all on that day.

Another change in mission type occurred on 8 June, when out of 59 sorties the number of CAPs and QRA scrambles remained roughly the same at 32, while the number of attack sorties was exactly that as on the previous day, 25. The balance of two sorties was a visual reconnaissance mission by Lieutenant Colonel Arlozor Lev and Lieutenant Avshalom Ran. However, by this day many of the attack sorties were in fact SEAD, namely, the attack of Egyptian SA-2 batteries. At least seven such sorties were flown. Pilot workload was roughly the same as the previous day: nine pilots flew three sorties each, 14 pilots flew two sorties each (including Captain Binyamin Romach who was killed on his second mission) and four pilots flew a single sortie each.

In the last two days the squadron flew another 58 sorties, to bring the total to 337, during which the squadron lost four Shahaks, a loss rate of one aircraft per 84 sorties. Of the four downed pilots, two were killed without (as far as is known) making an ejection attempt; two ejected safely, one of whom was killed on the ground by hostile Egyptian citizens, and the other, who ejected over friendly territory, was retrieved. The four losses had varied causes: the first was most likely shot down by an Egyptian MiG-21 with an AA-2 Atoll, the second was the victim of an Egyptian SA-2, the third was lost to Egyptian AA fire and the fourth was attributed to fuel starvation after an air combat.

All the 101 Squadron losses were over the Egyptian front, as were all its kills. The squadron was credited with 14 kills, of which 12 were claimed with cannon fire, although both the MATRA R.530 Yahalom semi-active radar homing AAM and the indigenous Rafael Shafrir IR AAM were in service. The former missile was designed for the interception of bombers and was probably not well suited for the tactical situations of the Six Day War. The latter AAM was not a mature weapon system and was rapidly succeeded by the far more successful Shafrir 2, with which 101 Squadron had a fruitful association in the coming years. The remaining two kills were an EAF MiG-21 which entered a spin and crashed on 5 June when threatened by Major Dan Sever (a kill without a weapon) and an EAF MiG-19 which entered a spin and crashed during an air combat versus 101 Squadron Shahaks on 7 June, with the kill awarded to the squadron but not to a specific pilot. The other 101 Squadron kills included two EAF MiG-21s, four EAF MiG-19s, a single EAF MiG-17, four EAF Su-7s and a single EAF Il-14. The squadron pilots virtually shot down everything they encountered, regardless of type.

The most interesting point of this air-to-air analysis is that 13 pilots claimed one kill each, unlike the other two IDF/AF Shahak squadrons in which pilots claimed five, three and two kills. Moreover, five of the 30 101 Squadron pilots on 5 June 1967 were credited with kills in the pre-Six Day War border clashes with the EAF and SAF, but none of them claimed a kill during the Six Day War.

The squadron entered the Six Day War on 5 June 1967 with five MiG-killer pilots and emerged from the war on 10 June with 17 MiG-killers (the 18th MiG killer pilot, Captain Binyamin Romach, was killed in the war). Of those 17 pilots, six became aces in the coming years including the two top-scoring IDF/AF aces, Giora Epstein with 17 kills and Iftach Spector with 15 kills. The two 101 Squadron Six Day War pilots who became IDF/AF commanders in later years – David Ivry (IDF/AF commander 1977-1982) and Amos Lapidot (IDF/AF commander 1982-1987) – were not credited with kills, although both were involved in a number of air combats during their long and distinguished careers as fighter pilots.

Top: Capt David Baruch was killed on the night of 7/8 June 1967 while flying the ex-119 Squadron Shahak 84. He had joined 101 Squadron from the Ouragan OTU.

Above: Maj Ezra Aharon led the formation to attack 101 Squadron's most distant target – Beni Suef on the first day of the war. He flew with 101 Squadron as a Hatzach.

Left: Standing in front of a F-16A Netz displaying 16 kill markings is Col Giora Estein. He retired as a Netz reserve pilot on 20 May 1997. He was a 101 Squadron Shahak pilot between 1966 and 1974.

An Industry of Prototypes

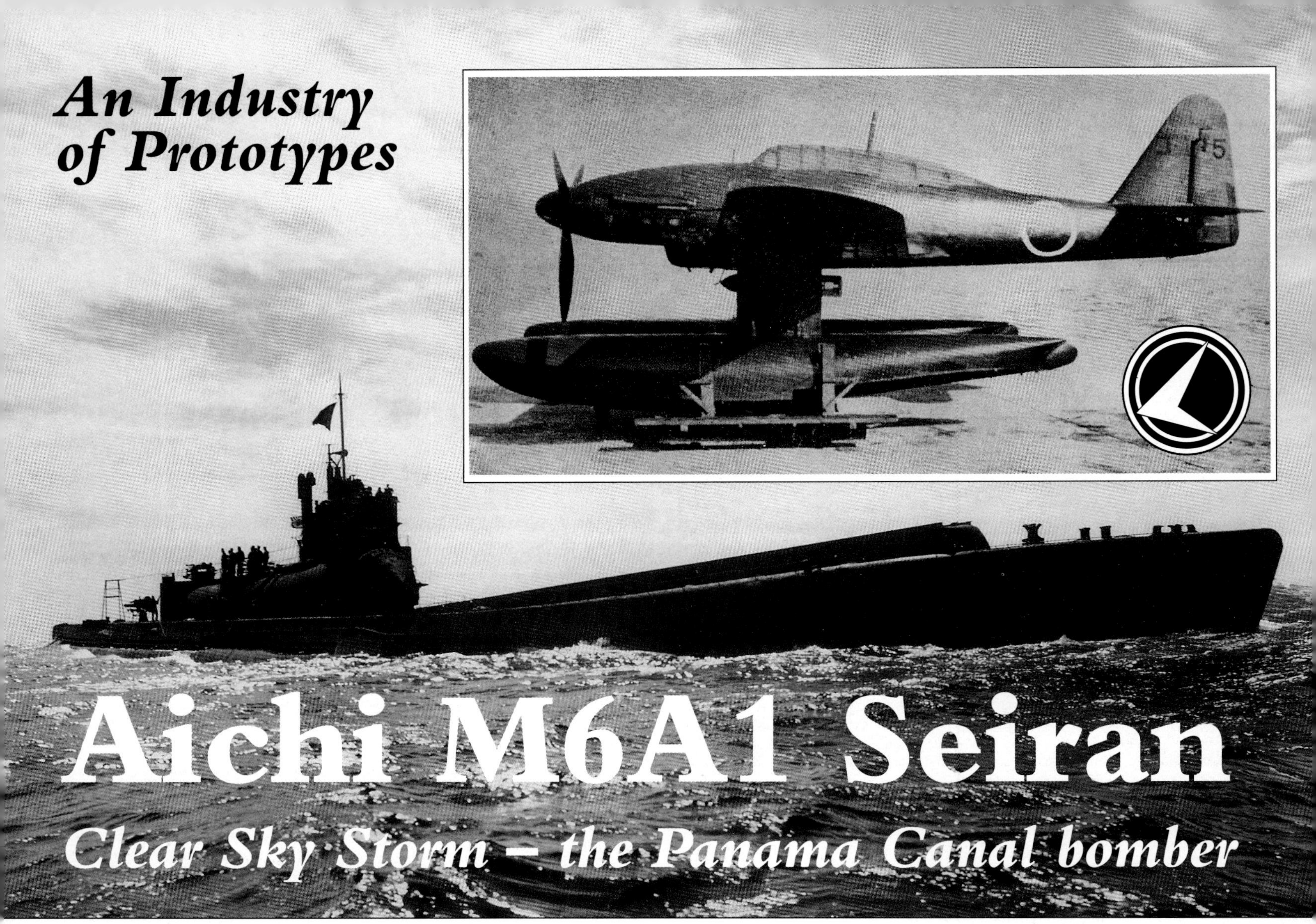

Aichi M6A1 Seiran

Clear Sky Storm – the Panama Canal bomber

In the final months of the Pacific war, world newspaper headlines came very close to reading "Japan Attacks the Panama Canal" – an event that would have been unbelievable at the time. Had the training of Japan's submarine-launched bomber force been completed as the Imperial Japanese Naval Headquarters had planned, it was not an unrealistic possibility that this Japanese attack upon the canal might have taken place.

Inset: The Seiran had pleasing lines for a seaplane, though it was originally conceived without floats. The aircraft shared a number of design features with the Aichi-built Yokosuka D4Y Suisei.

Above: When first sighted by the US Navy, I-400's bulk was almost unbelievable. Seen here on 28 August 1945, the giant sub was about to surrender to the USS Weaver. *Note the hangar tube and the catapult rail between it and the bow.*

This strategic plan made by the Japanese early in World War II would have had a damaging psychological effect on mainland America, much like that of American B-25 Doolittle raiders on Japan in April 1942. More importantly, since the war in Europe had ended and Allied forces were at Japan's doorstep, the need to block the canal had increased in order to slow this shift of military might to the Pacific theatre. Yet, in the final days, the plan had to be altered. The attack against the canal, which was nearly underway, was diverted to Ulithi Atoll, 1,600 miles (2575 km) south of Japan. It was here that Japanese planners thought the US fleet was at anchor, preparing for its final thrust at the home islands of Japan. The war ended a mere two days before the planned attack and this Japanese force of submarine aircraft-carriers surrendered at sea. To have hit loaded troop transports and major ships of the Allied fleet when so vulnerable while at rest in the water might have brought devastating results.

The weapon system of submarine aircraft-carriers and their unique aircraft was conceived

The Seiran's configuration when stowed aboard its submarine is clearly shown in this Japanese artwork.

Seiran's M6A1 designation explained

The Japanese navy's M6A1 designation assigned to the Seiran was unusual in the previously regimented system of identifying aircraft. M symbolised Special Purpose Plane, 6 meant the sixth design within this series, A was the manufacturer code for Aichi, and 1 indicated that it was the first version. The '6' implies that five preceding designs existed; however, none did. The designation was a compromise of various ideas. It was the opinion of Vice Admiral Misawa Wada, Chief of Yokosuka Navy Research and Development Arsenal, that the designation MXY6 was most appropriate: not only did the M signify Special Plane but MXY was in keeping with special design projects that emitted from Yokosuka, such as the concept of the Seiran. '6' was the next number in this series. The weapon delivery method of the Seiran was originally dive-bombing, and the Seiran's chief designer, Norio Ozake, felt that D6A1 was the rightful designation for the Seiran, D being the established designation for a carrier dive-bomber. This proposal was endorsed by Rear Admiral Jiro Saba, Chief of the Airframe Section, Yokosuka Naval Arsenal. '6' would have been the next number in the D series although the 5 was little more than a design concept. After considerable debate, a compromise was agreed upon. In light of the Special Plane type, M was substituted for D, which accounts for the numbering irregularity which becomes so apparent when listing aircraft alphabetically by the first letter designator. That the suggested MXY6 designation also contained a '6' was purely coincidental.

early in the war, yet remained unknown to the Allies until the very end. These I-400-class submarines were known as the Sen Toku, or Toku Gata Sensuikan, which literally means Special Type Submarine. Each vessel carried three single-engined bombers in an offset deck-level watertight hangar, an arrangement that placed the conning tower well to port. Although the primary purpose of these submarines was to carry and launch their bombers for aerial strikes, each was equipped with eight bow torpedo tubes and 20 torpedoes, in addition to deck guns.

These gigantic submarines were the largest in the world, measuring 122 m (400 ft 3 in) in length, and having a displacement of 5,222.8 tons (6,560 tons when submerged). This was far greater than the largest American submarine at that time, the 2,710-ton *Argonaut.* Range could be as far as 30,000 nm (34,500 miles; 55520 km) at 16 kt (18 mph; 30 km/h) or 39,500 nm (45,425 miles; 73,102 km) at 14 kt (16 mph; 26 km/h). With an operational endurance of four months, the submarines were capable of making a round trip to any part of the world. Eighteen of these giant submarines were originally planned, able to attack West Coast US cities as well as round Cape Horn to those on the East Coast. As the war progressed and resources were diverted from the planned construction of giant submarines, less ambitious plans were focused on the destruction of the Panama Canal.

Despite many construction problems, the *I-400* and *I-401* had been completed on 31 December 1944 and 8 January 1945, respectively, while *I-402* was nearly ready for service by the time the war ended. *I-404* had been launched and was scheduled for completion by the end of August 1945 but was sighted and sunk in June by US aircraft while being fitted as it lay in hiding against a sheltered island. At this point, only the keel was laid for *I-405* and *I-403* had been cancelled.

Clear Sky Storm

The aircraft to be carried aboard these submarines was the M6A1 Navy Experimental 17-Shi Special Attack Bomber, called Seiran. This name literally means Clear Sky Storm, though for many years it was translated as Mountain Haze. This model was the first aircraft designed as a bomber for submarine duty, all others having a primary role of reconnaissance. Aichi Aircraft Co., a builder of aircraft exclusively for the navy, was selected to design and build these special aircraft. An early consideration was to make the D4Y1 Suisei ('Judy') foldable for submarine duties. This was found to be impractical, so an all-new design was created around the inverted 12-cylinder liquid-cooled inline Atsuta 31 engine.

The Seiran was an all-metal monoplane with a crew of two, and could carry an 850-kg (1874-lb) bomb or torpedo when floats were not attached. To be able to fit inside the 3.5-m (11½-ft) watertight hangar-tube on the submarine deck, the wings of the Seiran would fold against the fuselage sides like that of the Grumman TBF Avenger. The outer portions of each stabiliser and elevator hinged at 90 cm (35 in) from the fuselage centreline and folded downward 90°, supported by stanchions connected to the fuselage. Vertical clearance was obtained by folding the tip of the fin to the right at 118°. It was the propeller that dictated the size of this tubular hangar, which gave only 15 cm (6 in) clearance at each tip.

The plan called for these aircraft to be used only once for an attack and for those returning to the submarines to be ditched alongside and the crews recovered. Twin floats were a late addition to the design for the purpose of ferry flights and crew training, but were not planned for combat use. Realising the success that might be gained with surprise attacks, a light weapons load of 250-kg (551-lb) bombs could be carried with the weighty floats attached so that returning aircraft could be hoisted aboard and serviced for follow-on attacks. Therefore, separate tubes for the floats became part of the submarine design.

By the autumn of 1944, with construction of submarines and aircraft well advanced, aircraft mechanics were selected to fill certain crew positions aboard these undersea aircraft-carriers. Those having previous experience aboard seaplane-carrying submarines were high on the selection list and these highly skilled men became the nucleus for training the many additional members who were needed. Their duties were also to include sailor responsibilities, so they were assigned and sent to their respective submarines at Sasebo and Kure Naval Arsenals, where they learned the intricacies of the submarine as it was being built.

The Seiran Kokutai (Air Corps) came into its own on 15 December 1944 at Kashima Air Base in Chiba Prefecture, when it was designated the

***Above:* One of the Seiran prototypes is seen here with a 250-kg semi-armour piercing high explosive bomb slung under its centreline. This was the maximum bomb load for a Seiran when floats were fitted. Without floats, an M6A1 was able to deliver an 850-kg bomb or torpedo.**

***Below:* This view from the conning tower of an *I-400* shows the catapult used to launch a Seiran, which sat on a 'launching car' which in turn ran along the catapult track.**

***Bottom:* I-400 and I-401 are seen here with the similar, but smaller I-14, in Tokyo Bay prior to scuttling. Again, the hangars and catapult tracks are clearly visible.**

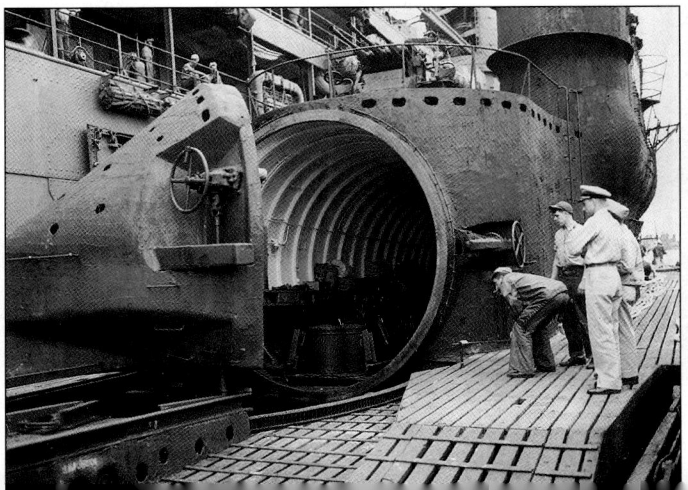

The hangar tube, large enough to house three Seirans, was positioned beneath the conning tower of an I-400-class submarine. Here an American boarding party inspects* I-400 *upon its arrival at Yokosuka following Japan's surrender. Plans existed for the construction of 18 of these vessels. In the event, of the first six (*I-400 *to* I-405*), the first three were completed and* I-403 *was cancelled (having possibly suffered damage in an air raid) along with* I-406 *to* I-417*.* I-404 *and* I-405 *remained incomplete.

Aichi M6A1-K Nanzan

When the Seiran project was first conceived, these aircraft were not to have a means of recovery since the missions would be one-way. However, there was a need for airframes suitable for flight testing and flight crew training, so two Seiran airframes were produced separately with retractable landing gear. They became M6A1-K, the 'K' signifying trainer, and were renamed Nanzan. Of unusual interest in the appearance of the Nanzans was the omission of the upper portion of the fin that balanced so neatly the profile of the Seiran. The absence of the large floats meant that tail surfaces could be smaller, so the folding upper section of the fin was omitted to simulate the directional stability of a Seiran with floats. The Nanzans were fitted with catapult attachment points and folding flight surfaces as on the Seiran. They, too, could have been launched from the giant Sen Toku submarines, either for training and test missions to be recovered at shore bases, or to be spent in combat.

631st Kokutai. In command was Captain Ryunosuke Ariizumi, a man who would become commanding officer of the 1st Submarine Flotilla, a unit consisting of these carrier subs and the Seiran bombers. All were assigned to the 6th Fleet headquarters at Kure, the only fleet to be comprised entirely of submarines.

When the submarines were ready to take on the Seirans, the 631st Kokutai moved to Kure where training began on 2 April 1945. It was soon apparent that these waters off Kure in the Inland Sea were too confining for the super-submarines to manoeuvre properly for operational training, and they were compelled to move into the open waters of the Sea of Japan. Training began at 02.00 (local time), for it was in these early morning hours that Seirans were to be sent against their real targets. Each attachment point on the Seirans was coated with luminous paint to facilitate assembly in the hours of darkness. Exercises – of swift surfacing, preparing and launching the Seirans, a crash dive, then resurfacing for the retrieval of the aircraft – seemed continuous. Once the 12-ton electrical crane had hoisted the Seirans from the water and all had been stowed aboard, the submarines would again settle quickly beneath the surface. This operation was repeated over and over, in ever-less time.

While the submarine was preparing to surface, the servicing of the Seiran would already be underway. Warmed engine oil and engine coolant were pumped from tanks within the submarine hangar into the aircraft's systems to minimise engine warm-up time on the catapult. Once surfaced, the heavy power-driven nose cover of the hangar tube was opened, and the first two Seirans on their launching cars were rolled out onto the catapult launch track; simultaneously, the floats supported on dollies were withdrawn from their storage compartments. The pylons were then attached to the floats, which in turn were attached to the now-extended wings of the aircraft. Ten men handled the float attachment phase, which took two and a half minutes to accomplish. In the early planning of the Seiran design, the floats could be jettisoned in flight, but when it was discovered that their weight would adversely affect the bomb or torpedo load, this feature was not developed. Instead, for optimum bomb loads, the Seirans would be launched without floats attached.

By the end of the six-week training period, the time to assemble and launch the first aircraft had been cut to seven minutes, and all three could be launched in just over 30 minutes. Since storage facilities for the third aircraft were an afterthought in the design of the submarines, it required 15 minutes to prepare it after the launch of the second. These times could be reduced during actual operations when launching the Seirans without floats.

In today's terms, the Seiran would be referred to as a 'hydraulic aircraft', for it had many actuators and hoses connected to various moving parts. However, all of the hydraulic activation was only necessary when preparing the aircraft for flight, and none was actuated by the pilot. The activation controls were accessed through a hatch on the left side of the fuselage at the waist, where the hydraulic pressure hose from the submarine was connected to the aircraft. The wings were extended hydraulically, controlled by a series of sequencing valves, and another actuator rotated the wing to its level position. The main locking pin was inserted into the main spar hydraulically, but the forward and aft spar locking pins had a screw device for manual insertion.

Operation Arashi

It was only after Captain Ariizumi brought his well-trained submarine group to its home port of Maizuru, confident that his task force was capable of neutralising the canal, that he learned the attack plan had been changed. This was disappointing news to all who had trained so well and so long to neutralise the canal, but their new mission was clear: there was reason to believe that the US Navy task force was at anchor at Ulithi Atoll, preparing for the invasion of Japan's home islands; the Seiran Kokutai was to attack the fleet by any means in order to cause maximum damage. The codename given to this mission was Operation Arashi, which in direct translation means storm.

Above: This heavily damaged Seiran was photographed in Japan soon after the surrender at Aichi's Eitoku plant, near Nagoya. It is believed to be one of eight prototypes that would have originally been painted orange overall, as was common practice with test aircraft. To the rear is an engineless D4Y4 Suisei.

Left: This Seiran was stored for many years at NAS Alameda, California and is seen here during a short term spell as an open air exhibit in October 1960. The blue spinner is believed to have come from a D4Y.

***Top left:* Under restoration at NASM's Garber Facility, the aircraft pictured opposite at NAS Alameda is expected to be completed in 1999.**

***Above:* A pair of restored floats awaits reunion with NASM's Seiran. In its primary tactical role, the Seiran would have flown without floats, which were fitted for ferry and training flights.**

Having relocated this flotilla to Ominato on northern Honshu for their new mission, one by one the four submarines of this task force departed for their destinations. First to leave were *I-13* and *I-14*, with a one-day separation. These were smaller submarines than the two I-400s with hangar tubes designed for two Seirans, but, for this mission, each carried two C6N1 Saiun (Myrt) reconnaissance aircraft. This part of Arashi was called Operation Hikari (meaning light), and the ships were headed for Truk Island, an outpost still under Japanese control that had been bypassed by advancing Allied forces. The aircraft would be assembled there, and on a predetermined date they were to overfly Ulithi and discover if the US fleet was there; Ariizumi did not want to launch his floatless force of Seirans on their one-way mission if their target ships were no longer there. *I-13* was intercepted by US carrier aircraft and was sunk, but *I-14* succeeded in reaching Truk.

The two I-400-class subs also came under air attack, but escaped damage. On 15 August, when they were near the waters of their respective aircraft launch locations, the Emperor announced to his people that their country had surrendered. For an undisclosed reason, Naval Headquarters merely radioed to the submarine force a message postponing the attack from 17 August to 25 August. At dawn on 16 August, however, the flagship *I-401* received a radio message from 6th Fleet Headquarters, this time informing them of the surrender and that the flotilla was ordered to return to the nearest Japanese port.

On 20 August 1945, an additional order was received to destroy all offensive weapons and important documents aboard the submarines. Difficult as it was for the men involved, ammunition was thrown overboard, and torpedoes were fired from their tubes. One torpedo circled and actively pursued *I-400*, passing dangerously close.

To the astonishment of the crew on one of these giant subs, the drill order was given to prepare the Seirans for catapult launch. In regimented order the bombers were withdrawn from the hangar, swiftly assembled, and catapulted from the ship. Their propellers were still, however, and the pilotless Seirans soon staggered in flight and fell into the sea. Their pontoons and fuselages had been punctured and soon they slipped out of sight. On the other submarine, the three unassembled Seirans were merely dragged from their watertight compartment, their metal skins were slashed, and they were pushed into the water.

This was the ignominious end of the long struggle for Seirans to prove themselves in battle.

An unconfirmed story has emerged in recent years – in at least three Japanese-language accounts of the Seiran – that adds a new twist to this intended attack. According to this account, while preparing to depart their base at Ominato, the Seirans were brought from their tubular hangars, painted silver and emblazoned with US blue and white stars and bars. So secret was this disguise that one crewman spread himself across the wing insignia when a Japanese aircraft flew overhead, not wanting to risk the American insignia being seen and the aircraft attacked. The intention was that their appearance would confuse Allied pilots into thinking the floatless Seirans might be P-51 Mustangs, and any resultant hesitation to attack would increase the likelihood that their attack mission would succeed. Evidence of the truth of this story now lies at the bottom of the sea.

The saga of the Seiran Kokutai and its near-surprise planned attack is hardly mentioned in the history of World War II. Aside from US Navy accounts and photographs of the Sen Toku submarines, there are no relics of their existence. After they had been sailed from Yokosuka to Hawaii by the US Navy and studied in some detail, orders were issued to dispose of the subs. Singly, they were taken to sea and used for naval gunfire targets. Even super-submarines could not withstand such pounding and inevitably they slipped beneath the waves. As one US Navy officer fittingly said of the boats, "These giant subs looked like prehistoric monsters. And like the Diplodocus or the mighty Brontosaurus of old, they, too, were apparently too big to survive."

Sole survivor

One Seiran remains, however, as testimony of this unique weapon system. Following the war, a large number and variety of Japanese aircraft were selected and shipped to the US for evaluation. Among them were one or two Seirans. As interest in former enemy equipment waned, only significant examples were retained for museums, including one Seiran. For many years it was stored at NAS Alameda, California, and exhibited on special occasions. In 1962 it was shipped to the National Air and Space Museum's storage facility at Silver Hill, Maryland. There it remained in outdoor storage for a number of years, like so many other aircraft, as indoor storage space was not available for the entire collection. In time, restoration began, and over a period of many years now nears completion, so hopefully this sole survivor of an audacious plan will be seen again.

Robert C. Mikesh

The pilot's station (right top) sported a Navy Type 3 Gun/Bombsight Mk 1, Model 1 – the most modern such device used by the Japanese navy in the Pacific war. The rear cockpit (right middle) featured a gyro-stabilised inclinometer, compass and command radio, with a 13-mm Type 2 machine-gun mounted facing aft.

0-61279

Convair F-102 Delta Dagger

Evolved from wartime German research, the Convair F-102A (and the two-seat TF-102A) was the first pure delta-winged fighter to enter service. Initial problems, including an unwillingness to go supersonic, delayed its introduction and forced a complete redesign. Its front-line career was brief, but three times as many 'Deuces' were built than its successor, and it saw service with far more units, including two foreign customers.

A classic overhead view shows the 60° delta planform of the F-102A. Overcoming the initial failings of the YF-102, Convair went on to build 1,000 delta-winged 'Deuces', and followed up with the successful F-106 and the less successful B-58.

Though it served briefly in combat in a distant foreign clime, the Convair F-102 Delta Dagger left a mark on history because of its long service with the US Air Force and Air National Guard on the home front. Among several fighters in the 'Century series' (those with designations beginning with 100 or more), the F-102A guarded North America during the years when an atomic attack was a real and immediate possibility.

The F-102 had a long and costly development that taught the world a great deal about supersonic flight and about integrated weapon systems. Once it began to reach operational squadrons, it developed a cult of pilots and maintainers who shrugged off its minor faults, revelled in its spectacular performance, and never lost the thrill of performing, seeing, or hearing an afterburner take-off with that J57 engine sending a plume of flame into the exhaust.

The first powered delta-winged aircraft to fly was Convair's Model 7-000, or XF-92A. Based on research by Alexander Lippisch in wartime Germany (who only got as far as testing gliders), the XF-92A was scaled up to produce the ultimately unsuccessful YF-102.

To repeat an appellation that pilots use too often for their mounts, many who flew this aircraft dubbed it 'the Cadillac of the skies'. Once teething troubles lay behind, it was stable, reliable, and lethal – and it gave pilots a trip like nothing they had experienced in the slower, clunkier aircraft it replaced.

For a time, it was one of the most advanced fighters in the world – and one of the most difficult to maintain. With its delta wing, it was the penultimate success in a story of technological progress that started with the XF-92, XF-92A, F2Y Sea Dart and B-58 Hustler and later culminated in its successor, the F-106 Delta Dart. It was the F-102 that introduced the area-ruled 'wasp waist' for sustained flight at supersonic speed. And the F-102 was a giant leap forward with many of its features, from radar to afterburner, from its weapons integration concept to its advanced missiles.

In addition to 14 prototype and pre-production specimens, 875 examples of the definitive F-102A single-seater were built, and no fewer than 111 TF-102A two-seaters, for a total population of precisely 1,000 airframes. The 'Deuce' (for no-one ever called it the Delta Dagger, a name which in any event came late in its career) and the two-seat 'Tub' were star performers at air shows and in mock air battles for two decades. In real air fights in Southeast Asia, in conditions for which it had never been designed, the glamour faded. Like the US itself, after Vietnam the F-102 was less a shiny ideal and more a maturing, practical entity that soldiered on in a less innocent world. And by the 1980s, the only F-102s left were those flying as drones.

History

On 8 October 1948, a US Air Force board of senior officers at Muroc AFB, California recommended that the USAF organise a competition for a new, all-weather interceptor, to be operational in 1954. From the beginning, before the size, shape or builder of the aircraft was known, it was dubbed as the '1954 interceptor'. The USAF announced approval of the board's recommendations on 4 February 1949 and ordered that the design competition be held in 1950. Searching for a new way to do business, in November 1949 the USAF decided that the 'weapons system' method would be used in developing the new interceptor. First, an appropriate FCS (fire-control system)

The F-102's most important role was probably providing 'top cover for America' from bases in Alaska, Canada, Greenland and Iceland. After the disbandment of the 31st FIS, the 317th FIS (seen above) became one of the largest fighter squadrons ever, with nearly 50 aircraft detached to locations all over the largest state in the Union.

would be designed. Then, an airframe compatible with the FCS would be developed. At the time, the USAF was fielding 'interim' jet interceptors to guard North America against atomic attack, namely the F-86D Sabre, F-89 Scorpion and F-94, which was later nicknamed Starfire only in its subsequent F-94C variant. A considerable portion of the air defence commitment was still being handled well into the 1950s, however, by day fighters such as the F-86A Sabre.

In January 1950 USAF Air Materiel Command (AMC) invited 50 firms to submit bids for the new interceptor. Some 18 of these companies responded, and a proposal submitted by one manufacturer had a price tag 10 times the amount proposed by another, a sign that the American aircraft industry was stepping into uncharted territory.

In May 1950 the AMC shortened its list of potential manufacturers to six. At the Pentagon, a board headed by Major General Gordon P. Saville looked at proposals for the FCS and farmed out some of its deliberations to an Air Defense Engineering Committee headed by Dr George E. Valley. After review of the recommendations of the Valley committee, the Saville Board narrowed FCS bidders to Hughes and North American by June 1950. Work on the new interceptor continued to be a top-priority item in the Pentagon despite the outbreak of war in Korea later that month. After a visit to the west coast, the Valley committee felt that the best answer was to award FCS developmental contracts to both Hughes and North American. The Saville board disagreed and declared that Hughes was the chosen contractor.

Convair (the name created by the merger of Consolidated and Vultee, later formalised in April 1954) had already done considerable work on delta-winged aircraft that might be applicable to the interceptor mission, among them two wholly different aircraft designated P-92. But Convair was no certainty for a contract award. On 2 July 1951, three winners were named for the airframe proposals. Convair, Lockheed and Republic were authorised to proceed through the mock-up stage. The most promising design of the trio was to be awarded a production contract and dubbed Project MX-1554. As it turned out, Lockheed dropped out, Republic continued through the mock-up stage, and Convair was given a contract for a '1954 interceptor' designated XF-102.

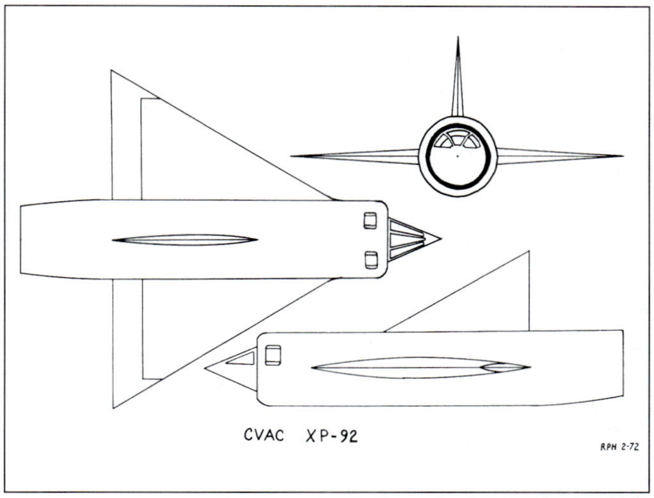

Left and below: Convair's delta-winged fighters, bombers and seaplanes originated with the 1946 XP-92 design for a short-range supersonic interceptor. The XP-92 contained so many radical features, including a compound rocket/ramjet engine, trolley take-off and a single control surface on each wing (dubbed the 'elevon'), that it was deemed sensible to develop a cheap low-speed test aircraft – the XF-92A – first. The XP-92 got as far as the mock-up stage.

Convair's biggest and smallest products are seen here brought together for a photo shoot. The XF-92 was built in Nashville and San Diego, and the B-36 at Fort Worth. The Fort Worth factory was later to create the B-58 Hustler, which owed much to the aerodynamic principles proved by the XF-92.

In the 1950s, the Convair company was equally busy with a range of civil aircraft products. Another shoot was arranged with the XF-92 and the prototype CV-240, first of a long series of 'Convairliners'. The CV-240 was borrowed back from General Motors which, in 1951, had converted it to turbine power with Allison T-38s as the Model 240-21 Turbo-Liner.

XF-92A

The aerodynamic test vehicle built as the Convair Model 7-002 took shape at Vultee Field near Nashville in late 1946 and early 1947. With the closure of the Vultee plant in the summer of 1947, the partially finished airframe was sent to San Diego for completion. After a long period of ground runs and high-speed taxying tests at Muroc, the 7-002 made its first flight there on 18 September 1948. E.D. ('Sam') Shannon became the first pilot to fly a true delta-winged powered aircraft. At the time, the design was still expected to lead to a mixed powerplant (turbojet-rocket) interceptor, but this requirement was dropped while the 7-002 was undergoing further tests in 1949. The engine fitted, a J33-A-23 of 5,200 lb st (23.15 kN) thrust was not powerful enough to push the 7-002 past the sound barrier, but the aircraft's performance was impressive enough to suggest that this would not be a problem given more thrust. The USAF cancelled the P-92 but adopted the 7-002 as a pure research vehicle, designated XF-92A with the serial 46-682. The XF-92A was re-engined with an afterburning 5,900-lb st (26.24-kN) Allison J33-A-29 with water/methanol injection increasing static thrust to 7,500 lb (33.36 kN). The aircraft could now be dived through the sound barrier, but performance and reliability were generally disappointing. A further change of engine, to the J33-A-16 of 8,400 lb st (37.37 kN) was made and the aircraft passed to NACA. A nosewheel collapse ended its flying career in October 1953.

Before any metal was cut, it had already been decided (though it did not exactly work out that way) that the XF-102, powered by the 10,000-lb st (44.48-kN) Pratt & Whitney J57 turbojet engine, would be an interim interceptor pending the advent of the ultimate interceptor, which would be the F-102B with the J67 engine, based on a British engine, the Bristol Olympus. The latter aircraft (with a different engine) became the F-106 Delta Dart and is the subject of a separate history in *Wings of Fame* No. 13.

There now began a seemingly endless series of problems with the fire-control system. The FCS being developed by Hughes and known as the MX-1179 was not going to be ready in time for the F-102A, so the USAF decided that a simpler FCS, dubbed the E-9, would be employed in the F-102. Already, before any F-102 had taken to the sky, on 7 January 1953 the Air Defense Command requested development of an MRIX (Medium Range Interceptor, Experimental) to replace the F-102A and F-102B (later F-106A) by October 1959. As it would turn out, the MRIX would not proceed and, as a result, the F-106A would become the last warplane built in the USA solely for the interceptor mission.

For all Convair's experience, as late as 1953 when the supersonic interceptor was supposed to be far advanced in its development, the company's work had little to commend itself to the Pentagon or anyone else. Indeed, the company produced the wrong aircraft, whose performance in its initial version was described by one expert as "abysmal", and the prototype was destroyed within a week of its first test flight. The goal of an interceptor capable of sustained flight at supersonic speed seemed out of reach, to say nothing of the ultimate goal of a fully supersonic, round-the-clock, all-weather interceptor created as a complete integrated weapon system with advanced radar and missiles. At one point progress on the original YF-102 design – also known as the Model 8-82, the version that was wholly inadequate in every respect – was so discouraging that D. E. Thompson of Hughes Aircraft, maker of the fire-control system, scribbled a note to his boss: 'This is not looking good for early resolution...'

The cancellation of the unpromising YF-102 – its 'Y' prefix signifying service-test duty – hung in the balance and it was obvious that the fighter would need to be completely redesigned if it was to have any chance of saving its San Diego, California manufacturer by winning a lucrative production contract. Another Convair document of the era shows an unnamed company member noting that, 'We are in serious trouble here'.

XP-92 design

The story really begins not in the mid-1950s but in the late 1940s, when Convair drew the task of exploiting wartime German delta-wing research to create a supersonic interceptor using mixed jet and rocket power. This P-92 'pursuit' aircraft (always accompanied by an 'X' for 'experimental' prefix so that it was first the XP-92 then the XF-92) resulted from Convair consultations with Dr Alexander M. Lippisch, German delta-wing pioneer, and from exhaustive wind-tunnel work.

The XP-92, also known by the company designation Model 7, combined internal rocket and ramjet power with an external rocket and was, as a Convair document in

Convair publicity photos show the Model 7-002 in its initial form, left, and after modification with an afterburner and other improvements as the XF-92A. The 7-002 first arrived at Muroc (later Edwards) in April 1948 and conducted a long period of taxi runs while pilots 'Sam' Shannon and Bill Martin got used to the sensitive handling characteristics. One short 'hop' was made in June 1948, three months before the official first flight. In 1951 the afterburning J33-A-29 engine was installed at San Diego. For a period, the aircraft remained in natural metal before receiving the overall white finish seen here.

August 1947 asserted, 'designed for the purpose of destroying attacking enemy aircraft and airborne missiles'. The pilot of this arrow-shaped aircraft sat inside a 'spike' to the round air inlet, looking out through a flush windscreen at air rushing into the ramjet engine around him. There were numerous unconventional features, to put it mildly, on the XP-92 design, and these included the 'take-off and alighting gear': the XP-92 was supposed to go aloft from a 'four-wheel, take-off cart, which is not an integral part of the airplane'. It seemed that 'when the airplane reaches a take-off angle of 18°, the cart is automatically disengaged'. After the XP-92 was aloft, the cart would automatically stop itself. The XP-92 was also equipped with a manually retractable, internal tricycle arrangement which gave new meaning to the term 'landing gear': it really was to be used for landing only.

Before returning to the XP-92, it should be noted that Convair was also creating other delta-winged fighters on its drawing boards. A 28 October 1948 proposal for a 'Class VA long-range special attack airplane' described a triangle-shaped aircraft intended for operation on the US Navy's forthcoming aircraft-carrier, the USS *United States* (CVA-58), which was later cancelled amidst bad blood in Washington over the merits of carriers versus bombers. This Convair delta was clearly meant for the nuclear mission at a time when the aircraft-carrier had not yet been ruled out as part of the US strategic nuclear force. Convair also intended the aircraft to be capable of launching from 'Midway'-class carriers and landing on 'Essex'-class carriers. For a while the US Navy's dream of a new class of carriers was still alive – the *United States* was a smooth-looking warship indeed, lacking the 'island' associated with most carriers, and the Convair aircraft shared this sleekness.

Below: The Howard Hughes-produced movie **Jet Pilot** ***is not regarded as a classic by film buffs or aviation enthusiasts. It might have been more memorable if the 'MIG 23', as played by the XF-92A, had not wound up on the cutting room floor. Although the film was completed in 1950, arguments between Hughes and the USAF over security issues helped delay its release for seven years.***

Left: Majors 'Pete' Everest and 'Chuck' Yeager (seen here) did most of the test flying on behalf of the Air Force. Yeager also did some of the flying for **Jet Pilot.**

The XF-92A suffered nose gear failure on 14 October 1953 while landing at Edwards piloted by NACA's Scott Crossfield. Considered not worth repairing, the airframe later became a travelling exhibit, ending up at the University of the South in Sewanee, Tennessee. It joined the USAF Museum collection in 1969 and is currently being restored for display.

What was not immediately obvious from the slick illustration on the cover of the 1948 report was that the 'Class VA long-range special attack airplane' was actually two flying machines – a small, dart-like mother craft otherwise known as the 'return component', and a droppable pod. The return component featured a 60° delta wing and vertical tail, and a single turbojet engine with afterburner. The enormous pod (the ordnance to be dropped by this aircraft) had three separate engines of its own. The big 'Class VA long-range special attack airplane' would also require six JATO (jet-assisted take-off) units to enable it to get aloft from the carrier deck. The composite aircraft had a take-off weight of 96,260 lb (43664 kg), but weighed only about half as much after dropping its powered load. (VA, it should be noted, was the US Navy's term for a heavier-than-air attack aircraft). The composite concept may have contributed later to the design of the B-58 Hustler bomber at a different facility (Fort Worth, Texas), but the US Navy never proceeded with the 1948 proposal. After briefly hitching its nuclear star to the Lockheed P2V-3C Neptune, which weighed only a little more than the Convair proposal and was strictly a 'one-way' aircraft able to launch from, but not land on, a carrier, the US Navy eventually settled after a series of attack aircraft on the submarine-launched ballistic missile as its contribution to the US nuclear force.

Power for the XP-92 was to have consisted of a combined ducted rocket/ramjet installation: 'Fifteen 50-lb [0.22-kN] thrust rockets discharge into a duct which is also the ram-jet combustion chamber. In addition to the main powerplant section, three 4,000-lb [17.79-kN] thrust unducted rockets are employed for high-power, short-period operation at take-off, in climbing, and for accelera-

The first YF-102, 52-7994, rests in a familiar pose for the Convair camera on the dry lake at Edwards AFB. It was destined to make only seven take-offs and six landings in its brief career.

This Convair montage shows the XF-92A with an early F-102 concept. The faired, almost NACA-type intake design contrasts with that actually used, while everything from the wing root aft is a simple scale-up of the XF-92A.

YF-102

With the principles of delta-winged jet flight proved by the XF-92, Convair's designers decided to take a low-risk approach and scale up the design to carry the MX-1179 weapons system (including the as-yet-unbuilt Falcon missile). The two YF-102 prototypes were essentially the XF-92A scaled up by a factor of 1.22, with lateral intakes, a lowered wing and an afterburning J57-P-11 turbojet giving 14,800 lb (6713 kg) maximum thrust. Dick Johnson flew the first example on 24 October 1953, but only nine days later it was written off when the engine flamed out on take-off, Johnson being unhurt. Testing continued with the second aircraft, but when the transonic region was probed, severe instability and buffeting occurred, and the YF-102 simply refused to accelerate past Mach 1.

Below: The crash landing of the first YF-102 on 2 November 1953, caused by an engine stall on take-off, delayed the flight test programme until January the following year. More importantly, it delayed the discovery that the design was difficult to fly at transonic speed and incapable of going subsonic.

The second YF-102 first flew on 11 January 1954 and, before long, proved that the design had been based on inaccurate or over-optimistic wind-tunnel calculations.

Model 8-82

After flight-testing with the second YF-102 had proved the need for a complete redesign, Convair was left with a second batch of eight aircraft on the production line too advanced to be completed to the new design. The company set out to see what could be done to squeeze some extra speed and improve the handling of the YF-102. A revised wing incorporating conical camber and a new elevon-fuselage junction was added, which reduced buffet and improved handling, but this revised version (Convair Model 8-82) remained subsonic in level flight, only being coaxed to Mach 1.29 in a steep dive.

The third of the eight reconfigured YF-102s (53-1779/1786) sits forlornly on the Muroc dry lakebed, apparently after a nosewheel collapse.

tion to supersonic speed'. A close look at detailed plans of the XP-92, which resembled the Flash Gordon rocket ships of 1930s motion picture serial fame, reveals absolutely no space anywhere on the 18,850-lb (8550-kg) aircraft which could have been used to accommodate radar, armament or, for that matter, sufficient fuel to travel very far. However, the company blithely asserted that the XP-92 – if it got off the ground at all – would have an armament 'of four 20-mm cannons installed in the forward section of the fuselage' with 824 rounds of ammunition.

Mercifully for Convair test pilots, as well as citizens residing on the slope above Lindbergh Field, the airport at the factory which even in the 1940s was situated amidst urban growth, the XP-92 was never completed as a design, let alone built or flown. After the 'P' for 'pursuit' designation had been changed to 'F' for 'fighter' on 5 June 1948, the USAF took the unusual step of reissuing the number 92 and assigning it to a totally different, far simpler – but in the end equally ineffectual – Convair delta-winged fighter.

Below left: This unusual view shows the heavily-framed mult-part windscreen of the YF-102s. The pilot preparing for a test flight here is Air Force Major Fitzhugh 'Fitz' Fulton who later was heavily involved in testing the Convair B-58.

This line-up shows three of the Model 8-82 YF-102s and the surviving original Model 8-80, third from front, which seems to have been fitted with a longer nose cone during tests. When the decision was taken to completely redesign the F-102, 20,000 of the 30,000 tools already purchased had to be discarded, an inevitable result of the early gearing up for production stipulated under the Cook-Craigie Plan.

Enter the XF-92A

The XF-92A (company Model 7-002 or, in some documents, 7002) was a completely different aircraft. It began as a mock-up cobbled together from parts of five other aircraft to save time and money. The aircraft itself was rolled out of the San Diego factory in September 1948. Powered by a 4,800-lb st (21.35-kN) Allison J33-A-23 centrifugal-flow turbojet engine borrowed from an F-80 Shooting Star (and none of the fancy rocket and ramjet gadgetry foreseen for its predecessor), the XF-92A (46-682) was now intended to be only a one-of-a-kind 'dogship' to furnish data from flight tests that would aid in the development of future aircraft, including the future F-102. Orders for two further aircraft (46-683/684) were cancelled before the sole example ever saw the light of day.

The XF-92A boasted a cigar-shaped fuselage housing the jet engine with the cockpit positioned just in front of the powerplant. The engine air inlet was a circular hole in the nose, no longer interrupted by the enormous spike that would have distinguished its predecessor. The XF-92A, initially flown in natural metal with no paint except for markings etc., had a delta wing spanning 31 ft 3 in (9.525 m) with an area of 230.0 sq ft (21.37 m^2). The XF-92A sat astride a rather intricate tricycle landing gear: the nose unit's leg (from a Bell P-63 Kingcobra) retracted forward, while the two main units' legs (from a North American

Below: 53-1784 was the sixth of eight YF-102s. Some vestiges of the XP-92 design remained by this stage in F-102 development, but the production F-102A was to be a very different machine.

After the failure of the YF-102s to go supersonic, Convair put a lengthened model with a relocated fin and wing through wind-tunnel testing. When this also fell short of expectations, they accepted Richard Whitcomb's theories of area rule, further extending and 'wasp waisting' the fuselage. Faced with the prospect of the entire programme being cancelled, Convair worked feverishly to build and fly this new design, the 8-90, in a record 117 days. This, the YF-102A, dubbed the 'Hot Rod', first flew on 19 December 1954.

This head-on view of the 'Hot Rod' illustrates the conical camber (downturned leading edge) that was used on all subsequent F-102s.

Back to the drawing board

Above: The YF-102A (left)was over 16 ft (4.9 m) longer than the YF-102. Other changes included a V-shaped windscreen and new canopy.

Right: Photographed during extensive taxi tests at Lindbergh Field, the first YF-102A, displays its 'Marilyn' fairings. which reduced drag in the transonic flight regime.

After its ground tests, the first YF-102A was taken to Edwards, where it made its first flight on 19 December 1954. Dick Johnson took it through the sound barrier on its second flight two days later. Early the following year, the Air Force rescinded its production hold order and by June the required altitude and speed figures had been met or exceeded.

FJ-1 Fury) pivoted inward about halfway up their struts before retracting outward into the wings. Other dimensions, including a height of 17 ft 8 in (5.38 m), were very similar to those of the earlier, more complex delta-wing design.

Convair had developed considerable sensitivity to the urban 'sprawl' growing on the mesa above Lindbergh Field, so the XF-92A departed San Diego not by air but by truck for the Mojave Desert. E. D. 'Sam' Shannon, a youthful 40 with 20 years of test-pilot experience, took the XF-92A aloft for its maiden flight at Muroc Air Force Base, California (soon to be re-named Edwards) on 18 September 1948. Shannon was sitting in an ejection seat that had been originally designed for the Convair XP-81 compound jet/propeller fighter.

After about 80 test flights at Edwards (and after being publicised along with other Convair products such as the B-36 bomber built in Fort Worth, Texas), the XF-92A was re-engined with a 5,200-lb st (23.13-kN) Allison J33-A-29 equipped with both an afterburner and a water/methanol injection system which increased thrust to 7,500 lb st (33.36 kN). The afterburner increased fuselage length to 42 ft 5 in (12.93 m), significantly altering the appearance of an aircraft that had previously looked puggish and blunt.

The XF-92A reached 590 mph (949 km/h) but apparently was not supersonic, even with the afterburner or even in a dive. USAF test pilot Major Charles E. Yeager praised it as one of the first jet aircraft with workable hydraulic flight controls. Long after Convair was proceeding with its subsequent F-102 – and making a host of mistakes in the initial design of the new fighter – the XF-92A continued to perform flight test duties for the USAF and in a gleaming cream-white paint scheme for NACA (National Advisory Committee for Aeronautics). Long before there was any Soviet fighter with such a designation, the XF-92A was filmed in matte-grey with the name 'MIG 23' painted in huge letters on its tail for the Hollywood epic *Jet Pilot* starring John Wayne – but, alas, this celluloid villain ended up on the cutting-room floor and the movie was released without it. Today preserved at the Air Force Museum in Dayton, Ohio, the XF-92A provided an enormous amount of aerodynamic data for the future F-102 but, ironically, some of the data may have been wrong and thus may have contributed to the tribulations that went into revising the F-102 design to make it supersonic.

Developing an interceptor

In January 1951, Convair entered the USAF's design competition by submitting its specifications for a delta-winged fighter that eventually became the F-102A. Convair was selected to carry out Phase I of a development programme, and in August 1951 entered into a contract for the F-102.

At this juncture, not distracted by the Korean War and focused strongly on the likelihood of war with the USSR, the USAF established the Cook-Craigie plan for the production and development of new combat aircraft such as the future F-102A. The plan was formally dubbed the ADTP (Accelerated Development Test Program) and called for two prototypes and the first 40 production aircraft to carry out all phases of development testing which had, in the past, been carried out by a maximum of six aircraft in a typical test programme. Convair saw two motives behind this scheme: firstly, the advent of sustained supersonic flight would require an almost total reinvestigation of all established criteria for testing aircraft, and secondly the ADTP would shorten the development of a new aircraft by a substantial period of time. The latter goal, especially, was to prove elusive, but it seemed a way towards getting the new interceptor into operational service more rapidly.

Accelerated production plans

More to the point, a slow initial production rate parallel to an intensive test programme would work the 'bugs' out of the new aircraft before hundreds had been built, while at the same time preserving the capability for higher-rate production once that happened. The USAF called for tooling that would produce 10 aircraft per month but could later accelerate to a production rate of 50 aircraft per month. Convair made a counter-proposal which called for a progressive tooling policy that would bring the manufacturer up to the capability for 50 aircraft monthly at a gradual pace. As part of these negotiations, Convair acquired Plant II in San Diego to manufacture the F-102, with A. P. Higgins as works manager.

For the engineering team, the creation of the new aircraft posed numerous challenges as it was designing a new aircraft around a new engine that was, itself, still in the design stage. When they sat in meetings with plant engineers, the designers did not yet know that their delta-winged aircraft would eventually introduce a modified cockpit, fuselage length and shape, wing tips, leading edges, and exhaust. All of these changes to the early F-102 concept were to occur while Convair was building a factory that could accommodate the planning and tooling peculiarities associated with the aerodynamics surface tolerances and contour control requirements inherent to supersonic flying.

The first two YF-102 (company Model 8-80) aircraft (52-7994/7995) began flight tests on 24 October 1953, when Richard L. Johnson took the first aircraft (52-7994) aloft. On 2 November 1953, during its seventh flight, a flame-out occurred during take-off and the YF-102 rose a scant 10 ft (3.05 m) or so, wallowed through the air briefly, then smashed into the runway, seriously injuring Johnson and itself being damaged beyond repair. The cause was later identified as a fuel system failure.

'Sam' Shannon (not Johnson, as often reported) first flew the second YF-102 (52-7995) on 11 January 1954, losing relatively little time as a result of the loss of the first machine. It quickly became evident that wind tunnel tests had been unduly optimistic. This aircraft went supersonic for the first time on 27 January 1954, achieving Mach 1.06, but only with difficulty and then in a dive. Even with the highly regarded 10,900-lb st (48.49-kN) Pratt & Whitney J57-P-11 axial-flow turbojet, which offered 14,000 lb st (62.28 kN) with afterburning, the YF-102 lacked the performance that had been predicted, which included the ability to sustain supersonic speed in level flight. A much-healed Johnson returned to the programme in April, and his experience with the original YF-102 design was summed up in the remark, "Performance found lacking". On 28 April 1954, Major General Albert Boyd became the first military pilot to fly the F-102: Boyd flew many types, and there is no evidence that the F-102 especially impressed him.

Wasp waist

The 'wasp waist' or 'Coke bottle' fuselage of the final YF-102A was the result in part of tests conducted on models and mock-ups in the transonic and supersonic ranges in June 1952 by NACA at Langley Field, Virginia. Richard T. Whitcomb of NACA showed Convair

With its distinctive original short fin, this is the first of four YF-102As, now preserved in New Orleans. The YF-102A was weapons-capable and met a particular milestone on 8 July 1955 when six Falcons and 24 rockets were fired in the space of 10 seconds.

The second YF-102A, 53-1788, reverted to the original heavily-framed YF-102 canopy for a period. Here it is seen partially painted in the grey scheme that was to be worn by the majority of Convair fighters to follow. It was preserved at the now-defunct Florence Air and Missile Museum in Florence, South Carolina. More recently it has moved to the Carolinas Aviation Museum in Charlotte, North Carolina.

One of the most visible improvements incorporated on the YF-102A was a two-panel canopy and a V-shaped windscreen. This latter item reduced drag but took some getting used to for pilots. Later a 'vision splitter' (a black sheet of metal) was added behind the leading edge of the screen to cut down reflections.

This is 53-1791, the first of 1,000 'Deuces'. It is seen here some time after its first flight while testing 230-US gal (871-litre) fuel tanks. These purely subsonic wing tanks were designed to increase the interception range, and were to be jettisoned along with the pylons when combat began. A later design made the tank independently jettisonable.

F-102A

The first production Model 8-10 F-102A followed the 8-90 (YF-102A), making its first flight on 24 June 1955. By this time around 190 aircraft had been ordered, even though YF-102A testing was incomplete. The F-102A had a number of detail changes, including a larger airbrake and redesigned intakes with external splitter plates.

engineers his area-rule principle. Wind tunnel tests showed that the original constant-taper fuselage could lose a tremendous amount of configuration drag – making the aircraft faster and more fuel-efficient – when revised with a pinched mid-section. This meant a design change (in contrast to the original F-102 design, which flew as the YF-102) with an extension of approximately 7 ft (2.13 m) to the rear of the fuselage with a corresponding movement of the vertical tail and an approximately 3-ft 3-in (0.99-m) rearward movement of the delta wing to maintain balance. In blunt words, the original fuselage was too bulky. Yet it would not be until August 1953 that Convair would accept the implications of area rule – while in the meantime manufacturing 10 almost useless YF-102 aircraft with the unwaisted fuselage.

While this was going on, Convair was becoming tooled up to produce the original F-102 design (as flown in YF-102 form) but a company document reported that, 'The performance gains with the J57 engine in the transonic speed range and in high speed at altitude [offered by the redesign of the aircraft] were sufficient to warrant serious consideration of a change in the F-102 configuration in as early in the production program as was feasible. Since this change would have an appreciable effect on the flight test program, [Convair] reviewed the change with all affected Air Force agencies in an effort to obtain a decision as to whether this change [area rule] should be incorporated. It was decided that the change would not have adverse effect' on the goal of having the new fighter in squadron service by early 1956. Nor would the change to the fuselage design jeopardise the ongoing development of the fire-control system.

In May 1954, the USAF decided that the F-102 needed a fire-control system more advanced than the E-9, which was already in service on the Northrop F-89H Scorpion, so the decision was taken that the Hughes E-10 system, soon redesignated as the MG-10, should be prepared for the F-102.

The second YF-102 posed with a block 60 F-102A (below) to show the many changes between the prototype and a late-production F-102A. Immediately obvious are the differences in fuselage cross section, the tall tail and the cockpit glazing. The intake splitter plates and airbrake were among the many other external changes. The YF-102 is fitted with an elongated nose section that contrasts with the stubby unit of the other early 'Deuces'.

Early operations

Rarely, if ever, had a warplane design seen so many changes as those which differentiated the YF-102 from the subsequent YF-102A, or Model 8-90. The outside observer could have been forgiven for thinking that the latter was a wholly new aircraft. On both aircraft, the 'Y' prefix indicated a service-test role, although the original YF-102 was in reality more of an experimental research vehicle.

On 20 December 1954, test pilot Johnson performed the first flight of the first YF-102A (53-1787), dubbed the 'Hot Rod' by some. This much-revised version employed the new area-rule technology and in its external shape closely resembled the production configuration of the new fighter. This aircraft also introduced a cleaned-up cockpit and canopy design, a lengthened fuselage and a modified exhaust area, all of which were retained on production machines, and the changes gave the YF-102A a look distinctly different from that of the YF-102 aircraft that had been flying for more than a year. The YF-102A had an interim powerplant in the form of the J57-P-41 turbojet

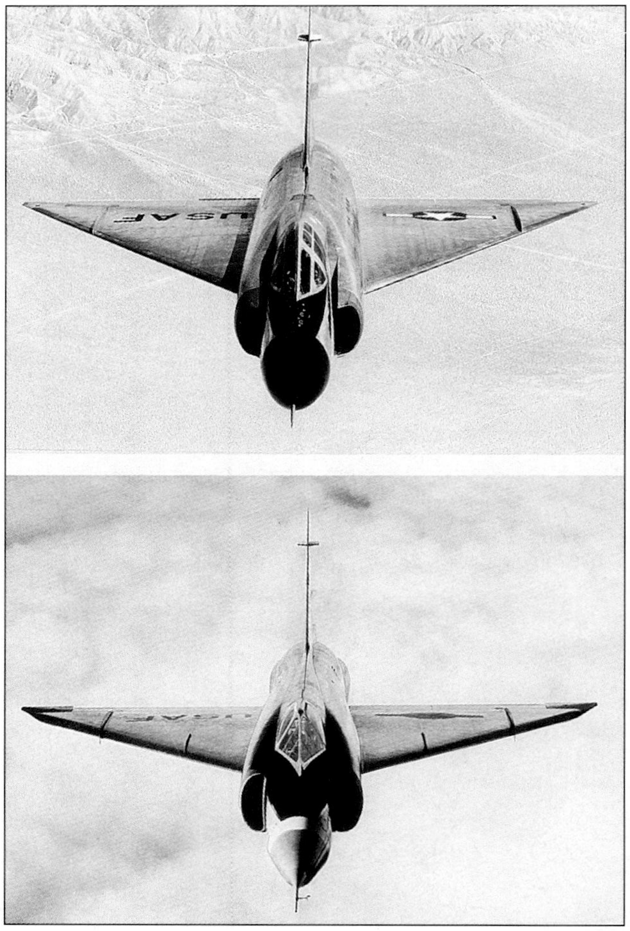

Convair also issued these comparison images of a YF-102 (top) and a YF-102A, showing the tubular fuselage of the YF-102 and the 'Coke bottle' area-ruled fuselage of its successor. Note also the extra wing fences on the YF-102A.

Seen turning finals for Wright Field, this early F-102A, the last of five F-102A-15s, was assigned to trials work with Air Research and Development Command. On this particular test, a KB-50 tanker had been spraying water over the 'Deuce' at high altitude as part of investigations into the type's icing characteristics. A small residue of ice is just visible on the underside of the nose.

and also the small fin associated with early 'Deuce' aircraft, and was one of the few aircraft in the series to fly in natural metal finish. 'CONVAIR UNVEILS NEW PLANE', headlined the *San Diego Evening Tribune* two weeks later on 5 January 1955.

The new aircraft also behaved differently: Johnson discovered that it needed less runway for take-off, could achieve Mach 1.2 in level flight, and was still climbing when the altimeter read 51,600 ft (15727 m).

While the YF-102A was being tested, Convair was exploring other ideas. In 1955, the company briefly explored the possibility, for the US Navy, of a carrier-based version of its new fighter, using laboratory models based on the original YF-102 design and studying the concept's use with the C-7 and C-11 American adaptations of the British-developed steam catapult. The company studied variations in catapult attachment point, catapult bridle length and other features. Had it been built, the US Navy version would presumably have been designated F3Y-1. Convair was later to go to even greater effort in mooting a carrierborne version of the subsequent F-106A, but neither the 'Deuce' nor the 'Six' ever came close to flying in naval livery.

Service test batch

Convair eventually turned out four YF-102A (53-1787/1790) service test aircraft. For reasons never made clear, the second of these retained the 'prison bar' braced canopy of the earlier YF-102 aircraft, while the other three adopted the new canopy shape. Phase I performance testing was conducted from 20 December 1954 through to the end of February 1955, and confirmed performance expectations for the new YF-102A configuration. The first aircraft achieved a speed of Mach 1.20 at 35,000 ft (10668 m) on 21 December 1954, on 29 December exceeded an altitude of 52,000 ft (15850 m), and on 21 January 1955 flew to the highest altitude yet reached, namely 55,130 ft (16804 m).

Phase II testing of the early 'Deuces', covering flying qualities, stability and control, lasted until March 1956. Thereafter, the first YF-102A was modified with the tailpipe shape intended for the F-106A interceptor and was flown until 25 April 1956 to evaluate this feature. The flight test programme for the YF-102A was completed on 2 October 1956. Fully a decade later, the first YF-102A would briefly reappear in a new role. In the mid-1960s, apparently after it was no longer airworthy, the aircraft became the first 'Deuce' to be painted in the T.O.114 camouflage scheme adopted during the years of the Vietnam War. It wore an early version of the 'camo' scheme which left the radome white and the radio call number (serial number) in white lettering on the tail. All F-102 warplanes that eventually acquired the green, brown and tan warpaint received it at Convair's Plant 2 in San Diego and were flown back to operational units from Lindbergh Field.

Right and below: A series of publicity photos was taken of a quartet of early F-102s shortly before delivery to the Air Force in April 1956. FC-792, and -794 were F-102A-5s and FC-795 and -796 were -10s. There were only four of the first block and three of the latter produced, indicating the high number of modifications requested and incorporated after early testing.

***Left:** Edwards Test Track Branch and Convair engineers adjust the rockets on an F-102A nose-section prior to another high-speed test.*

***Below:** (top left) The F-102A nose reaches peak velocity which is maintained by sustainer rockets, top right. The canopy jettisons and, by the last frame, the seat and pilot dummy are emerging. The time span covered by these frames is only a quarter of a second.*

Ejection seat

Unlike the later F-106 seat, there was no official requirement for the F-102 escape system to cope with ejection at high altitude and high Mach. A conventional explosive cartridge-fired seat manufactured by Weber was fitted, although there had been a proposal for an elaborate capsule system. F-102A ejection seat testing required the use of one of the first supersonic rocket sled tracks in existence, at the Air Force Flight Test Center at Edwards AFB. The TF-102 trainer offered particular challenges, being the first supersonic aircraft with side-by-side seating.

Space normally used for the weapons system on the TF-102 was used to mount test recording equipment on the nose section used in ejection tests. The high-speed test track was dubbed 'The Edwards and Western Supersonic Railroad'.

While the 'Deuce' was still a service-test type, Stanley Aviation developed a pilot capsule that would permit bail-out from the new interceptor at supersonic speed. A mock-up was completed using the braced YF-102 canopy configuration. The capsule enabled the pilot to eject upwards in a pressurised, air-tight and water-tight cocoon designed to shield him from wind blast and, if necessary, to keep him afloat at sea. Stanley hoped to sell the system not only for the F-102 but for other fighters in the 'Century' series. A working example was never built, and the idea was then abandoned in favour of a conventional ejection seat.

It is worth noting as a footnote regarding the earlier 'Deuce' prototypes that, at some point in the test programme, 52-7995 (the second YF-102 and oldest surviving aircraft in this series) was modified with the nose associated with the very different YF-102A, possibly to serve as a test ship for the MG-10 system. The new nose section was apparently painted in Dayglo colours. This aircraft did not, of course, have the area-ruled fuselage and other features found on the YF-102A, and retained the braced canopy found only on the YF-102 aircraft and a single YF-102A, but the new nose made it look more like the 'new' F-102 than the old.

F-102A model

When 53-1791 made its maiden flight on 24 June 1955, the 'Y' prefix vanished like a hot potato. Convair announced that this was the first production fighter in the series even though it was nothing of the sort. In fact, the

***Below:** In March 1956, the F-102A was, like most USAF aircraft before and since, sent to Alaska to prove its suitability for cold-weather operations. This early production aircraft is shown with cockpit and weapons bay exposed to the elements at Ladd Field.*

Service entry

The F-102A entered service with the 327th Fighter Interceptor Squadron at George AFB, California in April 1956. Even this date was seven months behind the revised delivery schedule agreed in March 1954. A month before this date, the USAF and Convair had decided on further design revisions, including enlarging the vertical fin, and the 327th was to be the only operational unit to use the 'small tail' F-102s.

Air Defense Command was eager to publicise its hot new interceptor and staged a series of fine publicity pictures, showing the 327th FIS at full strength and conducting a practice 'scramble'.

'weapon system' was nowhere near finalised as the FCS was still being refined and other production-standard features had not yet been installed. Flight testing for the F-102A, as distinguished from the YF-102A, began on 24 June 1956. Initially, 53-1791 and the airframes that followed soon after it still had the interim J57-P-41 engine, Case X wing with cambered leading edges and wing tips, an area-ruled fuselage and a small vertical tail surface.

During flutter tests 53-1791 demonstrated some unsatisfactory handling qualities above Mach 1.20. This led to extensive flight testing between July 1955 and January 1956 to determine corrective modifications. The result was an extended engine inlet ramp, beef-up of the engine inlet duct inter-wall, and bifurcation of the inlet duct wedge. After these modifications, the first F-102A demonstrated

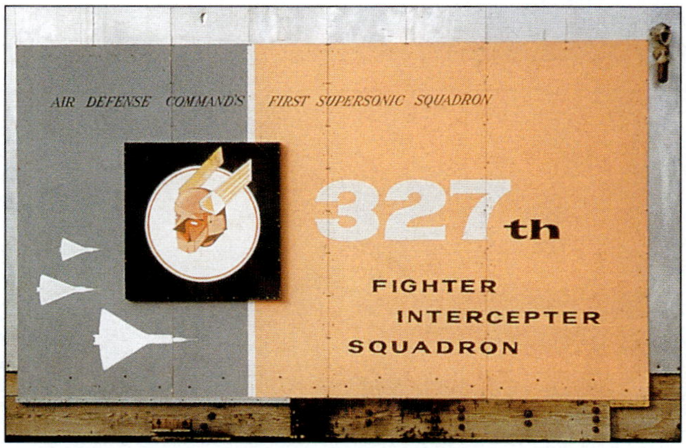

Left: The 327th was equally proud of its new supersonic interceptors, although the smart signage masked a number of frustrating teething problems. These included landing gear defects and disintegrating speedbrakes.

Left and below: The 327th's early F-102As were smoothed and polished and proudly wore the squadron's iron mask badge. Variations in markings, even on the very first aircraft, included the position of the national insignia and of the 'U.S. Air Force' titles. The squadron commander's aircraft received the one-off chequered tail pattern seen below.

An F-102A-41-CO shows off the exceptionally clean lines of the early 'Deuce'. The internal weapons bay, a feature that has returned on the latest US fighters for 'stealth' reasons, was the main reason for this purity of form. Later upgrades added external fuel tanks, an arrester hook, anti-collision beacons and an infra-red search-and-track sensor. This aircraft has the large fin, but retains the original small airbrake.

Perrin AFB, Texas was the home to USAF interceptor pilot training for many years under the auspices of the 4780th Air Defense Wing, whose 1959 markings are seen here.

The 327th FIS came up with this colourful tail marking after it received its tall-tailed F-102s. It was short-lived as the 327th soon exchanged California for Greenland and arctic red trim.

satisfactory performance up to the Mach 1.5 that had been part of the original specification. On 18 January 1956, the aircraft reached Mach 1.535.

Tank tests

Following Phase IV tests (operational suitability), 53-1791 was modified in September 1956 for the carriage of external tanks. External fuel tank testing was conducted in November and December 1956, and on 27 December 1956 a test pilot successfully jettisoned the tanks simultaneously at an altitude of 36,515 ft (11130 m) at the speed of Mach 0.953. The remainder of the programme so far as 53-1791 was concerned came to an end on 31 July 1957 after tests that were not related to performance.

On 10 December 1955, the 23rd example of the F-102A (53-1813) made the first flight with the larger fin (described below) that later became standard. The test programme consisted primarily of stability and control and flutter testing. The programme ended on 18 April 1956, and the large tail was adopted for the final production configuration. A later F-102A (54-1380) was assigned the task of powerplant and components development for the production J57-P-23A engine which replaced the interim J57-P-41. Engine tests were started on 13 June 1956 and concluded on 2 April 1957.

Evaluation of the Case XX wing was conducted with yet another F-102A (54-1317). Testing began on 28 June 1957 and continued through to 19 November 1957. This wing then became the production standard. The new wing appeared on all F-102 aircraft leaving the factory after October 1957, and was retrofitted on all others in operation. With it, the interceptor was capable of reaching 55,000 ft (16765 m), and also had much improved stability, especially at lower speeds.

The 64th FIS at McChord AFB, later Paine Field, Washington, was one of 16 ADC squadrons to equip with the 'Deuce' during 1957. One of the squadron's 'Tubs' is seen at McChord in September of that year.

TF-102A: the 'Tub'

In July 1954, while the F-102A was still undergoing modification to 'hot rod' configuration, the USAF ordered 20 of the Model 8-12 or TF-102A. Previous interceptors such as the F-86, F-89 and F-101 had been built only in single-control versions to that point. Neither ADC nor Air Training Command believed that pilots could safely transition to the delta-winged fighter directly from conventional jet trainers. At the time, flight training was mainly conducted on the T-33 and radar training in specially equipped B-25s. Following successful initial testing of the revised F-102A, a production 'hold' order was rescinded, and a further 28 TF-102As were ordered in early 1955. Eventually, one in every nine of all 'Deuces' was built as a two-seater, or 'Tub', for a grand total of 111. The side-by-side seating arrangement was chosen, despite the likely performance loss, to simplify radar training in particular. Unfortunately, severe buffeting problems proved impossible to solve by revising the canopy and windscreen design. In the end, rows of inelegant vortex generators provided a cure, but not until after another production 'hold' and a cut in the air force order. The similarly configured English Electric Lightning trainers (also colloquially known as 'Tubs') appeared somewhat later, design of the first, the T.Mk 4, beginning in 1957.

***Above:** A cynic might say that this classic 1950s publicity shot was an attempt to equate the portly lines of the TF-102A with those of a more popular two-seater, a Ford Thunderbird. Compared to the F-102A, the TF was no 'sports car', being more commonly referred to as a 'sled'.*

The prototype TF-102A takes shape among the single-seaters at San Diego. The mock-up forward fuselage, which was approved in early 1954, was constructed at Convair's Fort Worth facility.

***Below:** The first flight of the TF-102A on 8 November 1955 was five months behind schedule. Buffeting problems were not sorted out until the third aircraft, by which time the USAF had decided to cut its order by nearly 70 aircraft.*

Cold weather

In March 1956, the 11th example of the F-102A (53-1801) went to Ladd AFB, Alaska to undergo Arctic climate testing. The evaluation under real-life conditions had been preceded by artificial Arctic tests in an indoor climate hangar at Eglin AFB, Florida. This machine was probably the first 'Deuce' to wear brilliant Arctic red colours on rear fuselage and outer wing panels.

By June 1956 Convair was preparing for series production of three versions of the new aircraft, namely the F-102A single-seat interceptor, the TF-102A two-seat version with full combat capabilities (later to be called the 'Tub' by crews), and the F-102B (Convair Model 8-24, originally 8-21, also dubbed Weapon System WS-201B) with the more powerful J75 engine, inspired by the appearance of the Soviet Myasischyev M-4 'Bison' turbojet-powered long-range strategic bomber. On 17 June 1956, however, the F-102B was redesignated as the F-106A (see *Wings of Fame* No. 13).

The October 1955 debut of the TF-102A combat proficiency trainer, or Model 8-12, was not a rollout so much as a rollover – over the freeway, that is. San Diego was belatedly joining the rest of California in sprouting obscene, six-lane thoroughfares. Newly-built 'Deuces', mounted atop a large truck trailer, had to be transported past the main gate at Plant 2 (where a guard post had to be moved to make room for it to pass), then taken over a small narrow bridge which was the only way to cross the broad Pacific Highway (today's Interstate No. 5). The sight of a jet aircraft passing above freeway traffic eventually became routine, since this became the way all 'Deuces' began their travels, but at this juncture it drew considerable comment from press and public. The first TF-102A (54-1351) was

***Below:** This view across the cockpit of a TF-102A shows the roomy interior. The pilot is Mercury astronaut Gordon 'Gordo' Cooper on a proficiency flight with a NASA-assigned TF-102A. The new nose was 6 in (15.25 cm) higher than that of the A, and it increased the overall fuselage width by 11 in (27.9 cm).*

The Ricks Trophy event at McCarran Airport, Las Vegas in September 1962 saw the F-102s of a number of regular and Guard units gathered together alongside a dazzling collection of red-trimmed transports. The Ricks Trophy was and is awarded for outstanding airmanship by an ANG aircrew. In the 1950s it was awarded on the basis of a flying competition, (described as an 'air race'), today the award is most commonly given for handling a significant inflight emergency or for a humanitarian mission.

then taken by land to Edwards AFB where, on 31 October 1955, tests began with the performance of the first flight by Dick Johnson.

The 'Tub' was viewed as the answer to the knotty problem of familiarising an interceptor pilot with flying and fighting a complex supersonic weapons system. Initially, it was also billed as the solution to the criticism of the one-man all-weather fighter, because this version could be flown as a full tactical weapon by either one or two men. In fact, although it was fully capable of operating with the basic missile armament, the TF-102A lacked the MG-10 system fitted to the F-102A. In practice after the type became operational, the TF-102A was not used interchangeably with the F-102A on interceptor duties. And indeed it was not interchangeable, being marginally slower than the needle-nosed variant with one-man accommodation.

The very first TF-102A started out with the production J57-P-23A engine but had pre-production Case X wing with cambered leading edges and tips, the small tail and no vortex generators on the large canopy.

The two-seat model used a nose section manufactured at Convair's other factory in Fort Worth, Texas and trucked overland to San Diego to be mated to a fuselage in Plant 2. Early test flying revealed a problem not found in the single-seater, namely a buffet condition at Mach 0.85 to 0.90. Various fixes were tried, including balsa wedges on the aircraft's exterior in the canopy area, boundary-layer plough slats and many configurations of vortex generators. In April 1956, the USAF conducted a comparative flight evaluation of the original canopy configuration on the first aircraft and a cut-down canopy shape on the third (53-1353), of which the latter has apparently never been seen in surviving photos. The tests validated the original canopy configuration and this, with vortex generators installed, was selected for the production configuration. Buffet testing was completed on 28 November 1956 and the TF-102A was considered satisfactory to move ahead to service evaluation.

An early TF-102A (54-1380) was used for powerplant development work from 13 June 1956 to 2 April 1957, resulting in minor changes to the production engine. A subsequent TF-102A (54-1390) was the first with the large fin. The test programme for this configuration included stability and control, flutter and landing gear structural tests, and ran from 27 August 1956 to 23 October 1957. External fuel tank testing was performed with another TF-102A (54-1398) from 21 September 1956 to 9 April 1958, and this aircraft was also used to test some F-106A landing gear structural features.

The F-102 was very slow in development, flight test and deployment, and began to reach USAF squadrons only in April 1956, when the first arrived to join the 327th Fighter Interceptor Squadron (FIS) at George AFB, California.

By the time the 'Deuce' became operational, the development of the new interceptor had taken so long, and had involved so many airframes, that the USAF was littered with flying machines that were only partly up to the production standard. The effort to convert these ships from test versions to the tactical configuration was carried out by Convair in Fort Worth. It included changes to the radar system, missile bay doors, air inlet ramp and automatic flight control system. The 'Test to Tactical' programme added every feature, no matter how minor, that was now part of the definitive production standard. And, after all the years of work, the production warplane was a spectacle to behold.

A footnote to the story of a warplane that had in essence only two variants, namely the single- and two-seat versions, is that though the USAF assigned the designation F-102C, no operational aircraft ever took to the air as a 'C' model.

Almost as soon as it entered service, the F-102 began to appear in Air National Guard markings. 'Relegated to the Guard' would be the wrong expression, as the F-102 was close to state of the art in 1960 when the first ANG unit, the 182nd FIS at Kelly AFB received F-102s. The 'Deuce', was, however, the 'Interim Interceptor', and the 'Ultimate' F-106 was taking its rightful place in ADC. This 'Deuce' is from the 111th FIS, also of the Texas ANG, based at Ellington.

Rockets and missiles

The F-102 was designed as the airframe portion of the MX-1179 weapons system, of which the MG-10 was to become the fire control system (FCS) and the AIM-4 Falcon was to be the primary air-to-air weapon. These latter two elements were designed in parallel with the F-102 itself, but at the time Convair won the airframe contract, all they knew about the rest of MX-1179 was the maximum dimensions of the components. In the end, weapons system integration proved to be one of the least troublesome aspects of the programme and the F-102 was soon demonstrating the ability to fire all four AIM-4s and 24 rockets within seconds. The rockets, initially of both 2-in and 2.75-in types, were the 'Deuce's secondary armament, providing a 'shotgun' capabilty against targets that escaped the missiles.

***Below:* The F-102's rockets were mounted inside the missile bay doors. There were three tubes in each of four doors, into which pairs of rockets could be loaded, one behind the other. The aft pair was not usually loaded in peacetime for safety reasons, and later the capacity was reduced by half in order to accommodate the larger Nuclear Falcon in the weapons bay. This sequence, covering 'perhaps two-tenths of a second' according to Convair, shows a launch of all 24 rockets from one of the earliest production F-102As.**

***Above:* A 329th FIS F-102 flicks open its weapons bay and fires a salvo of AIM-4s. Infra-red and radar-guided missiles were usually fired in pairs, but firing all six at a single target in wartime might have been considered overkill.**

Convair proposed to use an upgraded J57 turbojet engine, the J57-P-47 with a titanium compressor, in an installation that would have extended the tail cone by 7 in (0.178 m), and the other major change would have been the revision of the missile bay to include provision for one MB-1 Genie unguided rocket projectile with a nuclear warhead. A number of F-102A aircraft were used in special tests, and one F-102A (53-1806), was photographed at Sheppard AFB, Texas marked as a 'YF-102C'.

F-102A described

The F-102A Delta Dagger interceptor, or Model 8-10, viewed from outside, was nothing less than a miracle of the pre-microchip industrial age. The powerplant was based on one J57-P-23A axial-flow turbojet engine rated at 10,200 lb st (45.37 kN) on military power at sea level and at 16,000 lb st (71.17 kN) with afterburning. Although it was considered an interim engine when it was introduced on the production 'Deuce', the J57 became the standard not only for the F-102 fleet but for most of the aircraft entering service in the late 1950s. The engine weighed 5,045 lb (2288 kg) and was equipped with an automatic, two-

Wearing a partial pressure suit, a USAF pilot looks longingly at an infra-red-guided AIM-4C. Behind him is a radar-guided AIM-4A. There were endless variations of this pose in 1950s Hughes publicity photos, which at least gave a good idea of the missile's size.

Air Defense Command

At the peak of Air Defense Command F-102 operations at the end of 1958, 25 squadrons were equipped with the type. Six squadrons had formed or transitioned in 1956 and 15 the following year. By 1959, the 'Ultimate Interceptor', the F-106, was coming on line, and the 'Deuce' was being handed down to ANG squadrons.

***Above:** The 482nd **FIS** from Seymour Johnson was one of the squadrons that worked up on the F-102 in 1956. It kept its mounts for a relatively long period – until 1965, but was then inactivated.*

***Above:** The 11th **FIS** at Duluth, Minnesota was one of the earliest F-102 users (August 1956) and one of the first to pass them on in favour of the F-106, in 1960.*

***Below:** The 27th **FIS** had an even briefer career with the 'Deuce', transitioning from the F-94C in June 1957 and receiving F-106s in February 1959.*

***Above:** The 48th **FIS** at Langley AFB, Virginia was proud of its new delta-winged interceptors, and emblazoned them with a 48-starred tailfin design. Within three years of accepting the F-102, the 48th transitioned to slightly less gaudy F-106s.*

***Above right:** The 332nd **FIS**, initially at McGuire AFB, New Jersey, operated the F-102 for nearly eight years, inactivating in mid-1965 at Thule, Greenland.*

position tailpipe first introduced on the first YF-102A. The afterburner nozzle unit was manufactured by another company headquartered in San Diego, subcontractor Rheem.

Fuselage and armament

The needle-nosed and area-ruled fuselage of the F-102A was 68 ft 1½ in (11.62 m) in length including the nose probe, while the TF-102A two-seater was a fraction of an inch longer. The fuselage structure of the F-102A was largely of light alloy construction but utilised titanium alloy frames around the area of the powerplant. The fuselage's central section was manufactured in left and right front and rear quarters. The final canopy design was of knife-edged windscreen glazed with stretched plastic which could not

*Cuba occupied ADC for a number of years. F-102s were first directed towards the island during **Operation Southern Tip** in 1961 and again in October 1962 during the **Missile Crisis**. This 326th **FIS** F-102A shows its planform over the Gulf of Mexico on a detachment to Key West.*

be shattered by impact, manufactured at different times by Beech and Goodyear. The pilot sat in a roomy cockpit on a lightweight Weber ejection seat. The ejection sequence could supposedly be completed in two seconds – first the cockpit depressurised, then the canopy unlocked and jettisoned, and finally the seat was fired. For normal cruising flight the cockpit was pressurised to 7.2 lb/sq in (0.5 bar), but USAF regulations required that for flight above 50,000 ft (15240 m) the MC-1 pressure suit was to be worn. The suit appeared on many recruiting posters in the 1950s and was frequently worn during test flying, but in an operational setting it was rarely, if ever, worn.

Immediately aft and below the canopy was the first of three missile bays, which in total carried six Hughes GAR-1 Falcon semi-active radar homing missiles (originally designated F-98, developed under Project MX-904, and later redesignated AIM-4 in 1962), designed to home on a target illuminated by the fire control radar of the MG-10 FCS. This early missile was soon supplanted by the improved GAR-1B (AIM-4B) version. Both of these radar-homing variants were later made interchangeable with the GAR-2A (AIM-4C) missile with infra-red homing. The Falcons were mounted on short rails which were extended into the airstream before the missiles were fired in a fraction of a second. The secondary armament on the F-102 was initially intended to be an unspecified number of 20-in (508-mm) T214B unguided air-to-air rocket projectiles. After developmental work on the T214B was abandoned at an early stage, the F-102A initially carried a secondary armament of twenty-four 2¾-in (70-mm) FFAR (Folding

***Above:** The F-102 line is seen on the night shift somewhere about one-third of the way through the production run. In all, exactly 1,000 aircraft were produced in just over three years, with F-106 production gearing up in the same period*

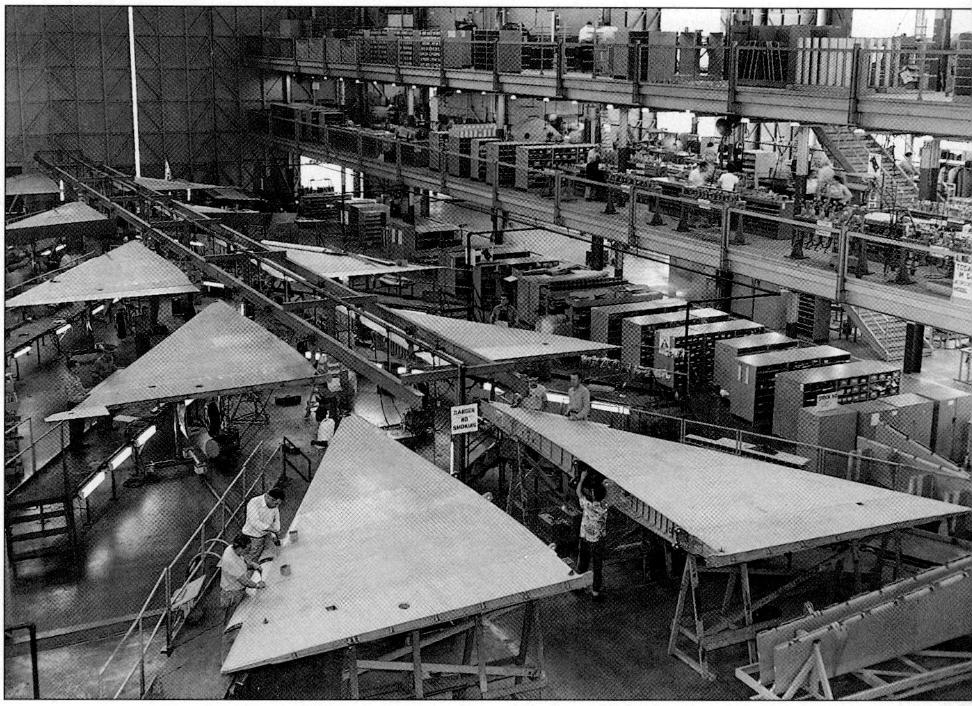

***Below:** The 'wing primary line' began with the basic structure panels, which were integral fuel tanks. By the end of the line, the wings were ready for attachment, with leading edges, doors, landing gear, wiring and elevons all fitted.*

***Below:** A latter-day 'Rosie the Rivetter' manoeuvres an F-102A windscreen frame into position on a forward fuselage section.*

F-102 factory

Convair's Plant 2 at Lindbergh Field, formerly used for B-24 production, was transformed from an empty building to an F-102 factory in 16 months. Initial production was exactly on schedule, but Convair admitted that they were delivering an "80 per cent weapon", rather than the fully-equipped fighter the new production line was designed to produce. Peak monthy deliveries were in June 1956, when 51 aircraft were accepted by the USAF. The peak year was FY57 when 372 (more than the total number of F-106s produced) were handed over. The Convair Service Center, also at San Diego, did a degree of refurbishment work and repainting of aircraft for the Air Force.

Although most overhaul work was conducted at Sacramento, the San Diego factory did some work on the 'Deuce'. In September-October 1965, aircraft destined for Vietnam arrived from Travis AFB for painting in the T.O.114 camouflage. This pair is seen leaving for Travis in late October, while others await their turn in the paintshop in the background.

North to Alaska

Deployment of the F-102 to Alaska (and to Europe) had to wait for the installation of TACAN equipment. The Alaska-bound aircraft were prepared first and two squadrons, the 31st and 317th FISs, were transferred to Alaskan Air Command (AAC) in August 1957. After a reorganisation in 1960, the 31st was disbanded and the 317th took over its aircraft, basing them at Elmendorf with detachments at Galena, King Salmon, Ladd and Eielson. Despite this dispersal of operations, the F-102s were hard pressed to defend Alaskan airspace and a number of Soviet intruders came too close for Washington's comfort. The 317th served with F-102s until 1969, but from 1963 they shared alert duties with rotating White Shoes/College Shoes deployments of the higher-performing F-106.

***Top:** The 31st FIS only served in Alaska from August 1957 to October 1958, when it disbanded and was absorbed into the 317th. The two squadrons were the first to be sent 'overseas' as Alaska was not yet a US state in 1957.*

***Above:** This 317th FIS F-102A, seen at Galena Airport in August 1960, later served with the New York ANG and eventually became a PQM-102B drone.*

Defence of the Distant Early Warning line and the Alaskan pipeline was part of the mission of the AAC F-102s.

Fin Aircraft Rocket) projectiles, which were replaced in later versions by the AIM-26 Nuclear Falcon. One F-102A (53-1797) was used to test the MB-1 Genie nuclear projectile at Holloman AFB, New Mexico in mid-1957, but the Genie never became an operational weapon aboard the 'Deuce'.

The Hughes MG-10 system was an extension of the interim MG-3 rocket and missile FCS which went into production in mid-1955. MG-3 development was initiated in late 1952 when it became apparent that the MA-1 system (then being developed under Project MX-1179 for use in the future F-102 and Republic F-103) would not be ready in time for delivery for the early production units of the F-102. The MG-10 system included, in addition to the basic MG-3 components, an automatic flight-control subsystem and a datalink subsystem. These gave the MG-10 capabilities approaching those of the more ambitious MA-1.

In addition to internal fuel, the F-102A and TF-102A were each capable of carrying two 215-US gal (179-Imp gal; 814-litre) or 230-US gal (191.5-Imp gal; 871-litre) external fuel tanks which, as the USAF cautioned its pilots, were 'solely to increase the subsonic range capabilities of the airplane'. The design limit speed of the tanks was Mach 0.95, and the tanks were to be jettisoned before combat.

Flying surfaces

The F-102A employed a delta wing swept at 60° 6' with a cambered leading edge extending from wing root to wing tip, and typified by a root chord of 29 ft 9¼ in (8.87 m), span of 38 ft 1 m (11.62 m) and area of 661.50 sq ft (61.45 m^2). The only other flying surface was the triangular vertical tail surface. The control surfaces, comprising two-section elevons on each half of the wing's trailing edge and a rudder inset into the trailing edge of the fin, were power operated. Convair referred to the wing employed on the YF-102 prototypes as the Case X wing, and this lacked the cambered leading edge. The YF-102A and a few early

***Below and left:** As in Europe, pilots sat long hours of alert in four-bay 'Zulu' hangars (these are at Elmendorf), ready to be airborne in five minutes. The 317th FIS boasted a three-minute reaction time from alert warning to aircraft airborne.*

F-102A aircraft also had a Case X wing in a form revised with cambered leading edges and tops. Most production examples of the F-102A and TF-102A had what Convair called the Case XX wing, which was simply the same wing, with the same dimensions, but incorporating minor improvements.

The camber was the direct result of flight tests. Modifications to install cambered wing leading edges with reflexed tips were completed on 14 April 1954, and minor handling problems were resolved. After testing throughout June 1954 which went up to Mach 1.29 (a speed attained on 2 May 1954), the decision was made to change the wing tips to full camber without reflex. In subsequent flying, Mach 1.33 was attained.

Enlarged fin

Early in the production of the F-102A and TF-102A, Convair changed and enlarged the shape of the fin, which was manufactured by Rheem. The original fin of the F-102 had been virtually the same as the triangular vertical tail on the XF-92A, and had left the aircraft vulnerable to roll-coupling. Rheem redesigned the larger fin design that became standard for this aircraft type. The original fin, found on early production aircraft, stood 8 ft 8 in (2.64 m) above the fuselage line by comparison with the figure of 11 ft 6 in (3.51 m) for the larger version. The original fin gave the aircraft an overall height of 17 ft 11⅔ in (5.47 m), a figure increased to 21 ft 2½ in (6.45 m) by the adoption of the larger fin. The smaller fin measured 15 ft 0⅛ in (4.57 m) in chord at its base, while the larger fin had a chord of 15 ft 10 in (4.81 m). The adoption of the larger fin resulted in a minor reduction in performance, but improved flight safety. The fin and portions of the wing made extensive use of resin-bonded honeycomb.

The landing gear of the F-102A and TF-102A was of the tricycle type with a single wheel on each unit. Each of the units was hydraulically actuated, the mainwheel units retracting inward into the underside of the wing roots and the nosewheel unit retracting forward into the underside of the fuselage.

In service with Air Defense Command

In the early 1950s, the US role in the defence of North America was divided among Alaskan Air Command, Continental Air Command and Northeast Air Command, the latter also responsible for operations outside the USA in locations like Goose Bay, Labrador and Thule, Greenland. This arrangement proved cumbersome, and at about the time the F-102 was coming on line the job was integrated

The 317th FIS was headquartered at Elmendorf, but dispersed its aircraft around the state. It was part of the 21st Composite Wing under Alaskan Air Command. Apart from a squadron badge, which was not always worn, the 317th usually carried distinctive fuel tanks marked with a lightning bolt, as seen here.

Left: An Alaska-based pilot is handed his helmet to top off his winter flying ensemble. Note the thick gloves – which must have made it hard to manipulate the smaller switches and controls – and the radar scope, which dominated the instrument panel.

Below: One concession to the environment at the various auxiliary fields used by the F-102 detachments in Alaska was the provision of 'nose hangars'. These allowed the weapons bays to be loaded and unloaded with reasonable protection from the elements.

Convair F-102 Delta Dagger

In order to practise interceptions against ECM-equipped Soviet bombers, Alaskan-based F-102s regularly flew with EB-57E Canberras acting as 'electronic aggressors'. The EB-57E pictured belonged to the 5041st Tactical Operations Squadron (until 1963 the 504th Radar Evaluation Squadron). It was lost in a collision with an F-102A during a practice intercept on 13 June 1969. All three crewmen involved ejected safely.

into ADC (Air Defense Command), which was itself a component of the joint US-Canadian NORAD (North American Air Defense Command). ADC enjoyed top priority, along with the Strategic Air Command, when the Pentagon handed out people and equipment. An Air Force hero of World War II and the Korean War, General Earle E. Partridge, was the boss at ADC when the F-102A was being developed. He summed up his own priorities in five words "Nothing's too good for ADC."

Partridge meant, of course, that he wanted the best for his men. But the remark also hints at a willingness to be patient with a seemingly endless series of technical bugs. Although it was known by various terms during its gestation (but not the Delta Dagger, a term that was retrospectively applied only many years later), the F-102A had always been regarded as the '1954 interceptor', and when it finally went on duty it was two years late.

Still, there were a lot of handshakes when the first true production example of the F-102A was formally accepted in June 1956 by Captain Alexander Butterfield, the assistant

The 327th FIS gave up sunny central California for Greenland in 1958. Some of the squadron are seen at bleak Frobisher Bay in Canada's Northwest Territories later that year.

Below: A partially painted 59th FIS F-102A formates with an F-105 over Spain in 1962. CASA performed overhauls on F-102s for USAFE.

Above: One of the deployments to South Vietnam was in anticipation of a coup against President Diem in October 1962. When it occurred, there was little the F-102s could do.

Left: A 509th FIS F-102A purges liquid oxygen (LOX) into the morning air at Don Muang in January 1962.

Right: Nose art was almost unheard of on F-102s and squadron markings tended to follow set patterns. The 509th was an exception, at least for a while, with the leaping tiger on the noses of its F-102. The pilot here is Captain Tom Halley.

Thailand

In 1961 F-102s of the 509th FIS were sent to Don Muang airport in Thailand to support the SEATO allies and the kingdom of Laos which was increasingly being drawn into the Vietnam conflict. From then on, a minimum of four USAF interceptors was kept on alert in Thailand. Rotations to Tan Son Nhut near Saigon began in March 1962. After May 1963, when the rotations were stopped, Thai-based aircraft were sent on a number of 'no-notice' exercises to test the ability of the F-102s to deploy quickly to Tan Son Nhut and Da Nang.

Camouflage

Technical order (T.O.) 114 issued in 1964 laid down a whole new system of camouflage for aircraft engaged in tactical operations in southeast Asia. It stipulated a pattern of tan, light green and medium green over light grey for each type of tactical fighter. Soon, the glossy 'ADC gray' colours of the F-102s vanished under the so-called 'SEA' or 'Asia Minor' camouflage. In Europe, camouflage was applied as aircraft went through major overhauls, the first appearing in 1965.

When camouflage came in Europe, squadron markings disappeared, and the 'Deuce' left USAFE before tailcodes became widespread. These aircraft from the 526th FIS illustrate old and new schemes.

A freshly-painted F-102A, ready for Vietnam service, is seen outside outside the maintenance hangar at McClellan AFB, California. The Sacramento Air Material Area (SAMA) was responsible for overhauling F-102s for Vietnam, including bringing them up to the latest modification standard. The IRST sensor on this aircraft indicates upgrade to at least FIG-8 status.

USAF plant officer in San Diego and project pilot on the 'Deuce'. In that same summer F-102A production aircraft began to reach the ADC's 327th FIS located at George AFB, California, and commanded by Lieutenant Colonel Charles E. Rigney, who rated the type "the easiest plane to fly I've ever been in". Rigney soon demonstrated the capabilities of the F-102A by flying from George to Oklahoma City, Oklahoma, a distance of 1,120 miles (1802 km) in 1 hour 22 minutes, beginning with a climb without afterburner and averaging a cruise of 711.7 kt (819.5 mph; 1318 km/h) at about 41,000 ft (12496 m). Rigney's 327th FIS forwarded to the USAF a proposal which had actually originated at Convair's Plant 2, which was the huge, rectangular building in San Diego that had once churned out B-24 Liberators and was now the assembly location for the F-102A. The suggestion was that the new warplane be given the popular name Lancer. The idea was rejected by the Pentagon for reasons that are difficult to fathom today, particularly since the name has subsequently been allotted to the Rockwell (now Boeing) B-1B bomber.

Good neighbours

In a community relations effort aimed at convincing taxpayers that the noisy J57 turbojet, which was always operated in afterburning mode during the take-off roll, was in fact the sound of freedom, citizens living near F-102A bases were given a free tour of ADC headquarters at Colorado Springs and a two-day instructional course at San Diego.

As if to compensate for the two-year delay in attaining operational status, the F-102A force expanded rapidly after the first arrival. The 11th FIS at Duluth, Minnesota was the second unit to get the delta-winged fighter, and many others followed so that by 31 December 1956 some 97 examples of the F-102A were in the inventory. The first airframes resulting from the Fort Worth 'Test to Tactical' programme were delivered to the 438th FIS at Kinross AFB, Michigan in July 1957 and by the end of that year the number of F-102A and TF-102A fighters in the ADC inventory had risen dramatically to 428. The ADC's highest number of 'Deuces' (the nickname assigned by pilots long after the USAF had rejected the name Lancer and before the appellation Delta Dagger was introduced) was 651 on 31 December 1958. Patience was a virtue, however: the downside was that, as of that date, ADC had sustained 62 accidents which resulted in 28 aircraft destroyed. By the end of the 1950s the ADC had already begun to equip with the F-106A – the former F-102B later named as the Delta Dart – and started to transfer some of its F-102A warplanes elsewhere. On 31 December 1959 the ADC mustered some 482 'Deuces', which now represented about 40 per cent of the ADC fighter force.

The first operational loss of a 'Deuce' occurred on 25 February 1957 when an aircraft (56-0976) of the 317th FIS

Left: The 509th FIS was headquartered at Clark in the Phillipines, but maintained detachments in South Vietnam, Thailand and Taiwan. This is one of the squadron's two-seaters, topping up its liquid oxygen supply before a sortie somewhere in southeast Asia during 1962.

Below: The 16th FIS at Naha, Okinawa played host to the first of many Phantoms deployed to Asia in December 1964. The 555th TFS, later to become famous for Vietnam MiG-killing, shared the base until March 1965.

Above and right: the Convair-designed refuelling installation was a fairly unsophisticated affair, with the probe raised high and forward by a large external brace for pilot visibility and to prevent intake fuel ingestion. As late as 1964, PACAF relied solely on hose-and-drogue refuelling (with KB-50s), and most TAC aircraft used the same method until well into the Vietnam war.

at McChord AFB, Washington suffered an engine failure and crashed. On 24 June 1957, two F-102A interceptors of the 327th FIS from George AFB, California, flew through the atomic mushroom cloud created by the 'Priscilla' shot in the Operation Plumbob series of nuclear tests in the Pacific. The fighters used in the tests were piloted by Major Budd Butcher and 1st Lieutenant Richard Satterfield.

Refuelling

Designed as a point-defence interceptor, the F-102 was built without provision for aerial refuelling. As the Vietnam conflict escalated, inflight refuelling was seen as a necessity to allow quick deployment of additional interceptors to southeast Asia. Convair developed a bolt-on refuelling probe kit that allowed refuelling from the same tank that was supplying the engine. The first F-102 units to make an air-refuelled deployment were the 64th and 82nd FISs who flew from California to Okinawa in January 1966 in Operation Thirsty Camel, but it appears to have been little used subsequently. Inflight refuelling was specified for a proposed RF-102 reconnaisance version which was never produced.

William Tell

The ADC launched its much-celebrated air-to-air weapons competition, dubbed William Tell, at Tyndall AFB, Florida during 1958 and had an F-102A category from the start. A team from the 326th FIS at Richards-Gebaur AFB, Missouri, won the first meet. The F-102 competitions at William Tell continued until 1974. Thereafter, William Tell saw the F-102A aircraft only as a drone. In a total of eight William Tell meets, 34 F-102A teams competed.

As the F-102A pressed on in its career, the USAF and Convair began a series of upgrades which brought minor changes and improvements, including the Configuration 5 modification programme which ended in December 1959 and the Configuration 6 programme that was completed in September 1960. Even as F-102A strength in ADC began to decline – there were 15 F-102A and TF-102A squadrons in the ADC on 30 June 1960 – a new milestone was reached when the first Air National Guard (ANG) squadron took delivery of the fighter on 1 July 1960.

Also in 1960, Convair began the Configuration 7 modification programme which added the GAR-11 missile, an improved version of the Falcon later to evolve into the AIM-26 Super Falcon. At the end of that year the ADC's F-102A and TF-102A squadron strength had declined to nine.

Right and below: The overcrowded nature of US air bases in South Vietnam and the lack of effective low-level radar made them tempting targets to the North Vietnamese Air Force. The US commanders believed they would have as little as one minute's warning of an attack on Da Nang. Aircraft were kept on five-minute alert at four bases in South Vietnam and Thailand with the rest of the F-102 force on one-hour alert. The 509th FIS F-102s at right were seen at Tan Son Nhut in May 1969. Below, a 64th FIS 'Deuce' taxis in at a typically busy US airfield in South Vietnam.

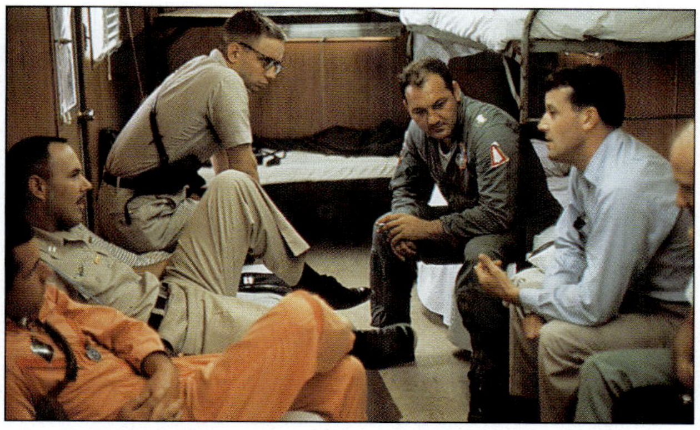

Above: Pilots of the 509th FIS chat with an NBC reporter in the alert trailer at Da Nang in 1968.

Left: 'C' Flight of the 509th was usually based at Bien Hoa with four aircraft and eight pilots. They had a more permanent structure as an alert pad.

The exact meaning of this very unofficial 'C' Flight, 509th FIS patch is obscure, but said to be unprintable.

This neat line of parked 64th FIS interceptors at Bien Hoa in December 1968 would not have been possible at Da Nang and some other bases, where Viet Cong mortar attacks took their toll on US aircraft, including F-102s.

Vietnam

Involvement in the Vietnam conflict for the F-102 began in 1962, long before US airpower was generally employed in combat in Southeast Asia. The Tactical Air Control System (TACS) radar network set up by the US in South Vietnam was picking up targets in the central highlands and four F-102s were dispatched from Clark to Tan Son Nhut on 22 March. The 'Deuces' rotated with Navy EA-1F Skyraiders every six weeks, but no targets were ever intercepted. Further F-102s were sent to Da Nang as soon as President Johnson authorised the US buildup following the Gulf of Tonkin incident in August 1964 under the codename Water Glass. During the war, the F-102s were primarily used for base defence at a number of locations. By the end of 1968, there were six aircraft on alert at Bien Hoa and six at Da Nang, with another 10 in Thailand (Udorn and Don Muang).

On 12 April 1961, the USAF began Exercise Southern Tip using the F-102A to counter possible nuisance raids by the Cuban regime under the communist Fidel Castro against the area of Miami, Florida, where many of Castro's domestic opponents had found asylum. In retrospect, it is impossible to separate this exercise from the catastrophic Bay of Pigs invasion of that month, but no connection can be proven. Six F-102A interceptors from Tyndall AFB were positioned at Homestead AFB, Florida (closer to Cuba) on two- to five-minute alert at all times. Following the failed landings at the Bay of Pigs, the Joint Chiefs of Staff directed that Southern Tip continue indefinitely, and as a result Homestead became home to a permanent detachment of interceptors.

The F-102 was employed at the start of the 1960s to judge the performance of a new, delta-winged bomber against air defences. Launched on 23 October 1961, Project

Below left: Seeing a need for air-to-ground firepower greater than the 12 2.75-in rockets in the weapons bay doors, Det. 3 of the 509th FIS conducted fit trials with a minigun pod hung from a TER on the drop tank mounting point. San Antonio Air Material Authority, the approving authority, was not happy with the installation's ability to withstand gun recoil and there were other practical reasons for its non-adoption. Only one was ever mounted on an F-102 and it was never fired as it was not wired to the aircraft's systems.

Below: 509th FIS F-102As fly over the defoliated and bomb-blasted terrain of South Vietnam. With little air threat, the F-102 was used as a B-52 escort and even in a limited ground attack role. A contemporary Aviation Week *account, quoting the* Air Force Times, *credited the 509th with the destruction of 106 buildings (with damage to 59 others), 16 sampans and one bridge in 199 sorties in a 45-day period.*

An F-102A from Det 1 of the 82nd FIS, then at Suwon, sees off an inquisitive Antonov An-12 'Cub-B' in June 1970.

Right: A fully-armed F-102A starts up in an alert hangar somewhere in South Korea, February 1971.

Above right: A trio of 82nd FIS 'Deuces' is seen high over South Korea during a deployment in 1970.

Korea

North Korean seizure of the spy-ship USS *Pueblo* in January 1968 led to the activation of several reserve units and the transfer of a number of active-duty units to South Korean bases. One of the first was the Naha-based 82nd FIS, which deployed to Osan before the end of the month. It was replaced by the first College Cadence deployment of F-106s at the end of February. Although the *Pueblo* crew was released in December 1968, F-102s made occasional deployments to Korea until 1971.

Dry Martini pitted defending F-102A and TF-102A warplanes of the 326th FIS against attacking Convair B-58 Hustler supersonic bombers. Lessons learned as a result of these intercepts helped both the bombers and the fighters to improve their tactics. The bottom line of the project, which ended on 5 January 1962, was that a big bomber with a configuration similar to that of the 'Deuce' was extremely difficult to stop.

At the turn of the year, on 31 December 1961, there had been 10 F-102A and TF-102A squadrons assigned to the ADC. Soon the ADC was operating the 'Deuce' even farther from home when the 57th FIS 'Black Knights' stood up in Iceland in July 1962. The squadron's claim to fame, long after Goose Bay and Thule had ceased to be familiar names in the air defence lexicon, was that it was the only ADC unit in a foreign country.

Flying the F-102

At air defence bases the F-102A was kept in the alert barns that had been built originally for North American F-86 Sabres, Northrop F-89 Scorpions and Lockheed F-94 Starfires. These barns were flimsy metal structures, barely strong enough to protect an aircraft from the elements and usually housing four aircraft, two on each side of an alert facility where pilots could lounge in flying gear while pulling alert duty. When the klaxon went off, the pilots were supposed to step smartly to their F-102A warplanes (there was no need to run) while ground crew assisted them in quickly starting up and taxiing out. All pre-flight checks were already finished. The job was to get the aircraft from the barn (located near the end of the runway) into the sky within three minutes. Lieutenant General Robert M. Lee, who commanded the ADC from 1 March 1961, is reported to have told an aide, "I want to hear afterburners [signifying a take-off roll] within three minutes of the klaxon. Any squadron that can't do that is going to have a new commander, and the old commander is going to be in charge of the Purple Water Fountain." This last is located in the basement of the Pentagon and while it exists for drinking purposes, in USAF jargon it signifies being demoted to the lowliest, most miserable desk job an officer can hold.

The 64th FIS was based at Clark AB in the Phillipines, but rotated aircraft in and out of the war zone as needs dictated. This F-102A was photographed at Yokota, Japan on 23 March 1969.

Right: Two-seat 'Deuces' carried missiles and rockets (in the yellow trolley) in Vietnam alongside the single-seaters. In ADC units, a proportion of TF-102s were not equipped with the weapons system or had it removed, and were only used as 'hacks'.

Below: When the 82nd FIS deactivated in May 1971, 18 of the squadron's 26 F-102s which had severe wing cracks and corrosion were scrapped at Naha. The remainder were flown back to the USA to join ANG squadrons.

Convair TF-102A-45-CO
82nd Fighter Interceptor Squadron
Naha, Okinawa 1968

82nd FIS
The 82nd FIS was one of the first F-102 users, becoming operational in July 1957. It became part of PACAF in June 1966. Its main role was providing air defence for Okinawa until it was deactivated in May 1971. Later, as the 82nd Tactical Aerial Targets Squadron (TATS), it was the last US F-102 user, flying PQM-102 Full-Scale Aerial Targets (FSATs).

This TF-102A-45-CO, the 17th-to-last two-seater built, has all the main features of a late F-102, including the 'Big Eight' IRST sensor and the Case XX wing. New antennas and external lights continued to appear on F-102s up to 1972. The aircraft was delivered on 25 May 1958 to the 326th FIS at Richards-Gebaur AFB. It subsequently served with the 4756th ADW at Tyndall AFB (from 24 August 1962), 325th FIS at Truax Field (from 1 April 1966), 326th FIS at Richards-Gebaur (from 13 June 1966) and 4780th ADW at Perrin AFB (from 23 November 1966). It then transferred to PACAF for service with the 82nd FIS at Naha from June 1970. It was scrapped there after the 31 May 1971 inactivation of the 82nd FIS.

Canopy and windscreen
The new wide cockpit section with its extensive glazing caused severe buffet problems when first flown. Tuft tests found that the airflow just aft of the canopy was actually moving forward. After some different canopy shapes were trialled, the solution chosen was to add two rows of vortex generators, one across the windscreen-canopy bow, and another across the midpoint of the canopy. This rather inelegant modification proved a satisfactory 'fix'.

War role
With little actual threat from North Vietnamese bombers, the F-102s were underemployed in their design role. They were sometimes used to escort B-52s flying 'Arc Light' missions over the south. On occasion, they went out at night searching for heat-emitting targets with the IRST and sometimes launched IR Falcons at them. Results are unknown, but it was an expensive way to destroy a truck or a campfire.

New nose
The new two-place nose on the TF-102A reduced the overall length by 55 in (140 cm) compared to the F-102A. The two-seater was about 250 lb (113.5 kg) heavier in an unloaded condition. Noses were produced at Convair's Fort Worth factory and mated to the rest of the airframe at San Diego.

Performance
The 'Tub' was supersonic like the single-seater, but only just. Maximum range was nominally the same, as there was no loss of fuel tankage, but climb rate and ceiling were slightly reduced due to the higher weight.

Quite early in the F-102's career, one aircraft was bailed to General Electric for use as an engine testbed. 54-1398, an F-102A-35, had a large pylon fitted in its forward weapons bay to which was attached a podded J85 turbojet (right). The testing, which took place at Edwards AFB in mid-1959, was conducted with an F-102 presumably because of the lack of supersonic wind tunnels at the time. The J85 was the engine used on the Northrop T-38 and N-156 (F-5), and the McDonnell AQM-20 Quail decoy missile. The aircraft above carries a J85 fitted in an AQM-20 fuselage, minus control surfaces.

After 1961 the F-102A was flown by pilots trained at Perrin AFB, Texas by the 4780th Air Defense Wing (Training) in a programme aimed at producing 120 'Deuce' flyers per year. Although the training course underwent numerous changes over the years, it was typically a 26-week combination of academics and flying which included 93 sorties totalling 146 hours 30 minutes of flying plus 293 hours of ground briefing, debriefing and simulator work. A shorter course retrained some pilots who had earlier flown the McDonnell F-101 Voodoo. Perrin was very much in the business of producing combat pilots, and the men who emerged from its classes were unlikely to be relegated to desk clerk duties by General Lee or his successors.

The F-102A did not intercept just any 'unknown' that appeared anywhere. The type was scrambled only when an unknown appeared in an Air Defense Identification Zone (ADIZ), one of several dozen regions around the US sea coast and land border that overlapped the likely approach route of Soviet bombers or, indeed, Cuban intruders. The F-102A did not carry wing tanks on alert status, and inflight-refuelling was not part of the scenario in the ground-to-air interception role. With a total internal fuel capacity of 1,085 US gal (903.5 Imp gal; 4107 litres) carried by four internal tanks in the spacious delta wing, an F-102A carrying three Falcon and one Super Falcon missile was able to get airborne in about 3,800 ft (1014 m) and climb to 17,400 ft (5305 m) in the first minute of flight. By this time, of course, the F-102A and the approaching intruder were like bullets fired at each other: when they converge, two objects come together at the speed of one plus the speed of the other.

Although the USA would soon field an automated system known as Semi-Automatic Ground Environment (SAGE) to decrease the human element in the interception process, the F-102A was guided to its targets in the old-fashioned Ground-Controlled Intercept (GCI) way. From a radar site, usually in a location quite separate from their air base, Delta Dagger pilots were fed information on the target's location, bearing, speed and altitude by the voice of a GCI operator bent over a radar screen and following a 'blip' with his eyes. It was expected that an F-102A would climb to 35,000 ft (10670 m) in about three minutes, and if

Sperry, which was the contractor on the Pave Deuce drone conversion programme, painted one QF-102 in its house colours and used it as a demonstrator. It is seen right, in 1978 and below, with its eventual successor in many squadrons, the F-16. The two generations of fighter were both built by General Dynamics (the F-102 by the Convair Division and the F-16 at Fort Worth), but share little in common except being single-engined.

Five-minute alert

The F-102 was designed for point defence (taking off and landing at the same base) and area defence (landing at another base). To this end, ADC and ANG squadrons were based in or detached to the majority of US states, as well as Canada, Greenland and Iceland for interception and identification of intruders approaching US airspace. Typically, a 25-aircraft squadron would have four flights with pilots on an eight-day cycle, two days on day alert (0800-1700) and two on nights in the 'Zulu' hangar, two days continuation training and two rest days. A scramble call would have the doors open and the engines started before the pilots reached the aircraft. As little as seven minutes after the call, the F-102s could be passing through 40,000 feet (12192 m) on a collision-course interception path with the unidentified aircraft or 'Zombie'.

Right: For many years, the 199th FIS at Hickam AFB provided the Hawaiian Islands' only air defence unit. This pair of 'Deuces' is seen in November 1976, in the twilight of the type's career.

Above: At established ADC bases, open-ended hangars of a variety of designs were built to allow a quick getaway. Usually there was room for four F-102s, such as these 482nd FIS examples at Seymour Johnson, South Carolina in 1965.

necessary reach maximum practical operating altitude of 54,000 ft (16460) in about 10 minutes. With fuel and armament, the 'Deuce' was capable of about 716 kt (825 mph; 1328 km/h) or Mach 1.25 in level flight at an altitude of 40,000 ft (12190 m). The expectation was that the interceptor would be fast enough, and its GCI guidance accurate enough, to allow a realistic interception of any bomber – even the new jet-powered Myasischyev M-4 'Bison' and Tupolev Tu-16 'Badger', of which US officials had become cognisant in 1955.

Heading upstairs on an intercept mission was not necessarily the most exciting flying in the world, but 'Deuce' pilots quickly became fond of their mount and celebrated both its merits and its quirks. Those who had flown Sabres, Scorpions and Starfires found that they had not only better performance but more cockpit space and, for the most part, greater ease of handling using the two-handled control stick that was a feature of Convair delta-winged fighters. One pilot called it "a real kiddycar to fly". The F-102A was not an aircraft to manoeuvre, however, and with its delta wing the type bled off energy at a dizzying rate when turning.

The ADC strategy was to send the interceptors up in what amounted to the shortest, straight-line route to the target. Pilots have different memories, today, of when and at what distance their on-board radar was capable of detecting and locking on to the target, the general impression being that it was useful only when the 'Deuce' closed to within 40 to 50 miles (64 to 80 km). While a first engagement from abeam was much preferred, it was neither expected nor assured, speed of interception being regarded as a higher priority. A speedy intercept might begin, however, with a 'lead-in pursuit pass' – a direct nose-to-nose collision course.

Crews of the 326th FIS run for their aircraft at Grandview AFB, Montana, 1960. By this time, ADC had over 25 squadrons of F-102s with numerous detachments spread around the USA.

Only thereafter, and here the manoeuvrability and airspeed of the F-102 were deemed sufficient, might the Delta Dagger re-engage from the side following the initial, head-on engagement. The ADC wanted to catch the foe some 520 to 695 nm (600 to 800 miles; 966 to 1287 km) off shore. In later years, when air-launched cruise missiles became a factor in the bomber-versus-fighter equation, the ADC did not believe the air-to-air radar on the F-102 would detect a cruise missile after launch. Guided to a GCI intercept, the F-102 would attack first with several Falcons or a single Nuclear Falcon, depending on the circumstance, and would attempt to re-engage if possible.

SAGE compatibility

In later years, the addition of datalink capability made the F-102A compatible with the SAGE system for which its successor, the F-106A, had been equipped from the outset. Late in its service life, the F-102A also acquired an IR seeker whose sensor protruded from in front of the windscreen.

Landing in the F-102A was easy, even if adrenaline churned when it was being done at night, in a rain squall,

The aircraft marked 'YF-102C' and seen at Shepherd AFB in 1960 remains a bit of a mystery, as no such designation actually existed. The proposed F-102C with the J75 engine and the MB-1 Genie missile armament of the F-102B (F-106) was never built, although some F-102As were used for related trials.

57th FIS 'Black Knights'

Probably the most famous 'Deuce' user was the 57th FIS at Naval Station Keflavik, Iceland which converted to the F-102 in July 1964. The 'Black Knights' of the 57th saw more 'trade' (unidentified aircraft) than any other ADC squadron. Mostly these were Soviet Tu-95 'Bear' bombers and reconnaissance aircraft, some of which were en route to Cuban or Angolan bases. In the latter days of their service, the F-102s were given datalink equipment, allowing them to make interceptions guided by ground radar or by EC-121 Constellations. Air Defense Command awarded the 'Black Knights' the Hughes Achievement Award for the outstanding interceptor unit in 1970, and the USAF flying safety award for 1968-71. The last regular squadron to operate the F-102, the 'Black Knights' returned their F-102s to the USA in July 1973. The last 'Bear' intercepted by the F-102 had been in June, when the squadron was in the process of transitioning to the F-4C.

Above: The 57th participated in William Tell 1972 having already been to Combat Pike, a live-firing exercise at Tyndall. Here, an F-102A breaks away after a Falcon shoot. It wears the later markings with 15 black/white squares on the rudder. Up to late 1969, the rudder markings were smaller blue/white chequers.

Right: International orange flight suits were a necessary accoutrement for flying over the desolate terrain of Iceland. The pilot carried his parachute on his back, unlike most later fighters where the 'chute was integrated into the seat.

As seen from a 57th FIS TF-102, one of the squadron's single-seaters banks over the hostile terrain. The 57th was the last active-duty F-102 operator in the USAF.

by radar control. The big delta planform was in most respects an assurance of good handling at low speed in the airfield pattern. Although the pilot often experienced an excessive sink rate just before touchdown, the ground effect smoothed out the landing nicely. The F-102A also suffered little effect from crosswinds. It was necessary to put the nose down quickly after initial impact when in a crosswind, but otherwise a landing in the 'Deuce' was virtually second nature, and the landing run was shortened by use of the drag chute located in a housing at the base of the fin's trailing edge.

Pilots complained that the knife-edge or inverted-V windscreen was a bar to good visibility, especially when taxiing in the rain. The pilot could not see his wing tips, so had to use dead reckoning to avoid any ground object that loomed too close to the taxiing warplane. Groundcrew also griped that the pneumatic brakes were a persistent maintenance problem.

Cuban missile crisis

The F-102A was an important part of the rapid build-up of US military strength that occurred during the Cuban missile crisis in October and November 1962. While the USA went 'eyeball-to-eyeball' with the USSR, to use the expression coined by Dean Rusk, President John F. Kennedy's Secretary of State, 'Deuce' squadrons, which had

The 57th FIS received its F-102s in 1962. By 1972, more than 1,000 'Bear' intercepts inside Iceland's Military Air Defense Identification Zone (MADIZ) had taken place. At particularly busy periods, over 100 were recorded in a single month. This intruder is a Tu-95K 'Bear-B' cruise missile carrier. The F-102A in the foreground was lost off the Icelandic coast on 22 January 1973.

The 57th had two 'Tubs'. This one, pictured in September 1969, wears a large unit citation ribbon above the national insignia.

Far left: The 230-US gal (871-litre) external tanks were essential for the missions flown by the 57th and made a suitable canvas for this artwork representative of the squadron's business – a jet-borne black knight chasing a Russian bear.

spent so much of their time preparing to defend North America from the north, now stood ready to mount a defence against attacks from the south. In the end, Moscow backed down from its plan to install nuclear missiles and Ilyushin Il-28 'Beagle' bombers on Cuban soil, the crisis was resolved without war, and Rusk concluded that, "The other fellow just blinked."

On 30 June 1963, with American attention beginning to shift from Cuba to Vietnam, the count was nine ADC squadrons equipped with the 'Deuce'. During that year F-102A interceptors and Lockheed RC-121 Warning Star airborne warning and control aircraft worked together in Exercise Cashew Tree, a readiness rehearsal in the Panama Canal Zone.

Cold War

By September 1961 the 'Deuce' was entering ANG service and the USAF decided to equip six ANG and ADC squadrons with the new GAR-11 nuclear-armed missile. This was the Super Falcon or, more commonly and to avoid confusion with other variants enjoying the 'Super' appellation, the Nuclear Falcon. The initial version gave way at an early stage to a model designated GAR-11B, which was shortened by about 1 ft (0.3 m) to facilitate accommodation in the weapons bay of the 'Deuce'. On 1 October 1962, the two missile types were redesignated as the AIM-26A and AIM-26B respectively.

Although they were developed primarily to carry a nuclear warhead, in effect using overkill to destroy an attacking bomber formation because the accuracy of non-nuclear missiles was still inadequate, the AIM-26A and AIM-26B were also widely used with conventional warheads. In its conventional guise, the AIM-26 was also sold to Sweden and Switzerland for use as the Rb 27 and HM-55, respectively, on the Saab 35F Draken and Dassault Mirage IIIS fighters equipped with Hughes Taran radar. The AIM-26B was 6 ft 11.6 in (2.07 m) long and had a fin span of 2 ft 0.4 in (0.62 m), at launch weighed 262 lb (119 kg), and used semi-active radar homing for an effective range of 6 miles (9.7 km).

In order to operate nuclear weapons, the ADC had to create and manage a PRP (Personnel Reliability Program) to exercise control over who had access to 'nukes'. Throughout the USAF anyone who dealt with 'nukes' had to be screened for PRP and the access was made a part of the individual's medical records. Midway through its career, when it became an ANG type, the F-102A retained its Nuclear Falcon capability. The decision to use an atomic

An advantage of the delta wing is that it remains controllable at low speeds. This was useful when trying to formate on a slow target such as a No. 202 Squadron, RAF, Hastings Met.Mk 1 on a weather reconnaissance flight over the GIUK gap. The 57th FIS 'Deuce' seen here is now displayed in the USAF Museum.

Less well known than the 57th FIS, which occupied Keflavik for 40 years, are the various other squadrons who operated in the even harsher climate of Thule AB, Greenland. This trio is seen above the partly-frozen Wolstenholm Fjord in August 1958.

Europe

Nearly 170 F-102As and TF-102As served with six squadrons in Europe between the years 1959 and 1970. The first aircraft arrived at Saint-Nazaire aboard a converted wartime escort carrier in January 1959. They were then towed to Sud-Aviation's facility at Montoir Air Base where their protective cocoons were removed and the aircraft were prepared for flight. By the end of 1960, three United States Air Forces Europe (USAFE) squadrons in West Germany, two in Spain and one in the Netherlands were equipped with the 'Deuce'. The three Germany-based squadrons formed the 86th Air Division (Defense) under the Fourth Allied Tactical Air Force (4 ATAF). They comprised the 496th FIS at Hahn, the 525th at Bitburg and the 526th at Ramstein. Spain had the 431st FIS at Zaragoza and the 497th at Torrejon under the 65th AD. The Soesterberg-based 32nd FIS was part of 2 ATAF, under the operational control of the Royal Dutch Air Force. Twenty-one USAFE F-102s were lost in over a decade of service, about 12 per cent of the inventory. This compared with the overall loss rate (F-102As only) of 14 per cent.

Uniquely, the 32nd FIS at Soesterberg was under tactical control of the Royal Netherlands Air Force. Here, the 'Wolfhounds' 'Tub' completes a line-up of Dutch airpower of the early 1960s. The relative size of the F-102, just shorter than a B-17 bomber, is evident here.

F-102s of the 32nd FIS (right) and the 526th (far right) line up on the ground and in the air circa 1963. F-102 squadrons of the period were large by modern standards, with up to 25 aircraft, including two or three two-seaters. The view at far right shows the runway arrester hook, developed for the F-106 and installed on USAFE F-102s from April 1961.

The great strength of the F-102 in Europe was its all-weather capability. This picture of an unidentified unit's F-102A can be dated to after the 1963/64 time frame by the IRST ahead of the windscreen which was added under project Big Eight at that time.

weapon on board an interceptor reflected the thinking of the time: under today's rules, nuclear weapons would not be released to ANG personnel. Release of nuclear weapons in wartime requires an order from the NCA (National Command Authority), meaning the President or Secretary of Defense. Moreover, there are no nuclear-tipped air defence missiles in today's USAF inventory.

By this juncture, the ANG was very much a part of the Total Force, to use a term coined in the Pentagon, and ANG personnel played a direct role in the air defence of North America and in deployments overseas. By 1964, the F-102A and TF-102A were in service with 10 ANG squadrons and, at the peak of this interceptor's ANG career in the late 1960s, no fewer than 22 squadrons were equipped with the type. This level was maintained until 1970, when the ANG began slowly decreasing its 'Deuce' force in favour of newer aircraft, including the F-106A. At least 500 Delta Daggers, or half of those built, served with the ANG.

The ANG story would in itself fill volumes. Guardsmen are much like military folk of a past era – bonded to a particular unit for decades, if not for life – part of a local community as well as trustees of a national mission. Offering both full- and part-time slots, with some assurance of the permanency not provided by active-duty military life, the ANG readily attracted former active-duty members with a wealth of experience for the F-102A cockpit and for the maintenance shops. A visitor to any ANG squadron in 1970 – a period coinciding with a time of civil unrest at home and a war in Vietnam – would have quickly detected that the unit was alert, neat and proud. In competitions, F-102A ground and flight crews of the ANG routinely beat the socks off active-duty folk.

In Europe

It was decided at an early stage that the 'Deuce' would have an air defence role in Europe, where NATO confronted the risk of a westward push on the continent by Soviet and Warsaw Pact forces. The US Air Forces in

A pair of 526th FIS F-102As is seen blasting off from Ramstein during September 1965. Ramstein was the HQ of the 86th Air Division. By this period, USAF 'Deuce' markings were smart rather than flamboyant, with the squadron and air division badges on either side of the fin.

Above: It might seem that France adopted the basic design of the F-102A for its succesful Mirage series, but it would be more correct to say that the French built upon XF-92 research to follow its own path to similar ends. The first contract for research into a 'Mystère Delta' reached Dassault in early 1952 and the resulting Mirage I flew in June 1955. Today's Mirage 2000 bears superficial resemblance to the Convair deltas, but engine, materials and control technology, not to mention the radar, put the Mirage in an entirely different league.
This 32nd FIS Delta Dagger was photographed at the 1965 Paris Air Show.

After the colourful 86th AD markings disappeared from the northern European 'Deuces', it was not long before squadron identity began to reassert itself. The wolfhound badge is prominent on this 32nd FIS aircraft, and a vestige of red, white and blue remains on the airbrakes.
The 32nd FIS won the F-102 portion of the 1965 William Tell fighter meet at Tyndall AFB.

Europe (USAFE) eventually operated six fighter interceptor squadrons using aircraft made available by the ADC. The first two squadrons, the 525th FIS at Bitburg Air Base and the 496th FIS at Hahn AB, both in Germany, were operational by mid-1959. Eventually, the F-102A interceptors had a datalink system enabling them to use the NATO Air Defense Ground Environment (NADGE) system, the European equivalent of SAGE.

In Europe the F-102A enjoyed a relatively long period of service, aircraft in late service wearing the same camouflage as that employed in Vietnam. Details of squadron assignments appear in the operator's section.

Left: The 497th FIS at Torrejon was based alongside Spanish Air Force Sabres and stood alert under large blister hangars such as this one. Like the other USAFE F-102 squadrons, the 497th travelled to Wheelus AB in Libya for live weapons firing.

In the Pacific

In Pacific Air Forces (PACAF) the F-102A became a fixture after 1959 at the very time Americans were taking their first tentative steps toward involvement in Vietnam. In 1959-60 the 4th, 16th, 40th, 68th and 509th FISs of PACAF converted to the Delta Dagger.

The long, slow descent into the hell of Vietnam had one of its early steps in Operation Water Glass, the temporary deployment of Delta Daggers to Vietnamese soil to guard against a perceived incursion by North Vietnamese aircraft, which were then of the propeller-driven type. Unidentified radar tracks over South Vietnam on 19-20 March 1962 led to deployment of four F-102A interceptors to Tan Son Nhut AB outside Saigon. In a quote that revealed how Americans were fooling themselves and would continue to do so throughout the 1960s, the hapless US commander in Vietnam at the time, General Paul Harking, announced that, "There is no air battle in Vietnam and there are no indications that one will develop."

The 'Deuces' deployed to Vietnam on 21 March 1962 and returned to Clark AB, Philippines a week later without making any active intercepts. Additional Water Glass deployments continued throughout the year, using two-seat TF-102A aircraft which were more effective against expected targets flying 'low and slow'. In July 1962 the mission was taken over by Douglas AD-5Q Skyraiders of the US Navy, but in November the TF-102A aircraft returned.

The temporary deployments continued until May 1963, and were then briefly resumed during November 1963 in Operation Candy Machine. F-102 pilots and ground crews

Although never based in the UK, the F-102 was a frequent visitor to Britain, especially for airshows. This 496th FIS, 86th Air Division 'Tub' was a visitor to RAF Lakenheath in May 1969.

The Upper Heyford Air Day 1969 gave the British public the chance to see at close hand a newly-camouflaged F-102A of the 526th FIS in rare British airshow sunshine. The 526th's aircraft began to receive camouflage as they were overhauled by CASA, the first being delivered in 1965 and the last in 1968. Most of the 526th's aircraft were assigned to the Connecticut ANG in 1970.

became familiar with Vietnam as a place to come and go. Later that year, 'Deuce' operations throughout the Pacific reached a pause when inspections of Naha-based aircraft revealed structural defects in the air inlet ducts caused by severe corrosion. Over the next three months, PACAF grounded 28 airframes and made repairs.

There was a resumption of F-102A deployments to South Korea in 1963 under the programme name Bone Deep. In that year 12 four-aircraft deployments were made. North Korea had an entire air division of Il-28 light bombers, to say nothing of 300 or more Mikoyan-Gurevich fighters, and the F-102A represented the only all-weather interception capability that was readily available.

Candy Machine resumed on 26 June 1964 with a 10-day deployment of three F-102A interceptors to Da Nang. Within two months, the Gulf of Tonkin incident would lead to an American build-up in Vietnam, eventually to reach 545,000 troops, and the Vietnam story would overshadow everything else in the region.

But even at the height of the Vietnam conflict, Korea never ceased to be a trouble spot. On 28 April 1965, a Yokota-based Boeing RB-47 Stratojet was attacked by two North Korean MiG-17 fighters as it undertook a reconnaissance mission 50 miles (80 km) off the Korean coast. The crew returned fire but the bomber suffered severe damage. F-102A interceptors of the 4th FIS scrambled to escort the crippled Stratojet back to Japan, but did not engage the MiGs.

The first inflight-refuelling of the F-102A and the deployment of the 'Deuce' to the Far East during the US build-up in Vietnam is described in detail in the entry for the 82nd FIS in the operators' section. Using the programme name Thirsty Camel, 'Deuces' of the 82nd FIS deployed to Okinawa where they arrived on 18 February 1966 and began alert duty five days later. At about the same time, beginning on 6 June 1966, the 64th FIS deployed from Hamilton AFB, California, to Clark Field, Philippines in a project dubbed Hot Spice.

When the spy ship USS *Pueblo* (AGER-2) was seized by North Korea on 23 January 1968, the 82nd FIS deployed its 'Deuces' from Naha to Osan AB, Korea, eventually being relieved there by the F-106A interceptors of the 318th FIS in one of the rare overseas deployments of the Delta Dart. The F-106A was rotated into South Korea until the last of the type departed on 12 May 1970, marking the end of the crisis period.

Vietnam

The F-102A and TF-102A were to become intermittent participants in the Vietnam War. In air-to-air combat, the

In April and June 1964, over 40 F-102s were returned to the US. Most of these were from the 431st FIS and 496th FIS. The 431st and fellow Spanish-based unit, the 497th FIS, transitioned to the F-4C Phantom in early 1964, and the latter unit's aircraft were swapped with those of the 496th at Hahn. Operation Krazy Kat saw the 'Deuces' flown across the Atlantic via Prestwick, Scotland, where the first group is seen here. Just visible, second from right, is an aircraft from one of the Hanscom Field test units that had been assigned to trials with the 526th FIS.

Convair F-102A-60-CO
525th Fighter Interceptor Squadron
86th Air Division
Bitburg AB, Germany
1962

56-1111 was originally delivered to the 482nd FIS at Seymour-Johnson AFB on 24 April 1957. On 23 October 1958 it joined the 86th FIS at Youngstown Airport, before reassignment to USAFE on 16 December 1959. By November 1960 it was flying with the 525th FIS. In early December 1969 it left Europe for a new life in the Guard, flying briefly with the 116th FIS before assignment to the 157th FIS. In September 1978 it was allocated to the drone programme, and was destroyed in a missile test on 15 May 1980.

Weapons
This aircraft has not yet undergone the modifications required for AIM-26A nuclear Falcon carriage as it retains the rocket tubes in both forward and aft weapons bay doors. The AIM-26A required new doors because of its greater size.

Squadrons
There were about 25 aircraft per squadron in this period. In NATO Sector 3, in which the 86th AD squadrons served, the F-102s operated with Luftwaffe F-86s at Langerkopf. Their mission was interception and identification of aircraft detected outside of the assigned air corridors. Usually these turned out to be straying airliners.

Upgrades
During the period of F-102 service in Europe, several local organisations were contracted to perform maintenance and upgrades on behalf of the Air Material Force European Area (AMFEA). Breguet at Chateauroux, France had the first contracts, incorporating modifications for the nuclear AIM-26A in 1958 and, in 1962, adding arrester hooks to those aircraft that had not already been modified in the US. Later that year, CASA at Seville won the contract, and among the work it undertook was installation of the IRST (1963), afterburner modifications (1964) and addition of anti-collision beacons (1967). Datalink equipment was added in 1965, the evidence of which was two small aerials under the rear fuselage.

Markings
This aircraft is representative of a 525th FIS F-102 between 1961 and 1963. The colourful 86th Air Division 'sunburst' markings began to disappear in the summer of 1963 as aircraft were given the FIG-8 (IRST) modifications The two F-102 silhouettes on the nose were a common marking that contained the names of the assigned pilot and crew chief. The 525th was the first USAFE unit to receive a camouflaged F-102, in October 1965.

Wings
This aircraft was built with the slightly-upturned Case X wingtips. Unlike some other modifications, the later Case XX tips were never retrofitted to older F-102s.

Greece

The Elliniki Polimiki Aeroporia (Hellenic Air Force) received 26 F-102s for use by the 114th Pterix at Tanagra in 1969. The aircraft comprised 20 F-102As and six TF-102As as follows: (F-102As) 56-0981*, 56-0988, 56-1001, 56-1007, 56-1011, 56-1016, 56-1024, 56-1025, 56-1031*, 56-1034, 56-1039, 56-1040, 56-1052, 56-1056, 56-1059, 56-1079, 56-1106*, 56-1125, 56-1232, 56-1233*. TF-102s: 55-4035*, 56-2326, 56-2327, 56-2334, 56-2335 plus one. Those marked * are believed preserved today. The Greek F-102s were phased out in favour of Mirage F1CGs in 1979.

Some of the Greek F-102s were delivered in southeast Asia camouflage, and retained this during their service.

None of the Greek F-102s was equipped with the IRST sensor. It appears that the units were removed prior to delivery. They were not fitted to Turkish 'Deuces' either, thus denying either of these potential adversaries a technological edge over the other.

'Deuce' was to suffer the indignity of a final score of 0 to 1 against the MiG-21 – i.e. the type sustained one combat loss while never shooting down any enemy aircraft. There were numerous other losses to other causes as the conflict grew.

The first Southeast Asia loss occurred on 24 November 1964 when an F-102A (56-1159) of the 509th FIS suffered engine failure on a flight from Tan Son Nhut. On 1 July 1965 three more F-102A warplanes (55-0371, 56-1161 and 56-1182) were destroyed during a mortar attack on Da Nang airfield. Altogether, counting the one air-to-air combat loss, 15 Delta Daggers were lost in Vietnam. Of these, 12 were counted as operational rather than combat losses (including those wrecked by mortar fire), two more were lost to ground fire, and one was the sole air-to-air victim.

In the last six months of 1965, the 509th FIS's 'Deuces' at Tan Son Nhut participated in Project Stove Pipe. Using its IR seeker, the F-102A (designed for nothing but interception) used 2¾-in (70-mm) FFAR projectiles and AIM-4D Falcon missiles against heat-emitting ground targets. When Project Stove Pipe ended in December 1965, the official finding was that the 'Deuce' could be used as a tactical air-to-ground weapon. But pilots who were there say that the results of this experiment were murky at best.

Pacific TDY

It was the strain on PACAF resources amidst the Vietnam build-up that brought ADC squadrons on temporary duty to the Pacific, beginning with the 82nd FIS and continuing with the 64th FIS, as noted above. Although these two squadrons initially 'backfilled' the alert commitment at Naha, Okinawa, they soon began pulling detachment duty at Da Nang. At the end of June 1966, no fewer than 22 F-102A interceptors were standing alert in South Vietnam and Thailand – a modest number of warplanes compared to the growing legions of Republic F-105

This view of the flightline at Tanagra shows a quarter of the Greek Delta Daggers. Speculation about 'Deuce' vs 'Deuce' air combats in 1974 seems to be unfounded.

Turkey

The Türk Hava Kuvvertleri (THK - Turkish Air Force) operated at least 35 F-102As and eight TF-102As which were delivered during 1968. Known F-102A serial numbers include: 53-1814, 53-1815, 54-1377, 54-1379, 54-1380, 54-1382, 54-1383, 54-1384, 54-1386, 54-1403, 55-3380, 55-3383, 55-3384, 55-3385, 55-3386*,55-3389, 55-3390, 55-3392, 55-3395, 55-3396, 55-3400, 55-3401, 55-3403, 55-3404, 55-3405, 55-3408, 55-3409, 55-3410, 55-3412, 55-3413, 55-3416, 55-3421, 55-3425, 55-3426, 55-3429, 55-3443, 55-3452, 55-3455 and 54-3461. TF-102As were: 54-1360, 55-4033, 55-4053, 56-2325, 56-2342, 56-2355 and 56-2368*. Preserved F-102s are marked *. It has been said that Turkish F-102As may have shot down a pair of Greek F-5As during the short war over Cyprus in 1974, although F-102 involvement in the conflict was minimal. 182 Filo transitioned to the F-100C and 142 Filo to the TF-104G during 1979.

Above and above right: The 114th Filo at Mürted was the initial Turkish F-102 operator. It later split into two 18-aircraft units, the 142nd and 182nd Filos with the latter moving to Diyarbakir. The landings on Cyprus in July 1974 led to a US embargo on arms and military aid, including spare parts. The F-102 units were particularly hard hit, as there was no-one willing to provide spares in the way that a number of European F-5 and F-104 users did.

This TF-102A wears the post-1972 roundel insignia. The earlier red/white square, used since 1945, was thought to be mistakeable for a Soviet red star in certain conditions. This example is one of two 'Deuces' preserved at the Turkish Air Force Museum in Ankara.

Thunderchiefs and McDonnell F-4 Phantom IIs that shared ramp space with them, but it was an important contribution nonetheless. The inclusion of the 'Deuce' in the Southeast Asian war effort was symbolised by the T.O.114 camouflage that adorned all PACAF F-102A and TF-102A aircraft by the end of 1966. In 1968, the three squadrons in the war zone acquired tail codes.

Air-to-air

The sole F-102A lost in air combat fell victim to the extraordinary success of the MiG-21 'Fishbed' fighter, which in 1967 and 1968 was prevailing against American fighters over North Vietnam with a success ratio of almost 4 to 1, at the very time American pilots were batting MiG-17 'Fresco' fighters out of the air like flies. On 3 February 1968, Captain Allen Lomax and 1st Lieutenant Wallace Wiggins of the 509th FIS were launched to escort a flight of jamming aircraft over Laos. When the jammers failed to show as scheduled, Lomax and Wiggins fell into a trap. Apparently, they did not know they were being intercepted and ambushed by MiG-21F-13 'Fishbed-E' fighters until Wiggins radioed, "There's something wrong with my aircraft." That was when an AA-2 'Atoll' missile hit him, failed to detonate, but kinetically ripped his Delta Dagger (56-1166) to pieces. Lomax also thought he saw cannon fire from a MiG-21 arching through the air around them. Too distant from the fast-moving MiG-21s for a clear shot, Lomax rippled off three AIM-4D-8 Falcon missiles anyway, believing (correctly) that he was unlikely to hit anything. When he shifted his gaze back to the Wiggins fighter he saw "a fireball, and then debris, falling everywhere". In the only air-to-air engagement by the F-102A that resulted in an aerial victory, albeit for the other side, Wiggins apparently did not manage to eject, and thus became the only F-102A pilot ever to be killed in air-to-air action.

The wind-down of the F-102's role in Southeast Asia began when the 64th FIS ceased its alert commitment on 15 November 1969. Half a dozen of its aircraft reached the other two squadrons in the war zone, but in early 1970 the 509th FIS, too, began to discontinue its alert detachments in Southeast Asia. The 82nd FIS departed the Vietnam region for Naha and was inactivated on 31 May 1971, its

Far left: When their operational days were over, 20 of the Greek Delta Daggers were 'put out to pasture' at their former base, Tanagra, and at Elefsis near Athens. All five Greek TF-102s were relegated to decoy duties at Elefsis. A small number of the total found their way to museums.

F-102 Colours

5th FIS

The tail markings of the 'Spittin' Kittens' changed from simple red and black lightning bolts to this design, with the squadron badge and stars. It was later adapted by the 526th FIS without the central badge.

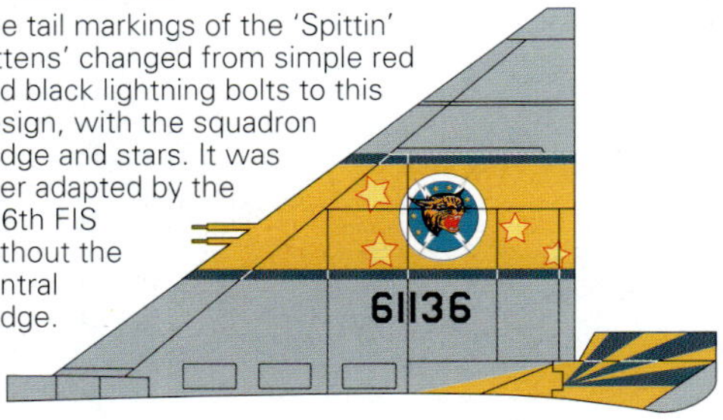

318th FIS

The 318th FIS's tail insignia was derived from the Chrysler Motors 'Way Forward' logo of the late 1950s. The squadron's dragon badge was often worn on the noses of its F-102s.

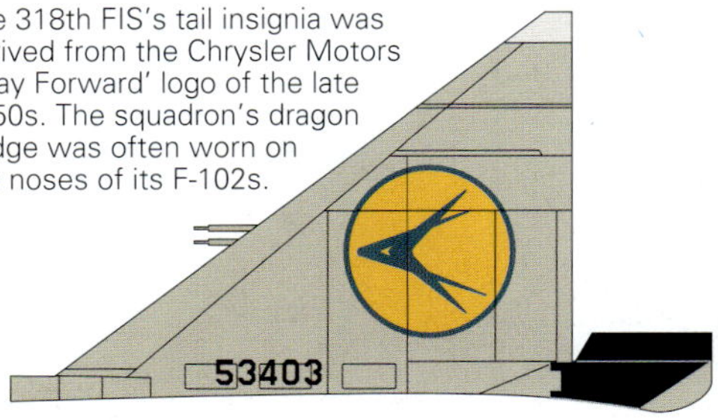

16th FIS

The 16th FIS at Naha also used a broad (black/white) chequered fin band, but distinguished itself from the 4th FIS with the squadron badge (a tomahawk splitting a stake) and the squadron designator.

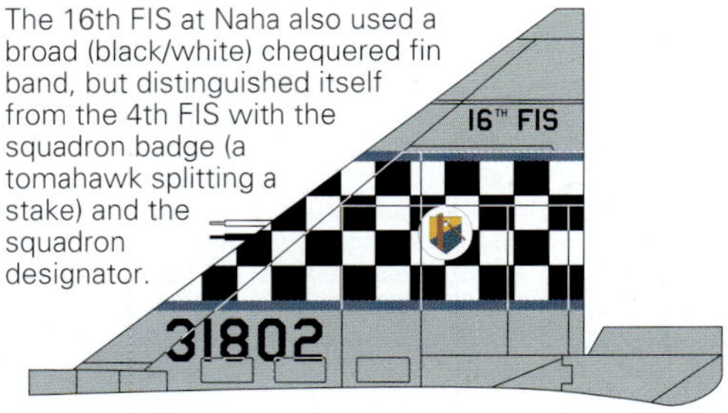

11th FIS

Some squadron commanders preferred to save on maintenance time by keeping the markings as small and as simple as possible. The 11th FIS charging bull badge and some red intake trim was all that 11th FIS F-102s carried.

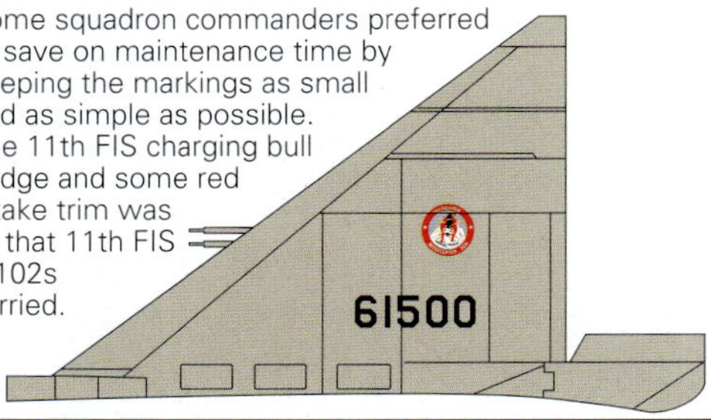

327th FIS

Most of the 'short-tail' F-102As of the 327th initially wore a simple badge on the nose. The commander's aircraft featured this chequered fin. 'Tall-tail' 'Deuces' briefly wore a different red and white design.

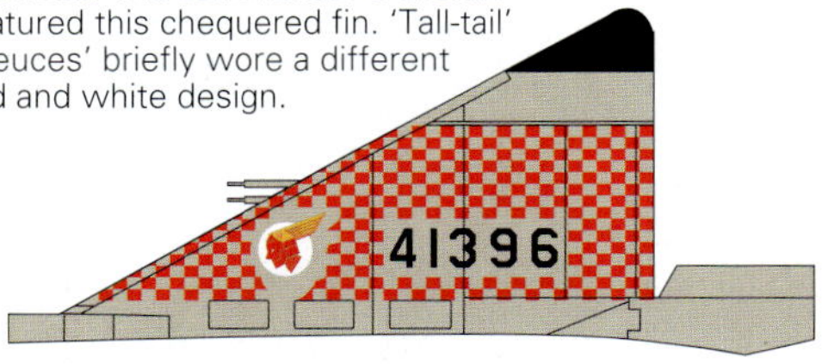

40th FIS

The 'Fighting Fortieth', based at Yokota, carried an especially large version of its regular squadron badge; a laughing devil's head.

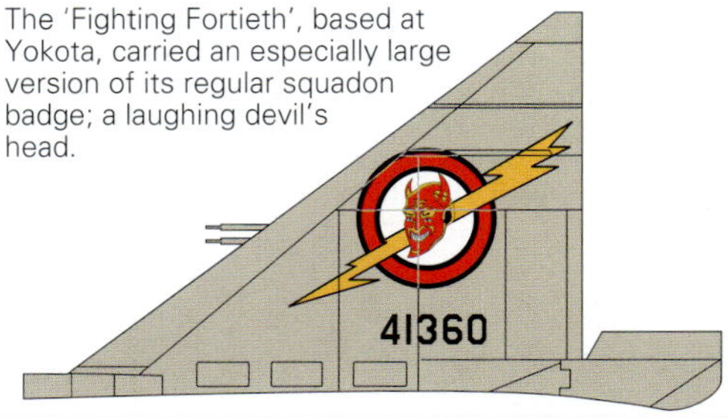

48th FIS

The spectacular 48th FIS tail design featured 24 Kelly green stars on each side of the fin (for a total of 48). The squadron's badge featured a red and yellow flash with four stars above and eight below.

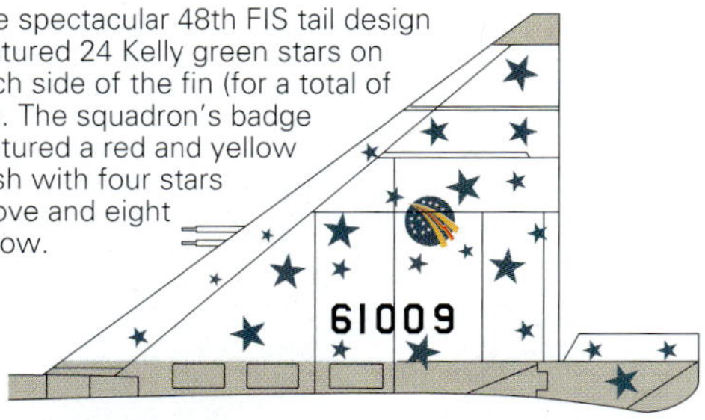

460th FIS

The tails of 460th FIS F-102s featured an enlarged squadron badge warning 'Beware of the Tiger'. The wing fences and, unusually, the wing tips were yellow on at least one squadron aircraft.

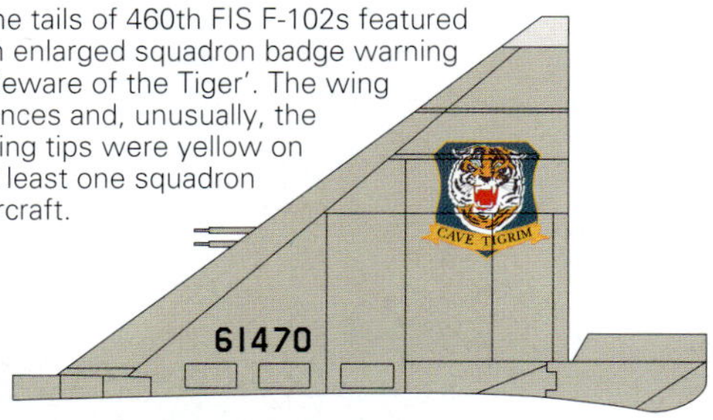

68th FIS

The famous knight insignia of the 68th, seen previously on F-61s, F-82s, F-94s and F-86s, appeared atop a large central red triangle on the squadron's F-102s.

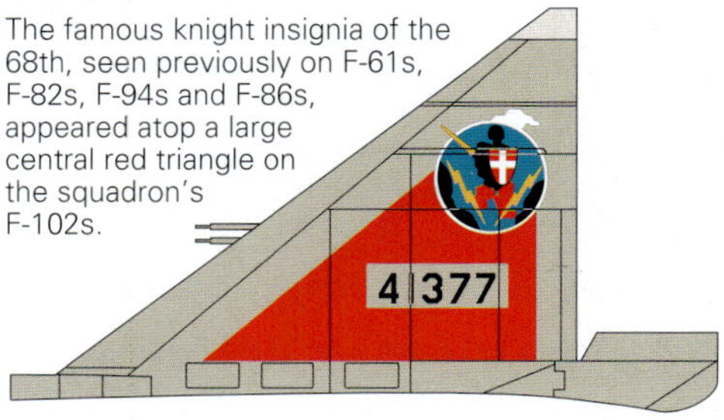

57th FIS

The 'Black Knights' (a nickname shared by the 525th FIS) wore the standard Arctic red wingtips and fins as had been seen on its F-89s. The F-102s added a chequered rudder to this pattern.

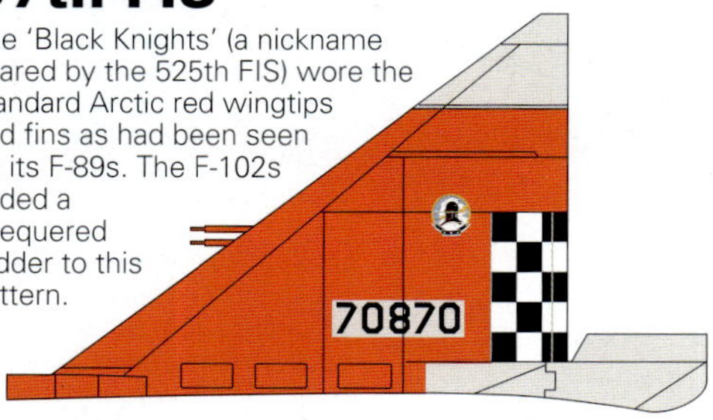

4780th ADW

The F-102A was the last of a long line of aircraft that trained interceptor pilots at Perrin AFB, Texas. This 'Deuce' had the 470th ADW's double chevron insignia, but no serial number on the fin.

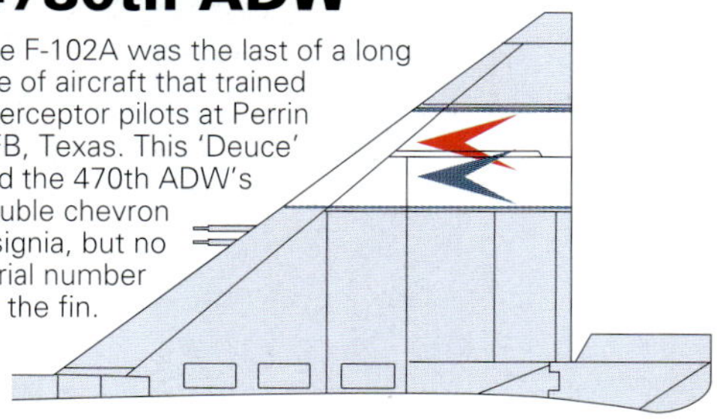

32nd FIS

The earliest markings of the 32nd FIS in Europe featured the colours of the Dutch flag over the whole fin. After mid-1963, the red, white and blue was restricted to the airbrake.

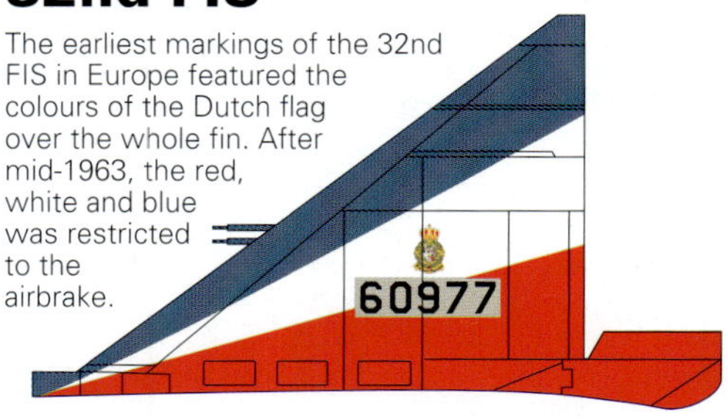

59th FIS

The 59th FIS was based at Goose Bay from 1952. Around the time it swapped its F-94s for F-102s, the unit also changed its dancing lion badge for the bat shown here.

ADWC

In the latter period of Air Defense Weapons Center F-102 use, this red and blue chevron with red/white rudder pattern was introduced. It was later applied, with variations, on ADWC F-106s.

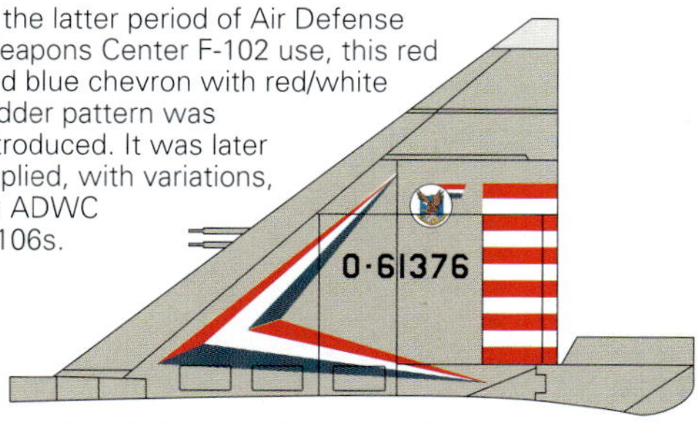

496th FIS

The sunburst marking of the 86th Air Division was seen on 496th aircraft from 1960 to mid-1963 when the general toning down began. In 1964, a broad band based on the 5th FIS markings appeared.

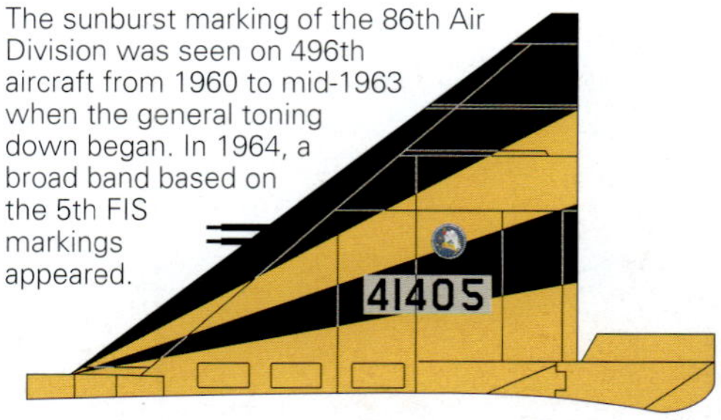

NASA

There was only one F-102 painted in full NASA colours with a NASA registration. The black of the central tail area continued along the fuselage to the air intakes.

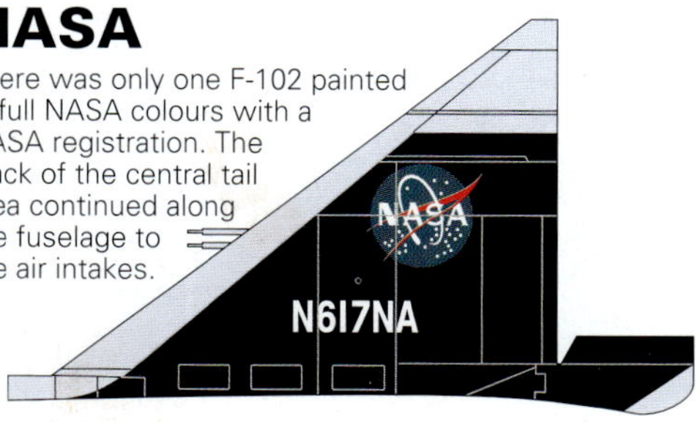

4th FIS

The 4th FIS at Naha on Okinawa used a broad red and black chequered band as a unit identifier, with no squadron badge.

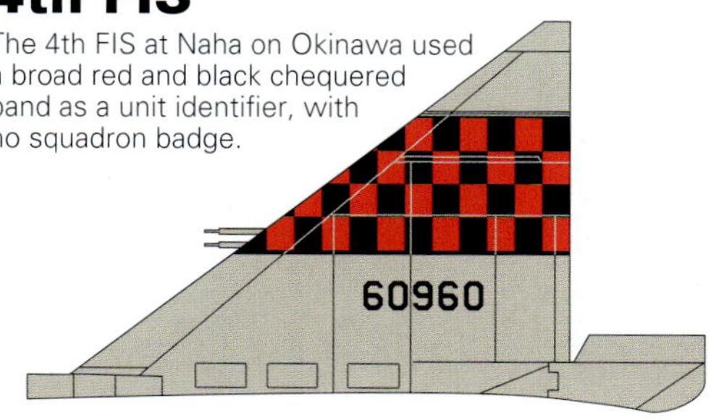

526th FIS

Flight assignment in the 'Black Knights' was denoted by the colour on the airbrake, either red, white or blue. The 526th was the first European unit to get camouflaged F-102s, in 1965.

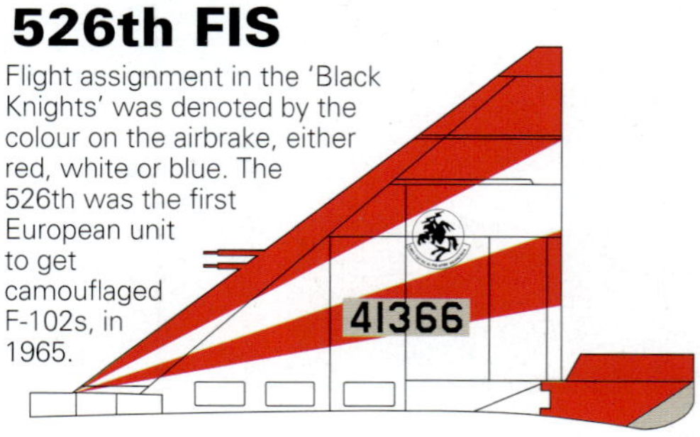

525th FIS

As with the 526th, airbrake colour on 'Bulldogs' F-102s denoted Red, White or Blue flights. The markings were later toned down to a badge on a grey fin.

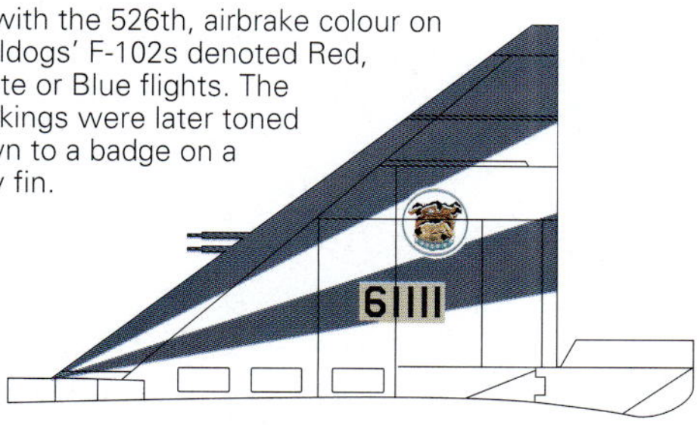

Pennsylvania ANG

The 146th FIS at Pittsburgh airport was distinguished by this striking black fin with striped rudder. A small tactical code number was often worn on the fin.

Minnesota

Although not an Alaska- or Arctic-based squadron, the 179th FIS at Duluth applied red tail and wing surfaces.The rudder was kept unpainted for balance reasons.

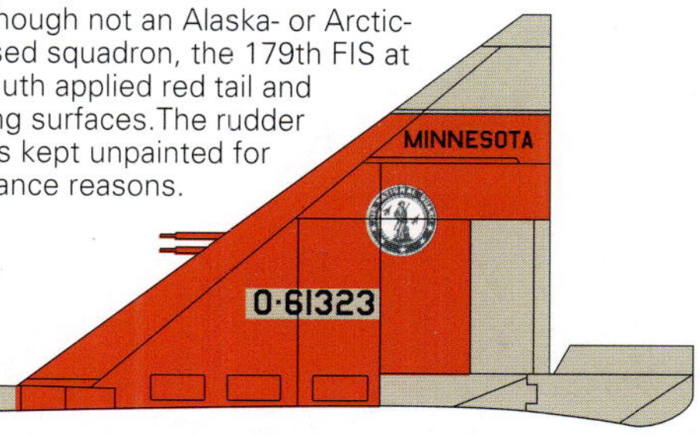

Texas ANG (111th FIS)

The 111th FIS carried the ANG badge on both sides of its F-102 fins, as well as the squadron's star and playing card badge. The badge dates from 1933 when the 111th was a Texas National Guard observation squadron.

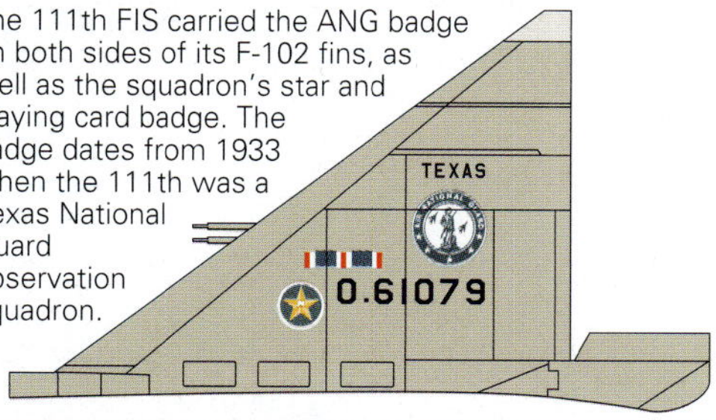

South Carolina ANG

Quite a few ANG F-102 users had variations of a band and stars, including the 157th FIS at McEntire which also had a coloured tail fin on some aircraft. Coloured air brake extensions were also seen.

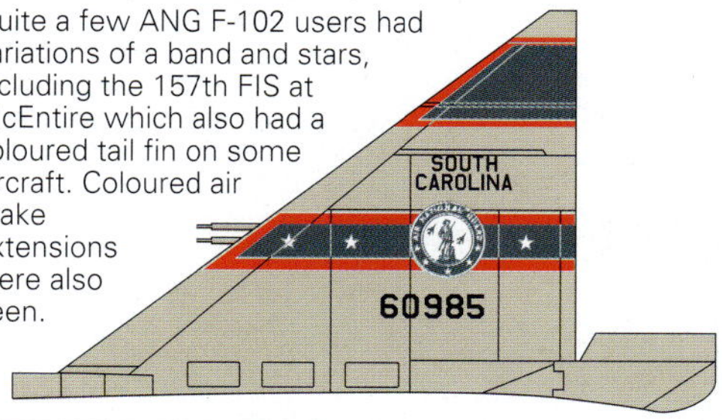

Montana ANG

Some ANG units used tactical code letters. The 'Big Sky Country' F-102s of the 186th FIS used an alpha-numeric system that had appeared on the F-89s previously used by the unit.

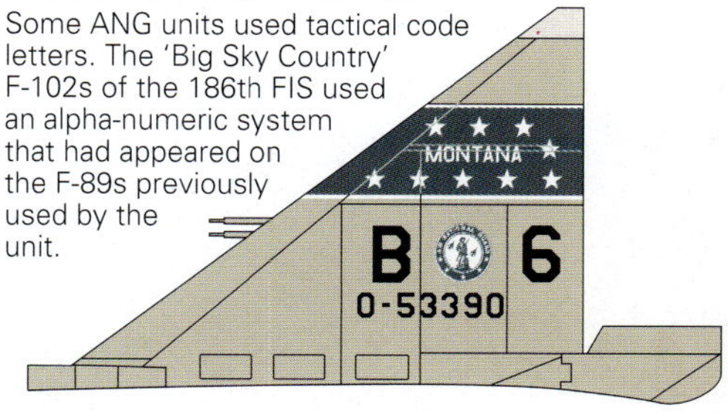

New York ANG

The 102nd FIS was one of the few squadrons to add any colour to the T.O.114 tactical camouflage scheme, in the form of a stylised seagull on a blue and white base.

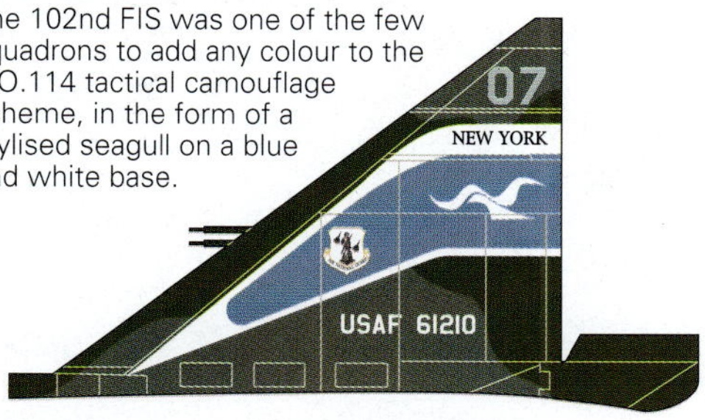

Florida ANG

The 159th FIS's F-102s wore this lightning flash in a blue band. The device was used, with variations, on the squadron's later F-106s, F-16s and F-15s. The abbreviated state name was unique to the 159th.

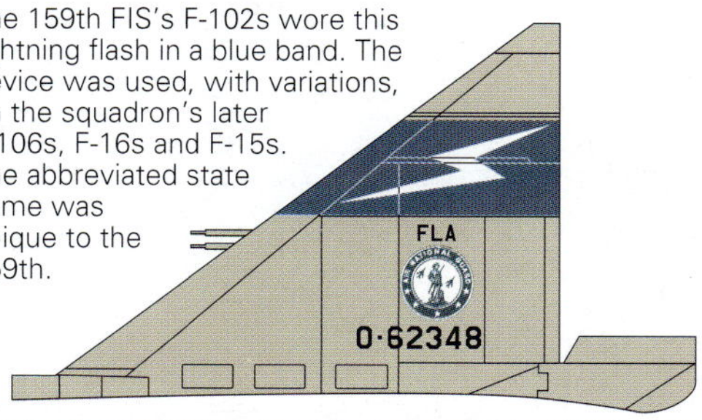

Idaho ANG

The 190th FIS was one of a small number of ANG units to have 'Deuces' in overall 'silver' finish. Its F-102s sometimes wore a numeric code on the rear fuselage.

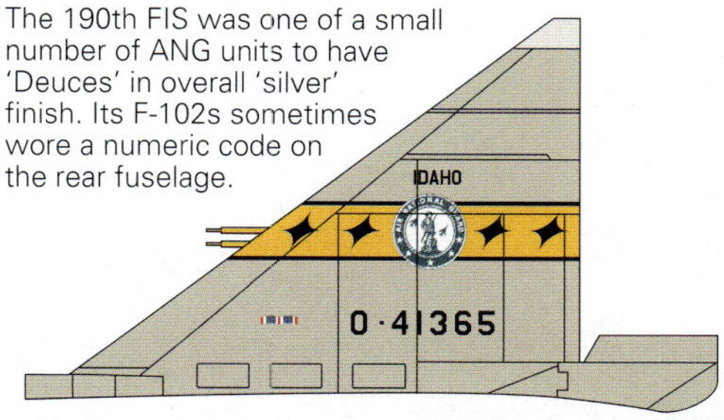

Connecticut ANG

Probably the cleverest design used on F-102 tail fins was the black and white stylised gull applied by the 118th FIS based at Bradley ANG Station. The 118th was an F-102 user from 1966 to 1971.

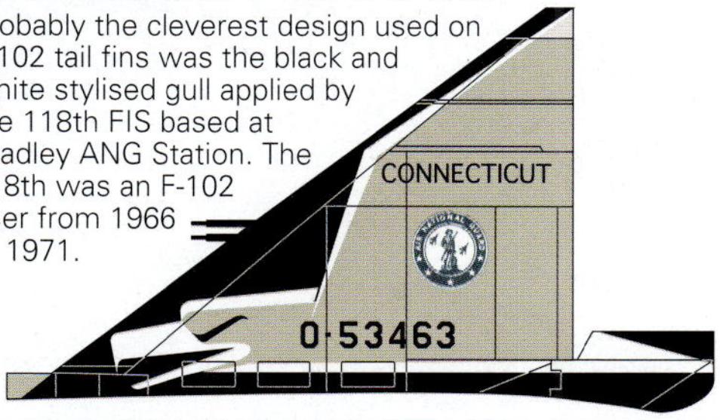

South Dakota ANG

The 175th FIS at South Dakota's Sioux City airport, which was one of the first ANG 'Deuce' squadrons, carried the state name on the fuselage (as S.DAK.AIR GUARD) rather than on the fin like other units.

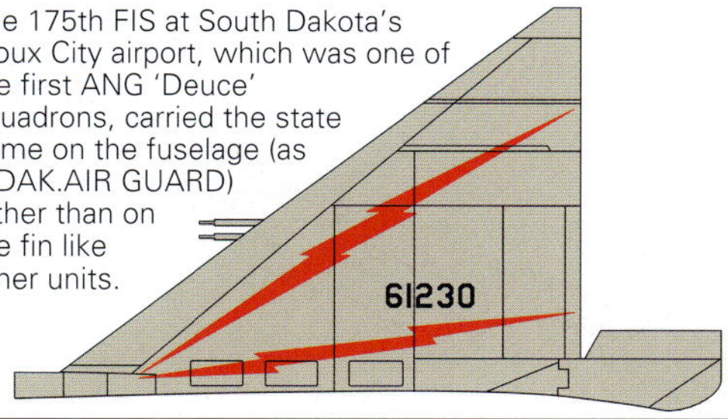

California ANG 196th FIS

The flamboyant stylised stars motif of the 196th FIS's F-102s reappeared on its later F-4 and RF-4 Phantoms. The 196th applied a natural metal finish to its F-102s for a period.

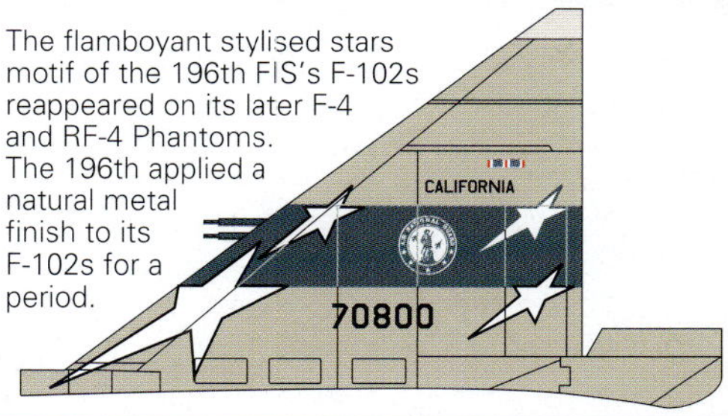

Oregon ANG

Like most ANG squadrons, the 123rd FIS, based at Portland Municipal Airport, wore the ANG badge on the port side of the fin and the squadron badge on the starboard side. The 'O' prefix to the serial indicated an 'obsolete' type.

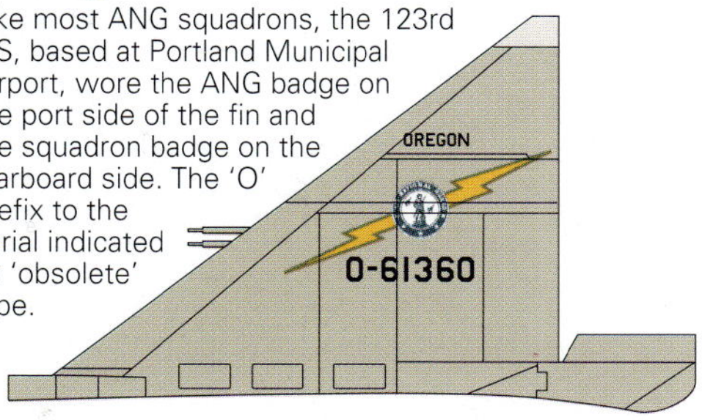

Wisconsin ANG

Like Pennsylvania's 146th FIS, Wisconsin's 176th marked its Delta Daggers with a full-colour fin, in this case red, with a red and white striped rudder. Large tactical numbers were also carried.

California ANG 194th FIS

In contrast to the 196th FIS, the 194th at Fresno used a simple small unit badge on its F-102s.

Vermont ANG

The 134th FIS 'Green Mountain Boys' used this simple green and yellow chevron on its aircraft. Sometimes the fin tip was coloured to denote flights within the squadron.

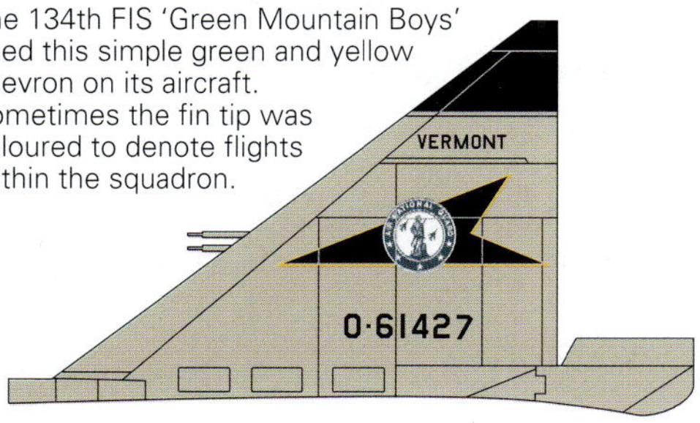

North Dakota

The 'Happy Hooligans' are said to have been so named after a boisterous trainng camp. The tail band was to appear on 178th FIS F-101s, F-4Ds and F-16s. A state law was passed to allow it to be worn on the 'low-vis' F-16.

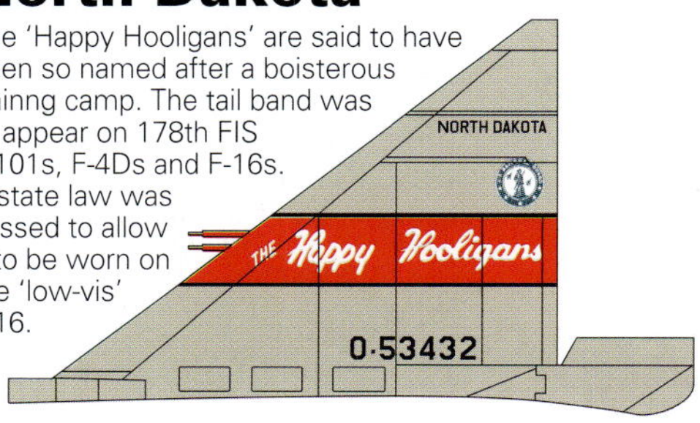

Hawaii ANG

The longest-lived ANG squadron, the 199th FIS F-102s wore a band based on a Hawaiian native basket design. It reappeared in reduced form on the later F-4Cs and F-15s.

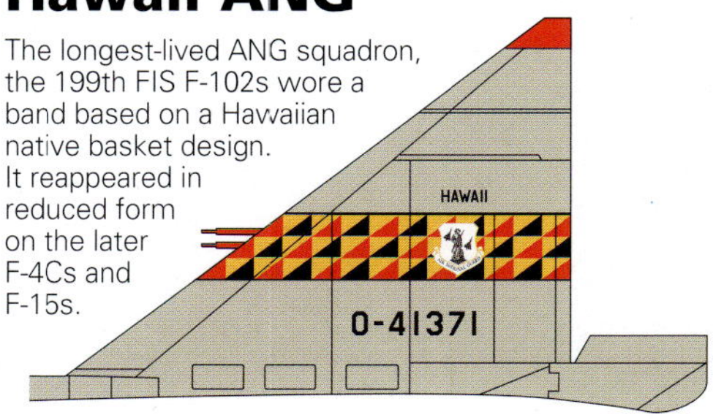

in many ADC squadrons, but unlike
the F-102A had a single crewman to fly
n. In order to fly the interception (when
the pilot had his face inside a rubber
aircraft with the (fixed) right-hand grip of
the left, moveable, grip. The throttle
cking the left grip from side to side
sed the beam on a target; lock-on was
e Falcon missiles and released them in a
achieved. Disengagement from the
tic.

Canopy and windscreen

The F-102A was not built with conventional dogfighting in mind, and thus all-around pilot view was sacrificed for greater aerodynamic cleanliness. With interception designed to be mostly 'automatic' with the pilot directing parts of the procedure head down in the cockpit, the view provided was judged sufficient to take-off, land and fly the aircraft in formation, rather than to visually acquire and track a target. The knife-edged windscreen featured prominent heating elements on each facet and the line of its central pillar followed on to a central canopy bar, allowing the canopy to be constructed in two halves. These were manufactured from stretched plastic, rather than cast acrylic, which proved shatter-proof when tested against 0.30-in calibre bullets, though the F-106, with an almost identical unit, was later retrofitted with a single-piece 'bubble' unit. 'A vision splitter', as found on the F-106, was refitted to F-102As, reducing internal reflections. The prototype YF-102A had a heavier 'birdcage' unit than those that followed, although the second through fourth YF-102s briefly reverted to this original canopy during testing.

Wings

The original wing fiited to the F-102A was known as the 'Case X' ('Case 10') wing. It was fitted to aircraft up to 56-1316, and could be distinguished by the squared-off tip to the wing, which was also slightly upswept, as seen here on 56-1279. The 'Case XX' ('Case 20') wing was tested in May 1957 and had been introduced into production by the end of the year. The new wing, with its downturned, pointed tips and leading-edge camber, increased the F-102A's ceiling, and improved manoeuvrability, glide angle and low-speed stability. Top speed was also increased by 0.06 Mach. However, despite these benefits, the 'Case XX' wing was not retrofitted to earlier examples.

The 'Deuce' was the first delta-winged fighter put into series production, and thus pioneered many of the features used on aircraft of this configuration today. It was in fact a scaled-up descendant of the very first powered pure delta, Convair's own XF-92A. Excluding the rudder, all control surfaces were mounted on the trailing edge of the wing. These comprised four elevons of primarily honeycomb construction, all hydraulically actuated, as were the missile bays and landing gear doors.

The wings were manufactured to a very close tolerance and were considered interchangeable between aircraft. Each contained two integral fuel tanks which were coated internally with Scotchweld sealant and assembled with Convair's patented Straylor rivets, which were then milled flush with the surface. The tanks were pressure tested to 7.5 lb/sq in (51.7 kPa) before installation. At least in early service, they were regarded as leak-proof, with no leaks or ruptures outside catastrophic aircraft accidents.

Radar
Like the F-86D/L that preceded the 'Deuce
most other 'all-weather' fighters of the day
the aircraft and operate the weapons syste
not under remote control from the ground)
hood watching the radar display, flying the
the control stick and directing the radar wit
was left alone, set to full military power. R
scanned the radar and tilting it forward foc
automatic. Holding down a trigger armed t
chosen sequence when correct range was
collision-course flightpath was then autom

Stopping the 'Deuce'
Mounted at the base of the fin was a clamshell-type speed brake. As well as slowing the aircraft in flight and on landing, the brake, in its retracted position, provided extra keel area, and thus stability in the yaw plane. As the fin area of the F-102A was increased after the earliest examples, so an upper fairing was added to increase the speed brake area and to strengthen the unit, which was prone to failures above 350 kt (403 mph; 642 km/h). Touchdown was usually made at 140 kt (161 mph; 259 km/h) although landings could comfortably made as low as 90 kt (104 mph; 167 km/h).

On the ground, the 'Deuce' was further slowed by holding the nose high for aerodynamic braking, using the wheel brakes, and by a relatively small drag chute which was neatly housed in a compartment between the two speed brake petals. Use of the speed brake and chute reduced the landing roll from about 2,450 ft (747 m) to about 1,780 ft (543 m) for a point defence (no external fuel) mission. Moisture leaking through the housing onto the parachute could cause the chute to freeze at high altitude, and it would fail to open on deployment.

As a 'last resort', the 'dog pecker' barrier engagement hook came into play. Fitted on the F-102 fleet by 1958, this device deployed from beneath the centre fuselage when the drag chute handle was pulled. Its function was to grab the runway-end barriers which were installed at most ADC bases. The barrier was flicked up by the nosewheel of an overrunning aircraft, but would normally fall back to the ground before catching the main gear, hence the barrier hook. From 1960, a Sheaffer runway arrestor hook, as developed for the F-106, replaced the barrier probe on most 'Deuces'.

Fin
Testing of the initial batch of F-102As revealed lateral instabilty and a tendency for roll-coupling (roll coupled with yaw, leading to departure from controlled flight). One month before the F-102A entered service, the decision was taken to introduce a larger fin to counter this. After the 65th F-102A, 55-3356, a new fin was introduced on production Block 41 and later retrofitted to the earlier aircraft. The larger unit was 95 sq ft (8.8 m^2) in area compared to the 68 sq ft (6.3 m^2) of the original. Comparative heights were 11 ft 5 in (3.48 m) and 8 ft 8 in (2.64 m), respectively. While increasing the stability, maximum speed was reduced by about 0.1 Mach with the addition of the larger fin. The fintip was made of a dielectric plastic material, and along with the horizontal aerial contained IFF and UHF antennas.

F-102 Colours

Vermont ANG

This F-102A of 'The Green Mountain Boys' has various items of green trim over its basic colours, including green wing fences. At different times, the 134th FIS marked flight assignment with coloured chevrons and/or fin tips.

California ANG (196th FIS)

Most F-102s were painted in overall 'Air Defense Command Gray': Federal Standard Colour 16473, like this one. The 196th FIS and a couple of other units operated 'natural metal' F-102s for some years. These appear to have been silver painted rather than bare metal.

Hawaii ANG

In their 15-year career with the 199th FIS, Hawaii ANG, the squadron's F-102s markings varied little. One addition to the basic scheme was red trim on the wing fences and fin tip.

Minnesota ANG

In common with F-102s and other interceptors based in Alaska, Canada, Greenland and Iceland, 179th FIS 'Deuces' were trimmed in Arctic red. The letter 'B' on the air brake of this example may have been a flight assignment or an individual code letter.

Florida ANG

Some ANG F-102 units, such as Florida's 159th FIS, had all-camouflaged aircraft in their later years. Some of these had seen service in Vietnam, while others had been repainted for USAFE units.

Turkey

Türk Hava Kuvvetleri (Turkish Air Force) F-102s retained their basic USAF colour schemes and even their serials. In the latter part of their service, the circular roundel replaced the earlier white-bordered red square.

Greece

Elliniki Polimiki Aeroporia (Hellenic Air Force) F-102s were mainly supplied from USAFE stocks, and included both camouflaged and ADC grey airframes. Like the Turkish AF aircraft, they wore their old USAF serials.

F-102 Details

The two YF-102s sported a heavily-framed cockpit windscreen and canopy design (far left), soon abandoned in favour of the YF-102A's smaller canopy, with less framework (left). Note also the redesigned engine air intakes which, on production F-102As, were again altered to include a splitter plate.

Below: The IRST, installed in F-102As from 1963 under Project Big Eight, was fitted immediately in front of the windscreen.

Convair F-102A Delta Dagger cutaway drawing

1 Pitot head
2 Radome
3 Radar scanner
4 Scanner tracking mechanism
5 ILS glideslope aerial
6 Radar mounting bulkhead
7 Radar pulse generator and modulator units
8 Nose compartment access doors
9 Static port
10 Lower IFF aerial
11 Angle of attack transmitter
12 TACAN aerial
13 MG-10 fire control system electronics
14 Nose compartment longeron
15 Infra-red detector
16 Electronics cooling air duct
17 Windscreen panels
18 Central vision splitter
19 Instrument panel shroud
20 Rudder pedals and linkages
21 Cockpit front pressure bulkhead
22 Air conditioning system ram air intake
23 Boundary layer splitter plate
24 Electrical system equipment
25 Port air intake
26 Nosewheel door
27 Taxiing lamp
28 Nosewheel, forward-retracting
29 Nose undercarriage leg strut
30 Torque scissor links
31 Intake duct framing
32 Nose undercarriage pivot mounting
33 Cockpit pressure floor
34 Port side console panel
35 Engine throttle lever
36 Two-handed control grip, radar and flight controls
37 Pilot's ejection seat
38 Canopy handle
39 Starboard side console panel
40 Radar display
41 Optical sight
42 Cockpit canopy cover, upward-hingeing
43 Ejection seat headrest
44 Boundary layer spill duct
45 Sloping cockpit rear pressure bulkhead
46 Air conditioning plant
47 Canopy external release
48 Canopy jack
49 Air exit louvres
50 Equipment bay access hatches, port and starboard
51 Canopy hinge
52 Radio and electronics equipment bay
53 Forward position light
54 Intake trunking
55 Missile bay cooling air duct
56 Missile bay door pneumatic jacks
57 Canopy emergency release
58 Liquid oxygen converter
59 Electrical system equipment bay
60 Fuselage upper longeron
61 Upper IFF aerial
62 Wing front spar attachment bulkhead
63 Pneumatic system air bottles
64 Bifurcated intake duct
65 Close-pitched fuselage frame construction
66 Engine bleed air duct
67 Anti-collision light
68 Starboard wing forward main fuel tank, total internal capacity 1,085 US gal (4107 litres)
69 Inboard wing fence
70 Fuel system piping
71 Centre-section wing dry bay
72 Wing pylon mountings and connectors
73 Starboard main undercarriage pivot mounting
74 Dorsal spine fairing
75 Intake duct mixing chamber
76 Engine intake centre-body fairing
77 Wing main spar attachment bulkheads
78 Intake compressor face
79 Forward engine mounting
80 Pratt & Whitney J57-P-23A afterburning turbojet engine
81 Engine oil tank, capacity 5.5 US gal (21 litres)
82 Oil filler cap
83 Starboard wing aft main fuel tanks
84 Fuel feed and vent piping
85 Ventral actuator fairing
86 Outboard wing fence
87 Cambered leading edge
88 Wing tip camber wash-out
89 Starboard navigation light
90 Fixed portion of trailing edge
91 Starboard outer elevon
92 Elevon hydraulic actuator
93 Trailing-edge dry bay
94 Fin leading-edge rib construction
95 Aerial tuning units
96 Fin attachment joints
97 Tailfin construction
98 Artificial feel system pitot intakes
99 Sloping front spar
100 Upper fin multi-spar construction
101 Fin tip aerial fairing
102 UHF aerials
103 VOR localiser aerial
104 Rudder
105 Honeycomb core rudder construction
106 Split airbrake panels
107 Airbrake pneumatic jacks
108 Airbrake, open position
109 Variable-area afterburner exhaust nozzle
110 Aft fuselage aerodynamic (area-rule) fairing
111 Exhaust nozzle control jacks (eight)
112 Tailcone attachment joint frame (engine removal)
113 Rear position lights
114 Afterburner duct
115 Engine bay internal heat shield
116 Brake parachute housing
117 Rudder hydraulic actuator
118 Rudder trim and feel force control units
119 Afterburner fuel manifold
120 Rear engine mounting
121 Inboard elevon hydraulic actuator
122 Engine turbine section
123 Bleed air connections
124 Bleed air blow-off valve
125 Engine accessory equipment gearbox
126 Wingspar/fuselage frame pin joints
127 Wing root rib
128 Port wing aft integral fuel tanks
129 Fuel tank dividing rib
130 Rear spar
131 Trailing-edge ribs
132 Runway emergency arrester hook, lowered
133 Elevon spar
134 Inboard elevon
135 Elevon rib construction
136 Outboard elevon
137 Trailing-edge honeycomb
138 Wing tip fairing construction
139 Port navigation light
140 Cambered leading-edge rib construction
141 Outboard wing fence
142 Wing rib construction
143 Main undercarriage mounting rib
144 Twin main spars
145 Main undercarriage side strut
146 Hydraulic retraction jack
147 Main undercarriage leg pivot mounting
148 Drag strut and pneumatic brake reservoir
149 Landing lamp
150 Port wing dry bay
151 Wing pylon mountings and connectors
152 Main undercarriage leg door
153 Port mainwheel
154 Torque scissor links
155 Port wing forward integral fuel tank
156 Inboard wing fence
157 Mainwheel door
158 Hydraulic reservoirs
159 Position of ram air turbine on starboard side
160 Missile bay aft section doors

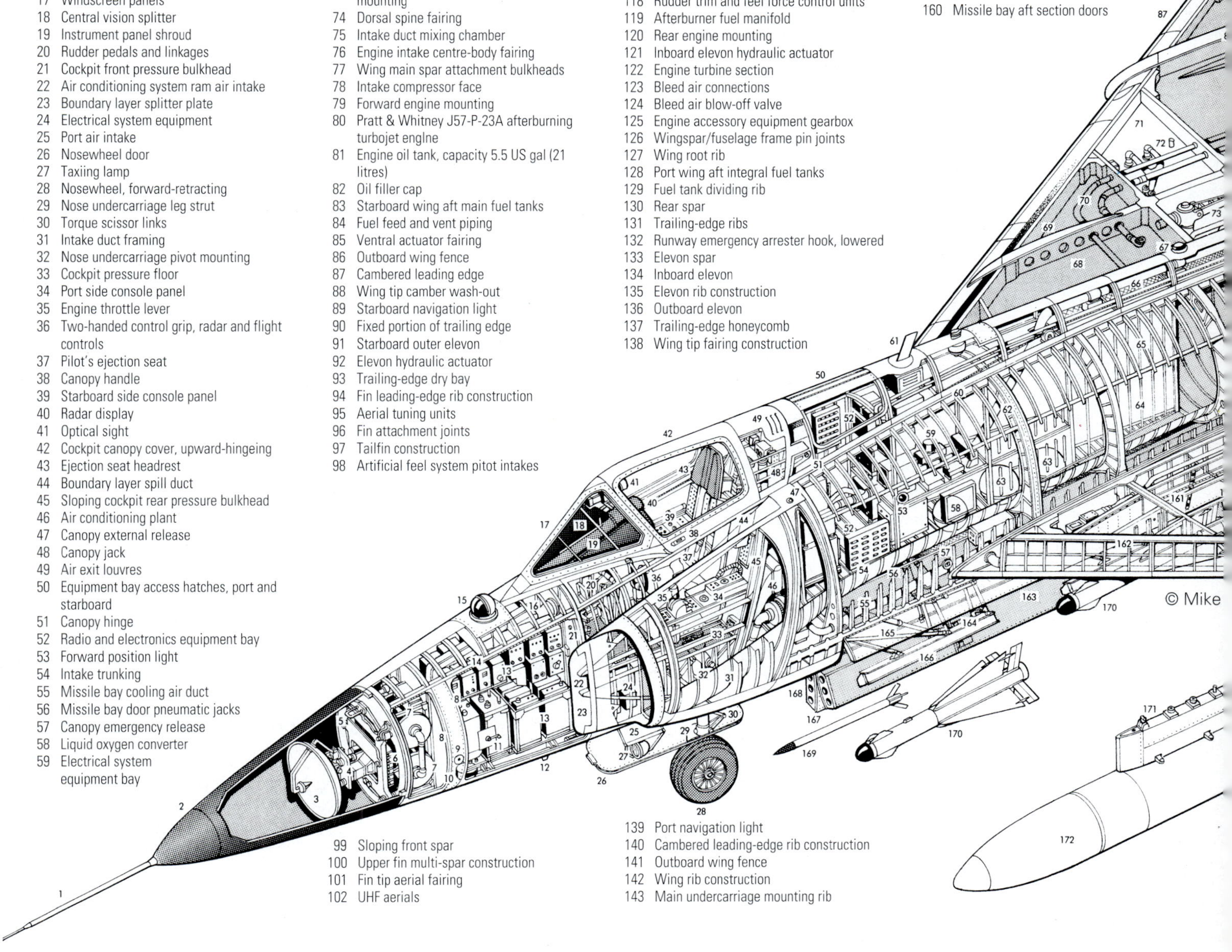

317th FIS

The badge of the 317th (approved in 1951) depicted sunshine, clouds, lightning, stars and rain, illustrating the all-weather, day-and-night role of the squadron, which had been formed as a day-fighter unit at Mitchell Field, New York in August 1942. Initially equipped with P-40s and forming part of the 325th Fighter Group, the squadron took part in combat in Algeria and Tunisia, before moving to Italy with P-47s and later P-51s. Known as the 'Checkertail Clan', the 325th produced 27 fighter aces. Inactivated in October 1945, the squadron reformed in August 1947 as the 317th Fighter Squadron (All-Weather) in May 1948 operating P-61 Black Widows until 1948 when F-82s arrived, followed by F-94s, F-86Ds and, finally, F-102s from 1956. Based in Washington state from 1948, at first as part of the 325th Fighter-All Weather/Fighter-Interceptor Group, then the 4704th Defense Wing, and eventually the 567th Air Defense Group, the 317th became part of the 325th Fighter Group once again in August 1955.

From August 1957, the squadron was detached to Alaska as part of the 10th Air Division, then the 5070th Air Defense Wing. The squadron became permanently subordinated to Alaskan Air Command (AAC) in October 1961. The 317th FIS was the primary interceptor asset of AAC, supplemented by 'White Shoes' rotations of CONUS-based F-106s from 1963 when it became clear that the F-102A had inadequate range to see off Soviet bombers probing the far reaches of Alaskan airspace. The 31st FIS served alongside the 317th in Alaska for only 13 months before its aircraft were handed over to the 317th, which became one of the largest fighter squadrons in USAF history with 46 aircraft, based in various locations including Elmendorf, Galena, King Salmon and Ladd AFB. The squadron was inactivated on New Year's Eve 1969. AAC itself was stood down in 1990 and its assigned units became part of 11th AF, in turn subordinated to Pacific Air Forces (PACAF).

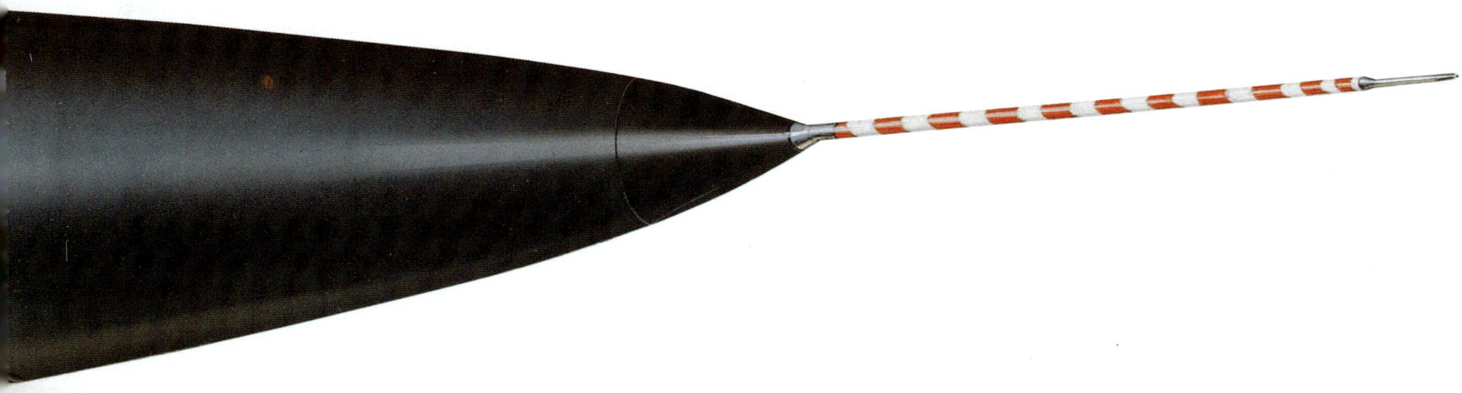

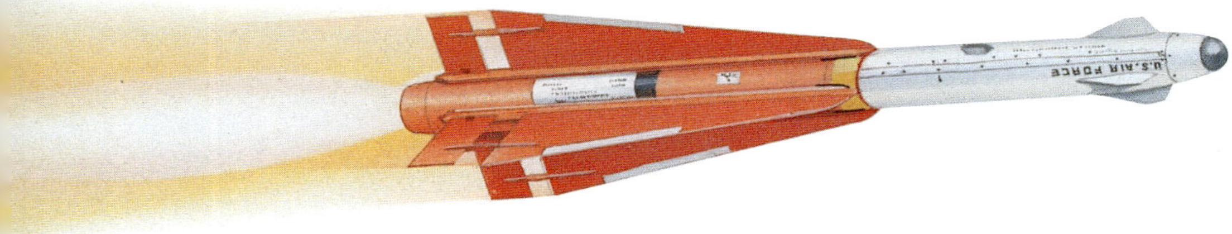

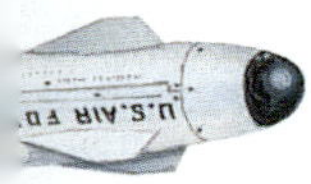

Weapons

An MB-1 Genie (then known as 'Ding-Dong') nuclear rocket was test fired from a YF-102 in May 1956, and consideration was given to equipping the F-102A fleet with this unguided air-to-air weapon, but this project was cancelled in early 1957, the Genie going to the F-101 and F-106 instead. The Dagger was to be equipped with the AIM-26A Nuclear Falcon. Originally known as GAR-11, Nuclear Falcon was designed by Hughes specifically for the F-102A, but provision for its use was not incorporated from the start, this being included in the modernisation phase by the fitting of kits to the centre missile bay, a process that was not completed until 1953, and then only to 450 aircraft (including trainers). The AIM-26A had semi-active radar homing (SARH) and essentially the same sub-kiloton warhead as used in the much larger Genie. Later modifications allowed interchangability of conventional and nuclear Falcons in the centre bay.

As a back-up to the relatively untried Falcon missiles, the Delta Dagger was able to fire up to 24 unguided rockets from launchers in the weapons bay doors. Aircraft delivered prior to December 1956 were capable of firing the 2-in and 2.75-in rockets, but after this, the USAF standardised on the larger weapon for the Delta Dagger, and teams from SAAMA modified up to 170 aircraft in the field. Nuclear Falcon-equipped 'Deuces' had the rocket tubes deleted from the centre bay doors, but could carry two rockets per tube in the other doors. Later, rocket capability was deleted altogether.

A typical weapons load was three semi-active radar homing GAR-1D/AIM-4A and three GAR-2A/AIM-4C or AIM-4G IR-guided missiles. This mix of radar-homing and infra red-guided missiles, fired in pairs consisting of one of each type, was pioneered in the F-102A and was later adopted as standard practice by most Soviet fighters.

For training, a Falcon-shaped device called a Weapons Evaluation System Missile (WESM) was often carried in the centre bay. This would remain attached to the weapons cradle which would pop out of the bay only long enough for the WESM to photograph the target aircraft. The addition of an infra-red search-and-track sensor under Project Big Eight, from 1963, assisted the Falcon in reliably locking on in heavy cloud and rain, which otherwise drastically reduced missile capability. As delivered, the weapons system contributed $219,876 to the $1.2 million flyaway cost of each Delta Dagger.

Convair F-102A-75-CO Delta Dagger
317th Fighter Interceptor Squadron
21st Composite Wing
Alaskan Air Command
Elmendorf Air Force Base, Alaska
1968

F-102A-75-CO Delta Dagger 56-1279
56-1279 was delivered new on 15 September 1957 to the 31st FIS at Wurtsmith AFB, Michigan, the unit moving to Elmendorf AFB, Alaska the following month. On 8 October 1958 the aircraft was handed over to the 317th FIS with whom it flew until 15 December 1969, when it was passed to the Wisconsin ANG (176th FIS) at General Mitchell Field, Milwaukee. The New York ANG (102nd FIS) at Suffolk County Airport, Westhampton Beach was the next unit to operate the aircraft, from 11 October 1974, though within six months it had been retired from active service and allocated to the 4950th Test Wing at Wright-Patterson AFB, on 18 March 1975. On 6 January 1976 the aircraft was written-off.

Structure and powerplant

The F-102 made more use than hitherto of heavy-pressed forgings. Complete fuselage frames, wing spars and longitudinal members were designed to be pressed from single large forgings. The main contractors for this work were Wyman-Gordon and Alcoa, and the use of the eight types of component these companies produced saved over 100 lb (45.3 kg) in weight, 273 components and 3,200 rivets. When the YF-102 failed to go supersonic, and it was deduced that the problem was failure to conform to the 'area rule', the nature of the Cook-Craigie production plan meant that changing the entire fuselage structure was considered impractical. A longer nose was fitted to improve the fineness ratio and large fairings were fitted to bulk out the rear fuselage. These were called 'Marilyns' in a tribute to the charms of a certain contemporary film star. Although these changes greatly improved the YF-102's performance, the air force called for further redesign. The resulting YF-102A was 14 ft (4.26 m) longer than the original YF-102 and was substantially different in most structural respects; two-thirds of the 30,000 tools purchased by October 1953 were discarded.

Other structural changes made to reduce transonic and supersonic drag included adding partial conical camber to the wing, which reduced high-altitude drag and improved handing at high angles of attack. During the enforced halt in the programme, Convair engineers took the opportunity to increase the accessibilitity of the engine and other internal components, improve the pilot's view by drooping the nose and making many other minor changes. These improvements, made possible by the original design's performance failings, transformed the F-102A into a much better weapon than would have otherwise resulted had production progressed based on the YF-102 airframe.

The F-102A's powerplant was a Pratt & Whitney J57-23A or -25 turbojet rated at 11,700 lb (114.7 kN) static thrust; 17,200 lb (168.7 kN) with afterburner. At the same time as the new, enlarged fin was added, intake splitter plates were introduced. This was a 'buzz fix' intended to reduce vibration, and cockpit noise levels rather than to smooth or regulate airflow into the engine.

Fuel tanks

As designed, the F-102A had no provision for external fuel, absolute 'cleanliness' of the airframe being seen as a priority for a supersonic interceptor. When 'Deuces' were based in Alaska, Iceland and Europe, it became clear that extra range was essential. Convair developed an external tank design which was fitted to all F-102As from 1958. The original design of the 215-US gal (814-litre) F-102 tank featured an integral pylon which was jettisoned along with the tank. In late 1966, the USAF flight-cleared a Convair-designed tank that could be hung from the standard Aero-7A rail, and this was put into production in July 1967. Convair also produced the refuelling probe kits needed for deployment to Japan, Vietnam and elsewhere. Internal fuel was contained in four wing tanks with a total capacity of 1,085 US gal. (4107 litres).

The F-102's massive nose cone (above left) contained its Hughes MG-10 fire control system (FCS) comprising a radar scanner (above) and associated electronics. Originally Hughes' E-9 FCS (later known as MG-3), as fitted to the Northrop F-89, was selected for the 'Deuce', but an aircraft with the performance of the F-102 demanded a better system and the MG-10 was chosen. MG-10 was effectively MG-3 with a addition of an AN/ARR-44 datalink, MG-1 automatic flight control system and AN/ARC-34 miniaturised communications set.

161 Retractable over-run barrier probe
162 Wing front spar
163 Port missile bay doors
164 Pantographic action missile displacement gear
165 Displacement gear hydraulic jack
166 Missile launch rail
167 Missile bay door integral rocket launch tubes

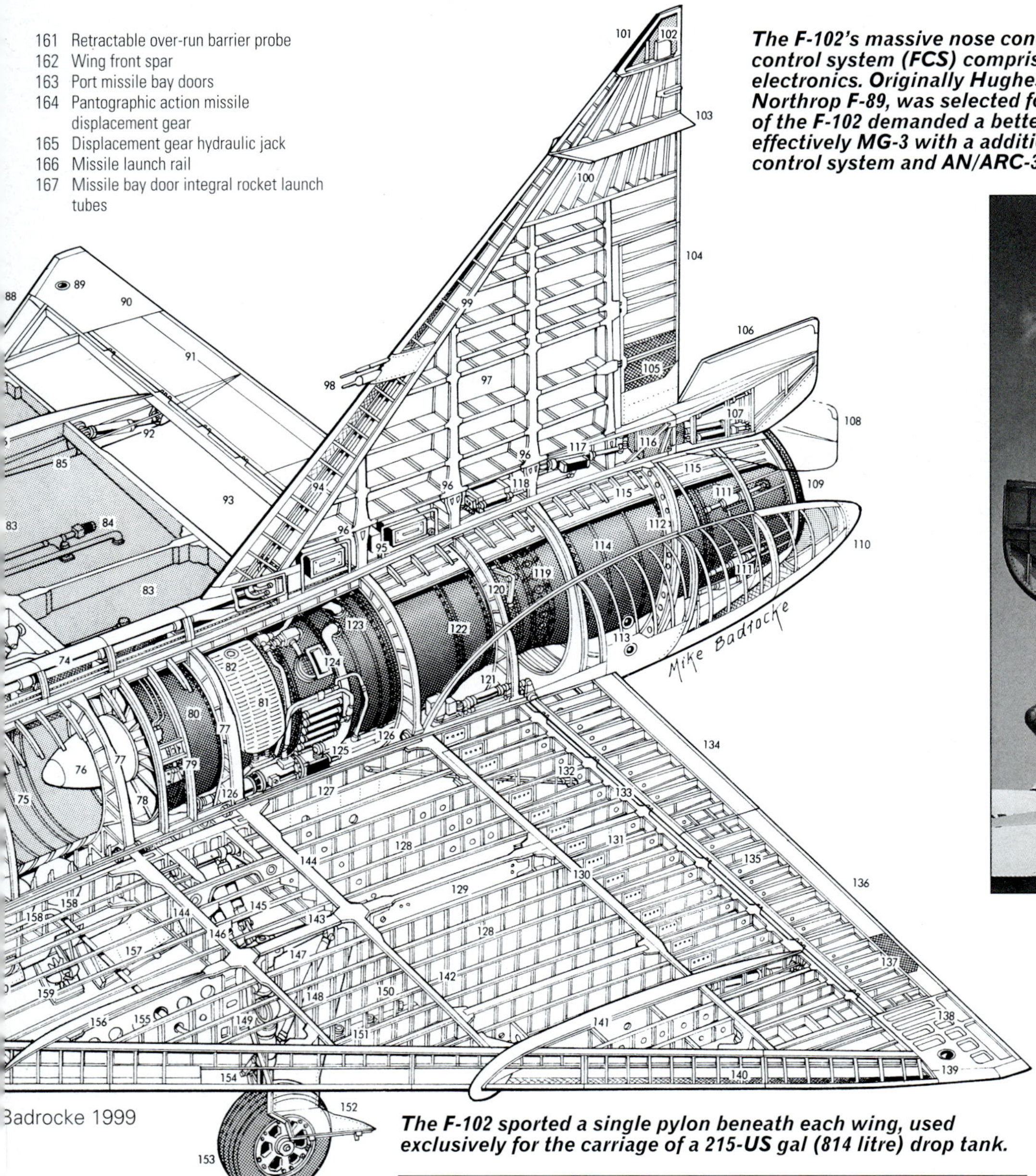

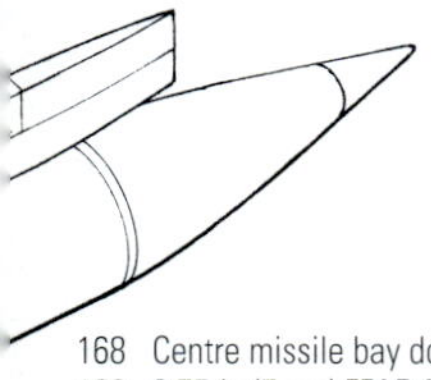

168 Centre missile bay door
169 2.75-in (7-cm) FFAR folding-fin rockets (24)
170 AIM-4D Falcon air-to-air missile (6)
171 Port wing fuel tank pylon
172 215-US gal (814 -litre) external fuel tank

These views of the YF-102A (below) and a production F-102A (above) show the aerodynamic fairings either side of the tail pipe, introduced when the fuselage was 'area-ruled' to reduce drag. Note also the smaller speed brake on the YF-102A. In the upper a Technical Sergeant packs the aircraft's braking parachute.

The F-102 sported a single pylon beneath each wing, used exclusively for the carriage of a 215-US gal (814 litre) drop tank.

F-102 Weapons

The 'silver bullet' in the Deuce's armoury from 1963 was the 'Falcon Model Y52A' or AIM-26 Super Falcon, in its nuclear tipped AIM-26A form also known as 'Nuclear Falcon'. Around half of the F-102 fleet was equipped to carry the missile at a modification cost of $10,000 per aircraft.

Above: As may be seen from this view of members of the Hughes Falcon AAM family (from left: AIM-26A, AIM-4C, AIM-4A, AIM-4G and AIM-4F), a typical AIM-4 was between 78 in (1.98 m) and 86 in (2.18 m) in length. The white leading edges on some of the missiles' fins are fuses to detonate the warhead.

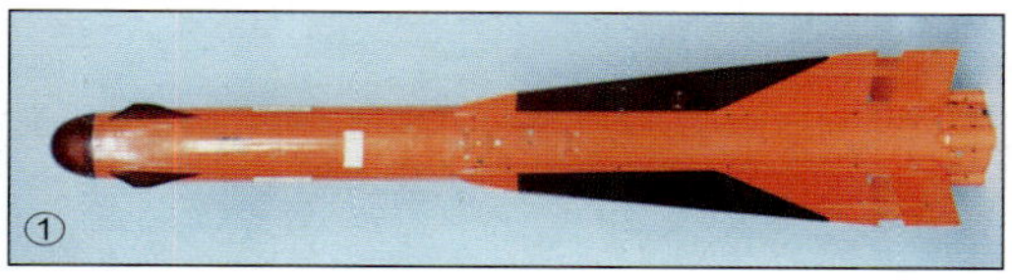

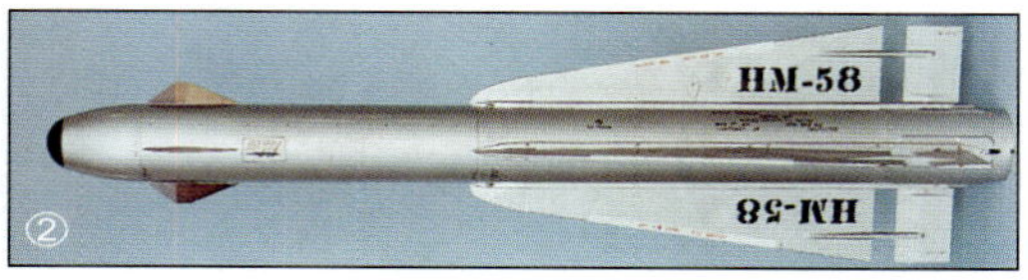

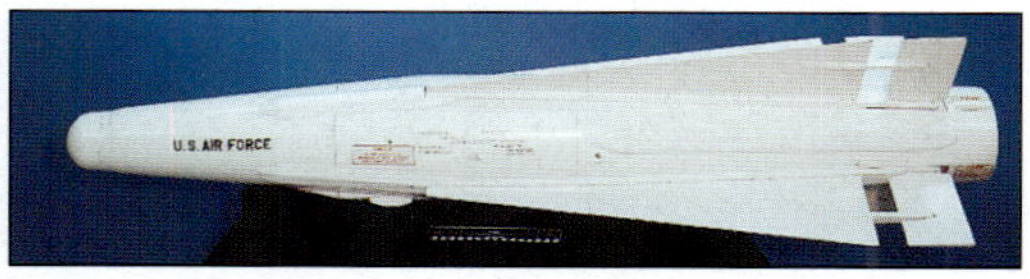

Above: More than 450 F/TF-102As were modified prior to 1963 under T.O. 1F-102A-620 to carry one or a pair of SARH AIM-26A (GAR-11) nuclear-capable AAMs in the centre bay. AIM-26A Super Falcon employed the same 1.5kT warhead as Douglas AIR-2 (MB-1) Genie and was proximity fused. AIM-26B (GAR-11A) was the nuclear Super Falcon's conventionally-armed equivalent. Though Convair proposed an 'F-102C' (originally 'F-102X') armed with a single Genie (and four Falcons), the unguided nuclear-tipped air-to-air rocket never formed part of the Deuce's arsenal, though F-102A 53-1797 was used to test the weapon at Holloman AFB, New Mexico in mid-1957.

The F-102's primary air-to-air weapon was the Hughes AIM-4 Falcon AAM (known as XF-98 in its prototype form and later redesignated GAR-1). Up to six missiles, usually three each of an IR- and radar-guided variant, were carried in pairs on rails in the aircraft's three weapons bays. The main AIM-4 models with which the F-102 was armed were, initially, the SARH AIM-4A (GAR-1D) ① and the IR-guided AIM-4C (GAR-2A, or HM-58 when exported) ②. These were superseded by the SARH AIM-4E (the first of the so-called Super Falcons, developed for use in the F-106 and originally known as GAR-3) and IR AIM-4F (GAR-3A) ③, respectively. Two other IR-guided Falcon variants saw limited use in the F-102. The AIM-4D (GAR-2B, middle right) was the last production Falcon, tailored for anti-fighter combat, while the AIM-4G (GAR-4A) was an AIM-4F derivative with a new IR seeker able to lock-on to smaller targets at greater distances. The other F-102A weapon option was up to 24 2.75-in (70-mm) folding-fin aerial rockets (FFARs) located in tubes in the missile bay doors. Aircraft modified to carry AIM-26 carried only 12 rockets, those on the two centre bay doors being deleted. Eventually the FFARs were removed altogether from F-102s.

Right: Each weapons bay contained two Falcon launch rails, each of which carried a single missile. During the firing sequence, the launch rails were hydraulically extended into the slipstream

Above: Typical of the IR-guided Falcons, AIM-4D was 79½ in (2.02 m) in length, 6⅜ in (0.163 m) in diameter, had a 20-in (0.508-m) span and a launch weight of 134 lb (61 kg). With a range of six miles (9.7 km), it had a top speed of Mach 4.

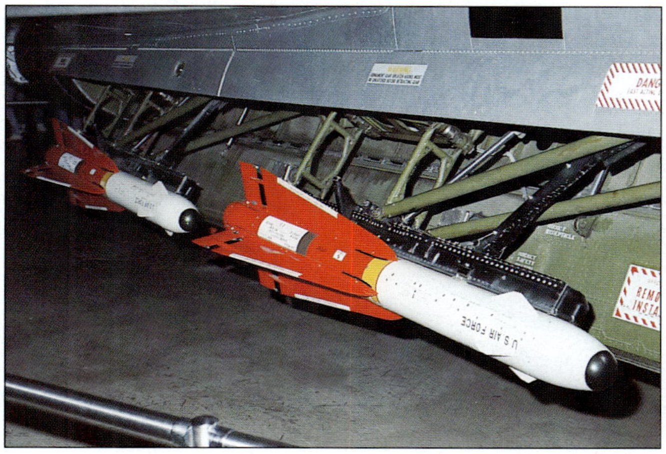

An F-102A of the Wisconsin ANG's 176th FIS (sometimes known as the 'Bushy Badgers') takes off during an Operational Readiness Inspection (ORI).

'Deuces' being consumed by the scrappers' torches at Naha in a busy three-week period.

At several junctures during the Vietnam War, Convair attempted to sell the USAF a major programme to modify existing 'Deuces' into what the company called a 'close support all-weather interceptor'. With inflight-refuelling capability, an unrefuelled ferry range of 2,506 nm (2,885 miles; 4643 km), and a ready supply and maintenance infrastructure, the new, dual-role version would have had six external ordnance stations in addition to the standard missile bay, and would have retained the existing MG-10 fire-control system. The 'close support' version would also have been capable of carrying up to three reconnaissance cameras, which would be interchangeable with the internally carried Falcon AAMs, and would have had wing pylons for two 750-lb (340-kg) and four 1,000-lb (454-kg) bombs, or alternatively for rockets. Possible weapon loads would have included the AGM-12 Bullpup ASM (by then determined by the USAF to be essentially useless but still being manufactured), 5-in (127-mm) Zuni rocket projectiles and fragmentation bombs. The general idea was that this proposal would offer a degree of flexibility deemed, by Convair at least, to be appropriate for the Vietnam setting. The USAF never bit, and there was never a 'Deuce' fighter-bomber.

The gradual weaning-down of the USAF's inventory of 'Deuces' continued into the 1970s. On 30 June 1971, Perrin AFB, Texas ended its long-standing role as Replacement Training Unit (RTU) for Delta Dagger pilots, and all F-102A and TF-102A training was transferred to the 111th FIS, Texas ANG.

A pair of 'Deuces' of the Louisiana ANG flies over its home town of New Orleans during 1965. Deficiencies in NORAD's coverage of the southern sector of the US led, in 1971/72, to an increased alert role for the Louisiana Guard.

F-102As of 'blue' and 'yellow' flights of the 134th FIS line up for a formation take-off.

In the late 1960s, a number of 'natural metal' F-102As appeared in ANG squadrons, mainly in the Oregon and Montana Guards and California's 196th FIS at Ontario (below). Fifty aircraft that passed through depot-level maintenance at Fairchild-Hiller's facility at Crestview, Florida from May 1969 were finished with a new silver acrylic lacquer paint. Although the resulting scheme was attractive and durable, it did not enter widespread service.

Above: Some TF-102s were not equipped with weapons or fire control equipment (or had it removed) and were mainly used for check-rides. Others, including this 199th FIS 'Tub', had a dual fire control system (FCS) fitted.

A Wisconsin ANG TF-102A glistens after an April shower. About half of the two-seaters were equipped with AIM-26A Nuclear Falcon capability, although it is unlikely that any ANG 'Tubs' ever carried the weapon.

The Cold War and the American face-off with Cuba continued. On 26 October 1971, a Cuban Antonov An-24 'Coke' twin-engined transport 22 nm (25 miles; 41 km) from New Orleans radioed the control tower requesting landing instructions. It was a defector, and the call was the first inkling that a Cuban aircraft was in the area. The 'Coke' was allowed to land and the press went into a frenzy, demanding to know what had happened to the southern air defence of the USA. To augment and beef-up this defence, three F-102 alert detachments of the ANG were created in Louisiana, Texas and Arizona.

The end of the F-102A Delta Dagger era in the ADC, which had been redesigned Aerospace Defense Command on 15 January 1968, came on 1 July 1973 when the 57th FIS 'Black Knights' at Keflavik AB, Iceland surrendered its 'Deuces' and filled its alert barns with F-4C Phantoms. The previous year, however, new life had been breathed into the Delta Dagger with a plan to fly a version that carried no pilot.

PQM-102A/B

In 1972 the USAF asked six aerospace contractors to submit proposals for a drone conversation of the F-102. On 31 March 1973, Sperry won a contract to convert six airframes. The programme became known as Pave Deuce.

The 'Deuce' drone was intended to replace the Ryan BQM-34 (*née* Q-2C) Firebee I and II drones, then being employed as high-speed, manoeuvrable aerial targets. The PQM-102A (which should have been designated QF-102A under the existing system for naming aircraft) made its first flight on 13 August 1974. It was billed, inaccurately, as the first full-scale pilotless target with an afterburning engine and hence the first able to simulate warplanes that might be encountered in actual combat.

In fact, the USAF had ordered the PQM-102A in part because of its lack of foresight with a previous full-scale, afterburner-equipped target. Earlier, the USAF had operat-

Air National Guard phaseout

The first F-102 squadron gave up its 'Deuces' as early as 1964, but the bulk of the 23 units so equipped phased them out in the 1969-71 period. When the F-102As were retired from the ANG, the squadrons that operated them transitioned to a wide variety of different types. Most stayed, broadly, in the fighter business, but only three made the logical step to the F-106. Five went to the F-100, six to the F-101, two to the O-2, one to the F-4 and one to the RF-4. Single squadrons acquired the A-7, F-84, KC-97 and EB-57. One became an air rescue squadron with HC-130s and HH-3s. The very last US user of operational F-102s was the 199th Fighter Interceptor Squadron at Hickam AFB, which retired them in favour of F-4Cs in January 1977.

The Texas Guard was the first and the last Continental US ANG users of the F-102, although different squadrons introduced the 'Deuce' (182nd FIS, July 1960), and saw out (111th FIS, January 1975) the Delta Dagger. Seen here with its replacement is an aircraft of the 111th. Note that both the F-102A and the F-101F have the 'O' for 'obsolete' serial prefix.

PQM/QF-102

Under a contract managed by the USAF at Eglin AFB, bidders were sought for the conversion of F-102s into unmanned targets. Bidders included Sperry Rand Flight Systems Division, Lear Siegler, Northrop, Celesco Industries, Lockheed and Hughes/Honeywell. The winner, in April 1973, was Sperry Rand, which, after converting and testing the first of six prototypes at Holloman AFB in August 1974, subcontracted Fairchild at Crestview Florida to do the remaining 24 conversions and maintenance. Following further contracts, conversion and maintenance was taken over by Sperry at a new facility at Litchfield Park near Davis-Monthan where large numbers of F-102s were stored

The first aircraft destined for conversion to PQM-102B standard is seen arriving at Litchfield Park. 56-1077 was an ex-Idaho ANG aircraft that had been delivered to AMARC in April 1975. The conversion process from 'boneyard' to drone took six months.

Flight Control Stabilisation System (FCSS) components replaced the F-102's old vacuum tube autopilot, while a manouevre programmer allowed evasive actions to be input by the ground controller.

ed the Lockheed QF-104 Starfighter, the drone target version of a fighter that had had a relatively lacklustre career in US service. But in a false economy move, the USAF had ordered only 22 QF-104 conversions and only very slowly, over a decade's time. It was a time of vigorous weapons testing, and the final QF-104 was shot down in July 1972.

The PQM-102A was purposely ordered in more robust numbers. Among other duties, the type was to serve as a realistic target for McDonnell Douglas F-15 Eagles in air-to-air engagements and, when flying from Holloman AFB, for US Army surface-to-air missiles launched from the White Sands Missile Range. Ultimately, by 1977, Sperry's Crestview, Florida facility transformed 65 former Delta Dagger interceptors into PQM-102A drones. Some 29 aircraft – it is unclear whether their number is included in the total of 65 or increased the total to 89 – were converted in Crestview by Fairchild. Of this number, 14 were owned by the US Army. Fairchild described the conversion process as follows:

"Crews at Crestview remove most of the original avionics equipment. After that, there is extensive re-wiring and refitting to install the Sperry-designed autopilots, flight controls, and low-altitude radar.

"Technicians also install a smoke system, designed by Fairchild engineers, which allows ground observers to visually track the drone at high altitude, even with the afterburner on. They also install a destruct system which controllers can use to blow up the drone in the event it goes out of control."

After completion, the PQM-102A drones were flown to Tyndall AFB by civilian pilots employed by Sperry. At Tyndall, Sperry removed the ejection seat and installed 'black boxes' in the cockpit so that the PQM-102A could no longer be flown by a human pilot.

Four of the 65, or perhaps 89, PQM-102A aircraft did not receive the cockpit modification and remained, throughout their service lives, capable of being flown either remotely or by a pilot. These four were the only aircraft to be designated QF-102A. The first QF-102A was the first 'Deuce' to make an unmanned flight, in this instance at Holloman AFB on 13 August 1975.

The first unmanned flight of a production-standard PQM-102A was also accomplished at Holloman AFB, where testing was delegated to the USAF Special Weapons Center's 6585th Test Group. Operations also took place at Tyndall AFB where a new 7,000-ft (2133-m) runway for drone work was constructed 4 miles (6.4 km) east of the main base, the drones being towed to the launch site over a newly built taxi strip.

Sperry's Litchfield Park, Arizona plant began making the PQM-102B model in 1978. In the 'A' model the remote control equipment was located in the cockpit. In the PQM-102B that should, by rights, have been designated as the QF-102B, the equipment was moved to the nose, mak-

Take-offs by drones were conducted by the mobile Ground Station (MGS). After five minutes' flight, the mission was handed over to a control centre on base and regained for landing (if the drone was recoverable) by the MGS about 10 miles (16 km) out.

Control consoles in the MGS were a representation of the F-102's original instrument layout. Two pilots controlled the drone, one handled throttle and pitch, the other direction.

NACA and NASA

NASA and its predecessor NACA made less use of the F-102 than they did of its 'Century Series' stablemates, the F-104 and F-106. The XF-92A, a YF-102, six F-102As and two TF-102As served with various NASA centres between 1953 and 1974, although only one of these wore a NASA number.

***Right:* NASA 617 (56-998) was based at NASA Lewis at Cleveland Municipal Airport on chase duties for the NF-106B NASA 616 which was flying SST research missions over the Great Lakes. It was retired to AMARC in 1974.**

***Above:* The last-but-one YF-102 53-1785 passed across the Edwards AFB flightline to NACA Dryden in 1954 and was used until 1958. It is displayed today at the nearby town of Boron and is the only surviving YF-102.**

***Above:* F-102A 56-1358 arrived at NASA Ames (Moffett Field, California) on 23 December 1957. It was used on explorations of 'fire control auto manoeuvres', until March 1960. Similarly, F-102A 56-1304 was used for 'auto attack evaluation'.**

***Left:* Astronaut Alan Shepherd arrives at a NASA facility in F-102A 55-3391. This aircraft flew nearly 500 hours in the 22 months it was based at the Johnson Space Center.**

After the Project Mercury astronauts had complained that they were being treated more like lab rats than test pilots, NASA's Manned Spacecraft Center at Houston acquired two F-102As (55-3391 and 55-3405) and two TF-102As (54-1338 and 54-1356) in September 1962. They were used for proficiency flying and for 'commuting' between various NASA and contractor sites. The 'Deuces' supplemented USAF-loaned T-33s, and were later replaced themselves by F-106s, the last being sent to Perrin AFB in August 1964.

Robert M. White is seen boarding NTF-102A 54-1354 in an MC-2 full-pressure suit

One of the original 'Mercury Seven', Virgil I. 'Gus' Grissom, stands by F-102A 56-1017 (not a NASA aircraft). Both he and Robert White died in the tragic Apollo I capsule fire.

Above: The F-104 Starfighter was known as 'the missile with a man in it'. The F-102 became something of a missile without the man when converted to drone form. This is a (non man-rated) PQM-102A.

Left: Live weapons were expended at various types of target drones at William Tell meets, including BQM-34s and AQM-37s. After 1978, the drones were more than likely F-102s themselves. In 1972, this 57th FIS 'Deuce' was still the hunter and not yet the hunted.

ing it possible for the aircraft to be flown manually by a pilot. Sperry produced about 145 examples of the latter version.

Operation of the drones was initially by Sperry under contract, and later by the RCA company. PQM-102A/B drones served the USAF for several years. The last PQM-102B mission was flown at Tyndall AFB on 14 July 1983 when such an aircraft (56-1175, call sign SPAD 793) completed the 500th mission in the programme. This aircraft and another were flown to Holloman AFB on 9 August 1983, and operations continued at Holloman AFB until 1986. It is believed that the final mission at Holloman AFB was flown by another PQM-102B (56-1072, call sign SPAD 800) in that year.

Civil 'Deuce'

The F-102A was so expensive to operate and to keep in flying shape that none is likely, ever, to appear as a restored museum piece on the warbird circuit. Indeed, although many are in museums, none survives today in a condition that even approaches being a candidate for restoration. There was, however, a civil F-102A for a six-month period.

An F-102A (57-0835) was given civil registry N300 and assigned to the Federal Aviation Administration (FAA) in

The last role of the F-102 included the indignity of being a target for its successor, the F-106. The 'Deuce' here, 56-1254, formerly with Wisconsin's 176th FIS, was one of the drones expended at William Tell 80. The 87th FIS F-106A in this picture was in turn converted to a drone and shot down, by an AMRAAM missile in May 1994.

William Tell

The F-102 made its first appearance at the biennial William Tell Weapons Meet in 1958, the year the competition moved to Tyndall AFB. The F-102 was the first supersonic interceptor to appear. The William Tell competition had no overall winner as such, but each squadron competed with those flying the same type. The first ANG squadron to win the F-102 category was Pennsylvania's 146th FIS in 1963, and the 32nd FIS took the trophy for USAFE in 1965. Guard squadrons won again in 1970 (Minnesota), 1972 (Wisconsin) and 1974 (Idaho), but by that time the *only* F-102s were in the ANG. The F-102 was absent in 1976, but returned in 1978 – this time in the form of PQM-102 target drones.

The squadron scoreboard at William Tell '82 is flanked by the drones used in that competition, the PQM-102 and the 'newer' QF-100D. This was the last year the 'Deuce' took part, the Pave Deuce programme concluding the following year.

'Deuce' destruction

F-102As served for nearly a decade in the drone role at both Holloman, New Mexico, and Tyndall, Florida. The Tyndall-based drones were used for air-to-air engagements, while those at Holloman more frequently faced SAMs fired from the White Sands missile range. On average, a PQM-102 survived four missile engagements (including inert warhead missiles that passed within 'kill' distance). Some 'lucky' aircraft survived 16 or 20. The last F-102 built, 57-0909, was shot down in March 1982 by an AIM-7E fired by an F-4D Phantom of the Michigan ANG, but 17 aircraft of the 213 converted remained when the programme ended in 1983. Of the 200 or so remaining F-102s that were not converted to drones, 20 were given to the New Mexico Institute of Mining and Technology for explosive testing, others went to China Lake for weapons tests and over 100 went to a scrap company in Arizona in 1976-77. One (56-1515) remains at Davis-Monthan.

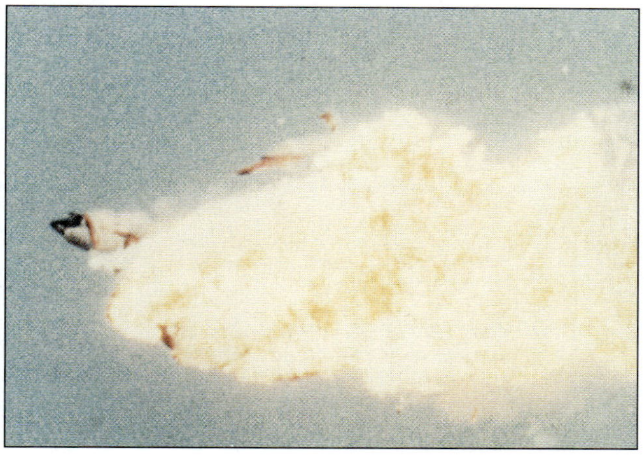

This sequence, recorded by a high-speed camera mounted on the tracking radar dish, shows the destruction of a PQM-102, possibly by a Stinger SAM (also a General Dynamics product). In the third image, hydraulic system damage appears to have caused the undercarriage to lower, precipitating the disintegration of the drone. The US Army were given the use of seven PQM-102s to expend in the Stinger and Patriot missile programmes.

June 1970. The aircraft carried out a six-month flight research programme at Edwards AFB to provide information for the development of airworthiness standards for the SST (supersonic transport) then planned by Boeing but later abandoned. Tests were directed at evaluation of low-speed performance characteristics to determine a suitable performance base-line that could be used in lieu of a stall speed for the SST, because delta-winged aircraft do not stall in the same way as straight- and swept-winged aircraft.

With test pilot Richard F. LaSuer doing the honours, the F-102A was modified with a wooden tail skid in order to restrict take-off rotation attitude to that of the proposed SST. Take-off and climb thrust were also limited to simulate normal thrust/weight ratios of the SST. In addition, the landing gear remained extended during tests to simulate the performance characteristics of typical SST designs. Speed brakes were then used to create landing gear drag. The programme yielded a wealth of performance that assisted with Concorde operations. It was probably the only appearance of the Convair F-102 Delta Dagger on the civilian scene. **Robert F. Dorr**

Below: Over 60 'Deuces' are preserved in the USA alone, with further examples in Canada, Greece, Turkey, the Netherlands and Germany. This F-102A, late of the 'Green Mountain Boys', is displayed at Burlington International Airport, Vermont.

F-102 Operators

Air Defense Command (ADC)

Between April 1956 and July 1973, ADC (Air Defense Command) operated 32 squadrons equipped with the Convair F/TF-102A. Midway through this era the interceptor acquired a nickname, the Delta Dagger, while ADC was redesignated Aerospace Defense Command. The aircraft and the mission remained little-changed throughout: the job was to defend North America against bombers and cruise missiles.

The focus was always on an attack from the Soviet Union, but during much of the 1960s, ADC was also preoccupied with Cuba, where the US sponsored a failed invasion by exiles in 1961 and forced the Soviets to remove missiles and bombers in 1962. From the very time Fidel Castro seized power, he had 'Deuces' aimed at him, and this condition persisted until 15 November 1969 when a longstanding alert detachment of eight F/TF-102As at Naval Air Station Key West, Florida, suspended operations. Even thereafter, a detachment of F-4 Phantoms was kept on alert for air defence against Cuba.

2nd FIS

The 2nd FIS at Suffolk County AFB, New York, operated the T/TF-102A from 29 January 1957 until 9 February 1960. The squadron was dubbed the 'Unicorns' but more frequently called the 'Horny Horses.' The emblem of a unicorn and the phrase 'Second to None' had previously adorned the F-86D/L Sabre. After the departure of the 'Deuce', the squadron continued in the air defence role flying the F-101B/F Voodoo.

55-3461 moved from the 5th FIS to the 2nd FIS in November 1958. Both squadrons were part of the 52nd FG.

5th FIS

The 5th FIS at Suffolk County AFB, New York, operated the T/TF-102A from 28 March 1957 until 21 March 1960. The F-86D/L Sabre had previously been the mount of the 'Spittin' Kittens' with their distinctive cat emblem and yellow/black trim. They progressed from the Delta Dagger to the next offering from Convair, the F-106A/B Delta Dart.

The 2nd and 5th FISs at Suffolk County wore 52nd FG colours rather than a squadron design.

11th FIS

The 11th FIS at Duluth International Airport, Minnesota, flew F/TF-102As from 27 August 1956 until 15 August 1960. One of at least two squadrons to use a charging bull as its emblem, the 11th FIS had previously operated the Northrop F-89H/J Scorpion. The squadron progressed in 1960 to the F-106A/B.

The 11th FIS CO's F-102A was marked with 'command stripes' over its otherwise plain finish.

18th FIS

The 18th FIS operated F/TF-102As from 27 August 1956 until 15 August 1960. Their emblem was a blue fox firing a machine-gun through the clouds. They were preceded at Wurtsmith AFB, Michigan by the F-89J Scorpion and replaced by the F-101B/F Voodoo, later becoming an Alaskan-based F-16 unit.

This F-102A of the 18th FIS, seen in 1958, has a band on the tail consisting of golden yellow and dark blue stripes, as well as a large squadron badge.

27th FIS

The 27th FIS, located during the 'Deuce' era at Griffiss AFB, New York, enjoyed the distinction of being the oldest fighter squadron in the Air Force, having been Frank Luke's unit in World War I. The 'Eagles' have operated everything from the Spad XIII to the F-15C/D Eagle.

The squadron began converting from the F-94C Starfire to the F-102A shortly after the first 'Deuce' arrived on 4 June 1957. The squadron remained an operator of the F/TF-102A until 18 February 1960. The F-102 was replaced by the F-106A/B.

When the 27th FIS transitioned to the F-106, it retained the yellow/black chequerboard and chevron markings used on its F-102s.

31st FIS

The 31st FIS at Wurtsmith AFB, Michigan had a brief interlude with the F/TF-102A from 1 December 1956 until 17 October 1957. The squadron employed a wolf emblem copyrighted by Walt Disney studios. The 31st dates to 1940 and was flying F-86 Sabres before the 'Deuce' came along. The squadron transferred to Alaskan Air Command, in 1957 and its further operations are noted in the section on AAC.

January 1957 at Wurtsmith gave the 31st a taste of the conditions they would soon find in Alaska.

37th FIS

The 37th FIS 'Green Mountain Boys' at Ethan Allen AFB, Vermont, flew the F/TF-102A from 3 January 1958 until 23 May 1960. The squadron derives its name not merely from the craggy peaks of Vermont, but also from a band of local patriots in the American war for independence. The 37th traces its origins to 1940 and was flying the F-86 Sabre prior to the 'Deuce'. The squadron later flew F-4D Phantoms and now flies the F-16C/D block 25 Fighting Falcon.

The 37th FIS was one of several ADC units to adopt arctic markings.

47th FIS

The 47th FIS at Niagara Falls International Airport, New York, was an F/TF-102A operator from 3 January 1958 until 25 May 1960. The squadron used a bumblebee or 'turnip termite' emblem, copyrighted by United Features Syndicate.

The squadron is one of only a couple to revert to an earlier aircraft. After flying the Delta Dagger in 1958-60, it reverted to the F-84F Thunderstreak.

Only the centre of these three 47th FIS 'Deuces' has the full squadron markings with the spade and dice insignia.

48th FIS

The 48th FIS at Langley AFB, Virginia flew F/TF-102As from 28 March 1957 until 28 September 1960. The Delta Daggers were replaced by F-106A/B Delta Darts. The squadron's symbol was a starburst broken by a bolt of lightning. Its history dates to 1917. It had F-94C Starfires before progressing to the 'Deuce'. Only after many subsequent years with F-106A/Bs and F-15A/B Eagles was the squadron eventually inactivated.

Seen at Langley in 1958, one of the 48th FIS's F-102As shows off its spectacular star-spangled tail markings.

57th FIS

The 57th FIS was the final ADC operator of the F/TF-102A, replacing its 'Deuces' with F-4C Phantoms on 1 July 1973. Before that happened, the squadron had a long and distinguished history flying the Delta Dagger. On 1 July 1962, the 57th FIS transferred from MATS (Military Air Transport Service) to ADC at Keflavik AB, Iceland. The following month, the squadron began converting from the F-89D Scorpion to the F/TF-102A. The squadron also operated T-33A Shooting Stars as 'hack' and electronic decoy aircraft.

One measure of the degree of activity in the 'GIUK Gap' (Greenland, Iceland, United Kingdom) was the enormous number of occasions when 'Deuces' from Keflavik intercepted and escorted Soviet bombers and reconnnaissance aircraft. In fact, on 15 September 1972, two F-102As of the 57th FIS made their 1,000th intercept of an unidentified aircraft. Sadly for those who gave their hearts to the 'Deuce,' on 1 July 1973 the F-4C Phantom replaced the F-102A on alert with the busy 57th. At this late date, the 57th FIS had the distinction of being the final active-duty unit to operate the Delta Dagger. The last F-102s left Iceland on 17 July 1973.

The squadron's emblem was a knight's head in a helmet. Its aircraft were frequently painted with black and white chequerboards.

A well-worn F-102A of the 57th FIS is seen on an interception mission in the 1966-67 period.

F-102 Operators

59th FIS

The 59th FIS was officially the 'Lions' for most of its existence, but informally dubbed the 'Black Bats' and also called the 'Black Watch' by troops. The squadron was located at Goose Bay, Labrador and transferred from Northeast Air Command to ADC when the former was disbanded and the latter took over the air defence role. The 59th FIS had been an operator of the F-94C Starfire when its first F-102A arrived on 24 May 1960. The 'Deuce' era lasted half a dozen years until 19 December 1966.

The squadron survives today as an operator of the F-15C/D Eagle at Eglin AFB, Florida with the 33rd FW.

One of the 'Black Bats' TF-102A proficiency trainers is seen on a visit to Andrews AFB in June 1965.

61st FIS

Located at Truax Field, Wisconsin, the 61st FIS flew the 'Deuce' only very briefly, from 9 October 1957 until 31 January 1958. The squadron emblem and mascot was an English bulldog.

The 61st began operations in 1941 and was flying F-89H/J Scorpions before graduating to the 'Deuce.' The ultimate fate of this squadron has proven elusive, but it is thought to have been retired following its F-102 era.

This 61st FIS F-102 has the arctic red trim extending along the spine.

64th FIS

The 64th FIS had the distinction of operating the F/TF-102A from two stateside locations before going overseas. The squadron is sometimes called the 'Scorpions' and has that creature as its emblem.

The squadron flew 'Deuces' at McChord AFB, Washington from 2 August 1957 until 7 June 1960, and at Paine Field, Washington from 8 February 1960 through 2 June 1966. That month, the squadron went temporarily to Hamilton AFB, California to prepare for overseas deployment. Its story is continued in the entry under Pacific Air Forces.

76th FIS

The 76th FIS at Westover AFB, Massachusetts flew the F/TF-102A from 3 March 1961 until 16 March 1963. The squadron's insignia of a tiger flanked by the Chinese characters meaning 'Vanguard,' relates to its origin as a follow-on to the American Volunteer Group, the 'Flying Tigers', of the China Burma India Theater in World War II.

The squadron had flown F-86D/L Sabres before the 'Deuce.' It subsequently flew the F-106A/B Delta Dart.

71st FIS

The 71st FIS at Selfridge AFB, Michigan operated 'Deuces' from 7 October 1958 to 22 November 1960. The squadron later flew the F-106A/B. Subsequently, on 1 July 1971, the 71st designation was transferred to Langley AFB, Virginia and the squadron lost its status as an air defence unit, becoming an F-15C/D Eagle outfit.

A simple squadron badge marked the F-102s of the 71st FIS at Langley. The aircraft otherwise wore completely standard ADC markings, with 'FC' buzzcodes and intake-mounted national insignia.

82nd FIS

ADC's 82nd FIS was stationed at Travis AFB, Calif. The squadron was a 'Deuce' operator from 3 July 1957. Almost a decade later, on 1 November 1965, as American attention became focused on Vietnam, the 82nd FIS ceased alert operations in preparation for a TDY (temporary duty) assignment which would transfer the unit from ADC to PACAF (Pacific Air Forces). The deployment overseas, because it would involve the 'Deuce' gobbling down fuel in mid-air for the first time, was given the programme name Thirsty Camel.

The 82nd flew its F-102A interceptors-- camouflaged, and with angle-braced air refuelling probes installed – across the Pacific in 1966, and the squadron became a component of the 51st FIW at Naha. This was the first deployment of the 'Deuce' using aerial refuelling. The 82nd FIS assumed the air defence mission for Okinawa (which had then not yet reverted to Japan) enabling the F-4C Phantoms of the 555th TFS 'Triple Nickel' to transfer to Udorn, Thailand. Twenty-three F-102As arrived at Naha on 19 February 1966 and three more on 22 February 1966. The story of this squadron's role in the Far East is continued in the entry under PACAF.

With an unusual white-painted radome, this 82nd FIS 'Deuce' was a participant at a March 1964 airshow.

86th FIS

After operating the F-86 Sabre, the 86th FIS adopted the F-102 in 1957 and operated it until 1960 at Youngstown Municipal Airport, Ohio. Its Indian in the clouds squadron badge was officially approved in 1959.

The 86th FIS markings consisted of a tiny red lightning bolt on the rudder, as seen on this 'Tub' at Youngstown in May 1959.

87th FIS

The 87th FIS, symbolised by a Walt Disney insignia of a bee carrying a machine-gun, but apparently never given a nickname, was an ADC unit on a SAC base at Lockbourne AFB (known today as Rickenbacker AFB) near Columbus, Ohio. After flying the F-86D Sabre, the unit acquired its first F-102A on 26 August 1958. It operated 'Deuces' only until 22 June 1960, when it began conversion to the F-101B/F Voodoo.

317th FIS

In its capacity as a component of ADC, the 317th FIS flew the F/TF-102A at McChord AFB, Washington for just a year, beginning on 3 December 1956. The squadron was transferred to AAC (Alaskan Air Command) in a process that began on 15 August 1957 and was completed on 24 December 1957. The squadron's subsequent story appears in the AAC entry.

95th FIS

The 95th FIS, known as 'Mr. Bones' and sporting an emblem of a skeleton in a high-hat, operated all-weather Sabres before becoming an F/TF-102A user at Andrews AFB, Maryland on 9 January 1958. The squadron's brief Delta Dagger era concluded on 12 August 1960. From the 'Deuce,' the squadron moved on to the F-106A/B Delta Dart.

Photographs of 95th FIS F-102s are rare. This view was captured at a 1958 airshow.

318th FIS

The 318th FIS at McChord AFB, Washington flew the T/TF-102A from 6 January 1957 until 25 May 1960. The squadron graduated from the 'Deuce' to the F-106A/B.

This F-102A of the 318th FIS sports the squadron badge on the forward fuselage and the Chrysler 'Way Forward'-inspired tail marking.

325th FIS

The 325rd FIS operated the F/TF-102A at Truax Field, Wisconsin from 6 February 1957 until 13 June 1966. The squadron emblem is a stylised young bull butting against the moon. The squadron had previously operated the F-86 Sabre.

In 1963, when these 325th FIS F-102As were photographed at McEntire AFB, South Carolina, the squadron was using tail insignia similar to that used on 1st FIW F-106s. The Dayglo bands are of interest.

326th FIS

The 326th FIS operated F/TF-102As at Richards-Gebaur AFB, Missouri briefly from 25 March 1957 until 5 January 1958. The squadron emblem was a snarling wolf.

56-1383, seen at Forbes (formerly Salinas) AFB Texas in May 1964, was lost after a mid-air collision on 22 December 1966.

327th FIS

The 327th FIS at George AFB, California had the distinction of becoming the first operator of a Convair delta-wing fighter when it took delivery of its first F-102A in April 1956, much later than had been planned. Once initial delays in the 'Deuce' programme were ironed out, the squadron operated the type at George from 24 April 1956 until 17 June 1958. The squadron also flew the Delta Dagger at Thule AB, Greenland. The squadron emblem was a medieval red iron mask.

The chequered tail, intake lips and command stripes on this early F-102A were unique to the 327th FIS commander's aircraft.

F-102 Operators

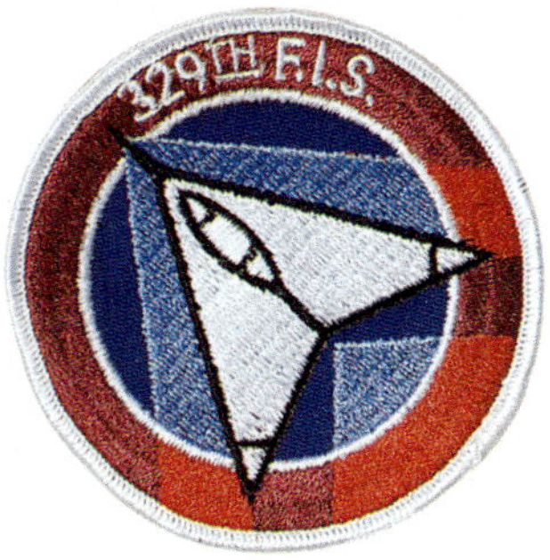

329th FIS

The 329th FIS operated the F/TF-102A at George AFB, California, from 22 March 1958 until 24 October 1960. The squadron progressed to the F-106A/B.

An even more stylised version of the 329th FIS's delta-winged aircraft insignia formed the basis of the squadron's F-102 markings.

331st FIS

The 331st FIS flew F/TF-102As at Webb AFB, Texas from 18 March 1960 until 21 May 1963. The squadron emblem was a stylised griffin.

Seen on Armed Forces Day 1960 at Peterson AFB ('Pete Field'), Colorado Springs, the markings of this 331st FIS 'Deuce' consisted of a blue-edged yellow 'swoosh' and star.

332nd FIS

The 332nd FIS is the only ADC operator of the F/TF-102A Delta Dagger to fly the aircraft at three locations. After graduating from the F-86D/L Sabre, the unit operated at McGuire AFB, New Jersey from 30 July 1957 until 30 October 1959, at England Air Force Base, Louisiana from 24 July 1959 until 25 August 1960, and from Thule AB, Greenland from 21 July 1960 until 16 April 1965. The squadron emblem was a white eagle.

Thule, Greenland was home to this 332nd FIS TF-102A in April 1964.

438th FIS

The 438th FIS at Kinross AFB, Michigan was an operator of the F/TF-102A from 4 March 1957 until 4 November 1960.

The squadron badge used Donald Duck, who is copyrighted by Walt Disney Productions. After its 'Deuce' period, the squadron continued delta-winged flying with the F-106A/B.

456th FIS

The 456th FIS operated F/TF-102As from Castle AFB, California from 15 April 1958 until 15 October 1960. The squadron emblem used a red octopus. The 'Deuce' was preceded by the F-86 Sabre and followed by the F-106A Delta Dart.

460th FIS

The 460th FIS operated F/TF-102As at Portland International Airport, Oregon, from 11 January 1958 until 25 February 1966. The squadron had a badge depicting a tiger. It went from the F-89H/J Scorpion to the 'Deuce.' The unit was inactivated after its F-102 era but was later activated to fly the F-106A/B.

The 460th FIS's large 'beware of the tiger' badge is seen here on an F-102A on 20 September 1962.

482nd FIS

The 482nd FS was stationed at Seymour Johnson AFB, North Carolina. The squadron flew the F/TF-102A beginning 24 April 1957.

In November 1961, reacting to tensions in the aftermath of the failed Bay of Pigs invasion of Cuba, the 482nd FIS established a permanent alert detachment at Homestead AFB, Florida. For a brief period prior to that date, the 482nd FIS operated at Miami International Airport while repairs to the Homestead runway were completed.

On 15 June 1963, the 482nd FIS moved its alert contingent from Homestead to Key West, Florida, the US city closest to Cuba. By then, the Bay of Pigs had been followed by the Cuban missile crisis, and tensions had peaked and begun to decline. In 1 July 1965, the 482nd ceased alert operations. The last F-102A apparently departed on 17 August 1965. The squadron was inactivated at Seymour Johnson on 8 October 1965.

A star of the Langley air show static park in 1960 was this F-102A of the 482nd FIS.

Air Defense Weapons Center

The ADWC at Tyndall operated F-102s from 1 January 1968 until June 1971. The centre had responsibility for developing Air Defense Command weapons and tactics, and operated all aircraft types in ADC inventory. Its constituent units included the Interceptor Weapons School.

4780th ADW

Located at Perrin AFB, Texas, the 4780th Air Defense Wing operated F-102s from 1 July 1962 until 29 June 1971. Perrin was the traditional training base for interceptor pilots for many years.

4756th ADW

The 4756th Air Defense Wing at Tyndall AFB, Florida was an F-102 operator for exactly a year, from January 1957 until January 1958. Its mission was primarily training rather than air defence.

Pilots and crew chiefs line up for an inspection with their 'Deuces'. Note the aircraft in the centre without markings or IRST sensor.

The double chevron insignia of the 4780th Air Defense Wing graced many interceptors, including this TF-102A 'Tub'.

Alaskan Air Command (AAC)

Alaskan Air Command remained separate from ADC and retained jurisdiction for its area of responsibility for decades longer than the short-lived Northeast Air Command. When the Convair F/TF-102A began operations (long before the belated Delta Dagger nickname was assigned), Alaska was still a territory of the United States, although it gained statehood two years later.

The F-102 was no stranger, having undergone arctic weather evaluation at Ladd AFB long before it returned to the region in a state of combat readiness. Serious F-102 business began when AAC became the 'gaining command' of the reassigned 317th FIS on 15 August 1957. This was the first transfer of an ADC F/TF-102A unit to another US Air Force command. The second 'Deuce' squadron to be assigned to AAC was the 31st FIS from Wurtsmith AFB, Michigan on 20 August 1957. These squadrons fell under AAC's 10th Air Division until the division was inactivated on 25 August 1960. After that date, the sole AAC squadron, the 317th, was subordinate to the 5040th Air Base Wing. Much later, on 8 July 1966, it became a component of the 21st Composite Group.

AAC operated forward bases and alert detachments for the 'Deuce' at Eielson AFB, Galena, King Salmon and Ladd AFB. Ladd AFB ended its long association with the USAF when it was transferred to the US Army on 1 January 1961.

The 'Deuce' era in Alaska coincided with increased Soviet aerial reconnaissance in the region, beginning in March 1958. In September 1958, F-102s attempted without success to intercept and escort a Soviet aircraft. Not until 5 December 1961 did two 'Deuces' scramble from Galena to achieve the first successful intercept of a pair of Tupolev Tu-16 'Badger' aircraft off the northwest coast. And when the 317th FIS failed to intercept an intruder during an actual overflight, as described in the entry for the squadron, the result was an unprecedented uproar in Alaska and Washington, especially in the Pentagon. Indeed, the furore caused nine F-106 Delta Darts to be deployed to Elmendorf in July 1963 to augment the AAC 'Deuces' on a temporary basis.

31st FIS

The 31st FIS, the second 'Deuce' unit in Alaska, transferred from ADC and brought its first aircraft to Elmendorf AFB, Alaska on 16 September 1957.

The squadron brought along its wolf emblem copyrighted by Walt Disney studios. But just a year after the squadron began flying in the cold north, the USAF made a decision to disband the 31st and to combine its existing 'Deuce' holdings into a single squadron, the 317th. The 31st had operated 23 'Deuce' airframes and had lost none in mishaps, when it transferred the fighters. The 31st was then inactivated on 8 October 1958. It has never returned to the USAF order of battle.

The 31st passed its aircraft on to the 317th FIS upon its inactivation.

317th FIS

On 1 September 1957, the first 317th FIS F-102A landed at Elmendorf AFB, Alaska. The arrival gave meaning to the transfer of the 317th FIS from ADC, which apparently had been official on 15 August 1957. It also marked the beginning of 12 years of 'Deuce' operations in Alaska by the 317th, which had transferred from McChord AFB, Washington. The unit's beginning at that base is noted in the section on ADC.

After losing two aircraft in mishaps, the 317th FIS was left with 23. When it acquired 23 more 'Deuces' following the 8 October 1958 inactivation of the 31st FIS, also at Elemendorf, the 46-plane 317th FIS became the largest squadron in the history of the Convair fighter. The successful intercept of two 'Badgers' in 1961 by Galena-based fighters proved to be a high-water mark for the 317th which soon encountered problems.

On 15 March 1963, a Soviet reconnaissance bomber overflew Nunivak Island and the west coast of Alaska. The 317th scrambled two 'Deuces' from King Salmon but the fighters had to break off 20 miles (31 km) from the target because of low fuel. As noted above, this much-publicited failure resulted in the arrival of F-106A Delta Darts on a temporary status to augment the 317th FIS' inventory of 'Deuces.' In the years that followed, F-102As made 13 successful intercepts and F-106As made 17 more before the squadron was inactivated on 31 December 1969. Its strength reduced to 27 aircraft earlier in the year, the squadron left behind only one (56-1282), which had a cracked wing spar and became a display at the Alaska Transportation Museum. During its years of operation, the 317th lost 14 Delta Daggers in mishaps.

The 317th's F-102s were decorated with squadron badges and lightning-flashed tanks in the latter part of their career.

US Air Forces in Europe (USAFE)

To confront the Soviet Union and the Warsaw Pact high above the plains of Europe, US Air Forces in Europe at one time operated six fighter-interceptor squadrons equipped with F/TF-102As. With one exception, namely the 32nd FIS (an F-100 Super Sabre outfit), all of these units were well prepared for air defence, having previously flown the F-86D Sabre.

The F-102s that reached Europe aboard US Navy carriers were ex-ADC ships that had gone through extensive maintenance at depots. Later, additional 'Deuces' reached Europe from the 317th FIS in Alaska. The first squadron in Europe to equip with the Convair fighter was the 525th FIS in West Germany. the last the 32nd FS in Holland.

In Europe, the F/TF-102A Delta Dagger began with plain markings, with only a squadron insignia on the tail. Markings became more colourful as the 1960s progressed, then went away altogether to be replaced by Vietnam-era T. O. 114 camouflage after 1965.

32nd FIS

The 32nd FIS 'Wolfhounds' arranged to be at Wheelus AB, Libya for initial training when it took delivery of its first F-102A fighters on 12 August 1960. With pilots who had no previous 'Deuce' experience (18 were checked out in the F-100C Super Sabre, four in the F-86D Sabre), the squadron operated temporarily under the mantle of the 86th FIW until a cadre of Delta Dagger-qualified flyers could be brought up to speed.

The squadron's usual home base was Soesterberg AB known to the Americans as Camp Amsterdam, Netherlands and the first eight F-102As arrived there from Wheelus on 18 November 1960. The squadron came under direct operational control of the Royal Netherlands Air Force. The squadron emblem was a wolfhound designed by Walt Disney studios.

The squadron operated a T-33A Shooting Star (52-9833) to tow a Delmar target for live-fire training of F-102 crews over the North Sea. After being the last squadron from Europe to participate in a William Tell competition, the 32nd FIS gave up its last 'Deuce' on 3 July 1969 and became an operator of the F-4 Phantom.

After a period of relatively austere markings, the 32nd FIS and other USAFE units introduced coloured tail bands.

431st FIS

The 431st FIS at Zaragoza AB, Spain accepted its first F-102A (55-3447) on 28 September 1960. Known as the 'Satan' or 'Devil' squadron, the 431st FIS had the shortest F/TF-102A tenure of any squadron in Europe. The unit gave up its aircraft on 23 April 1964. On receipt of its new F-4Cs, it was redesignated as the 431st Tactical Fighter Squadron.

Below: The stars on the 431st FIS badge and tail marking depict the Southern Cross. The squadron was formed in Australia in 1943.

496th FIS

The 496th FIS was the second European squadron to receive 'Deuces,' taking delivery of its first two F-102As and two TF-102As at Hahn AB, Germany on 9 December 1959, eleven months after operations began at Bitburg. A decade later, the 496th went out of the F-102 business in December 1969 and relinquished its aircraft to the Air National Guard.

In full 86th AD markings with a black and yellow tail, this 496th FIS F-102A displays a bay full of Falcons.

497th FIS

The 497th FIS began F-102 operations with the receipt of its first aircraft at Torrejon AB, Spain on 26 April 1960.

This squadron was under control of the Strategic Air Command's 65th Air Division until transfer to USAFE on 1 July 1960. The 497th continued to operate the 'Deuce' until giving up its last aircraft on 3 June 1964, its F-102s going to other USAFE units.

Normally based in sunny Spain, F-102s were seen at German bases in November 1963 on a strategic mobility exercise.

525th FIS

The 525th FIS 'Bulldogs' at Bitburg AB, Germany became the first Europe-based USAF squadron to receive the F-102 Delta Dagger when it took three F-102As and two TF-102As on charge on 3 January 1959. Soon afterwards, the 525th used borrowed F-102s to participate in the 1959 William Tell competition and reached second place.

The 525th FIS operated the F-102 until October 1969 when it transitioned to the F-4E Phantom.

A 'Bulldogs' F-102A is seen at a rainy Bitburg Air Base airshow in 1960.

526th FIS

The 526th FIS at Ramstein AB, Germany took delivery of its first three F-102As on 7 June 1960. It was the fourth combat unit in USAFE to receive the 'Deuce.' It lasted longer than all the others in Europe and gave up its last aircraft on 16 April 1970 when it became an F-4E user and a Tactical Fighter Squadron.

In early-period markings, this 526th FIS F-102A flies high over Europe, 1961. External fuel tanks were normally carried by European F-102s.

Pacific Air Forces (PACAF)

In PACAF (Pacific Air Forces), the F-102A became a fixture after 1959 and even before Americans took their first tentative steps toward Vietnam. In 1959-60, five PACAF squadrons – the 4th, 16th, 40th, 68th and 509th FIS – converted to Delta Daggers. First was the 16th FIS at Naha, and last was the 509th FIS at Clark Field in the Philippines.

As the United States began sending small teams of advisors to South Vietnam and eyeing the Pathet Lao in Laos, indications of hostile air activity began to show up even though no potential adversary in the region, not even North Vietnam had yet built a real air force. On 19 March 1962, a radar station at Pleiku, South Vietnam picked up seven unknown flight tracks over the Vietnamese central highlands. The only 'friendly' that could be scrambled was a B-26 Invader propeller-driven bomber. No contact was made, and hostile radar tracks were detected the next day, with the same result. The ensuing frustration led to the deployment of four F-102As to Tan Son Nhut AB outside Saigon. Thereafter, as described in the main text, the 'Deuce' was involved in Vietnam intermittently well into the late 1960s.

F/TF-102A fighters in the Pacific briefly enjoyed somewhat colorful markings until 1964. That year, all PACAF 'Deuces' lost individual squadron markings while remaining in 'ADC gray' with the PACAF emblem on both sides of the fin. After 1965, Vietnam-era T.O.114 camouflage became standard.

4th FIS

The 4th Fighter-Interceptor Squadron at Misawa Air Base, Japan, had a long tradition of night- and all-weather fighting, having been an operator of the F-61B Black Widow (until 1949), F-82G Twin Mustang (until 1951), F-94B (until 1954) and F-86D Sabre. The squadron moved from Naha, Okinawa to Kadena in 1954 and converted from F-86D to F-102A Delta Dagger in 1960. The badge for the 4th FIS shows the Okinawan god of wind, better known as a 'big bug' to Americans, flying against a backdrop of storm cloud and lightning bolt.

The last F-86D in PACAF (Pacific Air Forces) inventory went out of service on 8 March 1960. At Misawa, the F-102A provided greater speed and range, and enhanced the defence of western Japan against potential Soviet intrusions. Although farther from Korea than other units in Japan, the 4th FIS also deployed on occasion to Korea in a temporary deployment program dubbed Bone Deep.

On 28 April 1965, a Yokota-based RB-47 Stratojet was attacked by two North Korean MiG-17s on a reconnaissance mission 50 miles off the coast of North Korea. The RB-47 crew returned fire but the aircraft was severely damaged. F-102As of the 4th FIS were scrambled to the scene and although they did not make contact with the MiG-17s, they escorted the RB-47 back to safety.

As part of Project Clear Water, an effort to restructure PACAF units, the 4th FIS at Misawa stood down in 1965 (together with the 40th FIS on Okinawa), bringing to an end the role of the F-102A in the air defence of Japan. The Vietnam war was now escalating and in the late 1960s the 4th designation reappeared as the 4th TFS became an operator of the F-4 Phantom in Southeast Asia.

Red Striped Rascal ***was a rare example of a named F-102. Seen at Naha, Japan, it was the CO's aircraft of the infrequently-photographed 4th FIS.***

16th FIS

The 16th FIS, sometimes called the 'Tigers' or boasting the motto 'Every man a tiger' was located at Naha AB, Okinawa in 1959. The squadron had been one of the prime F-86 Sabre squadrons during the Korean War and had produced 16-kill air ace Captain Joseph McConnell. Now as the 1950s came to an end the 16th FIS converted from F-86D to F-102A.

The squadron received its first F-102A at Naha on 9 March 1959 and was declared operationally ready in September 1959. The squadron represented PACAF in the 1959 World-Wide Interceptor Weapons Meet at Tyndall AFB, Fla. The 16th FIS deployed its F-102As to Suwon AB, Korea for the first tiome on 18 December 1959 to participate in a local air defence exercise known as Bone Deep.

In 1964, in a reorganisation known as Project Clear Water, the 16th FIS was deactivated. The 'Deuces' belonging to the defunct 16th were transferred to the Hawaii Air National Guard.

The attractive chequered markings of the 16th FIS's F-102s are not often illustrated.

40th FIS

This PACAF squadron began to convert from F-86D to F-102A in 1960. For much of its existence, the 40th was located at Yokota Air Base near Tokyo, Japan. One of several squadrons to have a devil's face as an emblem, the 40th FIS was flying F-86 Sabres when it converted to the Convair interceptor.

The squadron stood down on 30 June 1965 when the air defence of Japan reverted to the JASDF (Japan Air Self-Defence Force). The withdrawal of the last F-102s from Japan marked the end of the reorganisation known as Operation Clear Water (see 68th FIS).

One of the 40th FIS's TF-102s, seen at its home base of Yokota, illustrates the squadron's devil's head and lightning bolt badge.

64th FIS

On 6 June 1966, the 64th FIS – which had been garrisoned at Paine Field, Washington and was unofficially dubbed the 'Scorpions' – made a deployment from Hamilton AFB, California, to Clark Field, Philippines in a project dubbed Hot Spice. The squadron was destined to keep Clark Field as its permanent duty station, with temporary jaunts to Vietnam, until being inactivated in December 1969.

F-102As of the 64th FIS are seen during the 1966 Hot Spice transit to the Phillipines.

68th FIS

The 68th FIS at Itazuke AB near Fukuoka, Japan began receiving F-102A fighters in 1960, replacing F-86D Dog Sabres. In 1964, in a reorganisation known as Project Clear Water, Itazuke lost its flying squadrons and the 68th returned to the continental US beginning 12 May 1970.

Despite operating the F-102 for a decade, the 68th FIS, whose Crusader emblem was made famous on the F-82 Twin Mustang, was rarely photographed.

82nd FIS

The 82nd FIS (assigned the tail code NV in 1968) formally transferred from ADC to PACAF on 25 June 1966 at Naha, Okinawa – following its expedition from the US which marked the first use of air refuelling by the 'Deuce.'

The 82nd deployed to Korea after the spy ship USS *Pueblo* was seized on 23 January 1968, returning to home base at Naha on 18 February 1968.

The 51st FIW at Naha transferred its serviceable F-102As to the ANG early in 1971. The remaining 18 F-102As which had severe wing cracks and corrosion, were reclaimed in place during March 1971 and dropped from the records.The official inactivation date of 31 May 1971 marked the end of the F-102's role in the Pacific, save only for those aircraft in Air National Guard service in Hawaii.

The 82nd FIS was the only squadron assigned to the 51st FIW at Naha, Okinawa.

509th FIS

The PACAF-based 509th FIS at Clark AB, Philippines (assigned tail code PK in 1968), began to receive the F-102A, replacing the F-86D, in 1960. The squadron was a component of the 405th TFW throughout its 'Deuce' period. The arrival of the last of the programmed F-102As at Clark on 3 March 1961 marked the end of the F-86D era in the Pacific region (three remaining 'Dog Sabres' went to the Philippine Air Force on 8 March 1961, the remainder into storage).

509th Delta Daggers deployed to Formosa (Taiwan) under Exercise Big Truck while the CNAF's F-104 Starfighters were grounded with engine problems. Big Truck terminated on 30 September 1961.

The 509th was apparently the first squadron to deploy F-102As to Tan Son Nhut AB, Vietnam in Operation Water Glass, a series of temporary movements that began in March 1962. It also sustained the first non-combat loss of a 'Deuce'. Later, the squadron maintained a detachment of F-102As at Bien Hoa until the practice was ended on 7 September 1968. The deployment had been a strain because the 509th was also making frequent deployments to Thailand and Korea.

As part of a reduction programme known as Project 703, the squadron's detachments at Taiwan (Formosa) and Don Muang (Thailand) were withdrawn. At its home base, Clark AB, Philippines, the 509th was inactivated on 24 July 1970. The squadron's F-102As were all flown to Itazuke and scrapped as this was cheaper than shipping them back to the US.

In the early days of the 509th FIS's involvement in South East Asia, its F-102s were decorated with a chequered rudder and a leaping tiger on the nose.

Air National Guard

By the time the F-102A Delta Dagger came on the scene, American air power was beginning its transition toward today's 'total force' concept in which members of the reserve component operate modern equipment and perform missions identical to those of active-duty airmen. This was a sea change from an earlier time when Air National Guard maintainers and flyers were dismissed as a useless cadre of 'weekend warriors.' In 1960, almost as much as today, it would have been inconceivable to conduct a military operation without the ANG being an integral participant. It should be noted that the same applies to the Air Force Reserve, although the latter was never an F-102 user.

So it was an important moment when, on 1 July 1960, the 182nd FIS at Kelly Air Force Base, Texas became the ANG's first F/TF-102A squadron. This was the result of a National Guard Bureau decision to build up four 'Deuce' squadrons beginning in fiscal year 1961 (which began on 1 July 1960). The four squadrons, beginning with the one in the Lone Star State, would take delivery of aircraft from active-duty units converting to the F-101B Voodoo and F-106A Delta Dart. Ultimately, however, Texas may become better known not for being first in the Guard, but for having a pilot who flew the F-102A in its other ANG squadron, the 111th FIS at Ellington Field near Houston – the state's governor and presidential aspirant George W. Bush.

As for the initial plan which brought the Guard into the 'Deuce' business, it was ambitious indeed. Back in 1959, NORAD (North American Air Defense Command) planners had proposed 19 permanent ANG alert units at points along the northern and southern borders and in areas where there existed gaps in ANG interceptor coverage. The plan assumed that the 19 squadrons would be equipped with F-102s, a total of no fewer than 475 aircraft. At the time, F-102s were also slated for PACAF and USAFE, meaning there would be scarcely a 'Deuce' to spare if the ANG plan were implemented.

It turned out that there were sufficient aircraft, barely, to begin the plan as conceived and the 111th FIS and 122nd FIS soon began acquiring their 'Deuces'. Others followed. Ultimately, the Guard operated not 19 but 25 F-102 squadrons.

During the Berlin and Cuban tensions of 1960 and 1961, some ANG units were activated, but the only deployments of Guard F-102s were to Alaska for annual training.

In every instance where an Air National Guard (ANG) squadron flew the TF/F-102A Delta Dagger, it functioned as an 'ADC-gained' unit meaning that, when carrying out its national mission, it came under the Air Defense Command (later Aerospace Defense Command) and was employed in the defence of the North American continent.

Arizona 152nd FIS

The 152nd FIS/162nd FG, Arizona ANG, flew F-102As, including TF-102A two-seaters, during a 43-month reign sandwiched between two periods when Tucson-based Guardsmen operated F-100 Super Sabres, these being the F-100A model until February 1966 and the F-100D version after 16 September 1969. A pristine 'Deuce' wearing the yellow tail blazer and yellow boundary layer fence, typical of 1966-69 operations, remains on display at the Tucson main gate today.

California 194th FIS

The 194th FIS/144th FIG, California ANG, flew F-102As from July 1964 until 11 July 1974. The earlier date marked the unit's transition from the F-86L Sabre to the F-102A, including the TF-102A model, at Fresno Air Terminal.

In January 1970, as part of an exercise dubbed Coronet East, the Fresno Guardsmen ferried 20 F/TF-102As from Hahn Air Base, Germany to their home base. Even after equipping with newer Delta Daggers, the 194th members were planning to receive a new aircraft. The last F-102 departed in July 1974 and the 194th converted to the F-106A Delta Dart.

The 144th FIW also operated detachment 1 of the 194th FIS at Davis-Monthan AFB, Arizona from 1971.

Fresno's Delta Daggers were 'plain Janes' compared with their cousins at Ontario Airport.

California 196th FIS

The 196th FIS,163rd FIG, California ANG, based at Ontario International airport near Los Angeles, was the second unit in the state to equip with the Convair delta-wing interceptors, flying them from May 1965 to 8 March 1975. The unit went directly from F-86A/L Sabres to the mighty F-102, and adorned its aircraft with white stars against a blue band on the fin, with the name of the state displayed prominently. Concern over noise pollution, plus anti-military feelings coinciding with the end of the war in Vietnam, forced the 196th FIS to exchange its 'Deuce' interceptors for Cessna O-2As and to become a forward air control unit beginning on the 1975 date.

In common with a number of units, the 196th painted the wing fences of its otherwise naturally-finished F-102s.

Connecticut 118th FIS

The 118th FIS/103rd FG, Connecticut ANG, flew F-102As at Bradley Field in Windsor Locks near Hartford beginning on January 1966. The 'Flying Yankees' converted from the F-100A Super Sabre and operated F/TF-102A interceptors until the final aircraft departed on 11 June 71. The Delta Dagger era was something of a departure for this unit, which has spent most of its career performing the air-to-ground mission. The 118th went from the F/TF-102A to the F-100D/F Super Sabre, but is better known in recent years as an operator of the A-10A 'Warthog.'

This F-102A of the Connecticut Guard was seen visiting Wright-Patterson AFB in September 1970.

Florida 159th FIS

The 159th FIS/125th FIG, Florida ANG located at the Thomas Cole Imeson Airport in Jacksonville, Florida, had briefly operated F-86L Sabres before converting to the F/TF-102A on 1 July 1960. The unit re-located to the Jacksonville International Airport on 24 October 1968. The Florida Guardsmen received upgraded Configuration 8 F/TF-102As in 1968 and continued to operate Delta Daggers until July 1974. Thereafter, the Jacksonville squadron flew the F-106A/B Delta Dart.

Detachment 1 of the 125th FIS kept F-102s on alert at NAS New Orleans, Louisiana, facing towards Cuba, from 1971 until 1974.

A small fintip lightning bolt and large tactical numbers identified Florida's Delta Daggers in June 1974, shortly before their retirement.

Hawaii 199th FIS

A ship carrying the first F-102As for the Hawaii Air National Guard docked at Fort Island, Pearl Harbor, on 5 December 1960. In Hawaii, the 'Deuce' was a replacement for the F-86L Sabre which had served the Guard for only three years. The first flight of a Hawaii ANG TF-102A occurred on 21 January 1961. F-102As replaced the F-86L on alert status at Honolulu's Hickam AFB in May 1961.

On 20 March 1965, Hawaii's 199th FIS received 20 newer F-102A fighters ('configuration 8' or 'Fig 8' standard, with infra-red devices, replacing aircraft of 'Fig 7' standard). These had been phased out by the deactivated 16th FIS at Itazuke AB, Japan.

On 31 March 1970, the same day the Hawaii Army National Guard deactivated its Nike missile battery leaving the 'Deuce' as the sole defender of the Hawaiian islands, the UE (unit establishment – authorised strength) of the 199th was cut from 24 to 18 aircraft.

The 199th received its first F-4C Phantom on 31 October 1975 and began the process of replacing its well-worn 'Deuces.' The last F-102A was phased out in October 1976.

In November 1975, when this F-102A was photographed at Hickam, the 199th FIS was phasing in the F-4C Phantom.

Idaho 190th FIS

The 190th FIS/124th FIG, Idaho ANG, flew F-102As from July 1964 to 19 November 1975. Located at Gowen Field in Boise, the unit had briefly operated the F-86L Sabre prior to the Delta Dagger's appearance on the scene. When its F-102 era ended, the Idaho Guard became a tactical reconnaissance unit and converted to the RF-4C Phantom.

This 190th FIS 'Deuce' was photographed at Williams AFB, Texas in June 1975.

Louisiana 122nd FIS

Known throughout much of its existence as the 'Coonass Militia,' a term reflecting local Cajun parlance and devoid of racial undertone, the 122nd FIS/159th FIG, Louisiana ANG, flew F-102As from July 1960 to 4 December 1970. Located at Naval Air Station New Orleans, the Louisiana Guard graduated into the F/TF-102A from the F-86L Sabre. A decade later, the 122nd converted to the F-100D/F Super Sabre.

This 'Deuce' was seen at Langley on 25 June 1970, in the last months of 122nd FIS F-102 operations.

Maine 132nd FIS

The 132nd FIS/101st FG, Maine ANG, flew F-102As from August 1969 to 17 November 1969. Located at Bangor International Airport, which had previously been the site of Dow Air Force Base (inactivated in June 1968), the 132nd FIS made the transition to the Delta Dagger from the F-89J Scorpion. Following the truncated, 15-month tenure of the Convair delta-winged fighter, the 132nd converted to the McDonnell F-101B/F Voodoo.

This F-102, which had previously served with the 32nd FIS in the Netherlands, was captured at Bangor in November 1969, the month the 132nd gave up its Delta Daggers.

Minnesota 179th FIS

The 179th FIS,148th FIG, Minnesota ANG, flew F-102As from November 1966 until 15 April 1971. The 'Deuce' made its debut with the 179th FIS on the heels of the F-89J Scorpion, flying at Duluth Municipal Airport. The five-year Delta Dagger era came to an end when the Minnesota Guardsmen began receiving F-101B/F Voodoo interceptors.

In September 1974, this Minnesota ANG F-102A awaited conversion into a drone at MASDC at Davis-Monthan.

Montana 186th FIS

Up in 'Big Sky Country,' the 186th FIS/120th FIG, Montana ANG, flew F-102As from July 1966 until 5 April 1972. The location was Great Falls Municipal Airport. The F-89J came before the Delta Dagger and the F-106A/B followed it.

The 186th FIS was phasing its F-102s out in favour of the F-106 when this TF-102A in its markings was seen at Fresno on 16 April 1972.

New York 102nd FIS

The 102nd FIS/106th FG, New York ANG, flew F-102As from 2 December 1972 to 14 June 1975. Located at Suffolk County Airport in Westhampton Beach (since named for World War II air ace Francis S. Gabreski), the unit had previously been an air refuelling outfit operating KC-97L Stratocruisers. Following its Delta Dagger period, this New York Guard unit became a combat rescue as an operator of the HC-130H/P Hercules and HH-3E Jolly Green.

Unlike many other Guard F-102 squadrons, the 102nd FIS added a splash of colour to the tactical camouflage scheme, as illustrated by these examples at Suffolk County in September 1974.

North Dakota 178th FIS

The 178th FIS/119th FIG 'Happy Hooligans,' North Dakota ANG, flew F-102As from June 1966 until 17 November 1969. The squadron has always operated at Hector Field, Fargo Municipal Airport. The F-89J Scorpion preceded the F/TF-102A in 'Hooligans' livery and the F-101B/F Voodoo followed it. During its 'Deuce' era, the 178th FIS also operated a VC-131D Samaritan transport.

As seen in 1967, this 'Happy Hooligans' F-102A marked its flight assignment with yellow on the airbrake extension.

Oregon 123rd FIS

The 123rd FIS/142nd FIG, Oregon ANG, flew F-102As from January 1966 to 8 March 1971. The squadron, which has a 'Redhawk' emblem, operated F-89J Scorpions previously and F-101B/F Voodoos subsequently. The location was Portland Municipal Airport.

The 123rd FIS retained aircraft in 'natural metal' as late as 1970, while many other squadrons were adopting camouflage.

Pennsylvania 146th FIS

The 146th FIS/112th FIG, Pennsylvania ANG, located at the Greater Pittsburgh (Coreapolis) Airport, was an operator of TF/F-102A interceptors from November 1960 to 12 April 1975. The 'Deuce' replaced the F-86L Sabre and was, in turn, replaced in Pittsburgh by the A-7D attack aircraft (named the Corsair II in its US Navy variant).

The black tails of the 146th FIS's aircraft made their aircraft instantly recognisable.

South Carolina 157th FIS

The 157th FIS/169th FIG, South Carolina ANG, flew F-102As from June 1963 until 5 April 1975. The 'Swamp Foxes' previously flew F-104A/B Starfighters. The 'Deuce' was subsequently replaced at McEntire Air National Guard Base by A-7D attack aircraft.

The South Carolina ANG's 157th FIS was one of several units to restrict its markings to a coloured fin band.

Tennessee 151st FIS

The 151st FIS/134th FIG Tennessee ANG flew F-102As from March 1963 until 5 April 1964. Located at McGhee Tyson Airport, the squadron converted from the F-104A/B Starfighter. After a decade in the 'Deuce' and nearly three decades in fighters, the squadron became a tanker outfit and converted to the KC-97G Stratocruiser.

South Dakota 175th FIS

The 'Lobos' of the 174th FIS/114th FIG, South Dakota ANG, flew F-102As from October 1960 until 23 May 1970. Located at Sioux Falls Municipal Airport, the squadron went from the F-89J Scorpion to the F/TF-102A to the F-100D/F Super Sabre, all in the span of just over a decade.

A small number of F-102s were seen with Dayglo radomes, including this 175th FIS example.

F-102 Operators

Texas 111th FIS

The 111th FIS/147th FIG, Texas ANG, flew F-102As from August 1960 until 11 January 1975. When the active-duty force ceased F/TF-102A training on 30 June 1971, the 111th FIS became the RTU for F-102 pilots.

One pilot who flew F/TF-102As with this unit was Texas Governor George W. Bush, considered a likely presidential candidate in 2000. The unit at Ellington Air Force Base had previously flown F-86L Sabres and T-33A Shooting Stars, and retained the T-33As for jet instrumentation school. During the Delta Dagger era, the squadron's base changed status and became Ellington Air National Guard Base in July 1968.

On 1 January 1970, the unit became the 111th Combat Crew Training Squadron and served as the Air National Guard's RTU (Replacement Training Unit) for the F/TF-102A, while also retaining the T-33A instrument training function. In May 1971, the unit added F-101B/F Voodoos and became the RTU for the latter type, while continuing as the Delta Dagger RTU. The F/TF-102As were phased out in January 1975 and the Voodoos remained.

The unit also operated detachment 1 of the 147th FIW at Ellington. The detachment was apart from the squadron in that it maintained constant alert status whilst facing towards Cuba.

The 1973 Patrick AFB air show saw an appearance by this F-102A of the 111th FIS.

Texas 182nd FIS

The 182nd FIS/149th FIG, Texas ANG, flew F-102As from July 1960 until 16 September 1969. The squadron enjoyed the distinction of being the first 'Deuce' operator in the ANG. Located at Kelly Air Force Base, Texas, like so many Guard units the 182nd went from the F-86L Sabre to the F/TF-102A Delta Dagger.

'We ran the check-out program for other squadrons,' remembers group commander Colonel Charles Quist. The 182nd FIS temporarily became the training unit for Guard F/TF-102A operators and, for a time, remained on alert status in the F-86L while training Guardsmen from other units in the F-102. There was no gap when the F-102A took up the alert role. Throughout its F-102A period, the unit also operated three T-33A Shooting Stars for training duties and a Convair VT-29 transport for 'hack' duties. The squadron had two TF-102A two-seaters.

The squadron's subsequent conversion to the F-84F Thunderstreak, however, was unique among 'Deuce' units, even if it was only a temporary measure until F-100D/F Super Sabres could arrive.

Seen in April 1969 alongside one of the squadron's T-33s, this 182nd FIS 'Deuce' has the 'last three' of the serial number repeated in the airbrake.

Vermont 134th FIS

The 134th FIS, 158th FIG 'Green Mountain Boys' of the Vermont ANG, located at Burlington, flew F-102As from August 1965 to 9 June 1974. The squadron is apparently the only Guard unit to go into the Delta Dagger from the F-89D Scorpion without operating the F-89J in the interim. Following completion of their F/TF-102A era, the 'Green Mountain Boys' took on the defence systems evaluation job – acting as decoys for the North American air defence network. Among 'Deuce' units, they were thus unique in converting to the EB-57B/C/E Canberra.

These Vermont Guard 'Deuces' exhibit coloured fin tips denoting the flights to which they belonged.

Washington 116th FIS

The 116th FIS/141st FG Washington ANG flew F-102As from May 1965 to 1 December 1969. The 'Ace of Spades' unit, located at Geiger Field, Paine, Washington, had previously flown the F-89J Scorpion. Following the 'Deuce' era, the squadron converted to the F-101B/F Voodoo and later moved to Fairchild Air Force Base, Washington.

Wisconsin 176th FIS

The 176th FIS/115th FIG, Wisconsin ANG, flew F-102As from May 1966 until 9 November 1974. Informally dubbed the 'Raggedy Ass Militia' for a time, the 176th FIS had previously flown F-89J Scorpions at Truax Field (the former Truax Air Force Base) in Madison, Wisconsin. Like California's 196th FIS, the 176th converted to the O-2A.

In common with Pennsylvania's 146th FIS, Wisconsin's 'Deuce' unit adopted a bold single fin colour to distinguish its aircraft.

Miscellaneous users

Left: The 6520th Test Group at Hanscom AFB, Massachussetts operated a number of F-102s on test work. At least one wore 'HH' tailcodes signifying 'Happy Hanscom'. This preceded the official adoption of tailcodes during the Vietnam War. The 6250th also operated F-106 Delta Darts at the same time.

Above: Air Proving Ground Command at Eglin AFB operated a small number of early F-102s. APGC's job was to test weapons and weapons separation and maintaining the Eglin ranges. The name changed to the Air Force Development Test Center in July 1957, and today this reports to Air Force Materiel Command.

Below: A number of Delta Daggers wore the markings of the Sperry company, usually a small tail logo. The F-102As were used during QF-102/PQM-102 development to test the drone control equipment. The TF-102As (sometimes called QF-102Bs) were used for checkout flights for trainee drone pilots.

Left: The Federal Aviation Administration operated a single Delta Dagger as part of research into supersonic transports (SSTs). The aircraft, registered N300, flew approach paths simulating a large delta-winged aircraft, in a programme to develop procedures for air traffic controllers. As seen here, it joined ANG F-102s in the 'boneyard' at Davis-Monthan AFB when its trials tasks had been completed.

Above: NACA and NASA operated at least nine F-102s, including a YF-102 and a TF-102A . Only one, 56-998 seen here, carried a NACA or NASA number (N617NA), and this served for four years at the Lewis Research Center, mainly as a chase aircraft for the ejection seat testbed NF-106B. Other aircraft were used for shorter periods at Ames on fire-control evaluation manoeuvres and at Johnson for astronaut pilot proficiency.

Greece (Elliniki Polimiki Aeroporia)

Greece began training pilots for its F-102A Delta Dagger fighters in Project Peace Violet when six Greek instructors began training at Perrin AFB, Texas on 30 September 1968. It appears that Turkish pilots had completed their work at Perrin by then, making it unnecessary for flyers from the two countries, hardly friends, to serve together in Texas.

Greece received 24 F-102s. The HAF (Hellenic Air Force), or Elliniki Polimiki Aeroporia, flew 20 F-102As and four TF-102As (plus possibly one or two more of the latter) beginning in 1969. The HAF was the subject of a temporary embargo on arms sales to Greece by the United States when the time came to find a 'Deuce' replacement, so Greece ordered 40 Dassault Mirage F1CGs to fulfil the interceptor role.

114th Pterix (Wing) at Tanagra was the sole Greek F-102 operator, flying the Dart from 1969 until 1979.

Turkey (Türk Hava Kuvvetleri)

Turkey began training pilots for its F-102A Delta Dagger fighters in Project Peace Violet when six Turkish instructors began training at Perrin AFB, Texas on 20 November 1967.

Turkey's air force, the Türk Hava Kuvvetleri or THK, received 38 F-102s according to one source, 39 according to another (36 F-102As and three TF-102As, and 46 according to a third (39 As and seven TFs). After preparation and workups, these equipped two interceptor squadrons, apparently 142 Filo at Murted and 182 Filo at Diyarbakir, both of which belonged to the THK's 1st Tactical Air Force, or Birinci Taktik Hava Kuvveti. The Turkish F/TF-102As had a relatively brief operational career and were replaced in the interceptor mission by the F-104G (142 Filo) and F-100C (182 Filo) in mid-1979.

Turkey's two F-102 squadrons had no distinctive identifying markings.

Curtiss F9C Sparrowhawk

The tiny Sparrowhawks achieved fame out of all proportion to their numbers due to their operation from the rigid airships *Akron* and *Macon*. The story of the F9C, the first Curtiss all-metal biplane to reach production, is intertwined with the USN's last rigid airships.

From the moment Lieutenant Commander Godfrey DeC. Chevalier recorded the maiden 'trap' aboard the USS *Langley* (CV-1), the US Navy's first aircraft-carrier, naval aviators became a special breed of airmen. Indeed, to this day carrier pilots are known as 'tailhookers', the contraption extending beneath their aircraft a symbol of the uniqueness of their operations. For a short time period during the 1930s, those who flew from carriers shared the stage with 'hookers' of another sort. Naval aviation's version of 'the daring young men on the flying trapeze', this select group operated from the giant rigid airships of the day, the hooks of their aircraft snagging a crane-like contraption lowered from the airship. The aircraft that made it all possible was as much an anomaly as its pilots but, like them, the Curtiss F9C Sparrowhawk represents a classic chapter from US naval aviation's Golden Age.

First Steps

Observing the success of German Zeppelin airships during World War I and realising the importance of long-range scouting in operations at sea, some US Navy officers advanced the cause of rigid airships in the years following the Great War. Five were produced for the service beginning in 1921, including USS *Los Angeles* built in Germany and operated between 1924 and 1939. It was aboard this airship that there occurred an experiment that would change the face of airship operations in the US Navy.

In the early morning hours of 3 July 1929, *Los Angeles* launched from the Naval Air Station Lakehurst, New Jersey and climbed into the darkness, and orbited above the east coast of the USA. As the first fingers of light stretched across the horizon, a speck appeared. With the airship turning into the wind, just as floating aircraft-carriers did when conducting flight operations, Lieutenant A.W. 'Jake' Gorton lined up his Vought UO-1 aircraft on the tail of *Los Angeles*. With an eye on the hook contraption affixed to the top of his machine's upper wing, the veteran carrier pilot approached the trapeze protruding from beneath the airship, and after labouring for

***Above left:** This line-abreast trio of Sparrowhawks represents 50 per cent of F9C-2 production.*

***Top:** The* Macon *dwarfs a pair of F9C-2s as they approach for the first operational hook-up, undertaken during exercises on 7 July 1933.*

***Left:** The XF9C-1 (Curtiss Model 58, BuNo. 8731) prototype failed to gain a production order as a carrier-based fighter, but was a pioneer of the airshipborne fighter concept during trials with the airship* Los Angeles *for which the aircraft was fitted with a 'cobra' hook.*

Below and right: The XF9C-1's carrier trials got off to a bad start when rudder and brake problems caused Lt Alfred M. Pride to put the aircraft on its nose on its first pass over the mock carrier deck at Hampton Roads, Virginia, 16 June 1931. After its rejection for carrier duties and trials in* Los Angeles*, the aircraft served as a spare machine in* Akron *and* Macon *before being scrapped in 1935.

six minutes to join the two, hooked-on. It was not the first time an operation of this nature had been attempted, both British and US Army pilots having previously experimented with the operation of aircraft from airships. Nevertheless, the event marked the first operation of its type by the US Navy from one of its rigid airships, and represented the beginning of an effort to perfect it that far outpaced those of the others.

Even before these trials, a decision had been made to include provision for aircraft aboard the US Navy's two newest rigid airships, the ZRS-4 and ZRS-5. Construction on the former, named the USS *Akron*, began at the Goodyear-Zeppelin Corporation in Ohio on 7 November 1929. Among the design features was an aircraft hangar located aft of the airship's control car. Separated from the crew's quarters and forward engine rooms by horizontal and longitudinal girders, the hangar measured 75 ft (22.86 m) in length and 60 ft (18.29 m) in width. The girders supported a series of rails that criss-crossed one another and supported the trapeze. Entrance to the hangar was via a T-shaped door. It was this facet of the structure that presented a problem for the US Navy, for the maximum length and wing span that an aircraft could have and still pass through the hangar were 24 ft (7.32 m) and 30 ft (9.14 m), respectively. In July 1931, with the *Akron* nearing completion, the US Navy set out to find the aircraft that could operate from her, and thus changed the fortunes of the F9C Sparrowhawk, an inconspicuous design recently produced by the Curtiss Aeroplane and Motor Company of Garden City, New York.

Three horses in the gate

The F9C Sparrowhawk began life in 1929 as a response to Bureau of Aeronautics specifications for a small, lightweight carrierborne fighter. Three companies submitted designs, including Berliner-Joyce with its XFJ-1 and XFJ-2, Fokker-Atlantic with its XFA-1, and Curtiss. The name Curtiss was synonymous with naval aviation. Maker of the legendary Hawk series of fighters that equipped both US Army and US Navy squadrons during the 1920s, the company certainly possessed the right level of corporate knowledge when it came to manufacturing fighters. Developed as the Model 58 in Curtiss parlance, the company's design featured an all-metal semi-monocoque fuselage and wing spars constructed of aluminium alloy, both of these 'firsts' for a Curtiss aircraft. The latter appeared only in circular section tubes, necessitating that they be run through rollers in order to shape them for use in the wings.

The XF9C-1 prototype, as it was designated by the US Navy, was powered by a 420-hp (313-kW) Wright R-975C (J-6-9) Whirlwind radial piston engine, giving it a top speed of 176.5 mph (284 km/h) and the ability to climb to an altitude of 22,600 ft (6890 m) at an initial rate of 5,000 ft (1524 m) per two minutes 36 seconds. Carrying on the tradition of its predecessors, the aircraft was christened Sparrowhawk.

The XFA-1 and the XF9C-1 possessed merit enough for the US Navy to procure one prototype of each, letting a contract for the former on 24 June 1930 and another for the XF9C-1 six days later. Work on the Sparrowhawk quickly outpaced that on the XFA-1. Modifications suggested by naval aviators and engineers during the examination of the mock-up of the aircraft constructed before the award of the contract were incorporated into the prototype. These included an externally mounted arresting hook for carrier operations, metal-covered control surfaces, N-shaped inter-plane struts, a tubular engine mount structure in place of a monocoque one, and an externally mounted compass.

Other changes appeared after the aircraft took to the air for it maiden flight over Mitchel Field, Long Island, on 12 February 1931, the first of 55 test flights conducted by company test pilot William Crosswell. Even before the aircraft was evaluated in the air, a Curtiss anti-drag ring cowling was installed around the

The first production model F9C-2 (BuNo. 9056) is seen at Buffalo, New York, the day before its delivery to NAS Anacostia. 9056's first flight was on 14 April 1932, at which point the aircraft had single main undercarriage struts. These were soon changed to the tripod arrangement seen here. Note that the aircraft also retained its original tailfin design; it was moved slightly aft with a small increase in area before the type entered service. Following the loss of both airships the surviving aircraft, including 9056, were redesignated XF9C-2 as they were of limited use without an airship from which to operate.

Airship support and 'Skyhook' training

Resting at NAS Lakehurst, F9C-2 BuNo. 9058 is seen prior to its move to Moffett Field. Note the N2Y-1 trainer in the background.

Above: Consolidated N2Y-1s were utilised as 'skyhook' trainers until replaced by a pair of Waco XJW-1s. Six (BuNos 8600-8605) were originally acquired to transport mail and passengers to/from the airships.

The XJW-1 was a standard Waco UBF three-seat, open-cockpit biplane, of which two (BuNos 9521/9522) were purchased as utility aircraft for the USS *Macon*.

engine, and flight testing affirmed the correctness of the decision for the maximum speed was thereby increased by 20 mph (32 km/h). Speed, believed by US Navy pilots of the day to be the most important attribute of any fighter, also figured in the installation of 'wheel pants'. Ironic given the future employment of the Sparrowhawk, these were called 'dirigible fairings' in the vernacular of the day. Finally, engineers changed the vertical tail surface, transforming the original rounded unit into a taller, more angular appendage.

Changing fortunes

Late in March 1931, the XF9C-1 arrived at the US Navy's flight test centre at NAS Anacostia outside Washington, DC, for its Board of Inspection and Survey trials, a final examination for any aircraft prototype with hopes of entering production. The members of the board conducted tests on the XF9C-1 during the period between 31 March and 30 June, ensuring that the aircraft met contract specifications and making recommendations for any changes that would benefit the design.

An important element of the flight testing was the arresting gear trials at NAS Hampton Roads. In the hands of Lieutenant Alfred M. Pride, the XF9C-1 nosed up during its first pass at the wires, suffering minor damage, but following repairs was able to complete the evaluation. Excessive tail rise and premature application of the brakes were determined to be the causes of the accident, and Pride recommended that the tailhook be moved one frame aft and that the brake pedals be made less sensitive and offset to prevent inadvertent use. The pilot's fields of vision appeared to be the major deficiency so far as suitability for carrier operations was concerned, and the relocation of the exhaust pipes to allow for some forward vision through the ring cowling during carrier approaches and the raising of the upper wing by about 4 in (10.2 cm) were among the suggested remedies.

The report of the other test pilots included 36 recommendations for improvement of the aircraft, and emphasised its poor fields of vision. Another major deficiency pointed out was the fact that the high wing and power loadings of the XF9C-1 made its performance inferior to that of other carrier fighters then in service, which were fitted with the Pratt & Whitney R-1340 Wasp radial engine.

Found wanting in visibility and power, the F9C's future did not look bright. However, just weeks after the pilots at Anacostia had put the aircraft through its paces, a decision in the Bureau of Aeronautics altered the destiny of the Sparrowhawk. On 20 July 1931 a conference convened with the goal of choosing a production aircraft to operate from the rigid airships *Akron* and *Macon*, the latter being the name selected for the ZRS-5. Both the XF9C-1 and XFJ-2 showed promise, especially as their low-mounted upper wings, which were gulled into the fuselage, were ideal for arrangement of equipment for hooking on to the airship. However, the assembled officers came down on the side of Curtiss, which could quickly deliver a second prototype incorporating the changes recommended following the XF9C-1 trials, thus hastening the arrival of production aircraft.

While the US Navy conducted initial testing of the skyhook application on the XF9C-1, Curtiss readied the XF9C-2 for its flight trials, which began in November 1931. However, the US Navy quickly cancelled them, desiring to evaluate a production aircraft from the batch of six already ordered from Curtiss. Results of the trials on the F9C-2, which began in May 1932, included two major changes to the design, namely a three-strut main landing gear arrangement to improve stability when applying the brakes, and an extension of the rudder hinge line aft a total of 9 in (0.23 m).

The men on the flying trapeze

Even before selection of the Sparrowhawk for service with the rigid dirigibles, men destined to serve in the Heavier-than-Air Unit arrived at NAS Lakehurst, the first of them early in 1931. They began logging hook-ups on the *Los Angeles*' trapeze using a Consolidated N2Y

Carrier operations were rare for the F9C-2s, but they did take part in an exercise based aboard Lexington (CV-2). The famous 'The Men on the Flying Trapeze' insignia, seen on this aircraft, was carried from early 1933 until late 1934.

Akron* and *Macon

Goodyear-Zeppelin and the United States government signed a contract on 6 October 1928 for the development of two 6,850,000-cu ft (193970-m³) rigid airships for the US Navy – USS* Akron *(ZRS-4, above) and* Macon *(ZRS-5, right). Intended to operate with the ocean going fleet and carrying three to four F9Cs each, they were the fastest rigid airships ever built, with a maximum speed of 84mph (135 km/h). First flown on 25 September 1931,* Akron *benefitted from a number of advances in Zeppelin design. Apart from being filled with helium gas, the use of this inert gas allowed the ship's eight 570-hp (425-kW) Maybach VL2 engines to be buried inside the envelope, cutting down on weight and drag.* Macon *flew on 21 April 1933, less than three weeks after* Akron *had been driven uncontrollably into a rough sea during a storm, at the cost of 76 of her 79 crew.* Macon *also came to an unfortunate end – suffering a tail unit structural failure on 12 February 1935 and crashing into the sea at Point Sur, about 100 miles (160 km) south of San Francisco. Four F9C-2s (BuNos 9058/61) were lost with the* Macon*, along with the USN's remaining confidence in the large rigid airship.* Akron *accumulated 1,695 hours flying time before its crash;* Macon *flew for a total of 1,798 hours.

training aircraft, until the modified XF9C-1 arrived in the fall. Accustomed to the difficult landings aboard an aircraft-carrier flight deck that pitched and rolled with the sea, the pilots found 'landing' on the trapeze comparatively simple. With the airship and aircraft travelling at the same speed, it was merely a matter of closing the distance and hooking on. Rough weather and material difficulties were the only real hindrances to the evolution.

Navy Day, 27 October 1931, marked the commissioning of USS *Akron* (ZRS-4), but its first nine months would not involve extensive use of the Sparrowhawks in exercises with the fleet at sea. Summer brought delivery of the first F9C-2, as well as four additional pilots to complement Lieutenants Ward Harrigan and Howard 'Brigham' Young. The first order of business was training the new arrivals in operating from the trapeze using the two-seat N2Y. "The first one, of course, is always a little touchy," Lieutenant (jg) Harold B. 'Min' Miller recalled of his indoctrination, "but as time went on, it was just an everyday occurrence, as though you were landing on a field." By August six more F9C-2 aircraft were in operation, joining the F9C-2 and XF9C-1 that had arrived earlier in the summer, and the pilots were able to fully assess the tiny biplanes. "It was a beautiful airplane to fly, even though it required constant attention," Miller wrote years later. "[It could] do literally anything...from a double roll to slow rolls, to rolls on top of a loop."

In time, the pilots also developed the techniques for operating from the 'flying aircraft-carrier'. Minimum altitude for trapeze operations was 800 ft (245 m), and the airship had to be travelling at a speed of between 68 and 70 kt (78 and 81 mph; 126 and 130 km/h) lest the aircraft stall during approach for a hook-on. As the pilots gained more proficiency, the standard approach was to fly alongside the airship's no. 1 engine, which was located roughly next to the trapeze, and using the F9C's rudder skid to a position underneath the trapeze. There, the pilot found himself looking up rather than straight ahead as he would in normal

Officers and enlisted men of the Heavier-Than-Air Unit pose for an official photograph in late 1932. The pilots (centre row, from left) were Lt (jg) F. N. Kivette, H. B. Miller, Lt D. W. Harrigan, F. M. Trapnell, H. L. Young and Lt (jg) R. W. Larson.

Left: Hook engaged, Lt Harold Miller makes sure he is secure before shutting down the engine of his F9C-2, which will then be winched inside the* Macon*, the shadow of which appears on the surface of the Pacific Ocean below.

Lt D. W. Harrigan approaches the* Macon *over New Egypt, New Jersey on 7 July. Clearly visible is the swing-arm cradle which steadied the rear fuselage as the aircraft was winched aboard the airship.

***Below left:* ① *Lt Howard Young approaches the trapeze aboard USS* Akron *in the XF9C-1 on 3 May 1932, the first day the Sparrowhawk operated aboard the airship.* ② *Safely locked-on, Young reaches out to guide one of the stabilising poles into the 'jaw' under the upper wing. With the engine switched off* ③ *and the aircraft safely tethered, the Sparrowhawk is raised into the* Akron*'s hangar* ④.**

horizontal flight. The bar of the trapeze became his horizon, and he concentrated on closing the distance. In rough weather the airship sometimes moved suddenly to the side or thrust downward, the latter forcing the pilot to close the throttle.

The hook atop the Sparrowhawk's upper wing was spring loaded. Thus when the aircraft hit the trapeze bar with any force, it locked on. Once that happened, the pilot needed only to get the aircraft to the centre of the trapeze bar, which he did by applying rudder and sliding the aircraft into position. This was important because the hangar entrance provided only 4 in (10.2 cm) of clearance at each wing tip, and the aircraft had therefore to be centred to make it through the gap. Once he felt the reassuring lock-on of the hook on the trapeze, the pilot could relax, though sometimes his senses betrayed him. "There were a couple of times when I thought I was locked on, and I'd sit back fat, dumb, and happy and just fall off," 'Min' Miller remembered. "That was no problem either; all I had to do was drop the nose a little bit and pick up a little flying speed and come back and go on again. But we learned to insure that we were on by giving a little burst of speed." To assist in lining up the aircraft for entry into the hangar, one of the unit's pilots, Lieutenant Frederick Trapnell, designed a brace known as the 'saddle' that pivoted down from the hangar and secured around the F9C's fuselage, keeping the aircraft from moving back and forth in the wind as it ascended through the narrow hangar doorway.

Defence without guns

The pilots were just as earnest in developing the tactics for tactical employment of the F9C as they were in perfecting the techniques for their aircraft's airship operations. In December 1932, Harrigan completed a report detailing the history of the Heavier-than-Air Unit's operations and offering opinions about how best to utilise the F9C. Using the term 'lighter-than-air carrier' to describe the *Akron*, Harrigan took as his central thesis that the role of the airship's aircraft was long-range scouting, with only a secondary mission as fighters. Harrigan believed that if an enemy force approached the carrier, the F9C's defensive mission was to warn her while the intruders were at extended range, allowing the airship to turn away from the danger. "As a fighter, its performance was obviously non-competitive with any carrier fighter that was in operation in those days," Miller remembered. "So that became the accepted mission of the airplane – to go on out and find out what was going on and keep the ship out of trouble."

It was aboard the *Macon* that the ideas espoused by Harrigan were put into practice. Tragically, the *Akron* went down at sea in a storm off the New Jersey coast on the evening of 3-4 April 1933. Among the 73 crewmen lost was Rear Admiral William A. Moffett, Chief of the Bureau of Aeronautics and the airship's greatest proponent. The *Macon* was commissioned on 23 June 1933, and following trials at Lakehurst flew to its new home base at Sunnyvale, California where it arrived on 15 October. In the following month the airship participated in fleet exercises off the US west coast, but its use was rather limited and it was ruled 'shot down' on three different occasions during the various phases of the exercise. Reflecting Harrigan's thoughts of months ago, the umpire aboard the airship during the exercises pointed out in his after-action report that the airship's aircraft should be employed in the scouting of enemy forces.

Development of a more effective way to navigate the F9C at extended ranges from the airship and better radio communications between the two were necessary before this could occur. This work was a key to the airship's very survival: as the new Chief of the Bureau of Aeronautics, Rear Admiral Ernest J. King, wrote early in 1934: "This is to be a critical year for airships...We must not be reckless, but if airships are to justify themselves, the Macon has got to show more than she has shown."

The *Macon*'s officers as well as those of its Heavier-than-Air unit immediately set out to develop a system to make the F9C a more effective scout. As early as 1932, Lieutenant Don Mackey, the *Macon*'s flight control officer, had devised a system that allowed the Sparrowhawk to operate at increased range from the airship. 'Min' Miller described the operation: "The ship would hold whatever the course was, at a speed of 50 knots. We would double the speed and search on a 60-degree angle to the airship's track. Any time we wanted to go back to the ship, no matter what side we were on, we would do a 120-degree turn that converged with the airship's track at 60 degrees."

An effort was also made to operate at the

Seen in July 1933, this trio of F9C-2s from* Macon *displays the colourful markings carried by these aircraft during the first months of their service.

same altitude as the airship, thus ensuring that both airship and aircraft were in the same wind conditions. Though having the disadvantage of placing the airship and her scouting aircraft on a set course, the system nevertheless for the first time allowed the Sparrowhawk to operate beyond visual range of its giant base.

Another innovation allowed even more freedom of operations for the F9C. Dr Gerhard Fisher and Lieutenant Howard N. Coulter, the *Macon*'s communications officer, teamed up to adapt the former's low-frequency radio direction finder to airship operations. Providing the operator with a visual indicator rather than an aural signal, which had to be translated into a bearing, the device was a veritable radio compass as well as a homing device, for the pilot could home in on a radio signal and follow it. Fisher and 'Min' Miller installed a homing set and radio receiver, which could be operated simultaneously, on two F9C aircraft using an antenna looped around the upper and lower wings. The success of the equipment extended the range of the F9C dramatically, allowing pilots to operate at even greater distances from the airship with the confidence that they could find their way home. Lieutenant Miller, who had succeeded Harrigan in command of the Heavier-than-Air Unit, also persuaded

The Sparrowhawk fleet

***Above left: Seen prior to receiving the more elaborate markings adopted shortly after it entered service, BuNo. 9056 (the first F9C-2) is seen not long after delivery to* Macon.**

Left: BuNo. 9059 inside* Akron *in May 1932, demonstrating the monorail system on which the F9Cs were stored within the airships. The aircraft gained its black section trim shortly afterwards.

Above: Lt F. N. Nivette is seen at the controls of BuNo. 9057 in July 1933, its white section markings clearly evident.

Below: F9C-2 BuNo. 9058 is shown carrying the name of USS* Akron*, aboard which it had recently been based. This aircraft later served within* Macon*, and was among the aircraft lost with the airship in 1935.

Left: BuNo. 9061 is seen in the configuration adopted for long-range operations over the Pacific when the type may have been required to land on aircraft-carriers in an emergency. An arrester hook has been fitted and fins added to the wheel spats to protect the undercarriage legs from missed wires. The aircraft's overall blue-black tail colour was adopted (briefly) to comply with Navy regulations concerning carrier-assigned aircraft based in the Pacific.

Right: BuNo. 9060's section markings were willow green, with blue band edging.

*Flotation bag compartments in the lower surface of the upper mainplane may be seen as square patches stencilled **FLOTATION**. The bags were inflated in the event of the aircraft ditching.*

The five main dials on an F9C-2's panel were (clockwise from left): tachometer, bank/turn indicator, air speed indicator, altimeter and engine temperature guage. The fuel gauge is lower left.

Lieutenant Commander Herbert V. 'Doc' Wiley, who assumed command of the *Macon* in July 1934, to operate the F9C without landing gear while at sea. Replacing the landing gear with a 30-US gal (113.5-litre) fuel tank increased the aircraft's range by 50 per cent.

To sea

As they solved many of the technical problems that had hindered airship operations in the fleet, the *Macon*'s crew operated steadily at sea during 1934-1935, mindful of the fact that the airship needed to prove itself in tactical exercises. One operation that drew the attention of everyone was Wiley's decision to take the *Macon* on an extended flight westward from California over the Pacific in an effort to locate the cruisers USS *New Orleans* and USS *Houston*, which were en route to Hawaii from Panama. Significant was the fact that President Franklin D. Roosevelt was aboard the latter ship, and Wiley's plan was to have F9C aircraft swoop down over the cruiser and drop newspapers and magazines, as well as letters specially stamped by the *Macon*'s mail clerk. The operation on 19 July 1934 was successful and one can picture one of those famous smiles stretching across Roosevelt's face as he dictated the message "WELL DONE AND THANK YOU FOR THE PAPERS THE PRESIDENT 1245."

The *Macon* completed 1934 just as it began what Admiral King had called its 'critical year'. To Wiley and his fellow officers, it appeared to be making headway. In one report he chastised those quick to condemn the airship, writing "it is believed that there prevails an erroneous impression of the vulnerability of the rigid airships...If planes are allowed one hit in ten, which is believed to be liberal, a squadron of 15 planes would be required to drop 30 bombs to 'sink' the airship." Unfortunately, as was the case with its sister, Mother Nature sank the *Macon*. While operating off the California coast on the afternoon of 12 February 1935, the airship was shaken by a series of wind gusts, causing one of its fins to break up and a series of helium cells in the after part of the airship to deflate. Despite efforts to keep it in the air, the giant airship fell tail first into the Pacific, and eventually sank, taking four F9C aircraft and two of her 83-man crew with it. With *Macon* went the future of the rigid airship in the United States Navy.

End of an era

With the platform for their unique mission gone, the three surviving F9C aircraft were relegated to general utility duty, and gradually disappeared from the fleet. Only one survives: painted in the colourful markings of the Macon's Heavier-than-Air Unit, it is currently on display at the National Museum of Naval Aviation, a tangible link to an era long since past.

M. Hill Goodspeed

Specifications

XF9C-1

Wing span	25 ft 6 in (7.77m)
Wing area	172.8 sq ft (16.06 m²)
Length	19ft 5 in (5.91 m)
Height	7ft 1 in (2.15 m)
Empty weight	1,823 lb (827 kg)
Gross weight	2,482 lb (1126 kg)
Maximum speed	176½ mph (284.04 km/h)
Service ceiling	22,600 ft (6888 m)
Range	328 miles (528 km)
Armament	two 0.30-in (7.62-mm) guns

F9C-2

Wing span	25 ft 6 in (7.77 m)
Wing area	172.8 sq ft (16.06 m²)
Length	20 ft 1½ in (6.13 m)
Height	7ft 1 in (2.15 m)
Empty weight	2,117 lb (960 kg)
Gross weight	2,779 lb (1260 kg)
Maximum speed	176½ mph (284.04 km/h)
Service ceiling	19,200 ft (5852 m)
Range	297 miles (478 km)
Armament	two 0.30-in (7.62-mm) guns

The fate of the three F9C-2s which remained in the USN inventory after the loss of Macon *in February 1935 was, for some years, shrouded in mystery. The three surviving airframes were **XF9C-2 BuNo. 9264** (which had been brought up to production standard) and two production **F9C-2s – 9056** and **9057** – attached to the **Battle Force Pool at NAS San Diego**. Due to their limited usefulness and unique design, all were redesignated **XF9C-2** after the airship's loss. In August, **9264** was flown to **NAS Anacostia** for 'general flying' duties, but the aircraft's limited range, tendency to ground loop and restrictions on aerobatics meant that it saw little use. The following year it became due for overhaul and the decision was taken to send all three machines to **NAS Norfolk**, where the two best aircraft would be overhauled with the third cannibalised for spare parts. En route from San Diego to Norfolk **9057** suffered two accidents, the second of which caused sufficient damage (left) for the aircraft to be stripped of useable parts and stricken. Once **9056** and **9264** had arrived at Norfolk (**9264** by truck, as it had also crashed en route) a survey of the two airframes was undertaken and the decision made to overhaul **9056** and strike **9264**. **9056** later saw about two years further service at **NAS Norfolk**, before being withdrawn from service and set aside for preservation by the **Smithsonian Institution (NASM)**. However, upon its restoration for display it was discovered that the airframe was in fact that of **9264**. The aircraft's identities had probably become confused during their survey prior to the overhaul of '**9056**'.*

Powerplant
A 420-hp (313-kW) Wright R-975C Whirlwind nine-cylinder radial powered the XF9C-1, but was replaced in the XF9C-2 prototype and F9C-2 production aircraft by the R-975E3, rated at 438 hp (327 kW) at sea level at 2,200 rpm. This drove a two-bladed Hamilton Standard propeller with ground-adjustable pitch.

Flotation gear
Flotation bags, 32 in (81.3 cm) in diameter and 56 in (142.2 cm) in length, were installed in bays under the upper mainplane and were inflated using a CO_2 bottle (housed in the lower forward fuselage) in the event of a ditching.

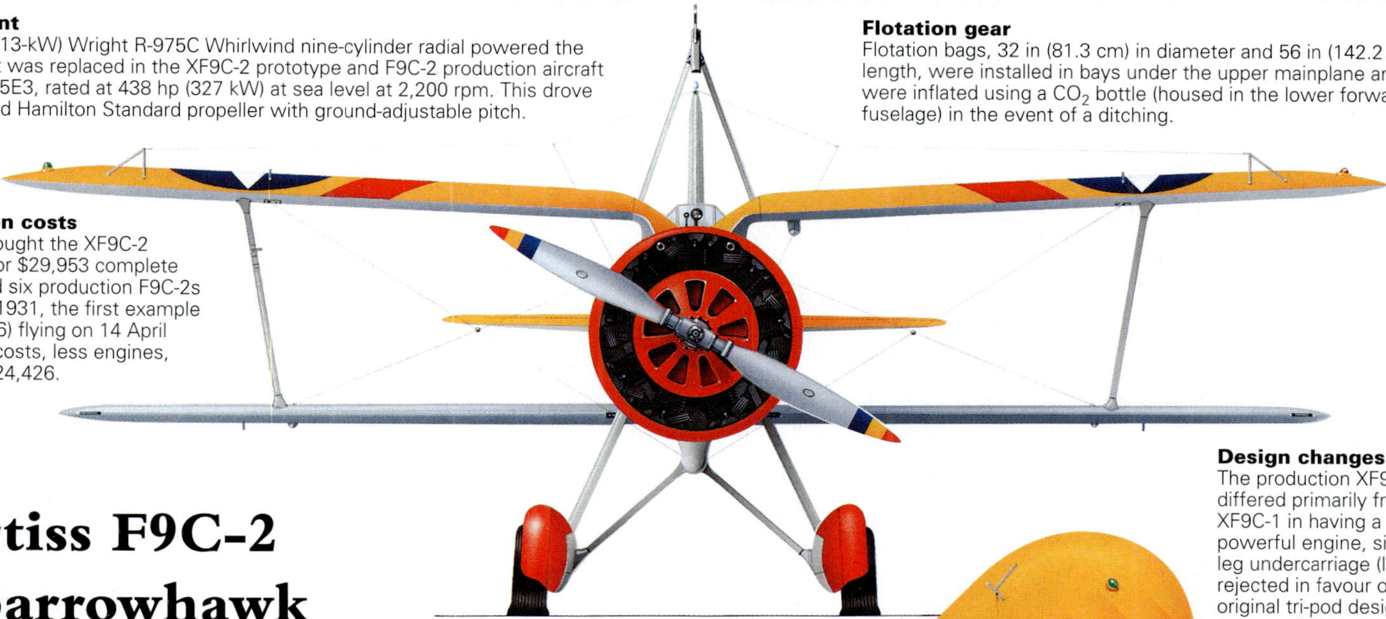

Production costs
The USN bought the XF9C-2 prototype for $29,953 complete and ordered six production F9C-2s in October 1931, the first example (BuNo. 9056) flying on 14 April 1932. Unit costs, less engines, averaged $24,426.

Design changes
The production XF9C-2 differed primarily from the XF9C-1 in having a more powerful engine, single-leg undercarriage (later rejected in favour of the original tri-pod design) and an upper wing mounted 4 in (10.2 cm) higher. In production F9C-2s the horn-balanced rudder was replaced with a conventional rudder positioned 8 in (20.3 cm) aft to increase fin area.

Curtiss F9C-2 Sparrowhawk Heavier-Than-Air Unit USS *Macon* (ZRS-5) US Navy 1933

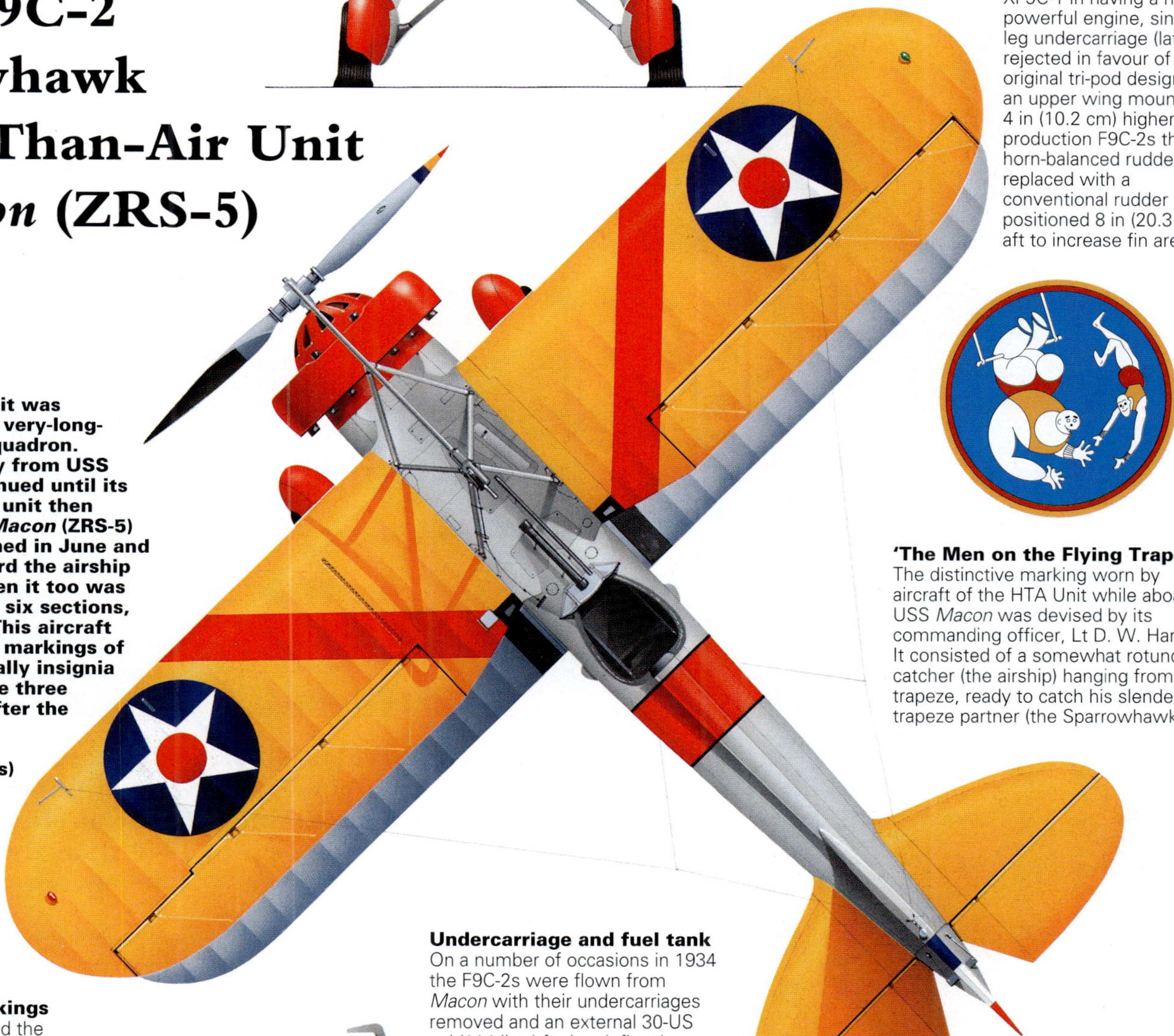

The Heavier-Than-Air Unit was established in 1932 as a very-long-range reconnaissance squadron. Operations began in May from USS *Akron* (ZRS-4) and continued until its crash in April 1933. The unit then transferred to the USS *Macon* (ZRS-5) when it was commissioned in June and continued to serve aboard the airship until February 1935, when it too was lost. The unit comprised six sections, each with one aircraft. This aircraft (BuNo. 9056) carries the markings of the lead flight, traditionally insignia red. 9056 was among the three aircraft that remained after the loss of *Macon* and was redesignated (with the other surviving airframes) XF9C-2 and finally stricken in November 1936, in the mistaken belief (it is believed), on the part of the Board of Survey at NAS Norfolk that it was the original XF9C-2 BuNo. 9264.

'The Men on the Flying Trapeze'
The distinctive marking worn by aircraft of the HTA Unit while aboard USS *Macon* was devised by its commanding officer, Lt D. W. Harrigan. It consisted of a somewhat rotund catcher (the airship) hanging from a trapeze, ready to catch his slender trapeze partner (the Sparrowhawk).

Undercarriage and fuel tank
On a number of occasions in 1934 the F9C-2s were flown from *Macon* with their undercarriages removed and an external 30-US gal (114-litre) fuel tank fitted on the forward fuselage centreline. (see scrap view). This reduced weight and drag and improved range at a stroke.

Overall colours and markings
The Sparrowhawk fleet carried the standard colours and markings of the day. Airframes were overall light grey (as per a directive of 1927), except for the upper mainplane and tailplane upper surfaces, which were chrome yellow and the upper surface of the lower mainplane, which was aluminum. The tailfin/rudder sported blue/white/red striping. Each of the six production F9C-2s carried a squadron section colour (introduced in June 1931), which was applied as it would have been to a section leader's aircraft in a conventional squadron (distinguished by a 20-in/50.8-cm fuselage band and full colour engine cowling). The section colours and the aircraft to which they were applied were as follows: 1st section (royal or insignia red) – 9056; 2nd section (white) – 9057; 3rd section (true blue) – 9058; 4th section (black) – 9059; 5th section (willow green) – 9060; 6th section (lemon yellow) – 9061.

Polikarpov
Biplane Fighter Variants

Before World War II Nikolai Nikolayevich Polikarpov was considered to be the principal designer of fighter aircraft in the USSR. His designs, encompassing aircraft of all types and roles, were built in greater numbers up to 1940 than those of all other Soviet designers put together.

Interestingly, this feat was achieved because he was also responsible for the development of the U-2, later renamed Polikarpov Po-2, a trainer and general-purpose biplane, which was prolifically produced over a long period of time; ultimately about 33,000 of the type were built in the USSR, Yugoslavia and Poland between 1928 and 1955.

Polikarpov was born on 10 June 1892 in the small village of Georgiyevskoye in Orel province, and was educated at the St Petersburg Polytechnic Institute. While there he worked in the local office of the Moscow-based Duks aircraft manufacturing company. On graduating in January 1916 he joined the Russo-Baltic Wagon Works to work under Igor Sikorskii (Sikorsky after this talented man had emigrated to the USA) and later joined the Military Air Fleet Board. By September he was head of the technical department of Duks. Shortly after this Polikarpov organised the development and production of the R-1 that was evolved from the British-designed Airco (de Havilland) D.H.4 and D.H.9. Production of this reconnaissance type eventually reached about 2,800 for service with the Soviet air forces. The R-1 was not just a copy of the D.H.4/D.H.9, but a complete redesign incorporating locally available materials, a different engine and new equipment allowing for a greater diversity of missions.

The recovery of the Soviet aircraft industry from the acute ravages of the civil war, which followed the assumption of power by the communists to create the USSR out of the formerly tsarist Russia, was slow and painful. But in January 1923 an aircraft design office was created at the former Duks factory in Moscow, now renamed GAZ-1 (*Gosoodahrstvennii Aviatsionnii Zavod*, or state aircraft factory), and Polikarpov was appointed its chief. His most important task was to design a fighter powered by the 400-hp (298-kW) Liberty engine. This situation at GAZ-1 was curtailed by his transfer on the 6 February 1923 to the design office of Glavkoavia (an acronym for the 'Main Directorate of the Amalgamated Aircraft Factories') and his place at GAZ-1 was taken by Dmitrii Pavlovich Grigorovich. Although the design of the fighter was transferred with Polikarpov, however, it was never built because the management at GAZ-1 was unenthusiastic – it was a classic example of the 'not invented here syndrome'.

Having caused something of a sensation with its restoration, in Siberia, of half-a-dozen I-16s, the first of which flew in 1995, the Alpine Fighter Collection, based at Wanaka in New Zealand's South Island, sponsored a similar project to rebuild three Chaikas. '10 Red' (c/n 6326) was the first of these and is seen here during testing in Russia in September 1997.

Below left: This rare air-to-air view shows a Chaika over the Baltic Sea during the Great Patriotic War.

Not knowing the true origin of their Chatos, the Nationalist air force called them 'Curtiss fighters' at first. Both sides in the Spanish Civil War operated the I-15bis.

Polikarpov's first fighter design to be built was a monoplane, called the IL-400 (*Istrebitel' [s dvigatelem] Liberty [moschchnost'yu] 400 [loshadinykh sil]*, or fighter with a 400-hp Liberty engine), which was completed by August 1923. This time Polikarpov had taken the diplomatic precaution of inviting I. M. Kostkin, the production manager of GAZ-1, to become joint leader of the project team.

The period of the 1920s was a decade of great transition in the aircraft industry as attempts were made to find the most effective blend of capable staff and appropriate organisation structures, and it was as a result of this, during August 1924, that Polikarpov was transferred from Glavkoavia back to GAZ-1 in the Khodynka area of Moscow. His new role encompassed the jobs of production manager and head of the factory design office, where he replaced Grigorovich. To improve the efficiency of the design office Polikarpov split it into several sections, each being given a clear task for which the section chief was accountable.

Reorganisations were also taking place at the national level, and trusts had become the favoured organisation for control of industries leading to the replacement of Glavkoavia by Aviatrest on the 7 January 1925. This was accompanied by the creation of a combined design office and experimental department, headed by Polikarpov, known as the OSS (Otdel Sukhopootnykh Samolyotov), the landplane component of the Central Design Bureau (TsKB, Tsentrahl'noe Konstrooktorskoe Byuro). By September 1926 this had become OPO-1 (*opytnii otdel*, or experimental department) of the TsKB, Aviatrest.

In the many design departments of which Polikarpov was head, about 40 aircraft projects were completed between 1924 and the end of 1928, and even though few of these reached the hardware stage, Polikarpov's prestige was greatly enhanced by the fecundity of his design work. He had even been permitted to visit France, Germany, the Netherlands and the UK to study the methodology of these countries' aircraft industries.

To accelerate the speed of new developments Zavod 25, also at Khodynka, was set up to accommodate OPO-1 and to provide it with dedicated production facilities. Polikarpov brought in his team on 24 February 1928 and was additionally appointed deputy director of the factory. (Note that aircraft factories were no longer called GAZ but in 1927 had been renumbered into a list of defence plants and were now referred to as *zavody* [factories] or *zavod* in the singular. Confusingly, the GAZ acronym from then onwards referred to the Gor'kovskii Avtomobil'nii Zavod, the automobile plant in Gor'kii [now Nizhnii Novgorod]!)

In September 1929 Polikarpov was arrested, falsely accused of being an industrial saboteur and condemned to death as an enemy of the people, but the sentence was commuted to 10 years' imprisonment in a labour camp. Many other aircraft designers, including Grigorovich, suffered a similar fate and in December 1929 a group of these designers, including Polikarpov, was gathered together in Butyrskaya prison, Moscow, and under the supervision of Goriyanov of the OGPU, as the Soviet secret service was known at the time, was set to work to design aircraft with Grigorovich as chief designer. It later transpired that this was a blatant attempt by the OGPU to demonstrate that repression was the best form of motivation and the most effective way to maintain control

The I-153 was no more fortunate than other Soviet air force aircraft in the first days of the Great Patriotic War; many were destroyed on the ground or captured by the advancing Germans.

I-153 '3 Yellow' was on display in Berlin in late 1941 as part of **Russenparadies**, *a collection of captured Soviet equipment on Unter den Linden Strasse. Note that the damaged interplane struts have been replaced by crudely fabricated structures of metal tube and fabric. A number of captured Soviet aircraft were shipped back from the front for evaluation by the Deutsche Versuchsanstalt für Lufthahrt (Research Centre for Aviation) at Berlin-Adlershof.*

of the industry. VT (*Vnootrennyaya Tyur'ma*, or internal prison) was the name given to these teams. Before long, in January 1930, they were moved to hangar number 7 in the grounds of Zavod 39 named after V. P. Menzhinskii. This factory was also located in the Khodynka area. At first the team was led by Grigorovich, but it was not long before he gave way to Polikarpov whose fighter design, the future I-5, had been preferred over a design suggestion of Grigorovich.

Further reorganisation

Further wholesale reorganisation took place on 3 March 1930, when Aviatrest and the other defence trusts were abolished and replaced on 16 April 1930 by Vsesoyznyye Obyedineniya (All-Union Associations) of which one, the Vsesoyooznoye Aviatseeonnoye Obyedineniye (VAO, or Aviation Association), was devoted to aviation and controlled by the Ministry of War. The next change was the absorption of Zavod 25 by Zavod 39 in August 1930, and the merging of the design teams from Zavody 22 and 28 into TsKB, VAO. At the same time the designers of the VT became part of the TsKB, VAO, but remained under OGPU control.

Polikarpov's luck changed for the better in June 1931, when Stalin was favourably impressed by the performance of the I-5 and observations which Polikarpov made at the Aviation Review which took place at the Central Airfield at Khodynka. Subsequently, on 7 July 1931 Polikarpov and some of his colleagues were granted an amnesty which allowed them their freedom, but the verdicts against them were not quashed until 1 September 1956, a time too late to benefit Polikarpov, who had died on 30 July 1944.

The number of experimental departments (OPOs), each of which had a design team, was constantly being increased at TsKB, VAO. There were 10 OPOs by September 1931 when the TsAGI (Tsentral'nii Aero-i Ghidrodinameecheskiy Institoot, or Central Aero- and Hydrodynamics Institute named after Nikolai Ye. Zhukovskii) took control of the TsKB and merged it with its own design team, AGOS (Aviahtsiya, Ghidroaviahtsiya i Opytnoye Stroitel'stvo, or aviation, hydro-aviation and experimental construction).

A design team within the TsKB, the TsAGI was now known as a *brigahda* (brigade) and Polikarpov was given charge of Brigade No. 3, a post which he lost after refusing the request of Andrei Nikolayevich Tupolev that he design all-metal aircraft. After Brigade No. 4 had been absorbed by Brigade No. 3, Polikarpov worked for a time as Pavel Osipovich Sukhoi's deputy. In order to achieve the directive of producing two fighters, a monoplane and a biplane, by mid-1933, two brigades had been formed, and Polikarpov was appointed head of Brigade No. 5, which was given the task of developing the biplane fighter.

Yet another reorganisation took place in January 1933 when the TsKB, although remaining at Zavod 39, was separated from the TsAGI. For this reason it was frequently referred to as TsKB-39 as well as TsKB, GUAP (Glavnoye Oopravleniye Aviatseeonnoy Promyshlennosti, or Chief Directorate of Aircraft Industry). Sergei Vladimirovich Il'yushin was appointed both chief designer and deputy factory director, and oversaw five airframe and two aircraft equipment brigades. Polikarpov was in charge of Brigade No. 2, which was to specialise in the design and manufacture of fighter prototypes.

'The King of Fighters'

At a conference of the aviation industry and its customers in August 1935, Polikarpov was congratulated on his fighter designs and he took advantage of the occasion to express concern over the physical separation of design offices from the production factories, and also over the lamentable lack of modern experimental facilities. His comments were well received and it was decided to base as many design teams as possible in production factories and to give each team its own experimental facilities. The result was the decentralisation of aircraft designing and the formation in 1936 of a number of Opytno-Konstrooktorskiye Byuro (OKBs, or Experimental Design Bureaux) based at aircraft factories. It was intended that the various OKBs should compete with one another to develop prototypes, the winning design then being mass-produced at the OKB's base factory. In this way the factory would have a strong incentive to co-operate with the OKB. Such was the prestige of Polikarpov, by now called 'the king of fighters', that he was appointed chief designer of two OKBs, at Zavod 21 in Gor'kii and Zavod 84 in Khimki near Moscow.

In 1937 Polikarpov and his OKB were transferred to the TsAGI plant for experimental designs, known as ZOK (Zavod Opytnykh Konstrooktsiy). This was located at Zavod 156 in Moscow where, after reviewing a range of projects with optimistic performance estimates, he settled down to build the I-180 fighter, a development of the I-16. Unfortunately the first prototype crashed but, when it was established that it was not as a result of any

Restored I-153 '10 Red' is seen, once again, during testing in Russia in September 1997. The AFC's I-16 and I-153 projects have been made all the more viable by the availability of Shvetsov ASh-62IR radial engines (manufactured in Poland by PZL as the ASz-62), of the type fitted to the ubiquitous Antonov An-2 transport. The ASh-62 is simply a modernised derivative of the M-62, as fitted to both fighter types and is similarly rated at 1,000 hp (746 kW).

Masters of the I-153 – Chaika pilots of the Continuation War

During the Winter War of 1939/40, five I-15bis and eight I-153 aircraft were captured from the Soviets and pressed into Finnish service. Another three fell into Finnish hands in the early months of the Continuation War (1941-1944), with a further 10 being obtained from captured German stocks in late 1942. So it was that, on a few occasions at least, I-153 met I-153 in the skies over the Gulf of Finland.

Above and top right: *A pair of olive drab 71st Fighter Regiment, Red Banner Baltic Fleet (71.IAP/KBF) Chaikas led by Capt. A. G. Batoorin take-off from Lavansaari on 22 August 1942. The aircraft each carry eight* ***RS-82*** *rockets for use in the type's primary ground-attack role. By this time Batoorin had claimed nine kills while flying I-153s and was awarded the Gold Star of the Hero of the Soviet Union on 23 October 1942. 71.IAP became 10.GvIAP/KBF (10th Guard's Fighter Regiment) soon afterwards and re-equipped with I-16s, Batoorin ending the war with 22 victory claims.*

Above and middle right: *71.IAP/KBF Chaikas '102 White' and '24 White' were flown by Major P. I. Biskup and Squadron Leader Captain K. V. Solov'yov, repectively. The latter became a Hero of the Soviet Union on 23 October 1942, with five German aircraft kills to his credit, but was killed in action on 27 December, having claimed another seven victories.*

Right: *'Olli' Puri was posted to 3/LeLv 6 (equipped with captured I-153s) on 25 September 1942. On 4 October he claimed a Soviet Chaika in air-to-air combat and added a Pe-2 bomber on 12 November – both while flying IT-18. In April 1943 he transferred to 3/LeLv 24, equipped with Brewster 239s, and by the end of the war had downed a total of 36 aircraft, latterly while flying Bf 109Gs.*

I-153 '50 White', Capt A. G. Batoorin, 71.IAP/KBF, Lavansaari, Gulf of Finland, summer 1942

I-153 '102 White', Major P. I. Biskup, Commanding Officer 71.IAP/KBF, Lavansaari, Gulf of Finland, August 1942

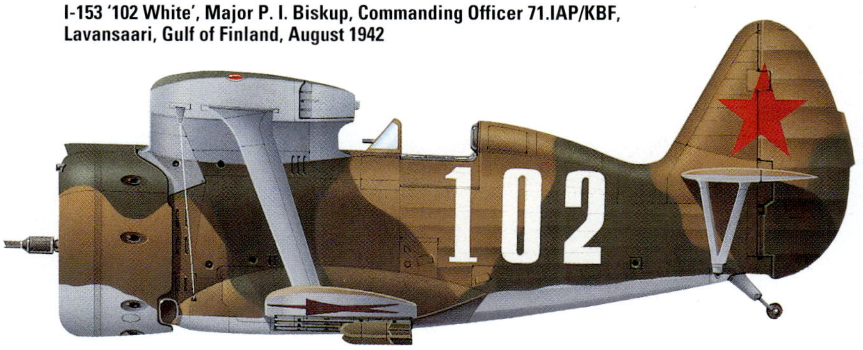

I-153 '24 White', Capt K. V. Solov'yov, 71.IAP/KBF, Lavansaari, Gulf of Finland, August 1942.

I-153 IT-18/'8 Grey', 2nd Lt Olavi Puro, 3/LeLv 6, Römpötti, November 1942

design fault, plans went ahead to build a second prototype. In February 1939 the OKB was transferred to Zavod 1, and it was there that the second prototype was built, but this too crashed as a result of a failure of the engine oil cooler. By this time Polikarpov's star was on the wane and a new generation of fighter designers headed by Yakovlev was exciting attention. After a visit to Germany, Polikarpov returned to find that a second design group, then an OKO (*Opytno-Konstrooktorskiy Otdel*, or experimental design section), with Artyom Ivanovich Mikoyan in charge, had been formed in Zavod 1. Furthermore, it had taken over the development of the I-400 (the future MiG-1), a design initiated by Polikarpov. Unable to reclaim his progeny and having lost 80 of his design staff to the new team, during July 1940 Polikarpov moved a short distance to Zavod 51 as director and chief designer.

Zavod 51 was not the large plant it is today, but rather a hangar which once housed the production workshops of TsAGI's 8th Department. It was located in a fenced-off region within the site of Zavod 1 in Khodynka. The OKB was intensively engaged in drawing up more fighter designs when the imminent arrival of German forces, advancing eastward through the USSR after the invasion of June 1941, required the OKB's evacuation to Novosibirsk. As Zavod 153 was already full, the OKB used the Oblavtotrans repair base at nearby Tolmachovo airfield. Work continued at this site on the I-185 fighter, as well as gliders and other types, and carried on after the return to Zavod 51 in July 1943. Regrettably, the I-185 fighter was rejected but, although ill with cancer, Polikarpov with unflagging enthusiasm worked on many new designs, including one for a projected rocket fighter, the *Malyutka* (baby), until his death on 30 July 1944.

Yefim Gordon and A. Dexter

Polikarpov Biplane Fighter Variants

2I-N1

The designation 2I-N1 was used for Polikarpov's first biplane fighter to be built. It was in October 1924 that design work started on this two-seat escort fighter which was also intended for the reconnaissance mission. Powered by a 450-hp (335.5-kW) Napier Lion W-type engine, the 2I-N1 was a sesquiplane with a semi-monocoque fuselage of oval section designed by Vladimir Denisov and constructed from glued layers of veneered wooden sheets (*shpon*) of 4-mm (0.16-in) thickness in the forward section tapering to 2-mm (0.08-in) thickness at the tail. The wings were covered by a skin of 1.5-mm (0.06-in) plywood and, instead of internal bracing wires, the structure had 3-mm (0.12-in) thick plywood ribs and multiple stringers 10-mm (0.394-in) square. Two spars in the upper wing and a single spar on the shorter lower wing were supported by Kol'chugaluminii (Dural) alloy struts with external steel bracing wires. The landing gear was fixed and a small ski was used as a tailskid. Armament consisted of one 7.62-mm (0.3-in) PV-1 (Pulemyot Vozdushnii, or machine-gun, aerial) fixed forward-firing belt-fed synchronised weapon and one DA ([*poolemyot*] Degtyaryova aviatseeonnii, or Degtyaryov's aviation [machine-gun]) of the same calibre ring-mounted in the rear cockpit for trainable use. The 2I-N1 was not only a handsome machine, but also one which was technically advanced for its time.

On 12 January 1926 the successful first flight took place and the chief designer was in the rear cockpit for the fourth and eighth flights. However, during the ninth flight on 31 March 1926, the skin covering of the right upper wing ripped off at a height of 100 m (330 ft), resulting in the collapse of both wings on the right-hand side and the destruction of the aircraft in the subsequent crash. Tragically, the pilot V. N. Filippov and observer V. V. Mikhaylov were both killed. The crash was attributed to manufacturing defects: large parts of the wings' skins were found to have been badly glued and areas of rib caps and stringers had been assembled with no glue at all. Many panel pins were discovered to be unattached to the structure and bradawl holes which should have been in the skin to equalise internal and external pressures had been omitted. As a result of the crash, subsequent aircraft, including the I-3, U-2, D-2 and R-5, were over-strengthened.

Further work on the 2I-N1 was cancelled, as was a projected single-seat variant, both because of the alleged unavailability of a suitable engine. Only the single 2I-N1 prototype was built.

2I-N1 specification

Span	39 ft 4½ in (12 m)
Length	32 ft (9.75 m)
Wing area	292¼ sq ft (27.15 m^2)
Weight empty	2,542 lb (1153 kg)
Weight loaded	3,748 lb (1700 kg)
Fuel and oil	1,205 lb (547 kg)
Maximum speed	166½ mph (268 km/h)
Time to 1000 m (3,280 ft)	1 min 48 secs
Time to turn	360° in 12 seconds
Service ceiling	23,295 ft (7100 m)
Range	497 miles (800 km)
Landing speed	57 mph (92 km/h)

Above and below: Seen before its short test flight career had started, the Polikarpov 2I-N1 was an extremely clean looking machine for the era. The observer's cockpit had a raised 'lip' onto which a single DA machine-gun could be mounted. The unusual rudder shape is also noteworthy.

I-3

The designation I-3 was given to the next fighter to be designed at GAZ-1 under the supervision of Polikarpov. Work started on this project in mid-1926 with the objective of creating a single-seat sesquiplane, and there was some discussion with Aviatrest on a suitable powerplant. The question as to whether to fit a liquid- or air-cooled engine was debated, but the first choice of a Wright Tornado III radial engine was vetoed by Polikarpov, who argued convincingly that it did not generate sufficient power, and finally the BMW VI Vee engine was accepted. Based on the design of the 2I-N1, the I-3 had an oval-section semi-monocoque fuselage; this time the thickness of the glued veneered sheets was increased to 5 mm (0.2 in) at the front tapering to 3 mm (0.12 in) at the tail. The wings were covered with plywood and fabric, and given the Clark Y aerofoil profile with two box-type plywood spars which had pine stringers and plywood caps; on this occasion internal bracing wires were fitted. All control surfaces consisted of a Dural frame covered by fabric, and of these surfaces all were cable-operated except the elevators, which were operated by pushrods; the tailplane's incidence angle was adjustable in flight. The ailerons were of a differential Frise-type design. The Dural wing struts now had a back-to-front N-shape with a teardrop section and adjustable end-fittings, and steel was used for the bracing wires. With 800 x 150-mm (311/2 x 5.9-in) tyres, the main unit of the fixed tailskid landing gear was pin-jointed and had rubber shock absorbers. The engine's coolant radiator extended below the fuselage immediately behind the rear landing gear struts. Armament comprised two 7.62-mm (0.3-in) Vickers fixed forward-firing synchronised machine-guns for the prototype, replaced by 7.62-mm (0.3-in) PV-1 weapons on subsequent aircraft.

Approval was obtained for the mock-up of the I-3 on 14 May 1927 and the first flight

Above: Constructed before the prototype I-3, this model differs in small details from the production aircraft.

In service some of the I-3s wore unit codes on the tails or other unit markings. These examples display a large white lightning bolt running down the length of the fuselage, while the nearest example wears a segmented red star.

Below: One of the I-3 prototypes is trestled for calibration of its twin machine-guns. The covers for the underside of the engine have also been removed.

Earliest designs

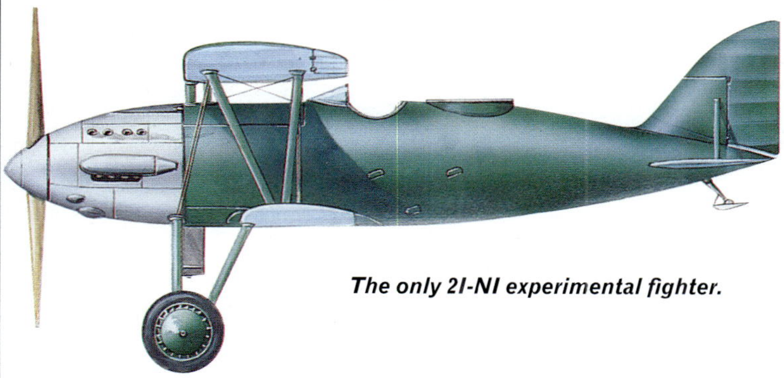

The only 2I-NI experimental fighter.

White '7', a production I-3 fighter.

of the prototype took place on 4 May 1928. The second I-3 prototype, which flew for the first time in August 1928, was experimentally fitted with a propeller specially designed for high speed and this increased the top speed to 283 km/h (176 mph) at the expense of a longer take-off run. Series production of the I-3 began later in 1928 and a total of 389 aircraft, including the above mentioned prototypes, was completed. All series aircraft were built with the Soviet-built 680-hp (507-kW) M-17 engine, a licence-built version of the BMW VI.

The I-3's operational history began in 1929, when the type began to replace the Grigorovich I-2 in service with the fighter units of the Byelorussian Military District.

The following units are known to have received the I-3:

– at Smolensk the 4th and 7th Aviaeskadril'ya, later redesignated as the 106th and 107th Istrebitel'naya eskadril'ya;

– at Bryansk the 13th and 5th Aviaeskadril'ya, later known as the 108th and 7th Istrebitel'naya eskadril'ya and the 9th Aviaeskadril'ya

– at unknown bases were the 17th and 19th Aviaeskadrilii, later called the 116th and 117th Isrebitel'naya eskadril'ya.

Deliveries to squadrons in the Ukraine started in 1930:

– at Kiev the 3rd Aviaeskadril'ya, later redesignated as the 109th Istrebitel'naya eskadril'ya and the 73rd Aviaotryad

– at Bobruisk the 91st Aviaeskadril'ya subsequently renamed 33rd Istrebitel'naya eskadril'ya.

The 1st, 2nd and 3rd Schools of Military Pilots also had some I-3 aircraft on their inventories.

By mid-1931 the total of I-3 fighters in the Soviet air force had reached its maximum of over 300, from which time it gradually decreased until about 1935 when, because its design had sacrificed manoeuvrability for speed, it was retired from front-line fighter units. It was succeeded by the I-5 and later the I-15, both of them newer designs which were better able to incorporate both these qualities.

I-3 production

Date	No. of aircraft built at Zavod 1 imeni Aviakhima
1927	2 prototypes
1928	35
1929	47
1930	250
1931	55
Total:	389

I-3 specification

Span	36 ft 1 in (11.0 m)
Length	26 ft 3⅛ in (8.01 m)
Wing area	299.78 sq ft (27.85 m²)
Weight empty	3,086 lb (1400 kg)
Weight loaded	4,070 lb (1846 kg)
Weight of fuel	462 lb (210 kg)
Weight of oil	73 lb (33 kg)
Maximum speed at sea level	174 mph (279 km/h)
Climb to 1000 m (3,280 ft)	1 minute 48 seconds
Service ceiling	23,620 ft (7200 m)
Range	364 miles (585 km)
Take-off run	241 ft (150 m)
Landing run	401 ft (250 m)
Landing speed	62 mph (100 km/h)

This line-up of Red air force I-3s highlights that the production aircraft had both spoked and disc wheels. The officer standing between the two nearest aircraft (who appears to be smoking a pipe) gives a rough indication of the size of the I-3.

D-2 (DI-2)

The designation D-2 or DI-2 (Dvookhmestnii Istrebitel', or two-seat fighter) was a two-seat version of the I-3 single-seat fighter designed in 1928 and completed in 1929 with a BMW VI engine. Its fuselage had an extra frame in the centre section, a longer wing cellule and an enlarged rudder. Additional armament comprised two 7.62-mm (0.3-in) DA trainable machine-guns on a Scarff ring mounting in the rear cockpit. Test pilot Bukhgolts successfully completed factory trials, but later in 1929 tailplane flutter in a dive caused the tail to break away and the aircraft crashed, killing the pilot, A. V. Chekarev.

Only one prototype was built.

D-2 specification

Span	38 ft 8⅙ in (11.8 m)
Length	26 ft 103/4 in (8.2 m)
Wing area	342.3 sq ft (31.8 m²)
Weight empty	3,433 lb (1557 kg)
Weight loaded	4,678 lb (2122 kg)
Weight of fuel	462 lb (210 kg)
Weight of oil	73 lb (33 kg)
Maximum speed	159 mph (256 km/h)
Climb to 3,280 ft (1000 m)	2 minutes 12 seconds
Service ceiling	20,670 ft (6300 m)
Range	317 miles (510 km)
Time to turn 360°	14 seconds
Take-off run	590 ft (180 m)
Landing run	820 ft (250 m)
Landing speed	62 mph (100 km/h)

I-6[1]

It was clear to Polikarpov that in order to create a fighter with better performance and manoeuvrability than the I-3 any new type must possess a powerful engine and must also be structurally lighter. Only in this way could a fighter be built with the power/weight ratio that would permit it to outclass its foreign rivals. At a sitting of the technical council of the Aviatrest that took place on 10 August 1927, Polikarpov was able to persuade its members to accept his recommendations and, as a result, he was asked in September of that year to start work on the new fighter which ultimately became the I-5. At another council meeting on 21 September A. N. Tupolev, the influential head of AGOS and deputy director of TsAGI, took the decision to pass over Polikarpov and give this task to P. O. Sukhoi whose section, under Tupolev's supervision, had designed the successful I-4 fighter.

After taking part in the 4th International Aviation Exhibition in February 1928, Polikarpov returned home to become chief designer and deputy director of the Zavod 25 factory, which had been specially equipped to build experimental aircraft. His first project there was to design a high-speed fighter developed from the I-3 but fitted with a radial engine.

The I-6 (Izdeliye [product number] 29) was the designation of this fighter which was to be fitted with a 600-hp (448-kW)

One of the two Polikarpov I-6 prototypes was adorned with a long arrow down the centre of the fuselage, and an unidentified emblem on the tail.

Bristol Jupiter radial engine. Polikarpov was determined to build this aircraft with the lowest possible weight and felt that considerable advantages could be secured in this respect by the use of an air-cooled engine which was shorter in length than any liquid-cooled engine of comparable power and required neither coolant nor radiators. Once again the semi-monocoque fuselage was constructed from glued layers of *shpon* but this time 5 mm (0.2 in) thick at the front tapering to 2.5 mm (0.1 in) at the tail. The wing cellule and interplane struts were of a design and structure similar to those on the I-3. The result was the I-6, whose empty weight was only 62 per cent of that of the I-3. The wooden propeller was given a spinner and the Dural-helmeted cowls of the engine's cylinders were left open at the front and top to facilitate cooling.

Polikarpov's arrest and imprisonment in September 1929 inevitably slowed the pace of the project and it was not until 30 March 1930 that the first prototype had its maiden flight. A second prototype followed shortly after this, and both machines were displayed at that year's May Day Parade. It is likely that the two aircraft were first equipped with imported 480-hp (358-kW) Jupiter VI engines, but these were subsequently replaced by the M-22 that was a locally developed and licence-built version. On 13 June 1930 one I-6 crashed after the test pilot bailed out, a measure which, in the opinion of the historian Vadim B. Shavrov, was without justification. The authorities spent the following 12 months comparing the I-6 with the I-5, which Polikarpov was also to end up designing, and the latter was finally chosen for series production. The most likely reasons for this choice were based on the I-5's stronger structure and faster rate of turn. Strange to relate, Polikarpov was not informed of its selection until released from the 'internal prison' in 1933.

Only two prototypes of the I-6 were built.

I-6 specification

Upper-wing span	31 ft 10 in (9.7 m)
Lower-wing span	24 ft 8 in (7.5 m)
Length	22 ft 4¾ in (6.8 m)
Wing area	221.67 sq ft (20.5 m²)
Weight empty	1,914 lb (868 kg)
Weight loaded	2,822 lb(1280 kg)
Maximum speed	174 mph (280 km/h)
Climb to 1000 m (3,280 ft)	1 minute 30 seconds
Service ceiling	24,605 ft (7500 m)
Range	435 miles (700 km)
Time to turn 360°	15 seconds
Take-off run	295 ft (90 m)
Landing run	656 ft (200 m)

I-5

To determine preferences between all-wood and mixed wood/metal construction, it was decided in mid-1928 to build the I-5 with a radial engine and mixed construction for comparison with the all-wood I-6. In addition to speed, the other two major factors for the designers to take into account were, firstly, the need to make the type highly manoeuvrable and, secondly, to ensure that the type would be readily adaptable to mass production methods. Instructions were originally given to have the I-6 prototype ready by 1 August and the I-5 by 1 September 1929, but these deadlines were not met. It is possible that this failure was interpreted by the OGPU as a case of industrial sabotage, rather than one of inefficiency, and this gave the OGPU an excuse to incarcerate Polikarpov.

As mentioned previously, design work on what was to become the I-5 was handed over to P. O. Sukhoi, but the formation of 'internal prison' design teams by the OGPU meant that someone more powerful even than A. N. Tupolev was influencing the choice of chief designer. While it is not known for certain why, the internal prison design bureau (VT), and not the AGOS received the job of designing the I-5. The most plausible explanation for this decision revolves around the influence of the OGPU. An alternative suggestion was that Tupolev preferred to concentrate on the development of heavy bombers and did not press the case for the AGOS to keep the I-5 project. D. P. Grigorovich was initially the chief designer at the VT, but Polikarpov convinced Goriyanov of the OGPU that his fighter concept was superior to that of Grigorovich and, as a result, he was placed in charge of the design team, which in January 1930 had moved to the hangar in Zavod 39 and was now known as the KBVT.

Formerly the ANT-12 of the AGOS, the I-5 was approved in mock-up form on 28 March 1930, and only a month later the first VT-11 prototype was completed and delivered to Moscow Central Airfield, Khodynka, for testing. It was a single-bay sesquiplane powered by an imported 450-hp (335.5-kW) Jupiter VII supercharged engine with a helmeted cowl and a propeller with a diameter of 2.9 m (9 ft 6¼ in). The machine was finished in silver with a red cheat line, and was adorned with a red star on the rudder.
logo inserted in the red star on the rudder.

Internally the fuselage had a gas-welded

***Above:** Ivan U. Pavlov sits in I-5 c/n 890403, carrying the slogan 'Za VKP(b)' ('For the All-Union Communist Party of the Bol'sheviks').*

***Below:** The first prototype of the I-5, the VTA-11. The Cyrillic VT within the red star on the tail stands for Vnootrennyaya Tyur'ma – 'internal prison'.*

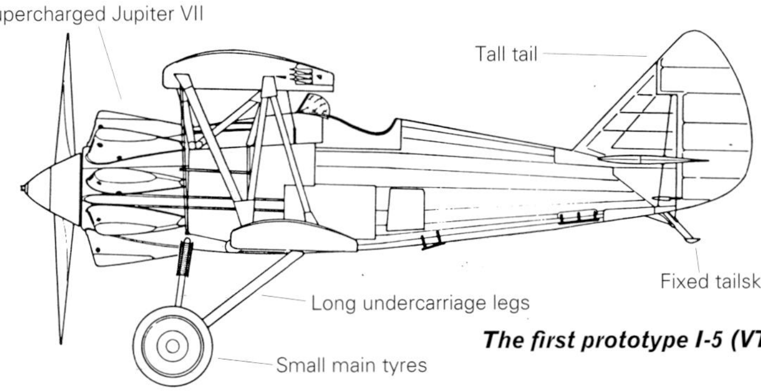

The first prototype I-5 (VT-11).

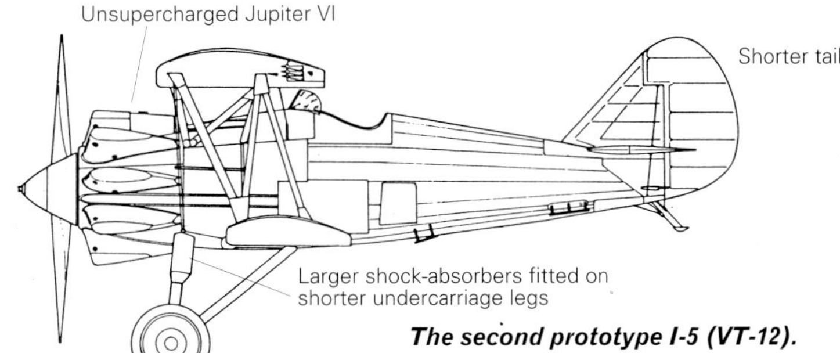

The second prototype I-5 (VT-12).

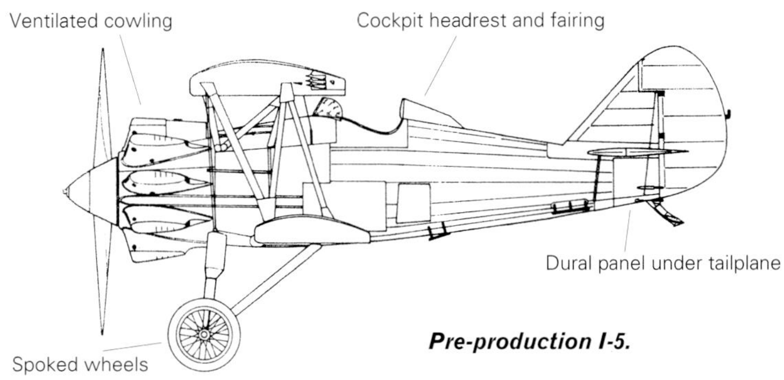

Pre-production I-5.

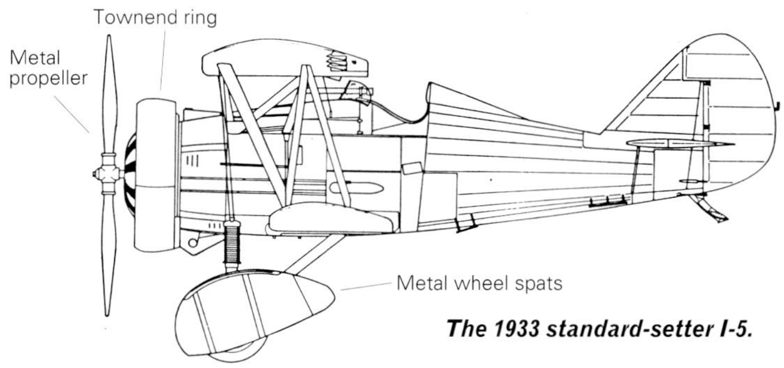

The 1933 standard-setter I-5.

***Below left:** Powered by an M-22, this I-5 displays a non-standard two-tone red star insignia.*

***Below:** This I-5 (wearing a large '2' on the tail) was involved in the RS-82 unguided rocket firing trials undertaken at the NIPAV KA (Artillery Weapons Research and Test Range of the Red Army).*

Polikarpov I-5s

The second prototype I-5 (VT-12), **Klim Voroshilov.**

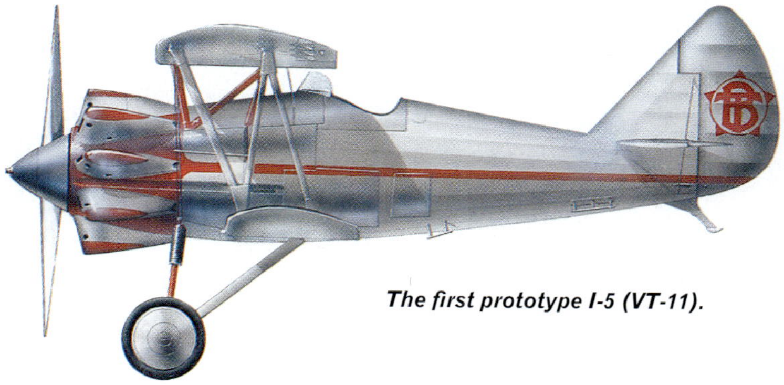

The first prototype I-5 (VT-11).

A late-production I-5 fitted with a Townend ring.

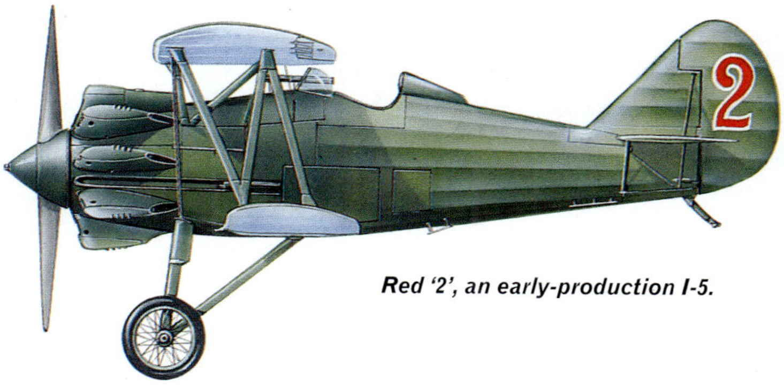

Red '2', an early-production I-5.

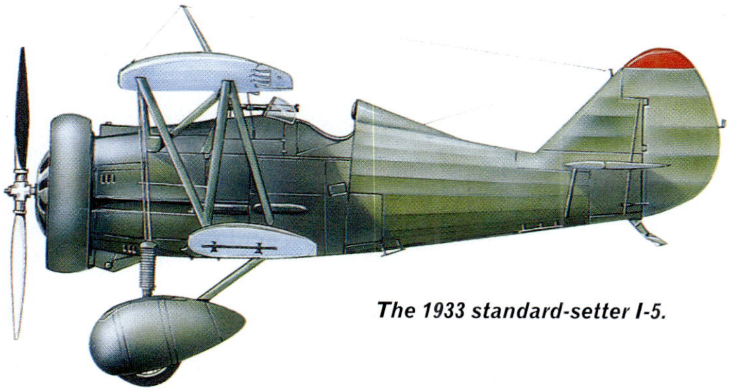

The 1933 standard-setter I-5.

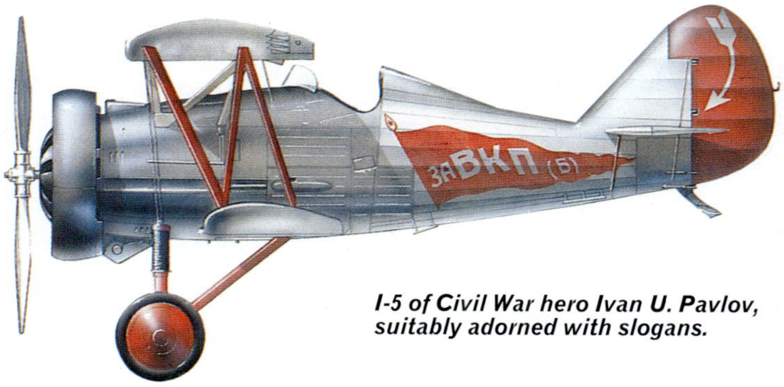

I-5 of Civil War hero Ivan U. Pavlov, suitably adorned with slogans.

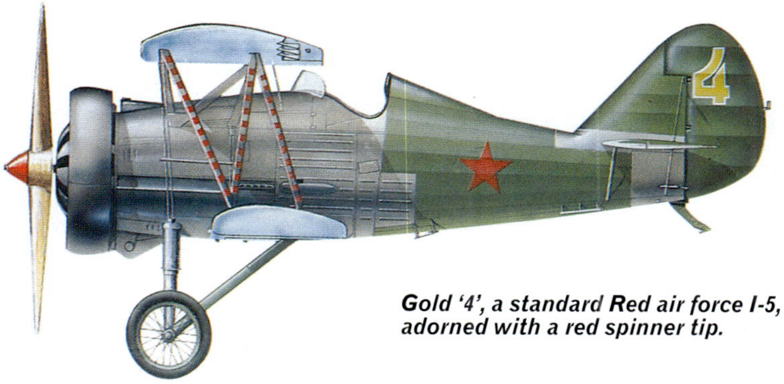

Gold '4', a standard Red air force I-5, adorned with a red spinner tip.

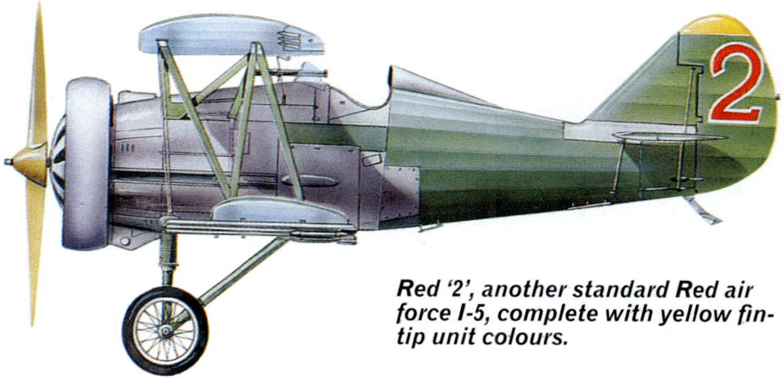

Red '2', another standard Red air force I-5, complete with yellow fin-tip unit colours.

I-5 SSSR-S2570 of Osoaviakhim, the parent society of Soviet aero clubs in the 1930s.

SSSR-S2590 was another I-5 used by Osoaviakhim in the 1930s.

Polikarpov Biplane Fighters

A pre-production I-5 hangs in the final assembly shop. The 'trench' for the PV-1 machine-guns and the break from Dural to fabric covering on the fuselage is prominent.

The 1933* etalon *(standard-setter) I-5, fitted with a Townend ring, metal wheel spats and a whip radio antenna, is seen during trials at the NII VVS.

tubular steel structure and internal bracing wires, and was based on four longerons with stringers to give the fuselage covering a streamlined shape. Light Dural panels, about 0.6-mm (0.02-in) thick, covered the fuselage from the nose as far back as the rear of the cockpit. The aft fuselage was covered with fabric, although from the second prototype all the aircraft had Dural panels below the tailplane to allow easy access to the tailskid's shock absorber. All panels were made detachable by affixing them to the frame with spring-loaded fasteners and steel pins. Lacing secured the fabric skin and seams were covered by mitkal' strips. Behind the engine, a fireproof bulkhead protected the 165-litre (36.3-Imp gal) fuel tank. A fire extinguisher was installed with outlets to the petrol pump, inlet pipe and carburettor, and a corrugated Dural frame supported the pilot's seat with his parachute acting as a cushion. The windscreen was of thick celluloid.

Both the upper and lower wings were constructed with two wooden spars, the upper wing comprising a centre section and two outer panels while the lower wing comprised two panels attached directly to the lower longeron on each side of the fuselage. The Dural interplane struts and steel bracing wires were similar to those of the I-6, the struts having the now-familiar 'reversed N' shape. There were 20 ribs in the upper wing and 15 in the lower wing, and the ribs were of wood. Ailerons were fitted only to the upper wing, each one attached by a set of three bracketed hinges. As on the fuselage, laced lacquered fabric with the seams protected by mitkal' strips covered the empennage and all of the wings except for the lower wing's roots, which were covered with plywood. The leading edges of the upper and lower wing were sheathed in Dural to points 150 mm (5.9 in) back from the leading edge. To provide the pilot with a better field of vision, the centre section of the upper wing was inversely tapered in thickness and chord (less severely on the leading edge than the trailing edge) so that the section immediately ahead of the pilot was thin and cut-away on its leading and trailing edges.

The tail surfaces had Dural frames and were covered in lacquered fabric, and where the tail unit's surfaces were attached to the fuselage the joints were covered by Dural fairings. The vertical tail surface was offset 3.5 mm (0.14 in) to port to compensate for the engine's torque.

Aircraft from the earlier batches had fixed tailskids, but later aircraft had smaller skids synchronised to move with the rudder. The compression shock absorbers of the main landing gear arrangement were constructed of 16 pieces of rubber each 20-mm (0.79-in) thick and, in some cases, covered by fairings. All the prototypes (and also the aircraft involved in the 'Zveno' parasite aircraft experiments) had longer mainwheel legs and smaller-diameter but wider 750 x 125-mm (29.5 x 4.9-in) tyres compared with the 760 x 100-mm (29.9 x 3.9-in) tyres of the standard model.

The gun armament initially comprised two 7.62-mm (0.3-in) PV-1 machine-guns with 1,200 rounds of ammunition and a PUL-9 synchronising mechanism, although it was hoped to change this arrangement on series-produced aircraft to four guns, two on each side of the fuselage, with a total of 2,400 rounds of ammunition. Aiming was undertaken with the aid of an OP telescopic sight. Unfortunately, the weight of production aircraft was greater than expected, and very few of these machines received four rather than two machine-guns.

A second prototype, known as VT-12, was built with a Jupiter VI unsupercharged engine, larger rubber shock absorbers on the main landing gear legs and a shorter vertical tail surface with a more rounded top. The machine was doped green with the dedication 'Klim Voroshilov' emblazoned in large white letters on the sides of the fuselage.

Each of these prototypes had a large spinner and the head of each engine cylinder was fully covered by a helmet cowling, but the third prototype, aircraft VT-13 that first flew on 1 July 1930, had no spinner but was fitted with a NACA cowling that fully covered the heads of the Soviet-manufactured 600-hp (448-kW) M-15 engine's cylinders. Radiator slats gave improved cooling and the rear fuselage from behind the cockpit was built up to enhance the aerodynamics and give the pilot better protection. This third prototype was doped silver with a red rudder and was given a large red pennant bearing the dedication 'Podarok XVI Partsyezdu' (A gift to the 16th Congress of the Communist Party).

Between 13 July and 13 August 1931 the second prototype successfully underwent its state acceptance tests, and on 13 September 1931 was formally ordered into production by Zavod 21 at Gor'kii and Zavod 1 at Khodynka, Moscow. Preparations for production, such as the ordering of machine tools and components, were already well in hand, but it was some time from the start of manufacture before an acceptable standard of finished product was achieved. The first production aircraft were used for in-service evaluation by the VVS (Voyenno-Vozdooshnyye Seely, or air force), and by 1 October 1931 some 54 I-5 fighters had been delivered. Zavod 21 had not been open for very long, and its inexperience presented many problems and, in particular, its inability to make a standard product meant that its I-5 fighters possessed performance lower than those of the prototypes. This shortcoming was a direct consequence of the factory's inability to maintain a consistently low airframe weight. All Zavod 21's production aircraft were built with the 480-hp (358-kW) M-22 engine and a Townend ring, but some imported Jupiter VI engines were installed on early models from Zavod 1 before it switched to the locally manufactured M-22.

Although it was intended to build the I-5 at Zavod 135 at Khar'kov, this time with the M-15 engine, none was built at this facility. No reason was ever given, but speculation connects it with the decision of the VVS not to use the unreliable M-15.

Meanwhile Zavod 39, having absorbed Zavod 25 in August 1930, had assembled about 10 pre-production examples of the I-5 between August and October, and was striving to improve the design with, for example, the following alterations: cooling holes in the crankcase fairing; a stronger tailskid; a pitot tube and static vent on the starboard upper wing; a head rest and fairing for the pilot; strengthening of the landing gear; and a Dural propeller with blades whose angle of incidence could be altered on the ground. Some aircraft were also fitted with wheel spats. All the pre-production aircraft had the Jupiter VI engine. The overall effect of these modifications was to increase the maximum speed over that of the second prototype at sea level by 17.5 km/h (11 mph), but this advantage deteriorated with altitude until at 5000 m (16,405 ft) the Zavod 39 type was slightly slower. It was unfortunate that the improvements had increased the total weight, resulting in a degradation of climb rate and ceiling, but nonetheless the modifications were accepted as the 1933 production standard at Zavod 21.

One fault that was noted in the state acceptance tests was the tendency of the aircraft to execute an uncontrolled 180° turn when landing in negligible wind conditions. Compensation with rudder movement broke the outer wheel on the turn, causing the fighter to tip onto its nose or flip over. Even experienced pilots such as the commander-in-chief of the VVS, Yakov I. Alksnis, experienced this problem. I. F. Petrov, an engineer of the NII VVS (Naoochno-Issledovatel'skiy Institoot Voyenno-Vozdooshnykh Seel, or Air Force Research Institute), suggested shortening the landing gear by 15 cm (5.9 in) and positioning it 12 cm (4.7 in) farther forward. This was tried and found to be effective, as Alksnis himself confirmed. All existing and future production aircraft given this revised main landing gear arrangement, and Petrov was awarded the Order of the Red Star for his ingenuity.

Above: The second I-5 (the VT-12) was named* Klim Voroshilov *in honour of the Red air force Commander-in-Chief and was doped green overall.

Left: At least one pre-production I-5 tested the carriage of 250-kg/551-lb bombs on underwing stations.

This is a late production I-5 powered by an M-25 engine, covered by a Townend ring and fitted with a metal propeller with ground-adjustable pitch. Like most I-5s, this aircraft has no spinner. The raised headrest is also visible.

In the expectation of improving manoeuvrability, a small number of aircraft had experimental streamlined leading wing struts which swivelled about their vertical axis in conjunction with rudder movement. This was not a success.

To reduce the number of accidents that had resulted from pilots being unable to control their aircraft after they had entered a spin, a spin test programme was carried out at the NII VVS. Test pilots Pyotr M. Stefanovskii, A. I. Filin and P. M. Stepanchonok were employed, and it was during this programme that Stepanchonok was forced to bail out when he lost control in an inverted spin. It was as a direct consequence of the bravery and skill of these and other tests pilots that a set of safe spin recovery procedures was finalised and issued. An interesting sequel was the formation of the first Soviet aerobatic demonstration team under the leadership of Stepanchonok.

Comparisons drawn up by the VVS of the I-5 and contemporary foreign fighters showed the Soviet fighter to be lighter than the Bristol Bulldog, Curtiss P-6E and Heinkel HD 37, and also superior to the foreign types in its rate of climb and manoeuvrability, but on the other side of the coin the Soviet fighter had a lower maximum speed. Its performance in simulated dogfights with available foreign fighters at the NII VVS convinced the Soviet authorities of the superiority of the I-5. The I-5 stayed in VVS service until 1942, although long before the spread of World War II (1939-45) to the USSR in June 1941 the type had been relegated to the role of advanced trainer.

The I-5's operational history with the VVS opened when new aircraft were delivered in late 1931. By the end of 1933 there were more I-5 fighters in service than any other fighter, and the type represented 40 per cent of the VVS fighter force. At first the I-5 fighters were concentrated in the Leningrad and Trans-Baikal Military Districts, but quickly spread to Byelorus, Moscow and other areas. During 1932, after reporting that his air defences were weak, the commander of the Moscow PVO (Protivovozdooshnaya Oborona, or anti-aircraft defence), N. V. Schcheglov, was given reinforcements of two fighter squadrons as well as two anti-aircraft and one searchlight regiments. Further strengthening occurred in 1933 when the 10th Istrebitel'nya Aviabrigahda (fighter air brigade) based at Lyubertsy and Ivanovo began to re-equip with the I-5. By the end of 1934 most of the I-3 and I-4 fighters in the VVS had been replaced by I-5 fighters, and deliveries of the I-5 had also begun to units of the VMF (Voyenno-Morskoy Flot, or navy).

Several new and innovative types of weapons were evaluated on the I-5. Small 8-kg (17.6-lb) anti-aircraft bombs were dropped on a towed target drogue by an I-5 of the 5th Aviabrigahda at Kiev during the summer of 1934. A primitive rocket missile known as the 'Flute' was carried in clusters of five under each lower wing of an I-5 and test fired. Another interesting experiment was the ground testing of RS-82 rockets fired from a triple underwing launcher attached to both inner and outer panels of the lower wings with the aircraft securely attached to a firm base. In this way the accuracy of the rocket could be accurately assessed. Later, six rockets were fired at both aerial and ground targets from each of two airborne I-5 fighters. Altogether 692 RS-82 rockets were expended in these trials and the weapon was used successfully in World War II.

During the 1930s the rate of aircraft development accelerated and this was brought home to the Soviets during a visit by Pierre Cotte, the French minister of aviation, in the summer of 1934. After his arrival at Kiev in a Caudron C.635 Simoun four-seat monoplane he was given an honorary escort of I-5 fighters for the next stage: the escorts could not keep up with their guest and had to turn back.

As a result of Japanese aggression in Mongolia during 1937, the 21st Squadron, with both interceptor and ground-attack flights, was deployed to Tamar-Bulak for border patrols. This did not deter the Japanese, however, for they had a strong force of Kawasaki Ki-10 (otherwise Army Type 92) biplanes and Nakajima NC (otherwise Army Type 91) parasol monoplane fighters at their disposal. There appears to be no evidence of confrontation between these Soviet and Japanese warplanes, which is just as well as the Japanese biplane was more manoeuvrable than the I-5 and the Japanese monoplane was faster.

Vladimir S. Vakhmistrov employed the I-5 for his 'Zveno' (in this case, flight, as a tactical unit) experiments which started in 1933. To protect long-range bombers from enemy fighters an I-4, later replaced by an I-5, was carried under each wing of a Tupolev TB-1 twin-engined bomber piloted by P. M. Stefanovskii. Flying the parasite fighters were I. F. Grozd and V. K. Kokkinaki. Further trials were conducted with Zveno 2, using the four-engined TB-3 with two I-5 fighters on top of the wing and a third on the fuselage. A display took place over Monino in November 1935 involving six aircraft: a TB-3 with two I-5 biplane fighters on the wing, two Polikarpov I-16 monoplane fighters under the wing and a Grigorovich I-Z monoplane fighter which flew onto an under-fuselage trapeze. All five fighters were safely released. While this concept was basically flawed in that the extra drag of the 'parasites' reduced the speed of the escorted bomber force to an unacceptable level, it did not stop the formation of a combat unit known as 'Zveno SPB', in which a TB-3 carried two SPB dive-bombers (I-16 fighters fitted with bombs). The concept's moment of glory came on 25 August 1941 with the destruction of a railway bridge over the Danube river at Chernovod in Romania, and a number of other operations were also completed from bases in the Crimea.

A fighter-bomber version of the I-5 was developed at the OKB of Pyotr Ignatyevich Grokhovski. Beam-type bomb carriers were designed for installation under the lower wing to carry two 250-kg (551-lb) bombs. One of the tests involved the aircraft diving down close to the target – the first time dive-bombing had been tried in the USSR. Unfortunately, the extra weight and drag of the bombs adversely affected performance to the extent that the fighter-bomber concept was rejected at the time, although it was resurrected during World War II.

As new and more potent fighters entered service with the VVS, the I-5 was increasingly used as a fighter transition trainer. Pupils started on the Polikarpov U-2, moved on to the Yakovlev UT-2 and completed a stint on the I-5 before graduating to the I-15 or I-16. The Air Force Academy named after Nikolai Ye. Zhukovskii received eight I-5 aircraft in 1933 but more were transferred to other flying schools in large numbers starting at Borisoglebsk and Kacha in 1936. By the end of 1937 all I-5 aircraft had been phased out of service with front-line units.

Enormous losses of aircraft in the opening attacks of the German invasion of the USSR and the subsequent disruption of aircraft production finally led to use of this obsolete fighter as a ground-attack aircraft and night bomber. This would be the first time the type had been used in action. Many of the surviving I-5 warplanes were given an additional two machine-guns during the war as an alternative to carrying bombs. Possibly the most desperate time for the USSR was at the end of 1941 and the beginning of 1942, when the shortage of aircraft was so acute that almost anything that could fly was pressed into service, and there are records of the 605th and 606th IAP (Istrebitel'nyye Aviatseeonnyye Polki, or fighter aviation regiments) using the I-5 on night bomber operations in the Battle of Moscow. Based at Bykovo, Pushkin and Klin, the type continued in this role until replaced by more modern aircraft in February 1942. In September 1941 the 2nd ShAP (Shtoormovoy Aviatseeonnii Polk, or attack aviation regiment) was formed from reserve air force personnel of the Crimean Front and equipped with 32 I-5 warplanes for service in the ground-attack role. These aircraft were taken from flying schools and returned to an airworthy condition by the regiment for use in the Crimea until January 1942, when the regiment was withdrawn to Chapayevsk for conversion to the Il'yushin Il-2 and redesignated as the 766th ShAP.

The pre-production I-5s (seen here at the NII VVS – Air Force Research Institute) differed from the prototypes in subtle ways, including the cowling and the adoption of the headrest first tested on the modified VT-12.

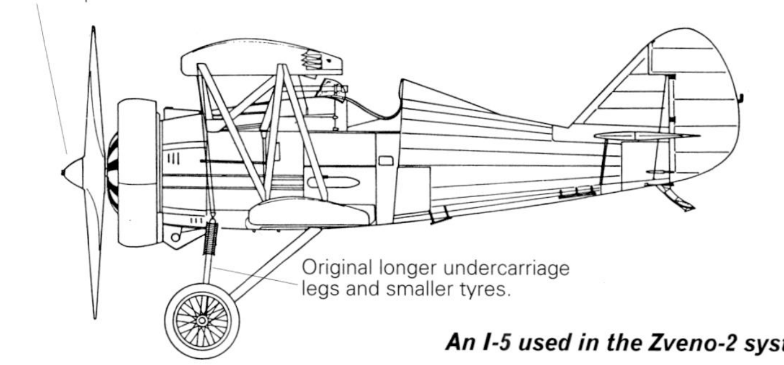

An I-5 used in the Zveno-2 system.

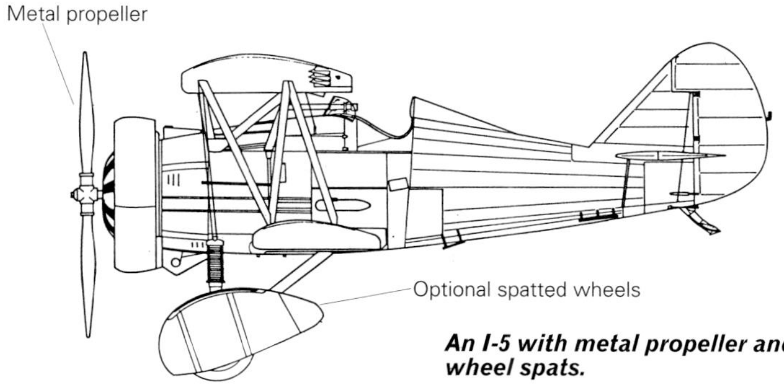

An I-5 with metal propeller and wheel spats.

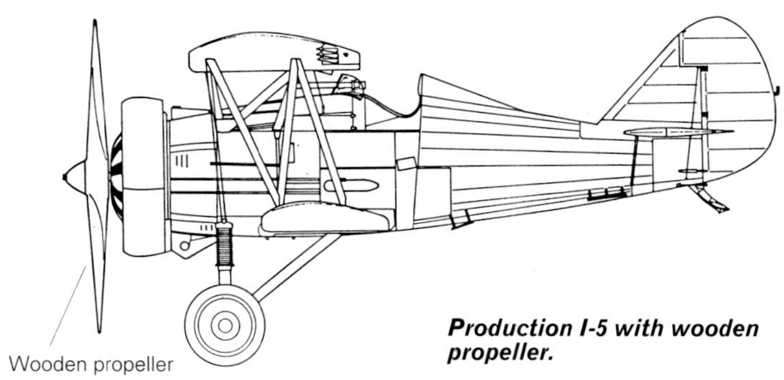

Production I-5 with wooden propeller.

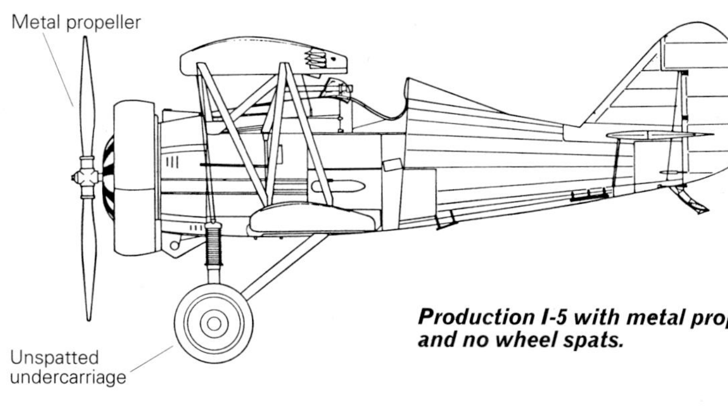

Production I-5 with metal propeller and no wheel spats.

I-5 '6' white, an aircraft built at the Gor'kiy factory in 1932, is typical of the appearance of the majority of production I-5s.

The Black Sea Fleet Air Force used refurbished I-5 fighters, and in November 1941 this type represented half the formation's entire fighter inventory, which in total was only 44 machines. One regiment was the 11th ShAP commanded by Major I. M. Rassoodkov, which covered the Red Army's retreat to Sevastopol'. Captain N. T. Khrustalev led 20 I-5 warplanes in ground attacks against enemy troops and armour in the Bel'bek valley and deliberately dived his blazing aircraft onto them when it was certain that he could not avoid crashing.

Regrettably no I-5 fighters are still in existence, but a three-quarter scale replica was built by NPP (Scientific and Production Enterprise) 'Antares' at Ivanovo in the late 1980s. It was first shown in the static line at the Khodynka air fest in August 1989, subsequently appearing in the static park at the Kubinka air base open doors day (11 April 1992) and the 1993 Moscow Air Show. The replica was powered by a 36-hp (26.8-kW) flat-twin engine from a Dnepr MT10-36 motorcycle and was accurately painted to represent the aircraft (c/n 890403) of Ivan U. Pavlov, a Soviet hero of the civil war. Specifications quoted by the manufacturer are as follows: span 7.4 m (24 ft 3½ in), length 4.7 m (15 ft 5 in), take-off weight 296 kg (652.5 lb), maximum speed 115 km/h (71 mph) and endurance 1 hour. The aircraft is stressed for +3.5/-1.5 *g* and is fully aerobatic.

I-5 specification

(Figures given below are for a series production I-5)

Span (upper wing)	33 ft 7⅛ in (10.24 m)
Span (lower wing)	24 ft 3½ in (7.4 m)
Length	22 ft 3 in (6.78 m)
Wing area	229.28 sq ft (21.3 m^2)
Aerofoil section	Gottingen-436
Weight empty	2,079 lb (934 kg)
Weight loaded	2,987 lb (1355 kg)
Weight of fuel	397 lb (180 kg)
Max. speed at sea level	173 mph (278 km/h)
Climb to 3,280 ft (1000 m)	1 min 48 sec
Service ceiling	24,605 ft (7500 m)
Range	410 miles (660 km)
Time to turn 360°	11 sec
Take-off run	328 ft (100 m)
Landing run	656 ft (200 m)
Landing speed	59 mph (95 km/h)

I-5 production

Date	No. of aircraft built at: Zavod 1 imeni Aviakhima	Zavod 21 imeni Ordzhonikidze
1931	66	–
1932	76	10
1933	–	321
1934	–	661
Totals	142	661

To these must be added the three prototypes and 'about' 10 pre-production aircraft built by Zavod 25.

I-5UTI

The I-5UTI (Oochebno-Trenirovochnii Istrebitel', or trainer fighter) two-seat dual-control trainer was manufactured in small numbers at one of the factories producing the I-5 single-seat fighter. It is believed that about 20 such aircraft were built to a standard that differed from that of the I-5 by the rearward movement of the cockpit so that a second cockpit could be placed in front of it.

I-6[(2)]

The second design to carry the I-6 designation was reported to be a modified I-5 with an experimental propeller fabricated from a new material. As the maximum speed was 20 km/h (12 mph) less than the standard model, trials were soon abandoned.

I-15 (TsKB-3)

I-15 (TsKB-3) was the designation of the next series-produced fighter to emerge from Polikarpov's design team. The designation TsKB-3 denotes the third design by the TsKB, and is confusing because at a later date there was another TsKB-3, this time the title referring to a third Central Design Bureau which was at Grivno and dedicated to the design of cartridges!

Officially freed from 'internal prison' as a result of the success of the I-5, but not exonerated, Polikarpov was to take part in the reorganisation of the TsKB which in February 1933 was removed from the control of TsAGI and now reported directly to GUAP. Polikarpov was now given charge of 'Brigahda' No. 2 and was responsible to S. V. Il'yushin for the design of fighters. For some time Polikarpov had been considering a replacement for the I-5 in which his primary aim was to maximise manoeuvrability in line with the VVS's newly formed concept of using a mix of highly manoeuvrable biplane fighters and very fast monoplane fighters. Polikarpov was to design both types.

The TsKB-3 prototype was completed in October 1933. It was finished in bright red, broken only on the rudder by a white circle containing a red star overwritten with the number '39' in black, this providing a reference to Zavod 39, the prototype's factory of origin. An imported Wright R-1820 Cyclone radial engine, rated at 630 hp (470 kW) at sea level increasing to 715 hp (533 kW) at 2000 m (6,506 ft), was installed as the core of the powerplant installation. A single-bay strutted biplane, the TsKB-3 was of mixed wood and metal construction with the upper wing attached to the fuselage in a gull-type arrangement, and it was this feature that gave rise to the type's nickname of 'Chaika' (seagull).

Welded KhMA chrome/molybdenum steel alloy tubes formed the main frame of the fuselage, which was similar in construction to that of the I-5. Again light Dural panels covered the nose as far back as the cockpit, and these were attached to the supporting stringers and bulkheads. Doped linen fabric covered the rear fuselage with double seam lacing and mitkal' strips. The cockpit was fitted with a windscreen but was otherwise open, and the pilot's seat was made of riveted Dural sheets allowing provision for a parachute. The wings were of internally braced two-spar wooden construction with ribs, but structural members were of steel and there was a set of 10 bracing wires. Steel tubes integrated into the fuselage structure inclined upward and outward at 30° to form the 'gull' junction. Large Frise-type ailerons were used, but these lateral-control surfaces were installed only on the upper wing. Apart from their leading edges, which were covered with plywood as far back as the main spar, the wings were covered with fabric. A novel feature was the use of streamlined I-shaped interplane struts.

A vertical tail surface slightly smaller than that of the I-5 was used on the prototype, but was replaced by a much taller unit on all subsequent airframes. The Dural structure of the tail unit, which also included a tailplane braced on each side by a Vee strut, was covered with fabric.

Cantilever struts were utilised for the main units of the fixed tailskid landing gear, and these struts incorporated oleo-pneumatic shock absorbers having a stroke

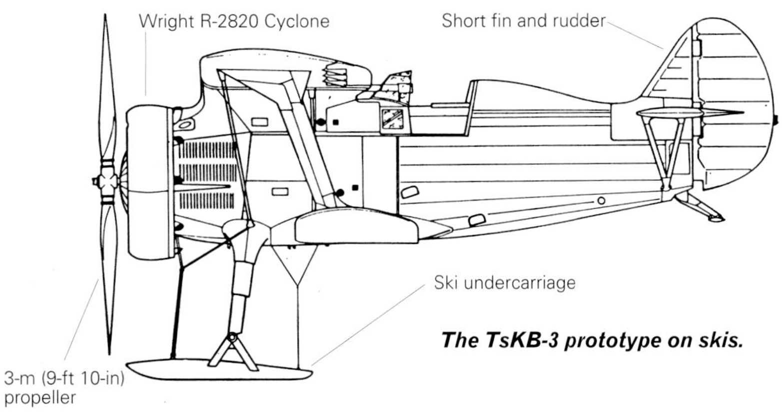

The TsKB-3 prototype on skis.

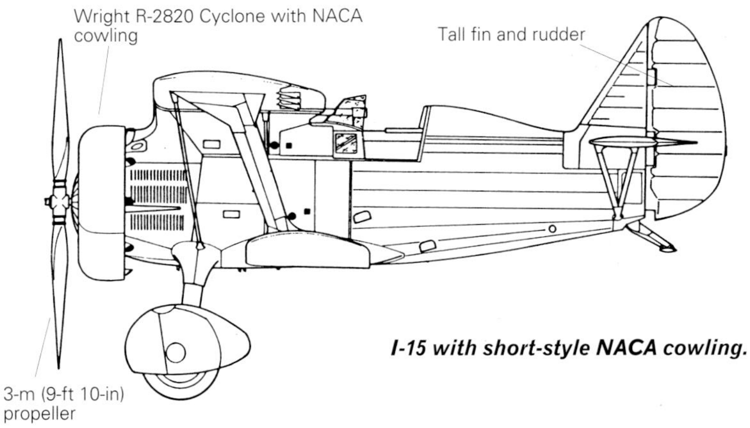

I-15 with short-style NACA cowling.

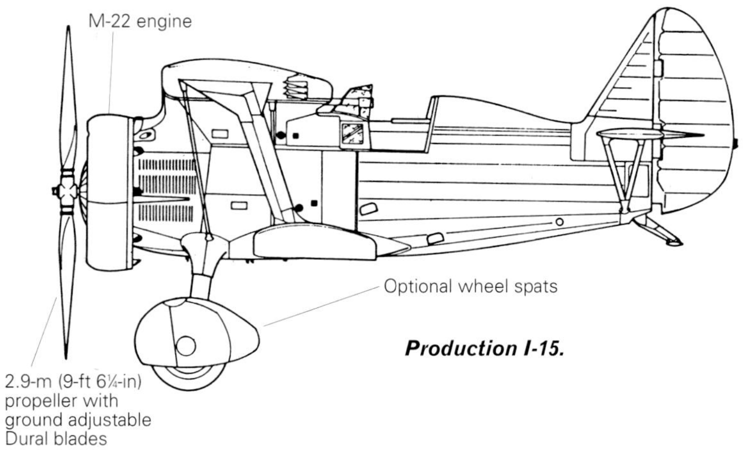

Production I-15.

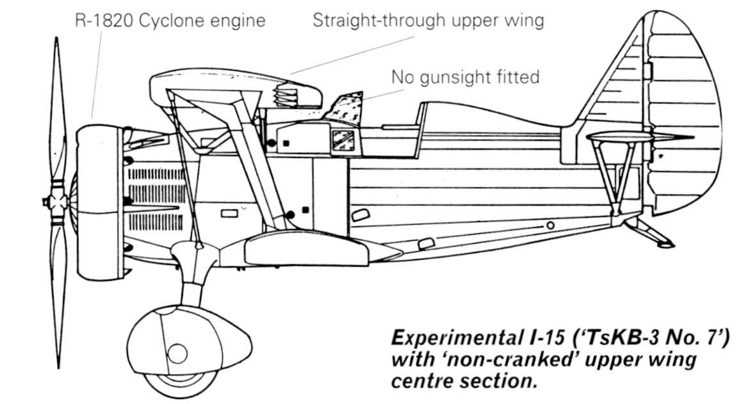

Experimental I-15 ('TsKB-3 No. 7') with 'non-cranked' upper wing centre section.

Polikarpov I-15s

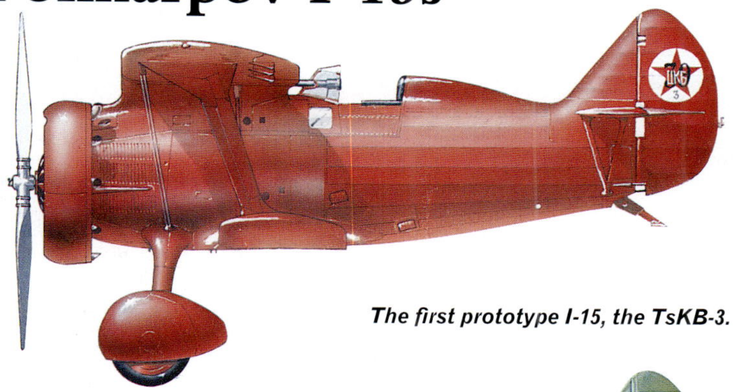

The first prototype I-15, the TsKB-3.

Ivan U. Pavlov's I-15 inherited the scheme and slogans of his I-5.

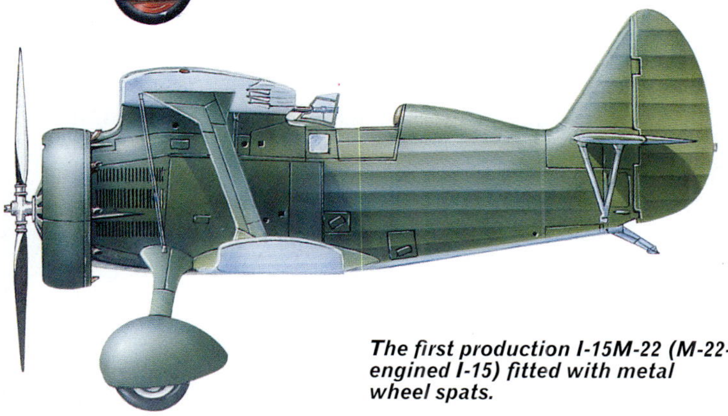

The first production I-15M-22 (M-22-engined I-15) fitted with metal wheel spats.

A production M-22 engined I-15 in a standard overall green camouflage.

of 190 mm (7.5 in). There was no axle connecting the two wheels. To prevent rotation of the oleo-pneumatic system's piston inside the cylinder, a torque link was provided. The wheel track was 1.6 m (5 ft 3 in) and the two main wheels had 760 x 100-mm (29.9 x 3.9-in) tyres. The prototype was built with 1650 x 370-mm (65 x 14.6-in) skis, which were also available for fitting to production aircraft when required. As on later models of the I-5, the tail skid moved in concert with the rudder.

The armament of production aircraft comprised four 7.62-mm (0.3-in) PV-1 synchronised machine-guns with an OP telescopic sight, and 2,600 rounds of ammunition were provided.

Factory evaluation tests and the first flight were carried out by Valerii P. Chkalov, who was very enthusiastic about the new fighter and particularly pleased with its incredible manoeuvrability. A new record was created when a 360° turn was completed in just over 8 seconds. These initial trials were successfully completed in only 26 days, but the prototype was destroyed in a forced landing after the ski landing gear had been damaged in flight. Happily the pilot was unhurt. One problem noted was a measure of directional instability at speeds exceeding 250 km/h (155 mph), but this was improved when a taller and larger vertical tail surface was fitted.

In December 1933 the second prototype was completed and used for the state acceptance trials, which took barely a month. This second machine had a green fuselage with a red '3' on the rudder, pale blue lower wing surfaces and green upper wing surfaces. Wheeled landing gear was fitted this time in place of the skis. Pilots taking part in the tests were V. A. Stepanchonok, Tomas P. Suzi and A. I. Filin, who all lavished praise on the new type's ease of handling, good control response and high climb rate.

Only two months later the Polikarpov TsKB-12 (I-16) monoplane fighter also started its state acceptance trials. This must have bolstered the self-esteem of the chief designer and his team, and in September 1933 it was even further elevated when Polikarpov's brigade was transformed into an OKB. It was not so long ago that many of the personnel had been in prison, and now they had two fighter designs likely to go into service with the Soviet air force.

Before the evaluations had even been completed, preparations had been launched for the mass production of the TsKB-3 at the two Moscow factories, Zavod 1 and Zavod 39. The TsKB-3 was redesignated as the I-15 for service in the VVS, and the first production aircraft from Zavod 1 were tested in November 1934 with those from Zavod 39 following from December of the same year. Once again poor weight control proved a problem, as typified by the fact that Zavod 1's aircraft were 30 kg (66 lb) and Zavod 39's 11 kg (24 lb) heavier than the prototypes. Performance was adversely affected, especially at low level, and the I-15's maximum speed at sea level was significantly lower than those of the prototypes. Other faults noted were an

The four PV-1 machine-guns fitted to later I-15s were located behind two fuselage panels. The tube-like device over the cockpit is the gunsight.

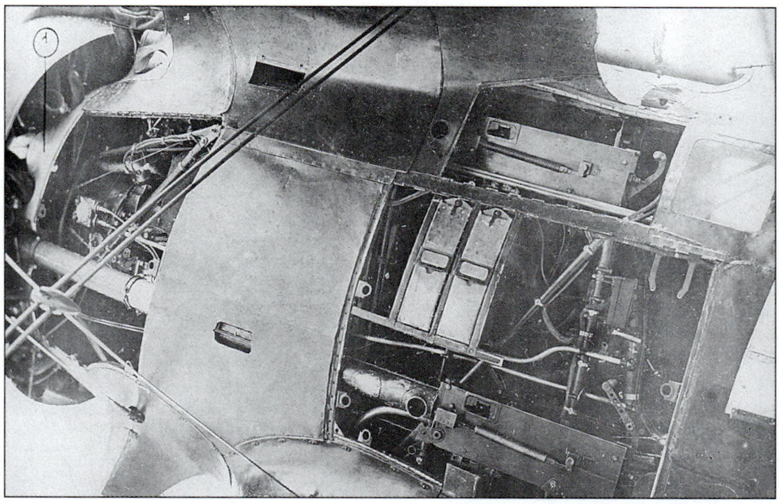

Above: A **Chaika** *with its fabric removed reveals the KhMA skeleton.*

Right: With the aluminium skin panels removed for maintenance, this view shows details of the cockpit construction.

The red-painted ski-equipped TsKB-3 was the prototype of the I-15. Although the production aircraft were built with wheels, the option to fit skis was retained.

unsatisfactory finish, the poor quality of the main landing gear attachments and, most importantly of all, the tendency of the wing skin to rip off during flight.

Production of the M-25 licensed version of the R-1820 Cyclone engine was slow to get under way, so after the prototypes and early production aircraft had been completed with imported SGR-1820-F53 engines, most production aircraft were completed with the M-22 rated at only 480 hp (358 kW), a change which resulted in a drastic degradation of performance. Townend ring cowlings were used, although one of the prototypes had a narrower-chord NACA type of cowling. In place of the prototypes' propeller with a diameter of 3.0 m (9 ft 10 in), production aircraft had a propeller with a diameter of 2.9 m (9 ft 6.25 in) and ground-adjustable Dural blades with three position settings.

The standard armament of two 7.62-mm (0.3-in) PV-1 synchronised machine-guns with 2,000 rounds of ammunition could be increased, when overload was acceptable, by the addition of four 10-kg (22-lb) bombs or chemical weapon containers on D-1 carriers under each half of the lower wing. At some stage, armour was also added to the pilot's seat.

A prototype of the M-25 engine was installed in an I-15 deliberately lightened for an attempt on the world altitude record, currently held by an Italian, Commandante Renato Donati, in a Caproni Ca 113 at a height of 14433 m (47,352 ft) set in April 1934. The M-25 engine used in the Soviet attempt on this record was rated at 635 hp (473 kW) at sea level and 700 hp (522 kW) at 2300 m (7,545 ft). Some instruments, all armament and the Townend ring were removed and a little extra weight was saved by replacing the pilot's seat with a leather sling. The drastic measures obviously paid off because in November 1935, with V. K. Kokkinaki at the controls, the machine reached an altitude of 14577 m (47,825 ft), breaking Donati's record by 144 m (472 ft).

Two more I-15 prototypes, both with Wright R-1820 Cyclone engines, were flight tested in 1937. One, with ski landing gear, was tested with six rocket projectiles mounted under the lower wing. Unfortunately, the extra drag reduced the top speed at 2400 m (7,875 ft) by 15 km/h (9 mph), the service ceiling decreased by 1400 m (4,595 ft) and the climb to 5000 m (16,405 ft) was increased by 2 minutes 48 seconds.

Above: The first production I-15 rests at Schcholkovo (now Chkalovskaya) airfield near Moscow.

Below: This spatted I-15 has had the type's usual Townend ring replaced by a shorter NACA cowling.

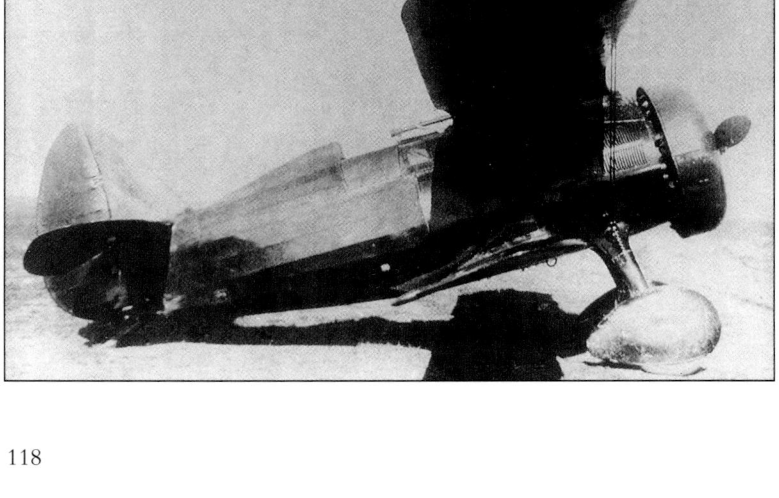

On the second aircraft a high-altitude pressure cabin, type SK-IV designed by A. Ya. Schcherbakov (SK = *strahtokapsoola*, or 'stratocapsule'), was installed in 1938. This cabin weighed 45.6 kg (100.5 lb) and featured rubber seals and circular windows. Test pilot Stepan P. Sooproon reported favourably on the cabin, but again it proved a fruitless project because only three flights were made, the highest being to 9450 m (31,000 ft).

Production continued throughout 1935 but contradictory reports were coming from the VVS. Many operational pilots were enthusiastic about the I-15 but the higher officials wanted production to stop and refused to allow the production rate to increase to its maximum. Among reasons given were the poor view from the cockpit during landing and take-off, and a directional instability so great that it adversely affected accurate firing of the guns. Polikarpov repeatedly tried to demonstrate that this criticism was groundless by conducting wind tunnel tests and demonstration flights, but the latter were inconclusive as a result of the lack of inertia-free flight data recorders at that time. Also, a special study conducted at TsAGI showed that the gull-wing configuration resulted in reduced directional stability as speed increased. With hindsight, it is clear that, rightly or wrongly, the gull-wing arrangement was not acceptable to the decision makers in the VVS, and production of the I-15 stopped at the end of 1935, the last two aircraft reaching completion in 1936. So strong were the feelings of many senior officers and officials that they demanded the withdrawal of the type from VVS service; Polikarpov only managed to avoid this by a personal appeal to Stalin.

A total of 384 I-15s was built in Russia. According to Alfonso Barbeta, a director of CASA, another 287 examples of the I-15 were built under licence by the Republican side during the Spanish Civil War (1936-39). This accords with the Nationalist's claim that 205 engineless airframes were found stored in the Reus factory and Republican records of approximately 80 Spanish-built I-15 fighters being delivered to their squadrons from August 1937. Assembly of the aircraft took place at State Aircraft Factories No. 3 in Reus and SAF No. 16 in Sabadell.

Apart from their 710-hp (530-kW) M-25 engines, the Spanish-built aircraft were intended to be identical to those produced in the USSR, but there were inevitably small differences. For example, there was a slightly different cowling and pilot's door, and the main landing gear units lacked the hooks that had been used to fasten the fairings. There were also reports of some aircraft having flaps fitted on the trailing edges of the lower wing. Whenever they were available, ShKAS machine-guns ([poolemyot] Shpital'novo i Komartnitskovo, aviatseeonnii, skorostrel'nii, or fast-firing aircraft [machine-gun designed by] Shpital'nii and Komartnitskii) with a rate of fire of 1,800 rounds per minute were fitted in place of the PV-1 which could only manage 750 rounds per minute. Soviet-built engines and machine-guns were the only components not manufactured locally.

Spanish-built I-15 fighters serving with the Aviación Militar of the Republican side carried on their fuselage sides black or white identification marks consisting of the letters CA (Construcciones Aeronauticas) followed by a number, while Soviet-built examples carried only a white number. Regardless of origin, the I-15 was known in Spain by the nickname 'Chato' (pugnose).

The operational history of the I-15 in Soviet service was surprisingly brief. Prejudice on the part of members of the VVS high command against the gull-wing layout led to the end of production at the end of 1935 (completed in 1936) after only 384 had been manufactured. Attempts were also made to withdraw the type from VVS service. Although this ploy failed, it comes as no surprise to discover that the I-15 was supplied in significant numbers from VVS stock to the Spanish Republicans and also probably to the Mongolian air force: when obeying a command to give something away, it is only human nature to give away what you do not want.

Those sent to Spain were in answer to a call for assistance from the Republican Popular Front government which was a coalition of socialist and communist parties. On 18 July 1936 the Falangist (fascist) Nationalist rebellion against the Republican government started, and during the course of the three-year civil war that followed Italy and Germany supplied help and arms to the Nationalists, and at the end of August 1936 Stalin agreed to the first delivery of aircraft to the Republicans. On 13 October 1936 the Soviet cargo ship *Starii Bol'shevik* unloaded at Cartegena the crates containing 18 I-15 fighters with M-22 engines. The crates were transported to Los Alcazares, where Soviet engineers quickly assembled the aircraft, together with another seven that had arrived on the *Lava Mendi* three days later. A further six disassembled aircraft were landed on 23 October from the *Georgii Dimitrov*.

These aircraft formed two squadrons (escuadrillas) of 12 aircraft each plus an attrition reserve. Flown at that time mainly by Soviet volunteers, the squadrons were named after their commanders: 'Palancar' was the *nom de guerre* of Major Pavel Rishagov and 'Antonio' the equivalent of Major Sergei Tarkhov. The squadrons were soon put into action in the 1st Battle of Madrid, the 'Palancar' squadron based at El Soto 26 km (16 miles) to the north-east of the capital and the 'Antonio' squadron at Alcala de Henares 29 km (19 miles) to the east. A number of Spanish pilots arrived to serve with the squadrons in November, and it was they who affectionately named the I-15 'Chato'. By March 1937 the 'Chato' pilots numbered six Americans, one Guatemalan and several Frenchmen. More Spaniards were training in the USSR but these did not complete their course until July 1937, after which appreciable numbers started to return to the fight.

A 'Basque' squadron was formed when 15 'Chato' fighters, also with M-22 engines, were unloaded at Bilbao on 15 November from the *Andrei*. Commanded by 'Boris' (Major Maranchov), this unit were based at La Albericia. A second batch of 15 or 16 'Chato' fighters was unloaded at Santander on 2 January 1937.

The 'Chato' fighters had achieved their first success on 4 November 1936, when one Junkers Ju 52/3m bomber/transport of Kampfstaffel Moreau and two Fiat CR.32 fighters were shot down by I-15 warplanes over Humanes; a second Ju 52/3m was so badly damaged that it made a forced landing at Esquivas. On the same day, 11 I-15 fighters led by 'Palancar' attacked nine Heinkel He 51 biplane fighters near Madrid and shot down four of them. In neither of these engagements did any of the 'Chato'

'Chatos' at war

Republican air force CA-006 was flown by Juan Comas, of the 3rd Escuadrilla de Chatos from Manises air base. It was the sixth Spanish-built I-15.

'Chato' '8-100' is believed to have been flown by the Nationalist's Staff Group at Getafe air base between 1940 and 1947.

fighters suffer anything but slight damage, although two landed behind Nationalist lines after running out of fuel and were captured.

An even greater achievement was recorded when half of the 'Palancar' squadron deployed to Aragon in late November. Under the leadership of Ivan Kopets, it destroyed the Nationalist side's first all-Spanish escuadrilla, which consisted of six He 51 fighters. One was shot down and four destroyed later when caught unawares on Caude airfield, while the sixth machine was written off in an accident. Led by 'Casimiro' (Anton Kovalevskii), the other half of the squadron had moved to Tabernas, near Malaga, in an attempt to stem the Nationalist drive up the coast.

For the rest of 1936 the other 'Chato' fighters defended Madrid with such success that the Nationalists abandoned daytime bombing of the city and resorted to night attacks. Historians attribute the Nationalists' failure to capture the Spanish capital in this offensive largely to the boost given to the morale of the defenders by the arrival and effectiveness of the Soviet fighters. A heavy price was paid by the two 'Chato' squadrons, however: nine aircraft were lost in battle and, tragically, Major Tarkhov was killed by Republicans who mistook him for a German after he had parachuted from his stricken aircraft.

Squadron commanders were frequently changed. In addition to the replacement of Tarkhov by 'Kozakov' (Major Aleksandr Osadchii), 'Palancar' was supplanted in December by 'José' (Major Ivan Kopets) who, when promoted in January 1937, was succeeded by Andres Garcia Lacalle.

On 8 March 1937 the Battle of Guadalajara began and an Italian motorised column attempting to encircle Madrid from the north-east was constantly attacked by Republican aircraft of which a significant number were 'Chato' fighters operating in the ground-attack role. The encirclement was averted and the Republican army gained a decisive victory, turning the retreat of the Italians into a rout.

When the Nationalists failed to capture Madrid they turned their attention to eliminating the Basque enclave in the north, beginning their offensive on 31 March 1937. In May, 15 'Chato' fighters of the 'Lacalle' squadron, with Spanish pilots, made several attempts to reinforce their beleaguered colleagues but, through a combination of bad weather and worse luck, only eight of the aircraft managed to reach their goal.

A delivery of 31 I-15 aircraft with M-25 or Cyclone engines from the *Aldecoa* on 14 February enabled the Republicans, in spite of large losses, to rebuild their stock to 30 machines by the end of March 1937. This number of airworthy aircraft was more or less maintained until the end of the year, after which it started to fall as a consequence of attrition from intensive ground-attack operations and a shortage of spare parts. Deliveries of the I-15 from the USSR continued until the end of July 1937, by which time two more consignments had docked. At least one, but probably both consignments, were of the 'Chato' version with the Cyclone or M-25 engine.

Aircraft were despatched from the USSR in batches of 31, which was the size of a VVS fighter Aviaeskadril'ya (air squadron); the regimental (polk) system was not introduced into the VVS until April 1939. There is some dispute among aircraft historians as to the number of I-15 fighters that arrived in Spain. One holds that there were five complete batches each of 31 making a total of 155, while another avers that one of the batches was incomplete and only 153 actually arrived, and yet a third maintains that the number was as low as 139. It is doubtful whether these discrepancies will ever be resolved because full records of the deliveries have never been found. For the purpose of this article it is assumed that 155 is the correct number.

As a result of the arrival of more aircraft a small detachment with William Labussière in command was formed at Carmoli in February 1937 for coastal patrol work, but was reabsorbed into the 'Lacalle' squadron in May. In addition, a fourth 'Chato' squadron was created for the Aragon front in April 1937 and based at Algete. It was commanded by Roberto Alfonso Santamaria.

A reorganisation took place in May and the squadrons were both re-formed and given numbered designations: the 1st Escuadrilla de Chatos was formed and commanded by 'Ramon' (Major Eremenko) at Teruel; the 2nd Escuadrilla de Chatos was led by Roberto Alfonso Santamaria and based at Castejon del Puente; and the 3rd Escuadrilla de Chatos with 'Kozakov' (Aleksandr Osadchii) in command was located at Campo Soto. At La Albericia the isolated Basque squadron commanded by Manuel Aguirre remained unnumbered.

At first the Republican 'Chato' squadrons had been part of Grupo de Caza (Fighter Group) 12 commanded by Arkadii Zlatotsvetov. In this unit the I-15 fighters were grouped with all the other Soviet squadrons flying types such as the I-16, Polikarpov R-5 and Tupolev SB. By December 1936 sufficient numbers of aircraft were available for the I-15 and I-16 fighter squadrons to be formed into a separate Grupo de Caza 21. Three months later Grupo de Caza 26 was created for sole control of the 'Chato' squadrons. Ivan Kopets was placed in command of this group, and remained in this capacity until April, when he was replaced by Yevgenii Ptookhin. From mid-October Grupo de Caza 26 was put under Spanish control with Juan Jose Armario as the commander although 'General Douglas' (Brigade Commander Yakov V. Smooshkevich) was in overall command of all Soviet aviation forces in Spain. In July 1937 Anatolii Serov, a flight commander of the 1st Escuadrilla, was provisionally given permission to form a Patrulla de Noche (night-fighter flight) with six I-15 fighters, and success followed when a Ju 52/3m was shot down on 26 July. Although the unit remained in existence till February 1939, scarce resources were being underused and therefore additional daytime ground attacks were introduced. The 'Chato' warplanes used as night-fighters had ring manifolds installed, redirecting the engine's exhaust underneath the fuselage to avoid impairing the pilot's night vision.

Modest supplies of Spanish-built I-15 fighters began to reach the squadrons in August 1937, and in September the 4th Escuadrilla de Chatos under Ladislao Duarte Espes was formed at Sabadell, Barcelona. In March 1938 José Falco Sanmartin attempted to form a 5th Escuadrilla de Chatos at Sabadell but after a few days it was disbanded when it was realised there were not enough aircraft to justify another squadron and still maintain an adequate attrition reserve. Battles continued to rage in the south and the Chatos were prominent in the Battle of Brunete, just to the south-east of Madrid. On one occasion two squadrons, together with three squadrons of I-16 'Mosca' fighters, about 50 warplanes in total, fought a pitched battle with 60 CR.32 and 12 He 51 fighters: for the loss of two 'Mosca' and three 'Chato' aircraft, the Republican force shot down eight CR.32 and one He 51 warplanes.

By September 1937 the 'Chato' was operating mainly in Aragon and Catalonia, and this situation prevailed until the end of the war. One spectacular success was achieved on 15 October when 15 'Chato' warplanes escorted by 43 'Mosca' fighters made a dawn raid on Garrapinillos airfield, near Zaragoza, and claimed the destruction of 26 Nationalist aircraft, including two Messerschmitt Bf 109 monoplanes that attempted to take-off to intercept them.

When the northern enclave was finally overrun by the Nationalists at the end of October 1937, the remnants of the 2nd Escuadrilla, unable to rejoin their comrades in the south, flew to neutral France.

Mid-December 1937 saw the opening of the Republican attack on Teruel with heavy participation by the four 'Chato' squadrons. The rate of losses was greater that the rate at which replacements were being made available, and by mid-March 1938 there were only 15 I-15 fighters left in flyable condition. Although no more 'Chato' warplanes arrived from the USSR, the Spanish factories at Reus and Sabadell were now supplying increasing numbers of repaired and newly built I-15 fighters, and the number of serviceable 'Chato' aircraft gradually built up to a maximum of 70 in October 1938. This number was unsustainable for very long, however, and losses once again mounted as an increasing number of ground attacks were made in desperate attempts to stop the advancing Nationalists. Republican airfields and aircraft plants were captured, thereby inhibiting

The original TsKB-3 was later fitted with a wheeled undercarriage. The star on the tail contains the figure '39' for Zavod 39, where it was built.

Above right: At least one I-15 was fitted with A. Ya. Schcherbakov's SK-IV 'stratocapsule' and tested at the NII VVS in 1937 (above).

repairs, and by the end of March 1939 the stock of operable aircraft was exhausted.

On 1 February 1939 the Nationalists had captured 18 examples of the I-15 on Vich airfield. Of these, six were airworthy, and by using them and others that had been captured and repaired, a squadron of 'Chato' fighters was formed. Designated at that time Grupo 1-G-8, the new unit was formed from 1-G-2, whose pilots had been flying He 51 fighters. In Nationalist service the 'Chato' was known as the Type 8. No evidence has been found to indicate that there was any confrontation between the 'Chato' aircraft of the Republicans and those of the Nationalists.

Slow-flying bombers, such as the Ju 52/3m, had been easy targets for the 'Chato' pilots, and the He 51 fighter, which was slower, less manoeuvrable and more lightly armed than the I-15, was also not difficult to defeat in air combat. Until the arrival of the Nationalist monoplane fighters, the only type whose capabilities matched the I-15 was the CR.32. This Italian machine was slightly faster on the level but lost out in climb rate and manoeuvrability, but its superior diving speed could often be relied upon to save its skin when confronted with the Chato's four 7.62-mm (0.3-in) machine-guns, which were more effective than the Fiat's twin 12.7-mm (0.5-in) machine-guns, particularly in close combat. The advent of the Bf 109 and the Fiat G.50 monoplanes later highlighted the obsolescence as well as the inadequacies of the I-15, but the monoplanes could be caught out if they ventured too close or their pilots became over-confident. Furthermore, when bombers such as the Heinkel He 111 monoplane arrived, they proved to be faster than the 'Chato', which then came to be used more frequently in the ground-attack role. The 'Chato' was very popular with its pilots, not only on account of its excellent manoeuvrability but also for its stout structure with the ability to absorb a great deal of punishment: aircraft were known to have returned to base with as many as 80 hits. An added bonus was the fighter's reluctance to catch fire, unlike its compatriot, the SB bomber. Another invaluable asset of the 'Chato' was its ability to take off and land in a very short distance, enabling it to use improvised and bomb-damaged airfields from which such types as the I-16 could not operate. Ground crews also appreciated the relative ease with which the type could be patched up and repaired: fuselage panels could be easily removed and the air-cooled radial engine was simpler to maintain than any liquid-cooled Vee engine. One serious design fault was discovered in tragic circumstances: the bomb-release lever was too close to the control lever for the engine cooling vents, and when José Cuatero was taking off for a bombing mission he inadvertently pulled the wrong lever and, in the resulting explosion, killed himself and the pilot of the aircraft in front of him. Both 'Chato' machines were destroyed and a third was damaged.

Misconceptions arose from the western observers' habit of referring to the I-15 as a 'Curtiss' simply because it bore a resemblance to biplane fighters manufactured by that American company. Journalists and experts, who should have known better, too readily assumed that it must be a copy of a Western type. The same mistake was made with reference to Japanese aircraft, and the Allied powers later paid a terrible price in blood for such ignorance. Several I-15 aircraft which had been flown to France and French North Africa at the end of the Spanish Civil War were returned to the new government after the final Nationalist victory. Others had been surrendered to avoid reprisals or were captured, and many were found incomplete at the Reus factory. After the war the Nationalists placed all airworthy 'Chato' warplanes, 44 in all, in the hands of Escuadra num 32, which was based first at Manises near Valencia but later moved to La Rabasa near Alicante. The escuadra was redesignated Regimiento de Asalto num 32 in 1940. After the end of the war, incomplete 'Chato' airframes found at the factory by the Nationalists were made airworthy and formed into Regimiento num 33 at Villanubla near Valladolid. By March 1940 the Ejercito del Aire had 53 'Chato' aircraft in flyable condition and another 72 retained in storage to be cannibalised for spare parts. The type code was changed to A4 in 1945, and the 'Chato' remained in service until the beginning of the 1950s. Its long service was attributable to the Allied embargo on supplies of military equipment to fascist Spain rather than to the excellence of its design.

There are no examples of the I-15 extant, but a replica is on show in the Museo del Aire in Madrid: one side is painted in Republican markings and the other in Nationalist colours.

The figures given below are for a typical Soviet-built series-produced aircraft of 1935 with the M-22 engine, while the data for the I-15 with the R-1820 Cyclone (licence-built as the M-25) engine are shown in parentheses:

I-15 specification

Span (upper wing)	31 ft 11 ⅞ in (9.75 m)
Span (lower wing)	24 ft 7¼ in (7.5 m)
Length	20 ft (6.1 m)
Wing area	253.5 sq ft (23.55 m²)
Aerofoil section	Gottingen-436
Weight (empty)	2,444 lb (2,166 lb)/1106 kg (980 kg)
Weight (loaded)	3,127 lb (3,070 lb)/1415 kg (1389 kg)
Wing loading	60.2 kg/m² (58.8 kg/m²) 12.4 lb/sq ft (12.1 lb/sq ft)
Max. speed at sea level	286 km/h (315 km/h) 178 mph (196 mph)
Max. speed at 9,845 ft (3000 m)	350 km/h (367 km/h) 218 mph (228 mph)
Climb to 5000 m (16,405 ft)	11 min (6 min 18 sec)
Service ceiling	7520 m (9800 m) 24,670 ft (32,150 ft)
Time to turn 360°	8.5 sec (9.0 sec)
Take-off run	230 ft (70 m)
Landing run	230 ft (70 m)

I-15 production

	No. of aircraft built at:-	
Date	**Zavod 1 imeni Aviakhima**	**Zavod 39 imeni Menzhinskovo**
1934	60	34
1935	273	15
1936	2	–
Totals:	335	49

CASA built a further 287 I-15s, for a total of 671.

'TsKB-3 No. 7'

A prototype was manufactured at Zavod 39 and in order to satisfy the customer, the VVS, Polikarpov used an upper wing with the same span as the I-15 but without the gull shape. No service designation has been recorded for this aircraft but it was known under the *'zavodskoye nazvanyie'* (manufacturer's designation) as the TsKB-3 No. 7. The structure was reinforced, four PV-1 machine-guns were fitted, various new pieces of equipment were added and the powerplant was based on the R-1820 Cyclone engine. The weight increased by 100 kg (220 lb) and the wing loading reached 62.6 kg/m² (12.9 lb/sq ft). This had the obvious adverse affect on manoeuvrability, and the time to required complete a 360° circle rose to 10 seconds. Likewise, the climb rate fell from 900 m (2,953 ft) per minute to 720 m (2,362 ft) per minute. This performance was not acceptable and a complete redesign of the fighter was then agreed, leading to the creation of the I-15bis.

RV (TsKB-42) project

RV (*Rekord Vysoty*, or altitude record) or TsKB-42 was the designation of a projected, but ultimately unbuilt record breaker. The plans included modifying the I-15 by installing a completely cowled R-1820-F54 Cyclone engine supercharged for maximum high-altitude capability, adding a cockpit canopy, and extending the span of the wing cellule by adding 2.25 m (7 ft 4½ in) to the upper wing and 2.0 m (6 ft 6¾ in) to the lower wing. No reasons were ever disclosed for the termination of the programme.

Early in 1936 Polikarpov was appointed chief designer of the OKBs at two factories: Zavod 84 in Moscow and Zavod 21 in Gor'kii.

The latter had, at that time, no facilities for the manufacture of prototype aircraft, and it took the whole of 1936 to create them. Nonetheless the replacement for the I-15 was developed.

TsKB-3bis (I-15bis, I-152)

TsKB-3bis was the OKB designation of the new fighter which the VVS called I-15bis or I-152. All these designations indicated a second version of the I-15 (TsKB-3). No details are known of the first flight but the revised type's state acceptance tests started on 2 July 1937.

The primary change was the elimination of the I-15's gull-wing layout but, among the many other changes that were effected at this time, the most important was the overall strengthening of the structure. Other changes included the adoption of the recently developed 750-hp (559-kW) M-25V engine with the much wider NACA cowling and the AV-1 metal propeller with a spinner, the modification of the cowling with adjustable louvres to control the airflow at different temperatures, and the introduction of a new type of exhaust collector ring. The wing span was also increased, and the aerofoil was changed to the Clark 'YH' type. The revised upper wing had its centre section, which was of riveted Dural construction over tubular steel spars, supported by cabane struts of the reversed-N type, but the shapely I-type interplane struts of the I-15 were retained. A radio transceiver could now be fitted when required, and the electrical supply was provided by a dynamo. To meet the new requirements that had been laid down in 1934, many structural items had also had to be strengthened, wheel spats were fitted as standard, the tyres were of the 760 x 120-mm (29.9 x 4/7-in) size, and the pilot was given added protection by the reinforcement of his seat with 9-mm (0.35-in) back armour.

The gun armament was still four 7.62-mm (0.3-in) PV-1 synchronised machine-guns, in this instance with 2,600 rounds of ammunition, and an OP telescopic sight was fitted for the aiming of these weapons, but the underwing bomb racks could now carry up to 150 kg (331 lb). Some aircraft were given the alternative of two 12.7-mm (0.5-in) BS ([poolemyot] Berezina sinkhronnii, or Berezin's synchronised [machine-gun]) weapons.

State acceptance tests at the NII VVS took place between 2 and 29 July 1937, and the results were disappointing. Maximum speed was the same as that of the I-15 with the R-1820 Cyclone engine, but climb rate and manoeuvrability in particular had deteriorated: this was inevitable, for without any increase in installed power the structure weight had been increased by 300 kg (661 lb). A new propeller was fitted but this failed to improve the situation, and the state commission reported regretfully that the I-15bis had failed its state acceptance tests. However, pressure from the VVS high command was sufficiently strong that approval was then given for the start of production pending further development of the basic concept.

Production started at Zavod 1 in mid-1937, but as deliveries did not begin until 1938 it is probable that the first batches were held back pending the incorporation of modifications. Progressive improvements were made after series production of the I-15bis had started: the fuel capacity was increased from 260 to 310 litres (57.2 to 68.2 Imp gal), and provision was made for the carriage of two 80-litre (17.5-Imp gal) external tanks under the lower wing.

During 1939 many new I-15bis prototypes were evaluated. One of these had a new VISh-6A propeller, a windscreen with a flat front panel, stub exhausts replacing the exhaust collector ring, a Townend ring cowling and self-sealing fuel tanks. Its higher service ceiling of 9600 m (31,495 ft) compared with 8980 m (29,460 ft) and other improvements ensured that it passed its state acceptance tests. Neither this nor any other new prototype was used as the pattern for series production aircraft, however, no doubt as a result of the fact that operations in the Spanish Civil War had vindicated Polikarpov's original belief in the

I-15bis markings

The I-15bis TK prototype as operated during the manufacturer's flight tests.

Spinner-less white '56' wears a typical camouflage scheme as applied to Soviet I-15bis aircraft during the late 1930/early 1940s.

An I-15bis of the Finnish air force, in an unusal black upper scheme with light blue undersurfaces.

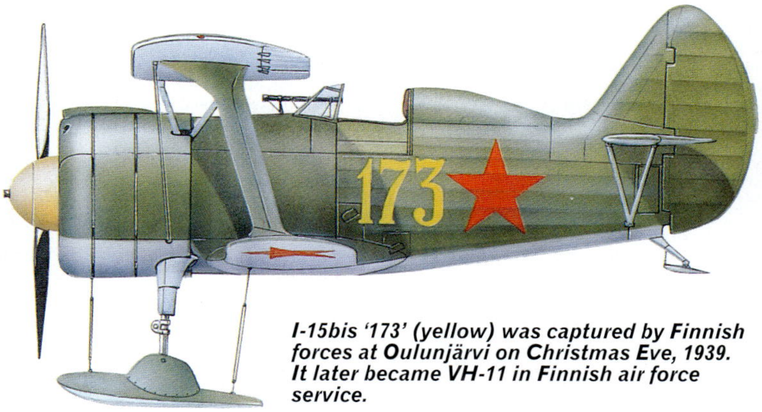

I-15bis '173' (yellow) was captured by Finnish forces at Oulunjärvi on Christmas Eve, 1939. It later became VH-11 in Finnish air force service.

305 is an I-15bis of the Chinese central government's air force operated around the Nanking area in 1938.

Wearing the old-style Spanish Nationalist markings, '2W-16' belonged to the Reus-based Regimiento de Caza 23, Grupo 24.

superiority of the gull-wing layout for the I-15, and it was in this configuration that the I-153 was now in full production.

The operational service of the I-15bis started when, in mid-1937, units of the VVS began to receive the type even before the completion of its state acceptance tests. By this time reports of the success and popularity of the I-15 in the Spanish Civil War forced the VVS High Command to prove the worth and superiority of the I-15's replacement, the I-15bis. The signing of the Sino-Soviet Non-Aggression Pact on 21 August 1937, with its secret clauses promising military aid to China, presented a good opportunity. Therefore, four 'volunteer' Soviet fighter squadrons were dispatched in November 1937 to the Nanking area to support the Chinese in the 2nd Sino-Japanese War, which had started on 7 July 1937. S. P. Sooproon led the Soviet contingent, whose primary opponent in the early stages of the conflict was the Imperial Japanese army air force's units equipped the Kawasaki Ki-10 biplane, official designation Army Type 95 Fighter Model 1. This was no match for the Soviet type and suffered heavy losses.

Disturbed by this setback, the Japanese high command replaced this biplane fighter with the Mitsubishi A5M2a (otherwise the Navy Type 96 Carrier Fighter Model 2-1) monoplane fighter operated by units of the Imperial Japanese Navy air force. This type proved to be the equal of the I-15bis which, although slower, was more manoeuvrable and had the added advantages of twice as many machine-guns, a stronger structure and seat armour protection. Therefore, the outcome of battles between these types depended on pilot skill, and in this respect the two protagonists were well-matched.

To provide the I-16 monoplane with more battle experience, two I-15bis squadrons were replaced by two others equipped with I-16 fighters in January 1938. Heavy losses sustained by the Imperial Japanese Army air force against the I-15bis encouraged a belief in the supposed ability of the biplane to hold its own against monoplane fighters, and was probably responsible for Soviet high command's decision to continue the production of biplane fighters after other countries, in particular their future enemy Germany, had phased out production of biplanes in favour of more advanced monoplanes.

I-15bis fighters were also supplied to the Chinese air force but, in spite of Soviet help, the training of pilots in general was poor and losses as a result of accidents and combat were very high. Two deliveries, totalling 186 I-15bis aircraft, were made to China in the first quarter of 1938, and these

Fitted experimentally with a 'straight-through' wing, this M-22-engined I-15 effectively became the I-15bis prototype.

Polikarpov Biplane Fighters

Left: This ski-undercarriage I-15bis tested an experimental drop-tank to increase the aircraft's range.

Above: This is the M-25V-powered first prototype I-15bis, painted in silver dope overall with red trim.

aircraft equipped the 5th and 6th Fighter Groups as well as serving in Soviet-manned training schools. The Japanese response was to deploy the new Nakajima Ki-27 (otherwise the Army Type 97 Fighter) monoplane to the Chinese theatre of operations. On 15 April 12 Ki-10 biplanes and three Ki-27 monoplanes fought 30 Chinese-flown I-15bis biplanes, and the Japanese claimed to have destroyed 24 of the Chinese aircraft without loss. The table was turned on 29 April when a mixed force of two Chinese and four Soviet squadrons claimed the destruction of 36 out of 39 Japanese fighters for a loss of 11 of their own.

At the end of 1938 Stalin personally authorised attrition replacements for the Spanish I-15 fighters and signed the order for three consignments, each of 31 I-15bis aircraft, to be sent to help the Republican side. Of these, 62 were detained at the French border but the remaining 31 entered service in January 1939 after being assembled at Sabadell. A wing of three squadrons, each comprising nine aircraft with a further four held as reserves, was formed. Emilio Galena Macias was given overall command of the wing and also command of one of the three squadrons: the other two units were put under the command of officers named Roderiguez and Mora. Two machines were lost in training accidents but no combat losses were recorded. It has been said that the aircraft were used for ground strafing, but there were no reports of aerial combat. Towards the end of the war, on 5 February 1939 the 29 surviving aircraft were to Carcassone in France.

Known in Spain as the 'Super Chato', the I-15bis was less manoeuvrable than the I-15 but this was to some extent offset by its faster acceleration in the dive. This gave the potential of redressing the balance in any dogfight confrontations with the Italian-built CR.32, which had always been able to outdive the 'Chato'. Republican I-15bis fighters were given three-digit registration numbers preceded by the letters 'CC'. Evidence suggests that the assembled aircraft were numbered CC-063 to CC-093, and this seems to indicate that they were considered to be the third batch.

After the end of the Spanish Civil War about 20 I-15bis warplanes were handed over by the French to the victorious Nationalists and, as the Type 2W, the I-15bis formed the equipment of Grupo 24, a part of the Regimiento Mixto de Caza num 23 at Reus in what became called the Ejército del Aire. In 1945 the designation was changed to Type C9, and the I-15bis served until the mid-1940s in the ground-attack role.

The ill-defined border between Soviet-occupied Mongolia and the Japanese puppet state of Manchukuo (ex-Manchuria) was disputed by the Japanese who, since 1936, had provoked skirmishes with Soviet and Mongolian forces along the Khalkhin Gol (Khalkhin river), and it was in 1939 that these skirmishes escalated into a full-scale but undeclared war when the Japanese appeared to be making preparations for an attack into Mongolia, outflanking the Soviet defences. The 'war' started on 11 May and continued until 16 September 1939. At first one regiment, the 70th IAP (Istrebitel'nyi Aviatsionnii polk, or fighter aviation regiment) commanded by Major V. M. Zabaluyev and equipped primarily with the I-15bis, was in action together with the 22nd IAP equipped with the I-16 monoplane. These regiments were later reinforced by another equipped with the I-15bis and two more with the I-16. The Japanese used mainly the Ki-27 monoplane that had previously fought against the Soviet volunteer squadrons in China. The Japanese fighter was superior in manoeuvrability and climb rate to the Soviet monoplane, and to the Soviet biplanes in speed. Large air battles took place over the Nomonhan plateau, often involving up to 200 aircraft, and wildly exaggerated claims were made by both sides.

By the end of the conflict the Japanese claimed to have destroyed 1,162 Soviet aircraft in the air and another 98 on the ground: this total claim of 1,260 destroyed is 2.5 times the total number of Soviet aircraft employed! To be fair, these claims have now been moderated to 400. The Soviet claims were less wildly exaggerated: their claim of 590 aerial and 55 ground 'kills' was still in excess of the 500 aircraft employed by the Japanese. It is worth comparing admissions from both sides of their own losses. The Japanese admitted 154 aircraft lost or damaged beyond repair, and the Soviets to a figure of 207 aircraft. Most uncommitted observers would call the result of the aerial battle an honourable draw.

However it soon became clear that the I-15bis, even when protected by the I-16, was just not effective enough. To remedy this fault, 13 examples of the newly developed I-153 were tested in battle in a mixed regiment alongside 45 examples of the I-15bis. Not only new aircraft but also new weapons were employed in this conflict. Five of the I-15bis fighters were each fitted with six 82-mm (3.2-in) RS-82 rockets for use against enemy aircraft. No information has been released of their success in destroying aircraft, but the threat of the projectiles was certainly extremely effective at dispersing enemy formations, allowing the I-16 fighters acting as top cover the opportunity to pick them off one at a time. During the USSR's so-called Winter War of 1939-40 against Finland, the VVS was not the only air force to operate the I-15bis. Five were captured by the Finns and served first in LeLv (Lentolaivue, or squadron) 34, and later in 2/TLeLv 34, of the Finnish air force, principally as fighter trainers with the serial numbers VH–1 to –5, later changed to IH–1 to –5. The aircraft survived in this role into Finland's involvement in World War II.

Germany's Operation Barbarossa invasion of the USSR opened with attacks on Soviet airfields. Many VVS regiments used a mix of I-15bis and I-153 fighters. Deliveries of the latter had begun in April 1941 and it was policy to supply only small numbers to each unit rather than totally re-equip fewer regiments. The 74th ShAP was based only 14 km (8.6 miles) from the border, and in the opening attack it lost all 47 aircraft on the airfield to artillery fire and bombs. Orders for the 66th and 164th IAP to take off were received just before dawn on Day 1 (22 June) but there was not enough time to achieve this before the bombs rained down, destroying 34 fighters, almost all of them I-15bis machines. Away to the south the 62nd IAP, reputed to be one of the best in the Kiev Special Military District, lost half its inventory.

On the southern flank, pilots of the 96th Independent Fighter Squadron were the first in the Black Sea Fleet to engage the enemy. The unit had 14 I-15bis and three I-153 fighters on strength, and when their Romanian opponents attacked Izmail in the afternoon of 22 June they were repulsed and the first blood fell to Lieutenant M. Maksimov. Captain A. Korobitsin was the proud commander of this unit, the first of the Soviet navy to be awarded the Order of the Red Banner of Combat.

In the north a ShAP commanded by Hero of the Soviet Union V. Belousov distinguished itself in the interceptor role when Captain M. Krasnolootski in his I-15bis rammed and destroyed a Bf 109 and was still able to limp home. For this act of bravery he was awarded the gold star of the Hero of the Soviet Union.

An example of extemporisation in the field occurred later, when the 65th ShAP discovered that when rocket missiles attached to the underside of the lower wings of the I-15bis were fired, fabric stripped off the wing and the structure warped. Undaunted, the mechanics attached Dural sheets to the underside of the wing, reinforced the spars and fitted additional ribs. Bomb racks were also installed but the effect of the additional armament and the use of ski landing gear reduced the top speed to 240 km/h (150 mph). These intrepid pilots needed to use all the excellent manoeuvrability of the biplane to avoid presenting an easy target for the Luftwaffe's Experten (aces) in their Bf 109 monoplane fighters. Another example of the ingenuity of regimental mechanics took

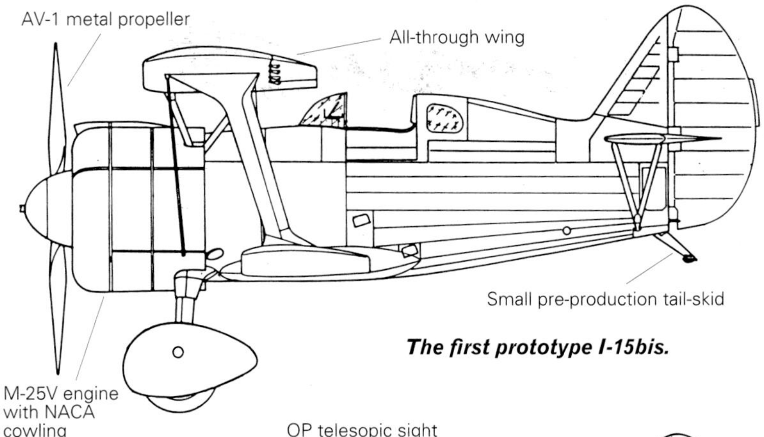

The first prototype I-15bis.

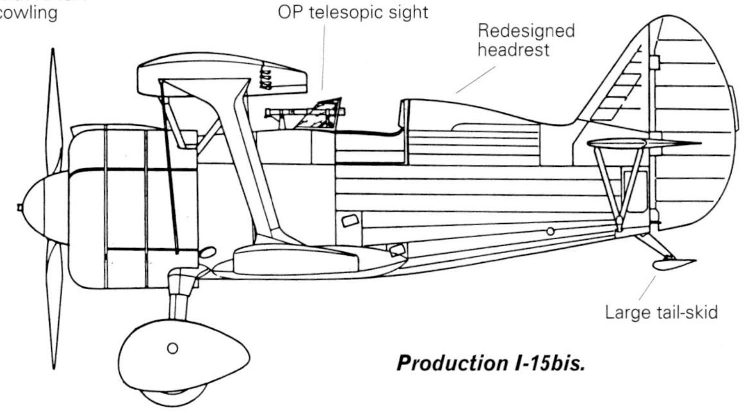

Production I-15bis.

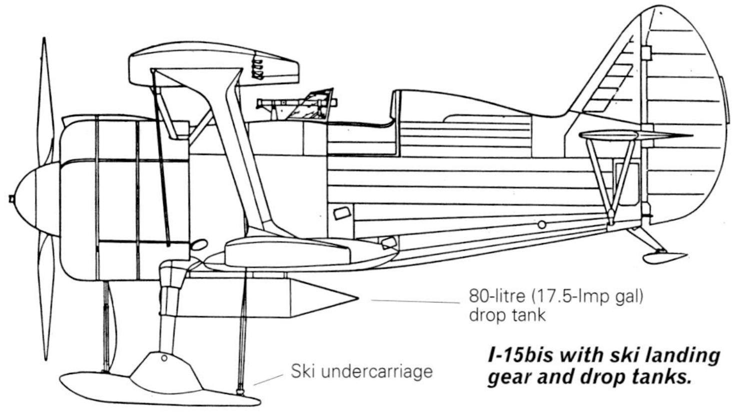

I-15bis with ski landing gear and drop tanks.

place in the summer of 1943 when, somewhat surprisingly, the I-15bis was still in use as a front-line warplane. Several such aircraft of the 5th Air Army received a second cockpit to be occupied by an observer when spotting for the artillery.

No example of the I-15bis exists today but there are two replicas, one marked '50 white' in the Air Force Museum at Monino and the other, '14 white', at the Central Museum of the Great Patriotic War in Moscow.

I-15bis specification

Span	33 ft 5½ in (10.2 m)
Length	20 ft 4 in (6.2 m)
Wing area	242.2 sq ft (22.5 m²)
Weight empty	2,747 lb (1243 kg)
Weight loaded	3,624 lb (1640 kg)
Wing loading	9.9 lb/sq ft (73.0 kg/m²)
Max. speed at sea level	197 mph (325 km/h)
Max. speed at 9,515 ft (2900 m)	228 mph (367 km/h)
Rate of climb	2,756 ft/min (840 m/min)
Service ceiling	29,855 ft (9100 m)
Time to turn 360°	10½-11 seconds
Range	323 miles (520 km)
Take-off run	525 ft (160 m)
Landing run	295 ft (90 m)

I-15bis production

Date	No. of aircraft built at Zavod 1 imeni Aviakhima
1937/38	1104
1939	1304
Total:	2408

Partially painted in olive green – the rest is in silver – with what appears to be a hand-painted '68' tactical code on the tail, this I-15bis was photographed during NII VVS trials.

I-152TK (I-15bis TK)

The I-152TK (*Toorbokompressor*, or turbocharger), otherwise known as the I-15bis TK, had two TK-3 superchargers driven via a divided pipe by the engine exhaust gases. The maximum speed at 6000 m (19,685 ft) was 435 km/h (270 mph), but the additional 140 kg (308 kg) of weight otherwise degraded performance to the level that no production was contemplated.

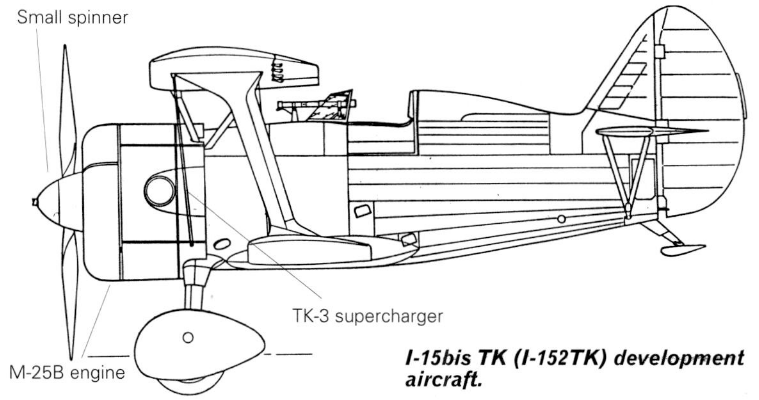

I-15bis TK (I-152TK) development aircraft.

Left: One of the I-152TK prototypes is seen parked in front of the factory hangar. It is painted white overall with red spats and engine cowling.

I-152GK

The I-152GK (Ghermeteecheskaya Kabina, or hermetically sealed [i.e. pressure] cabin) explored the potential of the latest pressure cabin designed by A. Ya. Schcherbakov. It was similar to one tested on an I-15, with rubberised fabric sealing an aluminium cupola to the fuselage. The additional weight of 67 kg (148 lb), coupled with the impossibility of opening the cabin at high speeds, led to the termination of the cabin's development, despite the fact that it was considered successful at the technical level.

I-152DM

The I-152DM (Dopolneetelnii Motor, or supplementary motor [i.e. booster]) was an I-15bis with the construction number 5942, which laid claim to fame in December 1939 when, with P. Ye. Loginov at the controls, it made the first-ever flight of a ramjet-equipped aircraft. Under each lower wing it carried a Merkulov DM-2 ramjet developed from the smaller DM-1. This engine had a diameter of 400 mm (15¾ in) and a length of 1.5 m (4 ft 11 in), and developed 0.187 kN (42 lb st) while running on the same fuel as the piston engine. An increase in maximum speed of 15 km/h (9 mph) was recorded and tests continued until May 1940, by which time 54 flights had been successfully completed.

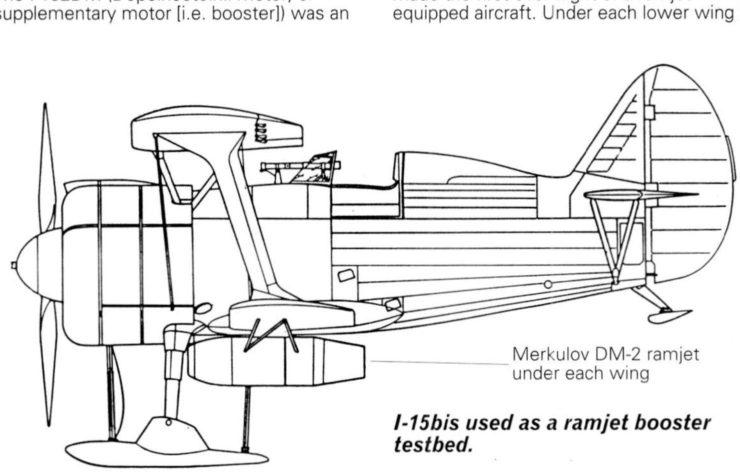

I-15bis used as a ramjet booster testbed.

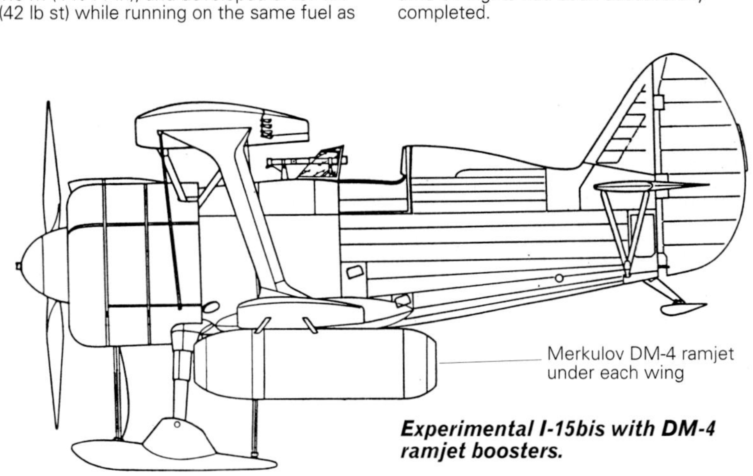

Experimental I-15bis with DM-4 ramjet boosters.

DIT-2

The DIT-2 (Dvookhmestnii Istrebitel' Trenirovochnii, or two-seat fighter trainer) was a two-seat trainer version of the I-15bis. Only one prototype was completed in 1939, but it was deemed unacceptable as a trainer because of its unsatisfactory spinning characteristics, although other aspects of stability and controllability were acceptable. Dimensionally almost the same as the single-seat fighter, the second cockpit and dual controls added 52 kg (114 lb) to the weight, in spite of the removal of the backrest armour and two machine-guns with their ammunition.

Unacceptable as a trainer, only one dual-control DIT-2 was built. Like many of the Polikarpov 'one-offs' it had red engine cowling and spats.

I-153 Chaika

I-153 Chaika was the designation of the last of the Polikarpov biplane fighters to be built in substantial numbers. The origins of the type can be found in the dissatisfaction of both the military and Polikarpov with the performance of the I-15bis, and as the VVS was still insisting on a mixed force of biplane and monoplane fighters, the OKB studied ways of increasing the maximum speed of the biplane without any sacrifice of its superior manoeuvrability. The results of this study were presented to the authorities in the autumn of 1937.

Polikarpov did not try to discourage this loyalty to the biplane concept, but concentrated instead on trying to break the vicious circle of increasing speed by the installation of a more powerful engine which then adversely affected weight and therefore reduced manoeuvrability. He indicated ways of minimising drag and structural weight so that he could still install the most powerful engine available and retain an acceptable level of manoeuvrability. His solution included returning to the gull-wing layout for the top wing and fitting a retractable main landing gear arrangement. The Narkomoboronprom (an acronym for People's Commissariat of the Defence Industry) and the VVS accepted Polikarpov's thesis, no doubt influenced by a report from TsAGI showing that with the Chaika configuration directional stability actually improved as speed increased. By this time, favourable comments from pilots using the I-15 in Spain had also reached the USSR.

Confident of the outcome, Polikarpov had already asked his deputy, Dmitrii L. Tomashevich, to design a biplane on these lines, and the provisional design for the I-153 received approval on 23 October 1937.

Ultimately, the decision to persevere with the biplane proved a costly error. France, Germany, Japan, the UK and the USA were all concentrating on the rapid and extensive development of monoplane fighters, and the only exceptions to this tendency among the major powers were Italy and the USSR. The result was that between 1939 and 1941 just under 3,500 biplanes were manufactured in the USSR when, instead, a similar number of monoplanes might have been built. Equally important was the Polikarpov OKB's waste on biplane development of the time and resources which would have been better spent on the I-16 and its successors.

When the design of the I-153 had been approved, Polikarpov was in charge of the OKBs at two factories. One of them, Zavod 84 at Khimki, was becoming involved with transport aircraft and would later build under licence the Douglas DC-3 as the PS-8 (later Lisunov Li-2). Zavod 21 at Gor'kii was just building up its experimental facilities. The obvious choice for the preparation of working drawings fell upon Zavod 1, which had been selected to manufacture the I-153. Unfortunately, this plant was struggling to start series production of the I-15bis and at the same time improve its unsatisfactory performance. Inevitably, there was a delay of several months before the drawings could be started and construction of two prototypes did not begin until the beginning of 1938.

From December 1937 Polikarpov was no longer involved with Zavod 21 and Zavod 84. He had been transferred to the ZOK (Zavod Opytnykh Konstrooktsiy, or Experimental Designs Factory), which was the experimental design plant of the TsAGI located at Zavod 156 in Moscow. Being successful enough to be called 'the king of fighters' had made many people envious of Polikarpov, an envy exacerbated by Stalin's apparent patronage. The shunting from plant to plant to which Polikarpov and his team were subjected from this point has been interpreted by many as a vindictive manoeuvre to clear the path for his less successful colleagues.

The first I-153 prototype had the 750-hp (559-kW) M-25V radial engine and made its first flight in the middle of May piloted by A. I. Zhukov; the second prototype was completed with the 800-hp (596.5-kW) M-62 radial engine and flew for the first time in the middle of June with A. Davydov at the controls. The M-62 engine had recently been developed by A. D. Shvetsov from the M-25V by the addition of a two-stage supercharger, a new induction system and numerous other improvements.

Successful state acceptance tests of the first prototype were completed by test pilot Pavel Fedrovi between 27 September and 15 October 1938, and the new design easily outclassed its predecessor, the I-15bis. For example, the maximum speed at sea level was 360 km/h (224 mph) compared with 325 km/h (197 mph), and the climb rate was 1050 m (3,445 ft) per minute compared with 840 m (2,756 ft) per minute. Several structural shortcomings were noted, but it was agreed to incorporate the appropriate modifications into the series production rather than build a new prototype.

Success also attended the tests of the I-153 second prototype with the M-62 engine, but it was decided, very wisely, to delay any production decision until the engine had entered series production and had become more fully developed.

Production of the I-153 with the M-25V engine started in October 1938 with a batch of 10 aircraft which, in November, were sent to Baku for service testing by operational as well as test pilots. One underwent further state trials from 21 March to 28 April 1939. These aircraft differed from the prototypes in having elevators of reduced area, a new control system, stronger landing gear units and other improvements. On 11 April one from this batch disintegrated in the air when the wing structure failed while the machine was being pulled out of a dive. In spite of this accident, the new tests were successful, the main complaint being the poor view of the ground from the cockpit.

Delivery of the I-153 fighters to operational units of the VVS began in 1939, and it was also possible that year to change to the M-62 engine on the production lines. During 1940 the M-62 was, in its turn, replaced by the more powerful 1,100-hp (820-kW) M-63 radial engine, although the expected improvement in maximum speed was in the event negated by the extra equipment and further reinforcements to the structure; the major performance improvement was in the climb rate, which was considerably enhanced. State trials for this variant, the so-called '1940 Standard', were completed on 30 November 1940. Several versions were tested, with and without external fuel tanks and with a wheel or ski landing gear arrangement.

Apart from the gulling of its upper wing's roots into the upper part of the forward fuselage, in structural terms the I-153 was very similar to the I-15bis with Clark YH aerofoil profiles and fabric-covered wooden wings with the same steel structure as on the I-15 to integrate the halves of the upper wing into the fuselage. Each unit of the main landing gear arrangement consisted of an oleo-pneumatic leg braced laterally by a diagonal strut, both pivoting to the rear on retraction, the wheel rotating through 90° to lie flat in a well on the underside of the wing root. On retraction, plates attached to the leg struts formed covers for the landing gear. Retraction was manually operated via a cockpit handcrank. Problems were expected with the new landing gear arrangement, but tests showed it to be reliable. The tyres were now wider at 700 x 150 mm (27.6 x 5.9 in), and the tailskid was replaced by a fixed tailwheel (with a solid tyre) that moved in concert with the rudder. Equipment included a battery, an engine-driven dynamo and navigation lights, and provision was also made for a radio.

The standard armament comprised four 7.62-mm (0.3-in) ShKAS synchronised machine-guns with 2,600 rounds of ammunition. In the course of the production run some aircraft were also built with the following gun selections: four 12.7-mm (0.5-in) BS machine-guns. two 20-mm ShVAK cannon; two 20-mm ShVAK cannon and two 7.62-mm (0.3-in) ShKAS machine-guns; or two 7.62-mm (0.3-in) ShKAS and two 12.7-mm (0.5-in) BS machine-guns. Following the success of I-15bis fighters with the RS-82 rocket in the Khalkhin Gol campaign, these weapons could be fitted to the I-153.

Tests were carried out at the NII VVS from 16 June to 16 August 1939 on an I-153 fitted with an M-62 engine comparing a fixed-pitch propeller with the AV-1 variable-pitch propeller which had already proved itself in Mongolia under combat conditions. There was no significant difference in top

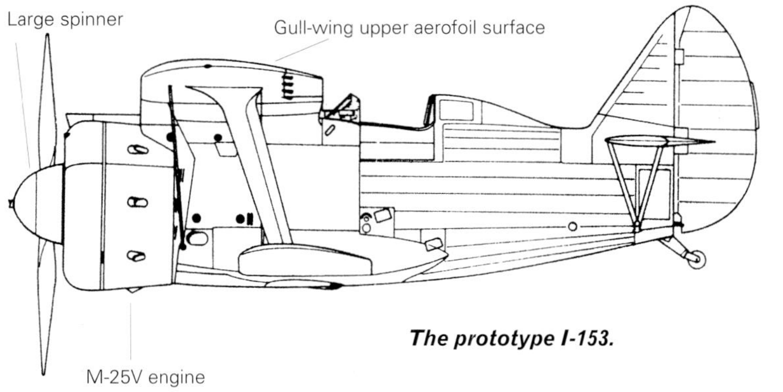

The prototype I-153.

Above: M-63-powered I-153 c/n 8019 was flown by A.I. Zhookov during spinning trials.

Below: One of the prototypes was fitted with a large spinner while participating in the NII VVS trials.

Polikarpov I-153s

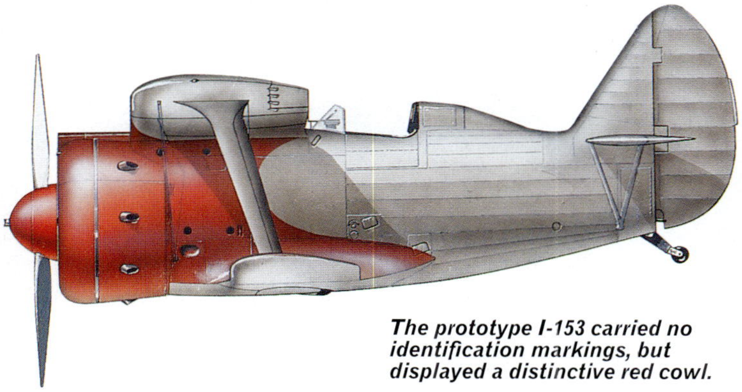

The prototype I-153 carried no identification markings, but displayed a distinctive red cowl.

Still in its summer camouflage, this production I-153 is equipped with skis.

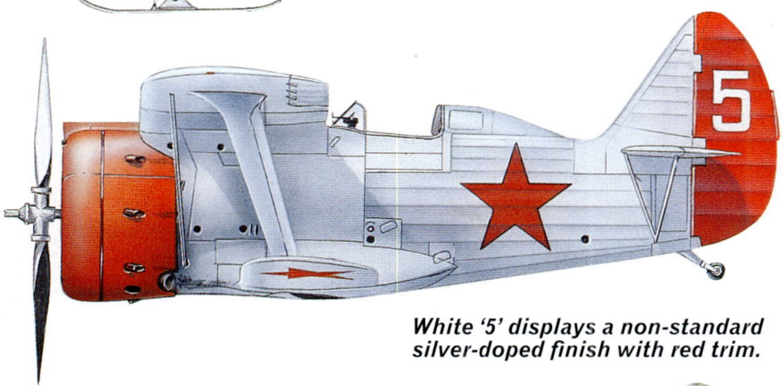

White '5' displays a non-standard silver-doped finish with red trim.

The crude mottled camouflage of Red '16' is the result of daubing green paint over the factory-applied silver finish.

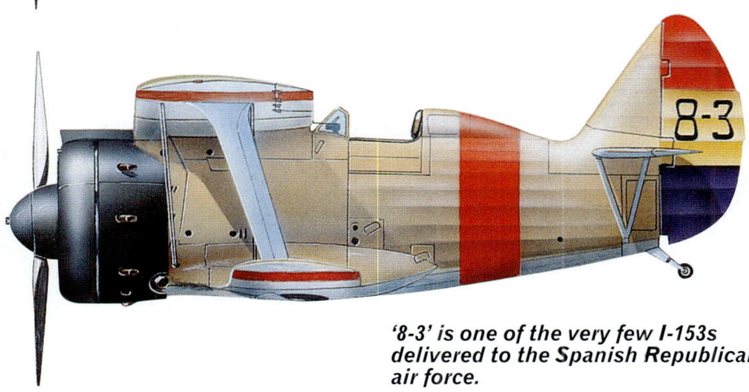

'8-3' is one of the very few I-153s delivered to the Spanish Republican air force.

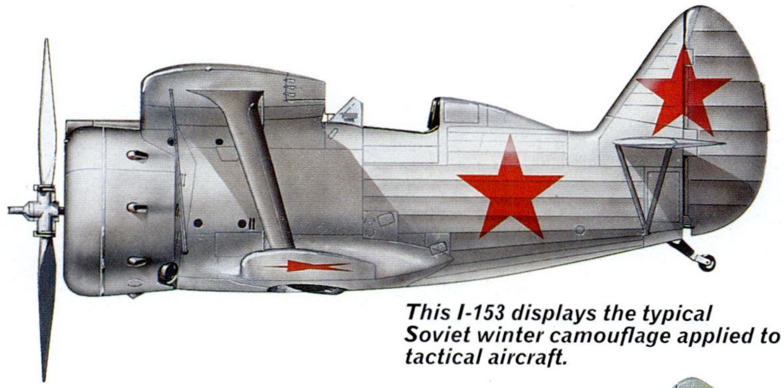

This I-153 displays the typical Soviet winter camouflage applied to tactical aircraft.

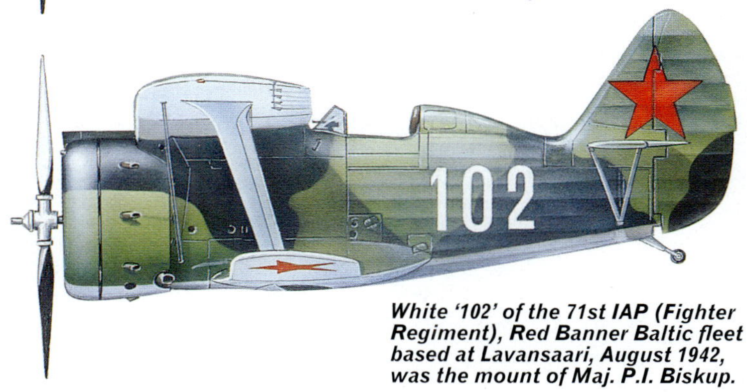

White '102' of the 71st IAP (Fighter Regiment), Red Banner Baltic fleet based at Lavansaari, August 1942, was the mount of Maj. P.I. Biskup.

The 8th Fighter Regiment of the Black Sea Fleet operated Red '6'.

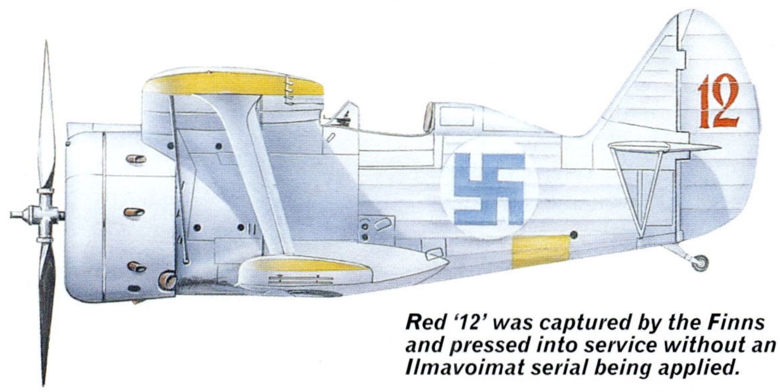

Red '12' was captured by the Finns and pressed into service without an Ilmavoimat serial being applied.

Painted black overall and with insignia on the lower wings only, this I-153 was operated by the Chinese forces.

Above right: A development I-153 tested twin TK-3 superchargers (below) fed by over-engine intakes. The aircraft was later modified to have a third intake for the TK-3s fitted (above).

speed at sea level, but at 5000 m (16,405 ft) the aircraft with the fixed-pitch propeller was 20 km/h (12 mph) faster. However, the variable-pitch propeller gave the aircraft a better climb rate and halved the landing run at the cost of slightly less endurance. Overall the advantages of this fixed-pitch propeller were insufficient to merit its installation on production models.

The start of the I-153's operational career is shrouded in mystery. Were any I-153 fighters sent to Spain? Spanish sources suggest that one or two aircraft were sent for trials, in the hands of Soviet pilots, towards the end of 1938 but there is still no firm evidence for this. The story relies for authenticity upon the appearance in France of an I-153 that now graces the Musée de l'Air, but it has also been suggested that this could have been taken there by the Germans as a war trophy.

As noted above, deliveries of the I-153 to the VVS began in October 1938, when 10 aircraft were sent to Baku for operational evaluation. Training units were the next recipients, and then the VVS commander, A. D. Loktionov, instructed that the first operational unit to receive the new type should be the 22nd IAP in Mongolia, which was to receive 13 such aircraft in replacement of some of its I-15bis fighters. Hero of the Soviet Union Stepan Gritsevets led a special group flying the I-153, and while delighted with the performance of his new aircraft was also horrified to find the synchronisation gear was broken on all of them. Fortunately, this discovery happened during ground firing tests and a new fire-control system was quickly devised and installed by regimental engineers.

Nine of these fighters were deployed for their first mission on 25 July 1939, when the main landing gear units were deliberately left in the extended position in a ploy to deceive the enemy. It was hoped that Japanese pilots would think the I-153 fighters were I-15bis machines, which had, of course, a significantly inferior performance. A similar number of Ki-27 monoplanes dived to attack, and just before they came into gun range Gritsevets gave the signal for the landing gears of the I-153 machines to be retracted. As the biplanes accelerated they quickly turned through 180° and mounted a frontal attack. Four Japanese fighters were destroyed without loss on the Soviet side. The Japanese will only admit to two losses but an incontrovertible fact was that they scattered in panic and ran for home. However, once enemy pilots gained experience with the strengths and weaknesses of the I-153 they devised different tactics to avoid close combat and losses in the biplane units mounted.

As operations in Mongolia continued, the I-153 revealed some structural weaknesses and more firing mechanism defects, both of which were put right in the field and on the production lines. What could not be rectified, however, was the inherent inadequacy of the biplane's speed when compared with that of a monoplane. To be effective, the I-153 had to go into battle together with the I-16 monoplane.

The overall result of the Khalkhin Gol campaign was a tactical victory for the Soviet forces under the command of General (later Marshal of the USSR) Gheorgii K. Zhukov, whose forces virtually annihilated the Japanese 6th Army. More importantly, it was a great strategic victory in that the Japanese lost the urge to expand into Mongolia and did not attack even when the USSR was at its weakest and the German army was at the gates of Moscow at the end of 1941. As a result, Stalin was able to order the transfer of divisions from the now less vulnerable Far Eastern sector and employ them in the defence of Moscow and later Stalingrad (now Volgograd).

The Chaika was extensively used during the Winter War with Finland and, according to Finnish claims, suffered heavy losses along with all the other Soviet types. Some 11 such fighters (eight during the Winter War and three in the so-called Continuation War [1941-44] in which Finland sided with Germany against the USSR) that were forced down behind the Finnish lines were repaired and used by the Finnish air force, together with 11 similar aircraft captured by the Germans in the USSR and later sold to the Finns. These aircraft were operated by LeLv 6 as Flight 3, providing fighter cover for this maritime patrol unit. In November 1942 the Chaikas became Flight 2 of LeLv 30. All were withdrawn from operations on 20 March 1944. Serial numbers VH-11 to 31 were given to 21 of these, which were later renumbered as IT-11 to 31. Five Soviet aircraft were claimed to have been destroyed for the loss of two Finnish I-153 fighters in combat and two in accidents.

Another country to receive the I-153, this time with the agreement of the Soviets, was China. A small number was flown by inadequately trained Chinese pilots without much success against Japanese Ki-27 fighters.

When the Germans attacked the USSR on 22 June 1941, over one-third of the Soviet fighters confronting them in the western part of the USSR were I-153 Chaikas. There were 179 in the Leningrad Military District in IAPs 7, 19, 26, 153 and 154. In the Baltic Military District 284 served with IAPs 15, 21, 38, 42, 49 and 148. The Odessa Military District had 143 of them in IAPs 4 and 55, and in the Western Military District 241 were in service with IAPs 122, 123, 127 and 129. By far the greatest concentration of Chaikas was in the Kiev Military District, where there were no less than 454 in IAPs 12, 20, 23, 46, 91, 92, 149, 164 and 165. Thus 1,301 I-153 machines were assigned to fighter regiments in this theatre. In addition, about 180 more I-153 aircraft served in ground-attack regiments nos 61, 241, 74, 62, 66 and 299 alongside

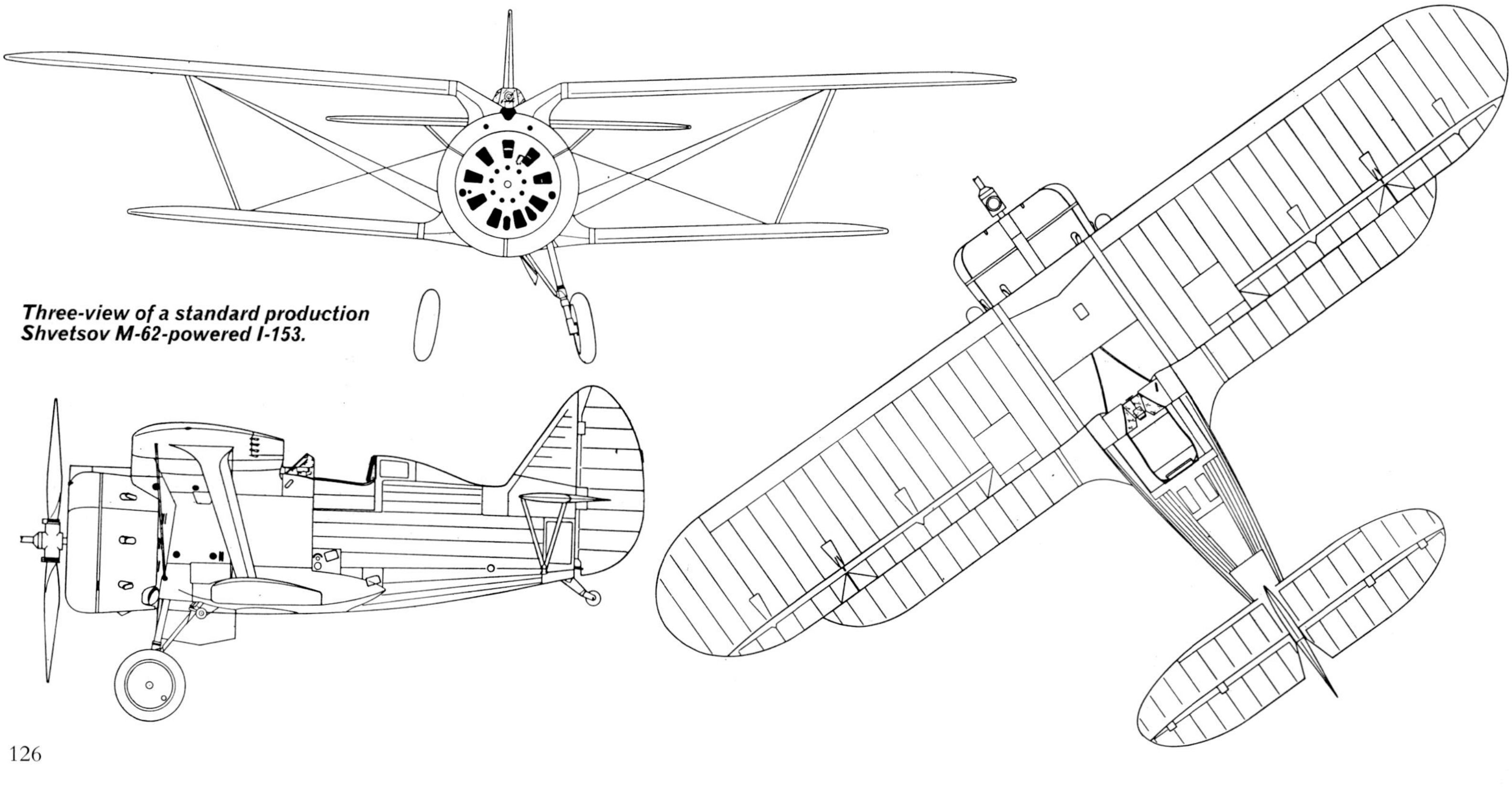

Three-view of a standard production Shvetsov M-62-powered I-153.

the I-15bis. The grand total was thus nearly 1,500 Chaikas out of the 4,226 fighters deployed in this theatre.

Figures for the naval air force showed 687 I-15bis and I-153 biplanes in its inventory at this time out of a total of 763 aircraft, the type therefore representing some 90 per cent of the navy's aircraft strength. Not all had yet been assigned to active fleet regiments, which had in total 148 I-15bis and 202 I-153 fighters. Of the latter, the Northern Fleet had 18 with the 177 IAP and the 72nd Composite Air Regiment; the Black Sea Fleet had 76 with the 8, 9, 32 and 96 IAPs; and the Baltic Fleet had 108 with the 71 IAP and the 12, 13, 104 OAPs (independent air regiments).

In addition to the first-line units in the west, the I-153 served with flying schools, reserve regiments and in military districts in other parts of the USSR, particularly in the Far East.

The first day of Operation Barbarossa saw huge losses inflicted on the VVS by the Luftwaffe. As recounted above, all of the 74th ShAP's aircraft were destroyed, a similar fate befell the 66th ShAP, and the 62nd ShAP lost half its inventory. One regiment not taken unawares was the 127th IAP at Avgustovo, commanded by Lieutenant Colonel Gordiyenko who, by camouflaging and dispersing his aircraft, succeeded in avoiding losses on the ground. Two of his pilots, Lieutenant S. Zhukovskii and Senior Political Instructor A. Artem'yev, flew nine sorties each that day and shot down a total of seven enemy aircraft. Fighters from the 122nd IAP joined the 127th in the fray, and together they claimed the destruction of 35 German machines on the first day.

Major Soorin, commanding the 123rd IAP, claimed the first Bf 109 at 0500 hours and at 0800 hours Captain Mozhayev, leading his flight of four, surprised another group of Messerschmitt fighters and shot down three for the loss of one of their own. This unit based at Steegovo destroyed 30 enemy aircraft and lost nine.

In spite of these and similar heroic actions the VVS fleet was decimated, with over 700 aircraft of all types lost. The Luftwaffe continued to attack airfields and by the end of June the Soviet armies' western front had lost 1,200 aircraft. The Germans had not achieved this victory without loss, however, and up to 5 July 1941 the Soviets claimed the destruction of over 800 machines, of which the lion's share fell to I-153 fighters. Thanks to their military success in Mongolia in 1939, the Soviets were able to rush reinforcements from the Far East, among which was the 29th 'Red Banner' IAP with a mixed bag of I-153 and I-16 fighters. After giving cover to the arrival by train of soldiers of the 29th Army as they, too, rallied to defend Smolensk, the regiment carried out low-level attacks on the advancing enemy. Its first aerial victory fell to Junior Lieutenant Yookhimovich, who intercepted and shot down a Junkers Ju 88. One incident displaying a tenacious defiance of danger deserves a place in any book of heroic ventures. Captain Tormorov and Junior Lieutenant Doodin were patrolling in the Velikiye Looki area, which required the carriage of drop tanks, when they came under attack from four Bf 109 fighters. Doodin shot down one of their attackers, but Tormorov's port drop tank was set on fire. He dived away to jettison it and the remaining three Bf 109 warplanes then concentrated on Doodin. After succeeding in jettisoning his drop tanks, Tormorov returned to the attack and shot down another German fighter and was able to return to base. Doodin went on to down a third by ramming it head-on and managed to parachute safely into the Soviet lines. It later transpired, when the wreckage was found, that the two pilots had also destroyed the fourth and last of their assailants. For this act of bravery and later victories Doodin was made a Hero of the Soviet Union in October 1941. Four other pilots in this regiment were also similarly decorated after gaining 10 or more victories.

Over a two-month period the 29th 'Red Banner' IAP claimed 47 enemy aircraft and mounted many ground attacks. For this and the heroism of its pilots the regiment was retitled the 1st Guards Fighter Regiment (Gvardeyskii Istrebitel'nii Aviatseeonnii Polk): this was the first occasion on which an air force unit had received this battle honour.

By August the German air attacks on Moscow were intensifying and the VI PVO Fighter Corps was formed with 783 interceptors for the defence of the Soviet capital. Of these interceptors, 94 were Chaikas but by the end of December only 11 of them were still operational. It was a similar situation in the defence of Leningrad, which was guarded by 242 fighters: of the 38 I-153 fighters available in July 1941, only five remained by the end of the year. Leningrad also enjoyed the support of other I-153 fighters from the Baltic Fleet and the VVS, a completely separate organisation from the PVO. On 19 August 1941 air reconnaissance reported that a strong German armoured force was attempting to complete the encirclement of the city, and the 7th IAP was ordered by Marshal Klim Ye. Voroshilov, now commanding the city defences on Stalin's insistence, to destroy the column. Eight I-153 fighters, now in ground-attack mode, first halted the force and then broke it up but the leader, Senior Lieutenant N. Svetenko, was forced to land his damaged aircraft in a shell-cratered field behind enemy lines.

It was at this point that an almost unbelievable act of heroism took place. Svetenko's second in command, A. Slonov, effected a landing between craters in spite of being under heavy mortar and shell fire and took off again with Svetenko clutching a wing strut, and both men miraculously landed safely at a nearby naval airfield.

I-153 fighters of the PVO, in defence of the cities of Moscow and Leningrad, suffered heavy losses in the first six months of the war and by the end of 1941 only 54 aircraft had survived.

Use of the I-153 in various secondary roles continued well into 1943, and it was in that year that another act of almost suicidal heroism was exhibited. Ramming an enemy aircraft is, in itself, a formidable act, but A. Sevast'yanov of the 26th IAP did just that but at night. On 6 November he rammed an He 111 bomber over Leningrad when he had exhausted all his ammunition. Debris from both aircraft fell on the garden of the

Above: A 1940-standard production ski-equipped I-153 was used to test wing-mounted drop tanks.

Below: Beginning in February 1941, Polikarpov tested an I-153 fitted with a supercharged M-62 engine.

Above: At least one Polikarpov I-153 was used to test VAP (vylivnoy aviatseeonnyy preebor – 'incendiary tanks for pouring liquid phosphorus') tanks.

Below: Red '5' is jacked up for undercarriage retraction tests. Of particular note is the trestle that supports the engine, resting on the extreme tip of the spinner.

Left: This I-153 has the majority of its M-62's cowling removed, leaving only the forward plate with the shutters in place. Easy access to the engine was a necessity on the primitive airfields from which the I-153 operated, where support infrastructure and even hangar space was at a premium. The 800 hp M-62 was a development of the M-25 and was later redesignated the ASh-62R, in recognition of the Shvetsov-led bureau's input.

An I-153 fitted with retractable skis was tested at the NII VVS.

Tauride Palace, but the Soviet pilot managed to escape by parachute.

An example of the successful use of RS-82 rockets against aircraft took place during an attack on Kronstadt naval base. Regimental Commissar I. I. Serbin, in a night attack at 1000 m (3,280 ft) on an He 111, destroyed it with a salvo of two rockets. On returning to base he saw a similar type of bomber outlined in a searchlight beam and also shot that bomber. Altogether, this pilot destroyed three He 111 bombers and claimed a share in a fourth.

By mid-1943 most of the I-153s still in service in the western theatre were with the Black Sea Fleet. Some were in the mixed inventories of the 3rd, 4th and 10th GvIAPs as well as the 7th Detached Flight, PVO. By this time the 10 I-153 fighters on Lavensaari Island were having to face the formidable Focke-Wulf Fw 190, and a switch was made to the 3rd GvIAP's Yakovlev Yak-1 monoplane fighters, which were far more capable of tackling the Fw 190 on equal terms. In the Caucasus, the VIII PVO Fighter Corps had 266 interceptors, of which 141 were I-153 machines, but the German offensive towards this area in August 1942 rapidly reduced this number until, by the end of November, only 20 of the biplanes were left. A separate PVO defence zone had been set up for Baku, the major port and oil centre for the region, and in the summer of 1942 an unexpectedly large number of I-153 fighters was transferred here as attrition replacements pending the availability of more modern types. It is worth taking account of the fact that this area was considered important enough to be second only to Moscow in number of PVO aircraft with which it was defended. As well as being an important oil centre, Baku housed many evacuated defence factories and was a vital *entrepot* for supplies from the UK and USA. By 1944 very few of the 3,437 I-153 fighters were left. Scattered survivors served in second-line duties amongst more modern aircraft. A Luftwaffe intelligence report of February 1944 suggested that only two regiments with which the Germans had come into conflict at that time had had any Chaika fighters left. In 1945 a small number could still be found serving with the Northern Fleet and several more in the Far East, well away from more potent enemies.

The I-153 was not the last type of biplane fighter, that dubious honour falling to the Fiat CR.42 Falco which entered service with Regia Aeronautica a few weeks after the I-153 joined the Soviet air force.

Notwithstanding the fact that the I-153 was considered by many to have been the finest biplane fighter ever to have been designed, it is a great pity that the type ever went into production as the USSR would have been better served by the production of more monoplane fighters. However, hindsight always provides an example of 20/20 vision.

Until recently, the last example of the I-153 still in existence was thought to be that which stands far from its native land in the Musée de l'Air et de l'Espace at le Bourget Airport outside Paris. In the mid-1990s, however, an I-153 was painstakingly restored to full flying condition from wreckage discovered in Russia. The silver-painted aircraft is owned by the Alpine Fighter Collection of New Zealand, and made its public debut at Wanaka, NZ, in 1998.

I-153 specification

Span	32 ft 9½ in (10.0 m)
Length	20 ft 2 ⅞ in (6.17 m)
Wing area	238.32 sq ft (22.14 m²)
Weight empty	3,031 lb (1375 kg)
Weight loaded	3,891 lb (1765 kg)
Weight of fuel	331 lb (150 kg)
Weight of oil	42 lb (19 kg)
Max. speed at sea level	227 mph (365 km/h)
Max. speed at 5100 m (16,730 ft)	264 mph (424 km/h)
Climb to 5000 m (16,405 ft)	5 mins 42 secs
Rate of climb	2,874 ft/min (876 m/min)
Service ceiling	35,105 ft (10700 m)
Range	348 miles (560 km)
Time to turn 360°	13.3 secs
Take-off run	360 ft (110 m)
Landing run	492 ft (150 m)
Landing speed	65 mph (105 km/h)

With the 920-hp (686-kW) M-62 engine:

Max. speed at sea level	276 mph (444 km/h)
Max. speed at 33,795 ft (10300 m)	298 mph (480 km/h)

With the 1,100-hp (820-kW) M-63 engine:

Rate of climb, short term boost	4,429 ft/min (1350 m/min)
Rate of climb, nominal power	3,346 ft/min (1020 m/min)
Time to 16,405 ft (5000 m)	5 mins 6 secs
Time to 34,775 ft (10600 m)	24 mins 30 secs

I-153 production

Date	No. of aircraft built at : Zavod 1 imeni Aviakhima
1938/9	1011
1940	2362
1941	64
Total:	3427

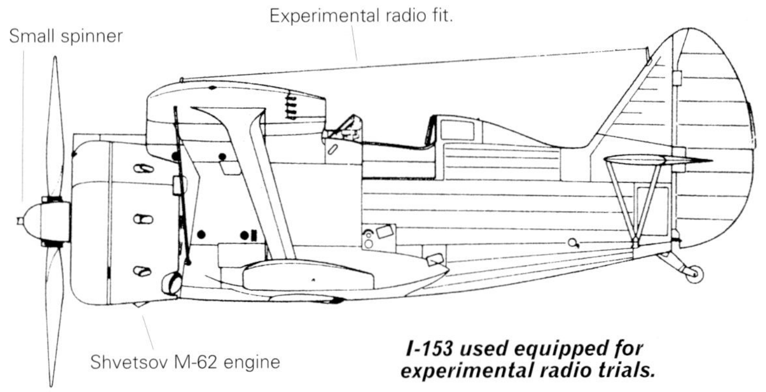

I-153 used equipped for experimental radio trials.

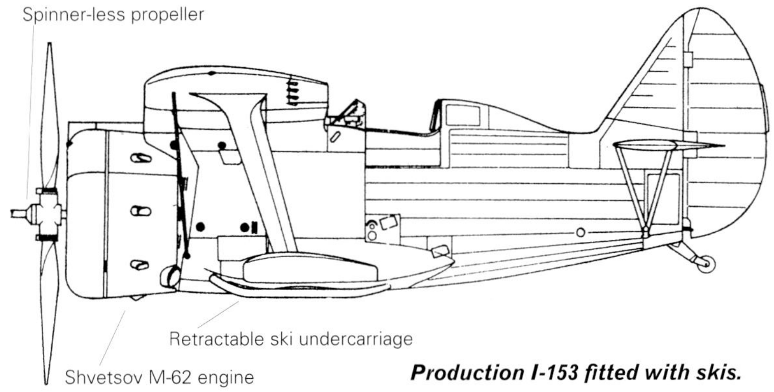

Production I-153 fitted with skis.

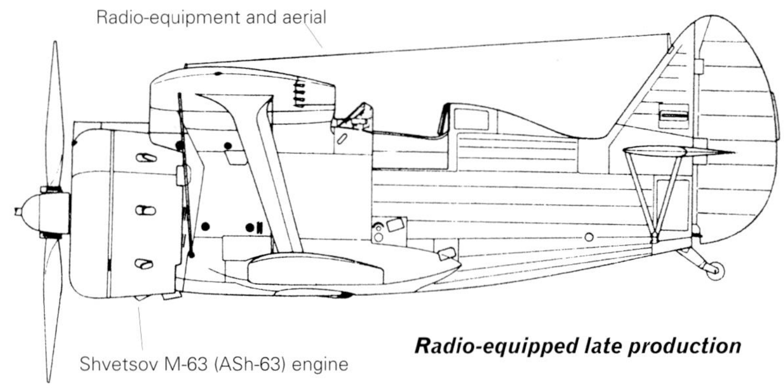

Radio-equipped late production

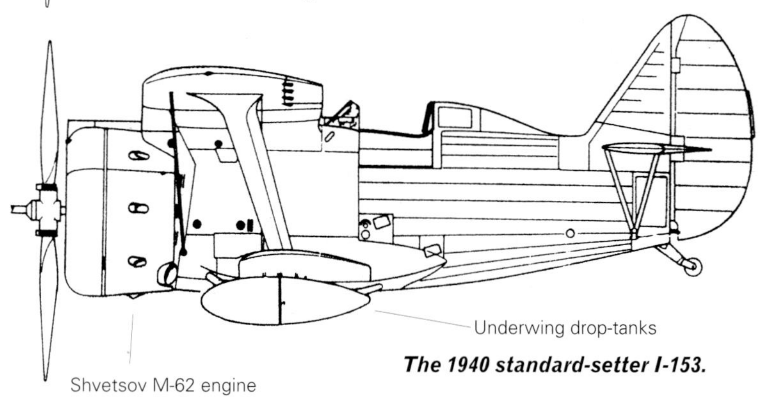

The 1940 standard-setter I-153.

I-153P

I-153P (Pushechnii, or cannon-armed) was the designation given to I-153 fighters armed with two 20-mm ShVAK cannon that were sometimes supplemented by two 7.62-mm (0.3-in) ShKAS machine-guns.

I-153V

The designation I-153V (Vysotnii, or high-altitude) was the designation of an I-153 with the M-62 engine and the latest pressure cabin designed by Schcherbakov. This cabin was fabricated from welded aluminium alloy and fitted with rubber seals over all apertures. A final airtight seal was achieved by cramping the hood to the rubber moulding around the sides of the cockpit's 6-mm (0.24-in) thick Plexiglas, and this heavily framed hinged hood improved the pilot's view compared to that of previous models. Once again the trials in June and July 1940 were successful but the overall weight increase of 190 kg (420 lb) degraded performance.

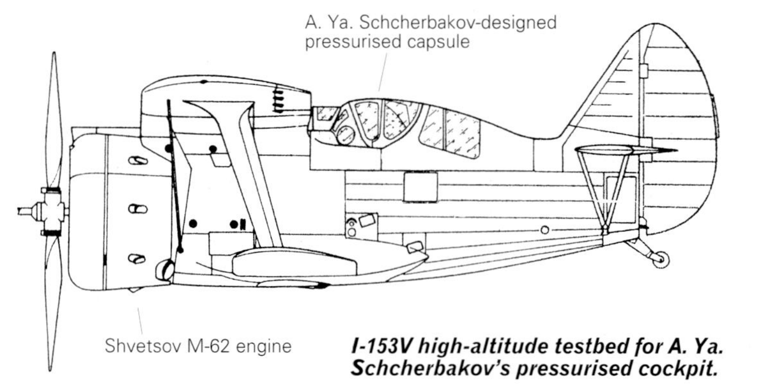

I-153V high-altitude testbed for A. Ya. Schcherbakov's pressurised cockpit.

The single Polikarpov I-153V (for vysotnyy – 'high altitude') was fitted with A. Ya Schcherbakov's pressurised cockpit. The aircraft was tested by Polikarpov (left) before being dispatched to the NII VVS (right) for testing by the Red air force in mid-1940.

I-153V-TKGK

The I-153V-TKGK (s Toorbo kom pressorami i Ghermeteecheskoy Kabinoy, or with turbochargers and pressure cockpit) was an I-153 with the M-63 engine modified late in 1939 with twin TK-3 turbochargers and a lightened and more flexible Schcherbakov pressure cabin. Trials had just begun when the newly formed NKAP (Narodnii Komissariat Aviatseeonnoy Promyshlennosti, or People's Commissariat for the Aviation Industry) ordered their end.

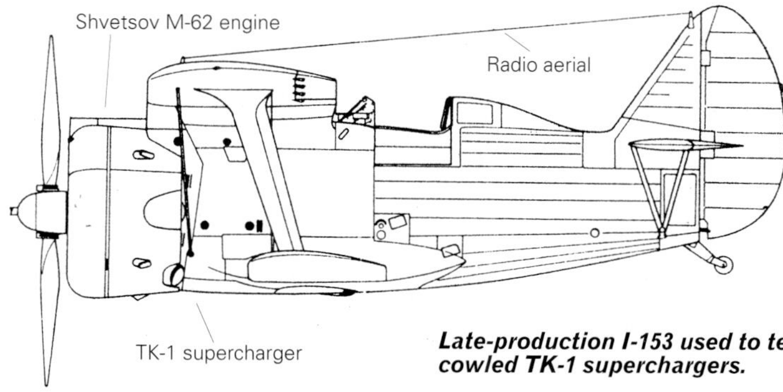

Late-production I-153 used to test cowled TK-1 superchargers.

I-153DM

The I-153DM was an I-153 (c/n 6034) to which, in September 1940, were fitted two underwing Merkulov DM-2 400-mm (15.75-in) diameter ramjets. A 30-km/h (19-mph) increase in maximum speed was recorded with the ramjets ignited during the course of trials flown by the test pilots P. Ye. Loginov, A. V. Davydov and A. I. Zhukov. In October of the same year trials were made with 500-mm (19.7-in) diameter DM-4 engines, with which a maximum speed increase of 51 km/h (32 mph) was achieved.

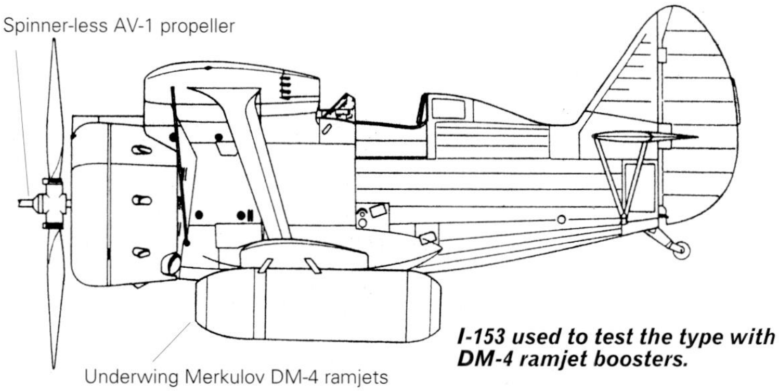

I-153 used to test the type with DM-4 ramjet boosters.

I-153 with TK-1 turbochargers

The I-153 with two TK-1 turbochargers on an M-62 engine was successfully tested between 15 May and 28 October 1940. It was faster than the standard I-153 above 5400 m (17,715 ft) but with the TK-1 inoperative it was slower at all altitudes as a result of the increased weight.

I-153 M-65

The I-153 with an M-65 engine was tested in 1940. No details of the engine or the tests are known.

I-170

The I-170 was a projected but unbuilt I-153 variant with a wooden fuselage and the M-106 liquid-cooled engine. Consideration was also given to the installation of the M-64 air-cooled radial engine and the Klimov M-105 (VK-105) liquid-cooled Vee engine.

I-190

The I-190 was developed over a two-year period as the successor to the I-153. It was powered by the M-88 engine designed by Sergei K. Tumanskii driving an AV-2L2 variable-pitch propeller. A larger vertical tail surface was fitted and the armament of production aircraft was to have been two 20-mm ShVAK cannon or four 7.62-mm (0.3-in) ShKAS machine-guns, plus up to 200 kg (441 lb) of bombs. The I-190 recorded its first flight on 30 December 1939 with A. I. Zhukov as pilot. Problems with the uneven running of the engine plagued flight tests and culminated in a successful emergency landing after the seventh flight. Testing was interrupted for a while in February after the aircraft had been involved in an accident but resumed when repairs had been completed. During mid-April 1940 an M-88R (Redooktornii) geared engine was installed together with a modified cowling, but constant overheating proved a serious problem. Yet another engine switch, this time to the M-88A, gave only a few more flights before the trials were terminated. A maximum speed of only 450 km/h (279 mph) at 7050 m (23,130 ft) had been recorded in these tests, this figure being worse than that being obtained from the I-153 with the M-62 engine.

In the meantime a second prototype I-190 had been built with the M-88 engine fitted with a TK-1 turbocharger. Work had also started on a variant with two TK-1 turbochargers and a pressurised cockpit, but the NKAP ordered that all development on the I-190 be stopped. It would be reassuring to believe that this decision was occasioned by the realisation that the biplane concept was finally outmoded, but a more likely explanation is to be found in the report delivered by Yakov V. Smooshkevich, head of the VVS, to the Communist Party Central Committee on 14 May 1940 declaring that the M-63, M-88 and M-105 engines were so unreliable that they had become obstacles to the development of new aircraft.

It is impossible not to feel pity for Polikarpov at this stage because the performance of the M-88 was also threatening his trials of the I-180, the intended replacement for his monoplane fighter, the I-16. Only two prototypes of the I-190 were built.

I-190 specification

Span	33 ft 5½ in (10.2 m)
Length	21 ft 4 in (6.5 m)
Wing area	267.28 sq ft (24.83 m^2)
Weight empty	3,882 lb (1761 kg)
Weight loaded	4,656 lb (2112 kg)
Weight of fuel	441 lb (200 kg)
Weight of oil	44 lb (20 kg)
Max. speed at sea level	233 mph (375 km/h)
at 23,130 ft (7050 m)	279 mph (450 km/h)
Climb to 16,405 ft (5000 m)	5 mins 54 secs
Service ceiling	40,680 ft (12400 m)
Range	447 miles (720 km)

Right and above right: Polikarpov tested the M-88-engined I-190 first prototype on skis, but the days of the fighter biplane were over.

I-195 project

The I-195 was projected in 1940 as a strengthened version of the I-190 with an enclosed but unpressurised cockpit. This unbraced sesquiplane was to have the much more powerful 1,500-hp (1118-kW) M-90 two-row radial engine driving a propeller fitted with a ducted spinner to boost the supply of cooling air. Other details known included a length of 7.65 m (25 ft 1 1/5 in), wing area of 28.0 m^2 (301.4 sq ft), loaded weight of 2916 kg (6,429 lb) and an estimated maximum speed of 590 km/h (367 mph) at about 7000 m (22,965 ft) reducing to 510 km/h (317 mph) at sea level. This was the final attempt by Polikarpov at designing a biplane fighter. He abandoned the work after metaphorically shooting himself down in flames by producing a paper attesting that vertical rather than horizontal manoeuvrability (i.e. climb rate), was the more important parameter in determining the victor of aerial combat.

Built in Buffalo

Aircraft of the Curtiss Airplane Division, Curtiss-Wright Corporation, 1940-43

By the time war had broken out in Europe in 1939, America's oldest aircraft manufacturer, Curtiss-Wright Corporation, was the world's biggest. Jack Kerr was a long-time Curtiss employee and documented much of the company's work, using 35-mm colour transparency film from 1938. Some of his colour images are shown here and concentrate on the activities of the company's Buffalo, N.Y. plant, with an emphasis on early 1941.

Top: *A sleeker aircraft than that which it was intended to replace, the* ***XP-46*** *was expected to be one of the 'hot ships' at* ***Buffalo*** *in early 1941 but its performance did not live up to its rakish looks and just two were built.*

Above: ***Curtiss test pilots of the period included (from left): B. T. Hulse, Ed Elliott, Herb Fisher, H. L. Childs, Bill Webster and Bob Fausel.***

Left: *It is July 1943 and in summer sunshine below a spectacular cloud formation, airframes fresh from the* ***Buffalo*** *production line await test and delivery flights. Sharing the flight line with a number of* ***P-40s*** *are at least three* ***Republic P-47Gs*** *(including* ***P-47G-1-CU 42-24950****). With the cancellation of the* ***Curtiss P-60A*** *contract in January 1942, production capacity at the* ***Buffalo*** *plant was filled with new orders for* ***P-40s*** *and a batch of* ***P-47s****. The 354* ***Curtiss-built Thunderbolts*** *were serialled 42-24920/25273 and though designated* ***P-47G*** *were simply 'razor-back'* ***P-47C/Ds*** *built under licence. The first were delivered in December 1942 – the last in March 1944. All were built with provision for a blind-flying hoods and were used principally in a Stateside training role.*

Right: Having gained US government permission to export a version of the US Army's P-36A fighter, Curtiss did a brisk business in the Model 75 (or 'Hawk 75'). The stripes and Arabic figures on the rudder of this otherwise unpainted machine identify it as one of a batch of 10 H75A-9s ordered by Persia in 1938/39. At least nine were delivered but were still in their crates when captured by British forces in June 1941. Shipped to India, they were assembled by the recently established Hindustan Aircraft Ltd and entered service as Mohawk Mk IVs with the RAF serials LA157/165. Given a training role, these much travelled aircraft served with 'A' Flight, No. 1 OTU (India), later No. 151 (Fighter) OTU, at Risalpur.

Above: The 'star and bar' insignia, outlined in blue, on these C-46 Commandos dates the photograph no earlier than August 1943. Though the Model CW-20 originated (as its model designation indicates) at the Curtiss-Wright Airplane Company's St. Louis plant, adoption of the airliner design by the US Army and US Navy (as the R5C) during World War II saw most built at the Buffalo facility, with the remainder turned out by a new Curtiss factory in Louisville and by the New Orleans plant of the Aircraft Division of the Higgins Boat Co.

Above: Early model P-40s share ramp space with a pair of USN SBC Helldivers (the last combat biplane built for the Navy) at Buffalo, probably during the winter of 1940/41. Two carrier squadrons of SBC-4s were in service at the time of Pearl Harbor, the Marine Corps retaining a squadron of land-based examples until 1943.

Left and below left: First flown on 18 December 1940, the second Curtiss naval dive-bomber to bear the Helldiver name could be said to have been one of those aircraft that 'did not look right' and, consequently, 'did not fly right'. Many observers at the time took the view that the XSB2C-1 (Curtiss Model 84) had an unusually close-coupled layout considering its intended role, one that required good directional stability for its successful execution. So it was that the production Helldiver (most of which would be built at a new plant in Columbus, Ohio) did not enter service until the end of 1943 and was plagued by aerodynamic problems. Here the XSB2C-1 prototype (BuNo. 1758) is seen having sustained damage in an accident during test flying in wintry conditions in February 1941. Though it was repaired, the aircraft was never tested by the Navy before being destroyed after suffering an in-flight wing failure on 21 December 1941. Of note in this view are the aircraft's automatic leading-edge slats, in the deployed position for landing, and split trailing-edge dive brakes/flaps. Ironically, the Helldiver was Curtiss-Wright's main product by 1945, the P-40 having ceased production in 1944 and there being little future for the C-46/R5C transport when the competition was the four-engined Douglas C-54. In October 1948, the last aircraft to bear the Curtiss name, the XF-87 Blackhawk jet fighter, was cancelled, sealing this once great company's fate. The Airplane Division was subsequently sold to North American Aviation.

With the P-40 entering production, Curtiss engineer Don Berlin began development of a potential replacement. This would draw on early British and French wartime experience and trends in European fighter design. Improvements in firepower and armour protection, as well as in performance, were primary objectives. The Model 86 (or XP-46) resembled the P-40 in its general arrangement but was smaller, had inward-retracting undercarriage, automatic leading-edge slats on the outer section of the wings (as fitted to the Messerschmitt Bf 109) and a new ventral radiator/oil-cooler. Armament was increased to four 0.30-in calibre machine-guns in each wing and a 0.50-in calibre gun either side of the engine, making the XP-46 the most heavily-armed American fighter at that time. Power came from a 1,150-hp (858-kW) Allison V-1710-39.

*The **US** Army ordered two **XP-46** prototypes on **29 September** 1939, and while the first aircraft (40-3053) would be completed to a more complete specification, the need to hasten flight testing led to the second aircraft (40-3054) making the type's first flight, on 2 February 1941. **Designated XP-46A**, this machine was completed without a radio, armament, self-sealing fuel tanks or additional cockpit armour. However, even in this 'stripped down' form, performance was less than electrifying, the aircraft only just managing to attain 410 mph (660 km/h) – the required top speed for a fully-equipped **P-46**! The **XP-46** finally flew on 29 **September**, but reached just 355 mph (571 km/h). **To** add insult to injury, the new design was slower than the **P-40D**, which was about to enter production with the same powerplant, and **XP-46** development was abandoned. These views of the **XP-46A** show the aircraft around the time of its first flight during a snowy February 1941. The reasons for the resemblance, in terms of its layout, between this aircraft and North American's **NA-73X** (later **XP-51** Mustang) have been the subject of debate. Though it is true that **NAA** (a company with no fighter-building experience) had access to all current data on **P-40** developments when designing its fighter, the Mustang turned out to be a very different machine with a laminar-flow wing, among other differences. In fact, it could be argued that the **XP-46** gave **NAA** more pointers as to the direction it should not follow in designing its own fighter!*

Left: Curtiss' Buffalo plant was the home of the P-40 family, the best-known of the company's wartime products. Deliveries of the first P-40s began in June 1940 and, from the fourth production aircraft onwards, were the first US Army fighters since the Curtiss P-1B to be delivered in full camouflage – olive drab with grey undersides. In this view, as a P-40 idles in the foreground, two Curtiss test pilots, discuss their flying duties. Note that these aircraft have yet to be fitted with their 0.30-in calibre armament.

Below: For longer-distance shipping this ingenious arrangement was devised, requiring simply the removal of the P-40's mainplane. The engine and other control surfaces remained in situ.

Above and above left: The somewhat ungainly Model 85 was a heavy, two-seat observation aircraft of a type that the US Army believed still had a place in the late 1930s. However, soon after Pearl Harbor the tactical reconnaissance role had been handed over to low-powered light aircraft of the Piper Cub type, while long-range Tac/R was entrusted to camera-equipped light bombers or fighters. Though it had not yet tested a prototype, the USAAC ordered no fewer than 203 examples in 1939, the first O-52 Owl taking to the air in February 1941. Once the US entered the war, however, the type was confined to training and other second-line duties. It is believed that 19 were later supplied to the Soviet Union. In these views early examples are seen, again during February 1941. Powered by a 600-hp (447-kW) P&W R-1340-51 Wasp, the production Owl carried a fixed 0.30-in calibre machine-gun in its starboard wing and had provision for a dorsal '50-cal'.

The introduction of the Allison V-1710-39 engine to the P-40 necessitated a redesign of the aircraft's nose, the spur reduction gear of the new Allison raising its thrust-line and shortening the engine overall. Introduced in the P-40D (designated Model 87 by Curtiss), the new configuration was retained on all subsequent P-40s, including the Packard Merlin-powered P-40Fs and Ls. The first USAAF P-40s to see combat were the P-40Es equipping five pursuit squadrons in the Philippines when the Japanese invaded in December 1941, the type remaining in use until the end of the war, though latterly in a fighter-bomber role. Including the Model 81 aircraft, 13,378 P-40s (and equivalant Model 87 export aircraft) were completed, the last P-40N-40 leaving the Buffalo plant on 30 November 1944. These views of a new P-40D or E (above) and aircraft awaiting their wings on the production line (left) are believed to be dated 1941.

Left upper: In all, 2,992 Model 87s were purchased directly by and supplied under Lend-Lease to the RAF. The first 560 aircraft were Model A87-A2s originally ordered by the French and were equivalent to the USAAC's P-40D. Known as Kittyhawk Mk Is by the RAF many, including this aircraft (left upper, serialled in the AK range), were destined for service in North Africa and were accordingly finished in two-tone desert camouflage. Seventeen were diverted to the Turkish air force (left) and 72 to Canada.

Above: Occasionally test flights ended this way, with a brand new aircraft in need of repair, most likely as a result of a mechanical failure of some description. Judging by the lack of apparent damage to the uppermost propeller blade, this P-40's engine had stopped before the aircraft touched down, in what appears to be a ploughed field, and nosed over.

'Pulsat Audaciter Die Noctuque'

Canberras of the Fuerza Aérea Argentina

The retirement of the last Canberra, conceived and initially built by English Electric (later absorbed into the British Aircraft Corporation which itself became a primary component of British Aerospace), and the only bomber in service in today's Argentine air force, represents the end of this country's strategic air power.

The Canberra was the pride of the Fuerza Aérea Argentina (FAA) until the 1990s, the strategic capability it provided allowing the air arm to project its power into any possible enemy country's interior for the destruction of that enemy's capacity to sustain a war.

Tested in combat during the Falklands/Malvinas conflict, the Canberra demonstrated this capability in an unexpected manner by bombing British troops by day and night. In this process it showed that, in the Canberra, the air force still had a potentially useful aircraft.

In 1999, just over 28 years after its arrival, the Canberra has not only lived up to the motto of Grupo 2 de Bombardeo ('Pulsat Audaciter Die Noctuque – 'he strikes bravely by day and by night'), but has demonstrated its ability in fulfilling a number of roles, including reconnaissance.

Soon after the withdrawal of the last Avro Lincoln in 1967, the FAA looked round for a replacement. That year a number of aircraft types, including the Canberra, were evaluated, and after a period a decision was made to order the British twin-jet bomber.

On 9 May 1968, the Commander-in-Chief's Resolution 03/5-68 determined the technical and operational details of buying 10 Canberra B.Mk 2 and two Canberra T.Mk 4 aircraft, all of them ex-RAF machines. These aircraft had been built in the 1950s and would be overhauled before delivery to the FAA, a contract being signed on 14 August by BAC and the FAA. The reworked B.Mk 2 aircraft would be redesignated B.Mk.62, while the T.Mk 4 machines had the revised designation T.Mk 64. At the time that the contract was signed, BAC also offered the FAA two Canberra PR.Mk 3 aircraft as reconnaissance platforms, but these were never acquired.

In January 1969 the Comando de Operaciones Aéreas (Air Operations Command) signed Resolution 01/1-69, creating the Grupo de Tareas Canberra (Canberra Task Group), commanded by Vicecomodoro Otto H. Schaub and formed with 23 officers and 29 non-commissioned officers. In July pilot training began in Argentina using Gloster Meteor F.Mk 4 fighters and locally built Morane-Saulnier MS.760 Paris counter-insurgency and trainer aircraft, and was completed in March 1970. Navigators were trained aboard the Lockheed C-130E Hercules. With local training complete, two crews were sent to Chiclayo, Peru, to receive further training on Canberra aircraft of the Peruvian air force. However, most personnel embarked for the UK where, between April and November 1970, further flying took place in BAC (Hunting) Jet Provost trainers at RAF Manby and Canberra machines at RAF Cottesmore, and also at the BAC factory at Warton in Lancashire. Meanwhile, technicians were trained on the Canberra's airframes and engines.

Farnborough appearance

Toward the end of 1970 the first two aircraft, B-101 and B-102, were being prepared for delivery. Both had been test flown, at first unpainted except for Argentine serial numbers and the British class 'B' registrations G-27-111 and G-27-112, respectively. Eventually, an Argentine grey/green camouflage scheme was applied, together with the British registrations G-AYHO and G-AYHP, the latter for an appearance at the 1970 SBAC air show at Farnborough in September – the aircraft's first public appearance.

Shortly after the completion of training in

Left: The unmistakable shape of the Canberra's wing is illustrated in this view of a B.Mk 62 over the Argentinian pampas. Late in its career the fleet lost most identification markings, while retaining the two-tone upper camouflage and white underside scheme throughout.

Above: An FAA Canberra pilot roasts under the perspex bubble that is the Canberra's cockpit canopy as the B.Mk 62 taxies at Paraná. Argentina's Canberra force has been relegated to a reconnaissance role in recent years, but has retained a bombing capability.

the UK, the first three aircraft, B-101, B-102 and B-103, were handed over to Comisión Canberra No. 1 and took-off for Argentina and their new assignment, the II Brigada Aérea at Paraná, in the province of Entre Ríos.

The delivery flight began on 17 November 1970, with escort provided by a C-130E. After stops at Sevilla in Spain, Isla de Sal (Cape Verde Islands), Recife in Brazil and Resistencia in Argentina, the three bombers and their escort landed at 6.15 p.m. on 20 November at Paraná, where a welcoming ceremony had been arranged.

On 19 February 1971, Comisión Canberra No. 2 left for the UK to collect B-104, B-111 and B-112 (the last two being T.Mk 64 trainers).

With the arrival of these aircraft, on 2 March, Grupo 1 de Bombardeo of the II Brigada Aérea (1st Bomber Group of the 2nd Air Brigade) was established. This group was later renamed Grupo 2 de Bombardeo and would, from then on, include Escuadrón I de Bombardeo (1st Bomber Squadron) or Escuadrón Canberra. On 10 May the first trials with practice bombs took place and on 21 May, as Comisión Canberra No. 3 left for the UK to collect another batch of aircraft, the first live bombs (1,000-pounders) were dropped by a Canberra over the Mazaruca range. Comisión Canberra No. 3 brought B-105, B-106 and B-107 back to Paraná, arriving on 31 May.

Six days before this, three Canberra aircraft had taken part in the air parade to mark the celebration of the May Revolution of 1810 that secured Argentina's independence, and on 20 June, the nation's flag day, six aircraft flew over the flag's commemorative monument at the city of Rosario. Trials and exercises continued. On 15 July, Canberra aircraft flew their first dive-bombing sorties at Mazaruca and, between 25 and 27 August, Canberra machines took part in exercises with other units of the air force for the first time. Co-ordinated by the Grupo I de Vigilancia Aérea (Air Vigilance Group 1), combat sorties were flown over Buenos Aires.

With its temporary British civil registration visible, B.Mk 62 B-102 is seen with an underwing load of four MATRA rocket pods. Although ordered to replace Lincolns in the level bombing role, the FAA Canberras were expected to also undertake anti-insurgency missions, though the MATRA pod was not a commonly used weapon.

B.Mk 62 B-101 (ex-WJ616, a Handley Page-built aircraft) was the first of the FAA's aircraft and was test flown unpainted with only a Class 'B' civil registration G-27-111 (left). Seen later with a coat of primer applied (middle left) B-101 is seen outside hangers at the British Aerospace Corporation's Samlesbury plant awaiting the application of a Fuerza Aérea Argentina camouflage scheme. Before departing for Argentina, B-101 (registered G-AYHO) made an appearance at the 1970 Farnborough airshow. In 1999 it is one of two surviving airworthy aircraft.

The last batch of aircraft, B-108, B-109 and B-110, arrived on 14 September, 10 days after Comisión Canberra No. 4 had left for the UK. The Escuadrón Canberra was thus complete.

Rocket launches were carried out on 24 September, again at Mazaruca, and on 8 October the first air-to-ground demonstration took place.

In order to give the aircraft a limited photo-reconnaissance capability, the Grupo Técnico 2 (2nd Technical Group) of II Brigada Aérea personnel began the installation of Carl Zeiss RMK-60 cameras on 22 July. Grupo Técnico 2 was also tasked with the installation of a compressed air engine starting system, used for the first time on 6 October in place of the original cartridge system fitted for use at air bases where the usual ground equipment was not available.

On 21 November came the first Canberra loss when, during a touch-and-go exercise, B-103 crashed; fortunately the crew ejected.

In 1972 the FAA's Canberra aircraft became fully operational. Exercises continued, a typical example being the Pesca ('fishing') exercise of 18 June, when four Canberra bombers and other FAA aircraft took part in maritime search and rescue missions. Other milestones during 1972 were the first flare launch on 20 November and the first bombing of a maritime target by a Canberra on 5 December.

On Air Force Day (10 August), the Canberra squadron flew Operativo Aniversario – a flight of four Argentine combat planes (for the first time) over the Argentine Antarctic territory, making low-altitude passes over the Vicecomodoro Marambio Antarctic air base.

By 1974 the first heavy maintenance on the Canberra fleet was carried out, engineers from Area de Material Río IV (Río IV Matériel Area), the main FAA workshop, helping II Brigada personnel in changing the main spar and other wing components on one of the Canberras.

The 1970s was a very difficult decade for Argentina as communist guerrillas waged a terror campaign, principally in the north of the country in the region where they hoped to establish a secure base area in which to prepare an advance against Buenos Aires. On 24 December guerrillas attacked the Batallón de Depósito de Arsenales Domingo Viejobueno (Domingo Viejobueno Arsenal Deposit Battalion) at Monte Chingolo, near Buenos Aires. To support the beleaguered army unit, one Canberra launched flares over the military base in an attempt to illuminate the surrounding area and thus assist the army to see and fight off its nocturnal foe.

On 5 February 1975 the government signed the secret Decree No. 261 which ordered the army, with the support of other armed forces, to neutralise the subversive elements operating in the country, especially in the northern Tucumán province, which was the core of the guerrillas' operations. The FAA went on to carry out 100 close support and bombing missions, in which the Canberra was to take part. Operations were generally made at the army's request, locally built Beech T-34 Mentor trainers operating in the forward air controller role to mark targets with smoke rockets for a section of two Canberra bombers, usually equipped with a pair of 1,000-lb (454-kg) bombs, which were dropped at around 500 m (1,640 ft) over the target. More than 20 missions were flown by Canberra bombers, the remainder being carried out by McDonnell Douglas A-4B Skyhawk, North American F-86F Sabre and MS.760 Paris aircraft. During 1976 the guerrillas' activities declined and the FAA's attack operations were halted.

The year 1975 had also seen the squadron's first overseas deployment, when seven aircraft took part in a flypast over Asunción to mark Paraguay's independence day on 15 May.

In March 1977 photo-reconnaissance operations and patrols over Argentina's frontier zones were made by Canberra aircraft for the first time, and in April two modifications were made to the Canberra fleet – the fitting of landing lights and a stand-by artificial horizon.

First crisis deployment

With the crisis between Argentina and Chile over the Beagle Channel late in 1978 looking likely to end in war, Argentina deployed armed forces to the south into the frontier zone with Chile. II Brigada Aérea created the Escuadrón Aeromóvil Canberra, which flew to Comandante Espora Naval Aviation Air Base, near Bahía Blanca, about 650 km (405 miles)

Above: Alongside B-101 at Farnborough was the second B.Mk 62, B-102/G-AYHP, seen here during practice at Samlesbury prior to the SBAC show.

Right: Fitted with tip tanks and ferry tanks on its underwing hardpoints, B-105 is seen, probably at Samlesbury, in 1971, awaiting its delivery flight.

south of Buenos Aires. This would have been the unit's operational base during the impending war. The Vatican intervened, however, and the confrontation ended in mediation rather than full-scale war, so during the first weeks of 1979 the Canberra bombers returned to Paraná.

On 22 March 1979 the Canberra force undertook another overseas excursion, five aircraft taking part in the Bolivian independence day flypast over the city of La Paz. Meanwhile, life in the unit continued normally until 4 December when, during a routine flight, the pilot of the B-106 lost control of his aircraft and crashed. Though the pilot ejected, his navigator lost his life.

New aircraft and modifications

By the end of 1981 British Aerospace, as BAC had by now become, had started the preparation of attrition replacements for the lost aircraft. Two ex-RAF aircraft (a B.Mk 2 and a T.Mk 4) were to be delivered to II Brigada Aérea, but the coming war with the UK meant that these machines were not delivered. At about the same time, the FAA was studying the possible installation of a Bendix RDR-1400 navigation radar to enhance operational capability. The project, named 'Pelícano', included the installation of a radome below the nose to enclose the antenna. The modification would be carried out at Area de Material Río IV during major inspections. In early 1982 B-101 was at Río IV and by March the aircraft's new installation had been completed.

The 'Pelícano' programme involved the testing of a Bendix RDR-1400 navigation radar in a number of aircraft. The first installation was made in B-101 which received one of the new sets in March 1982. In this view (right), taken after the aircraft's landing mishap on 5 June 1982 following a failed bombing sortie, the outline of the radome may be discerned under the aircraft's nose. Unexpected aerodynamic problems, which contributed to the loss of at least two aircraft, led to the eventual removal of the system. The above view shows B-101 after this work had been carried out, a blank having been fitted over the position occupied by the radome.

The first flight with the radar took place a few days later under the auspices of the Centro de Ensayos en Vuelo (CEV, or Flight Test Centre) at Córdoba City. Test pilots noted that the new radome produced a lateral force on the airframe and that more flap was needed for take-off. The CEV recommended removal of the radome until a solution to the problem was found. The installation of associated internal equipment continued, but the antenna and its radome were omitted for the time being.

At the beginning of the Falklands/Malvinas conflict, as testing of B-101 was carried out ,work on B-104 had reached an advanced stage. As it was difficult to remove the radar quickly and as the Canberra aircraft would be needed during the coming war, B-104 was delivered with the radome fitted. Both aircraft joined II Brigada on 8 April and were quickly sent to the Teatro de Operaciones del Atlántico Sur (TOAS, or South Atlantic Operations Theatre). These were the last aircraft to be deployed to Trelew Naval Aviation Air Base. A third aircraft, B-107, had just entered the radar installation programme and was therefore unavailable for war service. (The FAA Canberra's service during the war over sovereignty of the Islas Malvinas/Falkland Islands is described separately.)

Post-war service

After the war, radar experimentation continued, in the hope that solutions to the

Canberra at war: April/June 1982

Grupo 2 de Bombardeo crews are seen in happier times with four of their Canberra B.Mk 62s at Paraná in the 1970s. The aircraft nearest the camera – B-106 – was written-off on 4 December 1979.

During the South Atlantic conflict between Argentine and British forces, which took place in the months between April and June 1982, the Canberra bombers of Grupo 2 de Bombardeo flew almost 400 combat hours, dropped 39250 kg (86,530 lb) of bombs and lost two of their number. The episode was perhaps the swansong for this classic bomber, with the exception of the role played by Canberra aircraft of the Peruvian air force in the short border conflict with Ecuador early in 1995.

On the launch date for Operación 'Azul' – the Argentine amphibious operation to occupy the Falkland Islands – Grupo 2 had 10 Canberras on strength, of which seven (B-102, B-105, B-108/-112) were serviceable. Inquiries had previously been made with a view to purchasing 12 Avro Vulcan bombers, by then surplus to RAF requirements, with a view to providing the Fuerza Aérea Argentina with a long-range heavy bomber capability.

By the latter part of April the Canberra unit had deployed with its seven available aircraft to the naval air station of Trelew (also known as Almirante Zar), becoming known provisionally as Escuadrón de Bombardeo (B-101 and B-104 followed shortly afterwards, bringing the total complement to nine; B-107 took no part in the conflict). Almost immediately, three Canberras were detached to Rio Grande airfield in the extreme south for the first FAA combat mission – the bombing of British shipping taking part in the recovery of South Georgia. On Monday, 26 April, three Canberras departed Rio Grande shortly after mid-day. One aborted south of the Falklands after its tip tanks could not be released, while the others continued under guidance of a Boeing Model 707 of Grupo 1 de Transporte. Near the island the section was contacted by a Lockheed KC-130H from the same unit operating in the surveillance role, and the captain of this machine confirmed the target's position. But bad weather, including extremely low cloud, prevented the attack being pressed home and both Canberra bombers returned to Rio Grande after a round trip of some 4100 km (2,550 miles).

The events of that day are here described by 1st Lt Ricardo Proviero, one of the Canberra pilots on 26 April 1982.

[On Wednesday 21 April, the British destroyer HMS *Antrim* had approached the South Georgia group through a stormy ocean with snow squalls. At about 0700 hours, two Westland Wessex helicopters, carrying three groups of SAS commandos, were launched as the first stage in the British attack, which would culminate four days later through a joint effort that also included the frigates HMS *Brilliant* and HMS *Plymouth*, and the ice patrol ship HMS *Endurance*.]

"Many kilometres to the north at Trelew airfield, Majors Vivas and Escudero started to plan the mission with which Grupo 2 de Bombardeo, with its Canberra bombers, was tasked on the next day. That mission was to be made by two aircraft, while a third acted as airborne spare. Number one was crewed by the above officers, number two by 1st Lts Baeza and Cardo, and number three by 1st Lts Proviero and Moreno. One of the main problems with the mission was the distance at which the target was located, so it was decided to deploy the Canberra bombers to the mainland's southernmost air base, Rio Grande Naval Air Base, which offered a launch point 2000 km (1,243 miles) to the west of the target. Thus the fuselage bomb bay, which would normally carry up to six 1,000-lb (454-kg) bombs, was fitted with tankage for 3300 litres (726 Imp gal) of auxiliary fuel for a total of 13000 litres (2,860 Imp gal). Thus the armament was limited to two 1,000-lb (454-kg) Mk 17 bombs on the pair of underwing pylons. The target was a force of three ships, namely the Endurance, *the* Plymouth *and the auxiliary* Tidespring. *Later on we learned that the* Tidespring *was some 400 km (250 miles) away and the third ship was in fact the frigate* Brilliant, *with its deadly Seawolf SAMs, while there was also a fourth ship, the destroyer HMS* Antrim.

"The planned mission profile envisaged a climb to 11000 m (36,090 ft) using the fuel from the wing tip tanks which, when empty, we would drop to lessen drag as their retention would make it impossible for us to reach Rio Grande on the return leg. All in all it was a very scary mission! Before reaching the target we would descend to low level during the last miles of the inbound leg toward Cumberland Bay, inside which lies Grytviken Harbour. We had no photographic intelligence of the target's general area and the available charts did not provide any clear insight about the surrounding terrain. We only could ascertain that the bay was quite narrow, more like a fjord, with high walls on each side, thus it would be difficult to do fly the manoeuvres required to penetrate into the target area and make the bomb run if the targets were in port.

"On Sunday 25 April, Majors Vivas and Escudero went to Southern Air Command HQ, where they explained in detail how the mission was planned and received the appropriate clearance, although everybody knew that if we were faced with a headwind the conditions could be quite marginal, and in this eventuality we would not have enough fuel to reach even our emergency recovery base, which was none other than Port Stanley airfield, whose runway was

B-104 is seen at its dispersal at Paraná, prior to the installation of Bendix radar. This aircraft launched attacks on the British forces from both Trelew and, later, Río Gallegos. Though it survived the war it was lost in a crash in August 1982.

Complete with underwing stores and a pair of 1,000-lb high-explosive bombs awaiting loading is B-111 – one of the two T.Mk 64s – seen in May 1982 during the conflict. Both aircraft were deployed to Trelew during the war.

quite short for our aircraft. If we had to divert to Stanley, the idea was to take on fuel sufficient only to reach the mainland after a take-off that would require the full length of 3,900-ft (1190-m) runway. That Sunday in Trelew everybody was quite nervous and liberal quantities of coffee and cigarettes were consumed. It was the change from peace to war – all of us were ready for combat, but the waiting time until the first mission passed very, very slowly. Our minds reflected the images of our loved ones, and that damned Monday morning never arrived.

"Captain Casado, one of the Grupo's most experienced navigators, who would be shot down and killed on 13 June, handed my navigator a single-engine and no-engine performance chart on which we could find the distance which could be flown in each of these conditions before reaching sea level. For example, with both engines stopped through fuel exhaustion and maintaining a speed of 300 km/h (186 mph), we could run a distance of 295 km (183 miles).

"On Monday 26 April, before the sun rose through the eastern horizon, we started with a delicious coffee prepared by Carlos Seppey, the NCO in charge of our personal flight gear and survival equipment, who also shared those long readiness hours and always tried his best efforts to make us happy and well-fed. The deployment flight to Rio Grande was made without any problem and once there we were greeted by several air force and navy officers who took us to the mess, which also acted as a kind of operations room. We were informed that the weather conditions over the target area were not very good, then we met with the crew of the Boeing 707, which, having a better navigation suite than the old Canberra aircraft, would escort us until we reached the low-level approach leg. At 1200 hours we climbed into our aircraft, while the air force pilots deployed at the base, together with its CO, Colonel Corino, waved goodbye. We cranked up, taxied to the runway's threshhold and into take-off position, a fuel bowser filled up the tanks to the maximum, replenishing what we had used in starting up and taxiing. These litres were very useful as they meant the difference between reaching or not reaching Port Stanley's runway. The bombers took-off with a 10-second separation, joining up while we established an easterly heading, directly to the western side of the nearby San Pedro Island – in fact we took off with tailwind. While we climbed, the mainland started to dissapear behind and below us, then the last land seen before the infinite ocean was Los Estados island, to our right.

"We maintained radio silence, but the conversation between pilot and navigator never ceased – it was the way to make the flight shorter – while we made efforts to keep formation without touching the throttle as we knew that increasing or decreasing power meant more fuel used. When we where just south of the Malvinas [Falklands] we finished the fuel in the wing tip tanks, and then our leader gave the order to jettison them; numbers two and three did this normally, but the leader had a wing tip tank hang-up, so he could not continue with the mission as a result of the higher-than-expected drag. At this point number three, the airborne spare, took notice of the situation and assumed the role of mission leader. Meanwhile, the Model 707 signalled the route simply by its condensation trails, and the two Canberra aircraft, nicknamed 'Penélope' and 'Picasesos', followed it. The navigators made their best efforts to keep the route updated, but because of a small error before the flight, when fixing the Model 707's Point Charlie, this was not the same as ours, and from then on we had to make use of all our known navigation methods in order to confirm our en-route positions, as we could not call by radio to the Model 707's navigator. Then, at last, there arrived the time to separate from the four-jet transport, which did a graceful turn towards the mainland marked by its four white trails.

"Down there a little fleet of hostile ships was perhaps waiting for us, and our fear was not of the missiles, as a direct hit would finish an aircraft and possibly its crew, but of a near miss which could pierce our bomb-bay auxiliary tank, making it impossible to return home. While we were thinking on that and many other things, radio silence was broken and we heard the voice of the KC-130 aircraft commander, who said that his radar had located the ships grouped together within the bay and in front of Grytviken Harbour [in the South Georgia group of islands]. We continued to descend until we received the order to cancel the mission and return: the weather was quite bad and the targets were sheltered within the high walls of the narrow bay, whose nature did not permit the bomb run and escape leg of our return. Near the extreme western side of the westernmost island, we started our return climb heading for the Malvinas. From there the Model 707's navigator provided us with navigation data every three minutes, comparing this position with our course, until we tally-hoed it and closed in. About 150 km (93 miles) before reaching the Malvinas we did another fuel check and found out that there was enough to get to Rio Grande as we had not flown the planned low-level leg, which was the one which would have meant the highest fuel consumption. At 1900 hours we landed at

Seen outside the operations building at Trelew in 1982, Canberra aircrew model the two distinct types of anti-exposure flight suits worn by crews on the long flights over the bitterly cold South Atlantic.

T.Mk 64 B-111 taxies prior to a mission over the Falklands, with a 1,000-lb Mk 17 bomb beneath each wing but without tip tanks. Both of the Canberra trainers flew bombing missions during the war.

Rio Grande, after having logged 5 hours 30 minutes in a round trip of some 4075 km (2,530 miles).

"During that night the ground crews worked hard to fit new wing tip fuel tanks. On the next day, Tuesday 27 April, at 1200 hours the three Canberra bombers were again at the runway's threshold, ready to take off in better weather conditions, after a very careful mission planning briefing and with precise intelligence about where the ships were located, but just before we started our take-off run and without any explanation, the WOC (War Operations Centre) called us with orders to cancel the mission and return to the parking apron. Later we learned that the Argentine garrison on South Georgia had surrendered. Thus our desire to be the first to attack the British fleet was frustrated, although when we returned to Trelew we were received by the rest of our Grupo as if we had done it."

On 1 May, first day of the shooting war, the Escuadrón de Bombardeo launched six Canberra sorties from Trelew, in three-aircraft flights, against a supposed beach-head established by the British north of Port Stanley, and also against naval targets. The first sortie found nothing and returned home. The second was intercepted by BAe Sea Harrier fighters only some 90 km (56 miles) from the aircraft-carrier HMS *Invincible*, and at 1704 hours an AIM-9L Sidewinder fired by Lieutenant W. A. Curtis of No. 801 Squadron shot down Canberra B-110. The pilot, Lt Eduardo de Ibañez, and his navigator, 1st Lt Mario Gonzalez, ejected from the burning bomber, but were never found.

After this fiasco, in which the limited capabilities of the old bomber had been clearly shown, the Canberras of Grupo 2, equipped with Israeli-made chaff/flare dispensers, undertook most of their sorties by night.

During the conflict Grupo 2 flew a total of 54 missions, engaging in combat in 25 of them. The war's activities comprised surveillance and reconnaissance missions, tactical reconnaissance, long-range anti-shipping strikes, day bombing and night bombing missions. Some 395 combat hours were flown, and 39250 kg (86,530 lb) of bombs were dropped. FAA Canberra bombers had the dubious honour of taking part in the last combat mission of the war, and that mission is reconstructed here using interviews with the two crew members of the surviving Canberra and by assessing their report on the mission.

The story begins on Sunday, 13 June 1982, at Río Gallegos Air Base, where a flight of three Canberra aircraft had been deployed for the almost nightly bombing runs against British ground forces near San Carlos and Mount Kent. For crews in readiness awaiting the take-off order in their uncomfortable anti-exposure flight suits, it seemed that the war would continue until most of them were killed, so it came as no surprise when Frag Order 1326 arrived from Southern Air Command HQ (Comando Fuerza Aérea del Sur, or CDOFAS) at Comodoro Rivadavia Air Base. This required a bombing mission against British forces at Mount Harriet by two Canberra aircraft. The crews detailed were Captains Pástran and Casado with the callsign BACO 1 and 1st Lts Rivollier and Annino as BACO 2. OF-1326 also included two Dassault Mirage IIIEA fighters of Grupo 8 de Caza as escort: PLUTON 1 was flown by Major Sanchez and PLUTON 2 by Captain Gonzalez. All knew that the British controlled most of East Falkland Island. They also knew about the many and varied threats they faced from surface-to-air missiles (SAMs) and Sea Harrier interceptors.

At about 1900 hours the crews undertook an extensive briefing that lasted for more than an hour. At 2015 hours they headed for their respective aircraft to carry out the required walk-round inspection, and at 2130 hours they took off for East Falkland. Five minutes later the escorting Mirage fighters were airborne. The Canberra bombers climbed to 12000 m (36,090 ft), maintaining radio silence and communicating by a previously arranged system of lights. Over the ocean it was pitch black but cloudless, and the crews had to adapt themselves to the darkness, keeping their instrument lights dim. When the aircraft were about 370 km (230 miles) from the target area, the pilots turned off the navigation lights. As the Canberra aircraft crossed Falkland Sound between West and East Falkland, the escorting Mirage fighters were about 6 km (3.75 miles) behind in radar trail. Argentine radar near Port Stanley started to provide concise instructions while the Mirage fighters loitered in a high-altitude CAP (Combat Air Patrol) over the sea. The bombers arrived at their initial point, some 80 km (50 miles) south of Mount Kent, and turned left to head directly at the target. There were thin, broken layers of middle and low cloud over the area, revealing glimpses of a few

1Ten Annino (above, with B-104) and 1Ten Roberto Rivolier crewed B-109 on the last Canberra sortie of the war, on 13 June 1982, in which B-108 was shot down. Annino and Rivolier landed back at Rio Gallegos just after midnight on 14 June, completing the last Argentine sortie of the conflict. They had been in the air two and a half hours and had failed to hit their target.

***Right:* B-108 was the second of two Canberras destroyed by enemy action during the conflict, crashing at 0155 Zulu 14 June 1982 after being hit by a Sea Dart SAM fired by HMS *Exeter* in the lower front fuselage while undertaking a night bombing sortie. While the pilot, Captain Pástran, eventually ejected and was later captured by British troops, his navigator, Captain Casado, was killed in the crash. B-108 was photographed the day before its final flight.**

***Below:* Royal Navy Type 42 destroyer HMS *Exeter* launches a Sea Dart surface-to-air missile on the morning of 7 June 1982. This particular shot was responsible for downing Grupo 1 de Aerofotografico Learjet 35A T-24; a week later *Exeter* launched a Sea Dart at Canberra B-108 at 0150Z, 14 June 1982.**

lights in Port Stanley. Flares and tracers pierced the darkness, together with flashes from Argentine and British artillery fire.

The Canberra bombers' radio sets, on stand-by, picked-up noises from the jamming efforts of both sides, which disturbed communications with the Argentine radar controller. Both aircraft dropped their bombs at 2255 hours at an altitude of 13000 m (42,650 ft), and the 1,000-lb (454-kg) Mk 17 bombs exploded in the middle of gloomy flashes that gave the battlefield a diurnal tone. Both Canberra bombers then set a 180° heading and descended to 12000 m (39,370 ft) to gain speed in the thin air. But the British had the aircraft on their fire-control radars. Scarcely a minute into their escape leg, Roberto Pástran, the pilot of BACO 1, realised they had received a SAM hit, the tremendous explosion followed by an extremely violent jolt was wholly unmistakable. A Sea Dart, launched by HMS *Exeter*, had hit B-108's lower front section, probably right under Casado's seat. The effects were immediate: explosive decompression in the cockpit, no elevator response and the number one fuel tank, that nearest to the cockpit, on fire. The Canberra was doomed, but Pástran put both engines on idle, got the fire extinguishers ready – just in case – and deployed the air brakes. Knowing that any effort to abandon the aircraft under these circumstances could be fatal, he tried hard to regain control and prevent a spin. Then, through the glare of the onboard fire, Pástran saw that they were descending through 4500 m (14,765 ft) and yelled the order to eject. Casado's reply was clear but worried: "I am trying but it's stuck."

Pástran decided to wait until his navigator could find some way to bail out of the Canberra, which continued its descent followed by a trail of flame. At 3000 m (9,845 ft) the aircraft began to spiral. Pástran knew that time was running out and that he had to escape. He shouted his intentions to Casado but this time did not receive any reply. At 2400 m (7,875 ft), when the Canberra was in the third turn of its spin, Pástran ejected. The acceleration was so violent that he passed out. B-108 crashed – with Casado still trapped – into the sea near Lively Island.

Meanwhile BACO 2, flown by Rivollier and Annino, evaded several SAMs by dropping chaff, and at 0003 hours landed at Río Gallegos some 10 minutes after the Mirage section.

Pástran regained consciousness while he was falling. With one hand he tried to feel the seat, and only then realised that he was hanging from his parachute. He hardly had enough time to inflate the life vest before sinking into the freezing waters. Despite the shock and ingestion of sea water, he managed to remove his parachute. The time was 2355 hours: scarcely four minutes had passed from the moment that the Sea Dart had hit the Canberra. After several attempts he inflated his dinghy, in which he eventually reached land near Fitzroy. There he saw the smoking hulks of the British transports *Sir Galahad* and *Sir Tristram*, attacked some days previously by the A-4B Skyhawks of Grupo 5 de Caza. He started to walk on a roughly westerly heading, his only injury a wound on the back of the left hand. After nightfall on 14 June Pástran noted several British helicopters looking for him, but the terrain kept the Argentine officer hidden. Tiredness finally took its toll and the beam of a helicopter's searchlight marked the end of his freedom. He was well treated as a POW, returning to Argentina in mid-July aboard the ferry *St Edmund*.

Thus ended the FAA's last combat mission and also the last for the Canberra bombers of Grupo 2. The campaign had clearly revealed the obsolescence of this beautiful aircraft in the traditional bombing role. Little in the way of positive results had been gained and two Canberra bombers had been lost, but to add to the unit's bad luck a third Canberra was lost during a peacetime training sortie on 13 August, both members of the crew, Lts Cooke and Tejada, being killed. During the months after the war Grupo 2's serviceability fell as a result of the British embargo of spare parts, but about a year later serviceability was restored as the result of the receipt of spares from Peru, South Africa and Venezuela. **Salvador Mafé Huertas**

For a period post-war the Canberras continued to wear their mission marks (15 on B-109) below a map of the Malvinas. Grupo 2 de Bombardeo's badge appears next to the serial, with an unidentified badge on the crew entrance, alongside crash rescue markings.

One of the FAA's T.Mk 64s departs Trelew complete with a pair of Mk 17s under-wing, date unknown.

Canberra combat log

26 April

Frag number/call-sign: OF-?/?,'Penélope' and 'Picasesos' – three aircraft
Crews: Mayor Vivas and Mayor Escudero; 1Ten Baeza and 1Ten Cardo; 1Ten Sproviero and 1Ten Moreno
Armament: two Mk 17 1,000-lb bombs per aircraft
On 21 April British troops landed on the South Georgia, Argentina deciding on the 25th to bomb the shipping supporting the invasion. Flying from Base Aeronaval Río Grande, the three aircraft had a 2000-km flight to their objective and thus carried extra fuel comprising 2724 litres in a bomb bay tank and two 1109-litre tip tanks. All up this totalled some 12000 litres of fuel. For the return leg to the mainland the aircraft would have to land at Port Stanley/Puerto Argentino to refuel. During the flight the Canberras were escorted by a Boeing 707, providing navigation support, and a KC-130H surveillance aircraft. On 26 April the Canberras flew from Trelew to Río Grande, where they were refuelled on the runway and took-off again after midday. One aircraft returned to the base after problems releasing a drop tank, the rest of the flight continued to the Georgias. However, although the Hercules reported two targets in a bay near Grytviken, their location and deteriorating weather led to the mission being abandoned and the aircraft returned, non-stop, landing after 5½ hours in the air.

27 April

A renewed attempt at executing the mission of the previous day was planned, but the surrender of the Argentine troops on the Georgias brought its cancellation.

1 May

Frag number/call-sign: OF-1111/'Ruta' – three aircraft
Crews: Cap. Nogueira and Cap. Sanchez (B-102); Cap. Rodino and 1Ten Dubroca; 1Ten Lozano and 1Ten Cooke
Armament: four Mk 17 bombs per aircraft
Took off from Trelew at 4.05pm to attack landing ships near Puerto Argentino/Port Stanley. One SAM launched from an RN ship, this damaging the wingtip of B-102. Weather deteriorated and mission cancelled. All aircraft returned, landing at Trelew at 5.30pm.

Frag number/call-sign: OF-1117/'Rifle' – three aircraft
Crews: Cap. Baigorri and My Rodeyro; 1Ten Gonzalez and 1Ten De Ibañez (B-110); Cap García Puebla and Ten Segat.
Armament: four Mk 17 bombs per aircraft
Took-off from Trelew at 4.20pm to attack same objective as OF-1111. CAP of Sea Harriers spotted approaching head-on, forcing Canberras to turn back. Aircraft Nos 1 and 3 broke, but No. 2 (B-110), with the youngest crew, maintained course and was downed by an AIM-9L launched by Lt. W. Curtis in Sea Harrier XZ451. The Canberra crew ejected but were never found. The remaining aircraft returned to Trelew where they landed, at 7.20pm

3 May

Frag number/call-sign: OF-1159/'Lince' – two B.Mk 62s
Crews: My Vivas and My Escudero (B-102); 1Ten Baeza and 1 Ten Cardo (B-104)
Armament: four Mk 17 bombs per aircraft
Took off from Trelew at 3.40pm to attack shipping but on reaching objective discovered they were Argentine. Mission cancelled; aircraft returned to the base 5.50pm.

17 May

B-101, equipped with radar, and with three crewmembers, began reconnaissance operations under the 'Krill' call-sign; these were repeated on 20, 21, 25 May and 11 June.

21 May

After the British landings at San Carlos Water, a high-altitude raid by eight aircraft, each carrying eight Mk 17 bombs and escorted by Mirage IIIEAs was planned to attack the recently landed troops. The aircraft left Trelew but updated intelligence and intense Sea Harriers activity saw the mission cancelled.

26 May

Frag number/call-sign: OF-1240/? – three B.Mk.62s.
Crews: Cap. Freijo and Cap Marín; 1Ten Mauad and 1Ten Siri; Cap. Bredeston and Cap. Sisco.
Armament: ?
This, the first night mission, began at 3.35am from Río Gallegos air base. All three aircraft returned at 4.40am, as the weather had deteriorated.

27 May

Frag number/call-sign: OF-1240/? – two B.Mk.62s
Crews: Cap Freijo and Cap Marín; My. Vivas and My. Escudero
Armament: four BRP and two Mk 17 bombs per aircraft
Took off from Río Gallegos at 3.20am to make a low-altitude attack on the British camp at San Carlos. Bombs were successfully dropped at 800ft, the aircraft returning at 6.00am. This was the first successful bombing mission by Grupo 2 de Bombardeo during the war.

29 May

Frag number/call-sign: OF-1260/'Charrúa' – two aircraft
Crews: Cap Villada with 1Ten Pagano and 1Ten Rivollier with 1Ten Annino.
Armament: four Mk 17 bombs per aircraft
The aircraft took off at 1.00am to attack troops near San Carlos and in spite of fog, the bombs were dropped from 700ft and were seen to explode. All aircraft returned to Río Gallegos at 3.00am.

31 May

Frag number/call-sign: OF-1269/'Charrúa' – two aircraft
Crews: Cap Pastrán and Cap Casado (B-108); 1Ten Sproviero and 1Ten Moreno (B-101)
Armament: four Mk 17 bombs per aircraft
En route to San Carlos, B-101 returned to base having lost the lead aircraft, which successfully dropped its bombs from 600ft.

Frag number/call-sign: OF-1270/'Odín' – two aircraft
Crews: Cap Bredeston, Cap Sisco (B-105); 1Ten Mauad, 1Ten Acosta (B-109)
Armament: four Mk 17 bombs
Taking-off with OF-1269 and destined for the same target, these aircraft hit at least two installations, including the telephone exchange.

1 June

Frag number/call-sign: OF-1273/'Huinca' – three aircraft
Crews: My Chevallier and Ten Lozano (B-108); Cap Bertoldi and 1Ten Reyes (B-105); Cap García Puebla and 1Ten Segat (B-109)
Armament: three Mk 17 bombs per aircraft
With the British advance to Puerto Argentino/Port Stanley, the decision was taken to attack Mount Kent, where British troops were concentrated. These night attacks continued until the end of the war, the first taking off from Río Gallegos at 3.59am. Aircraft No. 2 returned with mechanical problems, the others dropping their bombs successfully in the face of AAA and SAMs. The two bombers returned quickly to their base and landed at 6.30am.

4 June

Frag number/call-sign: OF-1275/'Lince' – three B.Mk 62s
Crews: Cap. Nogueira and My Rodeyro; 1Ten Baeza and 1Ten Cardo; 1Ten Sproviero and 1Ten Moreno.
Armament: ?
Took off at 5.23pm, after one hour delay due to bad weather. (see below)

Frag number/call-sign: OF-1276/'Puma' – two B.Mk 62s
Crews: Cap Freijo, 1Ten Pagano; 1Ten Heredia, 1Ten Gerez
Armament: ?
Took off with OF-1275, both groups attacking Mount Kent in heavy AAA/SAM fire. In spite of this, the Canberras dropped their bombs and returned to base at 8.00pm

5 June

Frag number/call-sign: OF-1278/'Pato' – two B.Mk.62
Crews: Cap Bertoldi, Cap Sanchez; Ten Gonzalez, Cap Hernandez.
Armament: ?

Frag number/call-sign: OF-1279/'Gaucho' – two B.Mk.62
Crews: Cap. Bredeston, Cap Sisco; 1Ten Mauad, 1Ten Acosta (B-101).
Armament: five Mk 17 bombs
Both flights departed at 5.00am but, due to intensive SAM activity, both aborted. B-101 returned to Río Gallegos on one engine and went off the runway on landing, its right undercarriage collapsing.

In an attempt to halt the Canberra's night-bombing campaign the British conceived 'Operation Canbelow' on 6 June, whereby HMS Invincible and HMS Brilliant were positioned 100 miles (160 km) west of the Falklands to wait for Canberra movements. However, none was detected as, due to the weather, the Canberras did not take-off that day.
Answering the threat posed to their continued operations, four Canberras ('Negro' flight – B-102, B-105, B-108 and B-109) were deployed to Mar del Plata with impressed HS.125 biz-jet LV-ALW (as a radio relay aircraft) for anti-shipping strikes.

8 June

Four Canberras, C-130H TC-68 and the HS.125 took off from Mar del Plata to intercept a ship (the Liberian-registered tanker *Hercules*) detected by two Boeing 707s from the I Brigada Aérea between Ascension Island and the Georgias. The target was found 1,000 miles (1609 km) off the coast, the Canberras beginning their run into the target. However, alerted to the proximity of a CAP, they aborted the mission, though one aircraft had already dropped its load – two Mk 17 bombs which hit the ship but did not explode.

9 June

Canberras made long-range reconnaissance missions from Mar del Plata and Río Gallegos. On the next day the aircraft from Mar del Plata returned to Río Gallegos via Trelew, to resume the bombing campaign over Mount Kent. On the night of this day two flights were prepared:

Frag number/call-sign: OF-1308/'Tigre' – two B.Mk 62
Crews: Cap. Bertoldi and Cap Sanchez; 1Ten Heredia and 1Ten Gerez.
Frag number/call-sign: OF-1309/'Leon' escadrille – two B.Mk.62
Crews: Cap Martinez Villada, My Escudero; 1Ten Rivollier, 1Ten Annino.
1Ten Heredia and 1Ten Rivollier were unable to take-off due to mechanical problems, the remaining escadrille leaders reforming as 'Tigre' escadrille. However, with intense AAA/SAM fire, they were unable to attack and returned to base.

12 June

Frag number/call-sign: OF-1310/'Tauro' – two B.Mk 62
Crews: My Vivas and 1Ten Foco; Cap Pastrán and Cap Casado.
Armament: four Mk 17 bombs per aircraft
Took-off from Río Gallegos at 0.20am to attack objectives in Bluff Cove, near Mount Kent. As both aircraft were unable to jettison one of their drop tanks, they were forced to return to base.

Frag number/call-sign: OF-1311/'Acuario' – two B.Mk 62
Crews: Cap. Freijo, 1Ten Dubroca; Cap Bredeston, 1Ten Mondino.
Armament: two Mk 17 bombs per aircraft (due to delays in arming the aircraft)
Took-off with 'Tauro' flight and, though the lead aircraft was forced to return to base, the remaining machine continued to Bluff Cove where it dropped its bombs, returning to base at 2.30am.

Frag number/call-sign: OF-1315/'Roma' – one B.Mk 62 and one T.Mk 64
Crews: 1Ten Rivollier, 1Ten Annino; 1Ten Heredia, 1Ten Gerez (T.Mk 64)
Armament: ?
Took-off at 7.01pm (leaving a third aircraft behind with mechanical problems. The target was the British command HQ at Port Harriet House, near Mount Kent, but the presence of Sea Harriers, bad weather and the failure of the Argentine land radar system casued the mission to be aborted.

Frag number/call-sign: OF-1316/'Berlin' – two B.Mk 62
Crews: Cap Villada and 1Ten Pagano (B-104); Cap García Puebla and 1Ten Segat (B-102)
Armament: ?
Left Río Gallegos at 11.00pm with the same objective as OF-1316. B-104 returned to base when near the islands, the other aircraft continuing alone. Dropping his bombs, near the command HQ, Captain Garcia Puebla was alerted to the presence of a CAP and turned for home. However, a Sea Harrier pilot had spotted the fleeing bomber and gave chase. Captain Puebla descended to low level at full power to escape and was successful in shaking off his pursuer, though he was forced to keep his speed down as the aircraft still had its drop tanks aboard, as these were now becoming scarce on the squadron. Setting course for home, the Canberra crew realised they were lost, but were eventually guided back to base by Río Gallegos radar.

13 June

Frag number/call-sign: OF-1326/'Baco' – two B.Mk 62s
Crews: Cap Pastrán and Cap Casado (B-108); 1Ten Rivollier and 1Ten Annino (B-109)
Armament: five Mk 17 bombs per aircraft
Taking-off at 9.30pm, escorted by two Mirage IIIEAs ('Plutón' flight), the mission was another attempt to hit the command HQ, Port Harriet House. Approaching the target from the south, the aircraft's bombs missed the target by only a few metres. Destroyers HMS *Exeter* and *Cardiff* launched Sea Dart SAMs, one of these from the latter hitting B-108. At 15,000 ft Captain Pastrán ordered his navigator to eject, but Captain Casado said that his seat would not fire. At 7,000ft the pilot ejected and was picked up by a British helicopter the following day. Meanwhile, B-109's crew fired chaff and flares and managed to evade a CAP. At 00.05am (14 June) the aircraft landed back at Río Gallegos, the last Argentine combat aircraft to complete a sortie during the short war. A few hours later, the Argentine troops on the islands surrendered.

On 20 June the Escuadrón Canberra returned to its base at Paraná having flown 58 missions (including 9 reconnaissance sorties) over 395 flight hours. Eighteen sorties had found their target, 85000 lbs of bombs being dropped. Two aircraft and three aircrew had been lost.

Above: Though a compressed air starting system was fitted to the FAA's Canberras, the original cartridge system was retained for use at bases where the necessary air-start equipment was unavailable. Here, white smoke billows from the cartridge starter on the starboard Rolls-Royce Avon RA.3 Mk 101 of T.Mk 64 B-111 on 13 August 1987. By this time the fleet had lost not only its mission symbols but most other markings, including most of their national insignia.

Right: During the Falklands war a flare/chaff dispensing system of Israeli origin was fitted to the Canberra fleet to provide a measure of self protection from British SAMs.

stability problems associated with the first installations could be found. B-107's radar fit had been completed during the conflict, and this machine was joined by B-102 during July. On 13 August, during a routine navigation training flight, B-104's pilot was forced to shut down his starboard engine as a result of low oil pressure. He elected to return to base and make an emergency landing, but the fact that the aircraft was laden with fuel combined with the control problems associated with the radar fit to create considerable asymmetric flight difficulties. As a result, the pilot lost control and immediately ordered the navigator and his student to eject. However, the aircraft's attitude and proximity to the ground meant that only the navigator survived.

Radome problems persist

As a consequence of this accident, the Junta Superior de Investigación de Accidentes (Accidents Investigation Superior Bureau) decided in 1984 that the remaining radar-equipped aircraft (B-101, B-102 and B-107) would be extensively tested and the instability problem resolved once and for all, and also that the installation programme for the remaining aircraft would be cancelled. Eventually it was discovered that on a Canberra flying with only one engine, it was impossible to lower the flaps and accelerate at the same time without losing control of the aircraft. The pilot of B-104 had lowered his flaps for landing, but soon realised that his speed had dropped too low. Raising his flaps he applied power, but the flap response was slow and the aircraft 'departed' to starboard and crashed.

On 1 July 1983, B-107 suffered an accident at Paraná during a training flight in which asymmetric flying was carried out. Although it could not be determined whether the aircraft's radar was a contributing factor, the programme received another body blow and was finally cancelled altogether in late 1984.The radar equipment fitted to B-101 and B-102 was removed.

In order to overcome the British embargo on trade and ensure a continued supply of spare parts for the aircraft, the FAA sought and received the considerable assistance of Peru, and were thus able, with Peruvian and other assis-

Above: Having turned down the offer of a pair of reconditioned Canberra PR.Mk 3s, the FAA installed Carl Zeiss RMK-60 cameras in some aircraft to provide a limited PR capability. Two aircraft were given a more comprehensive reconnaissance equipment fit in the mid-1990s.

Seen post-war, B-102 displays 15 mission marks above its nose wheel. As B.Mk 2 WJ713 from August 1953 until February 1968, the aircraft had seen service with the RAF Flying College, College of Air Warfare and Nos 85 and 360 Sqns.

1999 – the Argentine Canberras' last year?

With only one aircrew current on the Canberra in late 1999 and a budget ceiling for a mere 100 hours of flying, the days of the Canberra in Argentine service are undoubtedly numbered. Their eventual retirement will further reduce the world's population of operational examples. While Ecuador is believed to have dispensed with its last examples, Peru and India are believed to retain small fleets, though their exact status is open to conjecture. The RAF's five PR.Mk 9s, two T.Mk 4s and two B.Mk 2(TT)s are to fly into the 21st century, possibly until 2005. These recent views show the last of the surviving Argentinian aircraft prior to the grounding of B-111 in late 1998. Of note is the general lack of markings on the aircraft, other than a small flag on the fins. Other forms of identification were seemingly abandoned in the mid-1980s.

tance, to operate a force, albeit a shrinking force, of Canberra aircraft for the 15 years of the embargo, which was partially lifted in 1998.

On 26 June 1985, a major deployment was made to Mar del Plata for anti-aircraft and low-level night bombing exercises, the latter with the aid of flares. These took place at the Mar Chiquita range, near the base of the same name. This was the last major exercise involving the Canberra until 1989, as the problems of the aircraft's serviceability increased. On 17 April 1989, three bombers were deployed to Patagonia to take part in Operativo Chispazo, undertaking photo-reconnaissance missions for the Comando de Operaciones Aéreas. During this exercise, in which other FAA units took part, the Canberra squadron successfully completed its tasking, PR having become the Canberra's main role, for which F95 and RMK-60 cameras were fitted.

Spares supply problems and a shrinking budget finally led to the deactivation of the Canberra squadron on 15 November 1990, though there remained two crews trained on the type and its mission. On 3 December these crews were ready for action in support of the government in the face of an unsuccessful *coup d'état* by a branch of the armed forces. Then, on 23 March 1992, came the unexpected reactivation of Escuadrón 2 Canberra and the training of new crews. By this stage however, it was proving impossible to have more than three aircraft operational at once. This situation was complicated further by the loss, on 30 March 1993, of another aircraft. B-112 suffered an accident on the runway at Paraná: the damage could have been repaired, but the aircraft was stricken off charge. The aircraft was restored to display condition and became a riverside monument in Paraná City on 7 October 1998.

Inevitably, the end of the Canberra's FAA career was close, but the few remaining

Above and right: B.Mk 62s B-101 and B-109 pose for the camera during 1998/99. Above the prominent blade aerial forward of the bomb-bay on the aircraft nearest the camera, a port for camera equipment, fitted in 1995, may be seen. Towards the end of their career, these aircraft have retained a bombing capability but have been largely confined to a PR role. Note also that the nearer aircraft is not fitted with a chaff/flare dispenser, as seen on the other aircraft.

Bottom: The last T.Mk 64 and the most recent retirement as of late 1999, B-111, rests in the sun at Párana air base.

airframes remained active. On 7 October 1994, during Ejercicio Operativo COA '94 at the Antuna bombing range in San Luis province, Canberra bombers posted the highest score in the bombing competition. New equipment was also introduced. In 1995, the type's 25th year in FAA service, B-109 was fitted with a new camera with a range of some 80 km (50 miles). The same type of equipment was also fitted to B-101 in the following year.

The 40th anniversary of the MS.760 Paris in FAA service and the 30th anniversary of the FAA's air fighting school were marked on 12 November 1998 by a flypast in which the last three Canberra machines (B-101, B-109 and B-111) took part. On 3 December these aircraft made their last flight together, and B-111 was then grounded after falling due for an airframe inspection that was not deemed economically viable.

By 1999 the Canberra aircraft were very much on borrowed time. On 15 March the two aircraft participated in a flypast to mark the withdrawal of the last Douglas A-4B/Cs from FAA service with the V Brigada Aérea, at Villa Reynolds in San Luis province, while on 10 August, to mark Air Force Day, a single aircraft flew over El Palomar Air Base. This was likely to be the last public appearance by a Canberra in 1999 and possibly the last of its career. By this point, only one crew was still trained on the type and a budget ceiling had been set at a further 100 hours flying time. Whether this would allow operations to continue beyond the end of 1999 remained to be seen. Either way, the last bomber of the Fuerza Aérea Argentina has enjoyed a remarkable career in war and peace – another testament to the 'rightness' of the original design of this classic Cold War bomber design.

Juan Carlos Cicalesi and Santiago Rivas

Canberras of the Fuerza Aérea Argentina

serial	variant	service date	RAF identity	(Class 'B' reg'n)	status
B-101	B.Mk 62	20 Nov 70	B.Mk 2 WJ616	(G-27-111)	*in service mid-1999*
B-102	B.Mk 62	20 Nov 70	B.Mk 2 WJ713	(G-27-112)	retired late 1998; to Museo Nacional de Aeronáutica
B-103	B.Mk 62	20 Nov 70	B.Mk 2 WJ714	(G-27-113)	crashed at Paraná, 22 Nov 71
B-104	B.Mk 62	19 Feb 71	B.Mk 2 WH913	(G-27-114)	crashed at Paraná, 13 Aug 82
B-105	B.Mk 62	31 May 71	B.Mk 2 WH702	(G-27-115)	retired late 1998
B-106	B.Mk 62	31 May 71	B.Mk 2 WJ609	(G-27-116)	crashed 4 Dec 79
B-107	B.Mk 62	31 May 71	B.Mk 2 WH727	(G-27-117)	crashed at Paraná, 1 Jul 83
B-108	B.Mk 62	14 Sep 71	B.Mk 2 WH886	(G-27-118)	shot down 13 Jun 82 by Sea Dart from HMS *Exeter*
B-109	B.Mk 62	14 Sep 71	B.Mk 2 WH875	(G-27-119)	*in service mid-1999*
B-110	B.Mk 62	14 Sep 71	B.Mk 2 WJ619	(G-27-120)	shot down 1 May 82 by AIM-9L from Sea Harrier XZ451
B-111	T.Mk 64	19 Feb 71	T.Mk 4 WT476	(G-27-121)	grounded for overhaul Dec 98; retired
B-112	T.Mk 64	19 Feb 71	T.Mk 4 WT875	(G-27-122)	crashed at Paraná, 30 Mar 93; displayed at Paraná city

Notes: The two attrition airframes ordered in mid-1981 but not delivered as a result of the Falklands conflict were ex-RAF B.Mk 2 WH914 and T.Mk 4 XH583. Converted to B.Mk 92 (Class 'B' registration G-27-373) and T.Mk 94 (Class 'B' registration G-27-374) standard, respectively, both remained in storage at Samlesbury in 1991, though it is thought that the T.Mk 94 may have been scrapped.

The standard four-part code (in this case 'T5+BU') was usually displayed on the lower wing surface. On this He 111 of Wekusta/Ob.d.L. the code replaces the original factory-applied service delivery code/call-sign, HP+AO, clearly legible despite overpainting. 'T5' was primarily the code for AufklGr(F)/Ob.d.L. and when this unit established its own weather reconnaissance squadron, the same 'T5' code was used, but in conjunction with the final letter 'U' to indicate Wekusta.

Luftwaffe Markings: Part 2

Tactical Symbols, Markings and Identification Codes of German Military Aircraft 1918-1945

As the Luftwaffe took the new world war to the Allies, it evolved new markings systems (to which there were numerous exceptions) to identify aircraft and their position within a fighting unit.

The Messerschmitt Bf 109 was to have a much greater influence on the development of fighter markings than was at first realised. Even as the General Staff was seeking simply to adapt the biplane markings system to suit the new machine, a group of young pilots was busy evolving a whole new set of fighter tactics. The first examples of Professor Willy Messerschmitt's monoplane fighter had been sent to Spain for operational evaluation tests late in 1936. By the following spring the first Staffel of Bf 109Bs was in action against Republican forces. And it was 'Legion Condor' pilots such as Werner Mölders and his peers who developed, and perfected, the new tactical fighting formation of four aircraft (a Schwarm) made up of two mutually-supporting pairs (a formation belatedly adopted by the RAF as the 'finger-four', and which subsequently became the norm throughout the world's air forces).

Operationally, this was to make the Stabskette of three machines something of an anachronism. And the increasing use of new four-aircraft Stabsschwarme (later sometimes increased to six) brought with it a whole new system of tactical Stab markings.

The definitive fighter markings ... and the wartime anomalies

With the gradual adoption of the Schwarm (four aircraft) in place of the earlier Kette (three aircraft) as the basic fighter unit, the new-style markings – again based upon the tried-and-tested chevron and bar symbols – now indicated an officer's function within the Stab's ground organisation (e.g. adjutant, technical officer, etc.) rather than the actual position in which he flew when the Stabsschwarm formation took to the air. The composition of individual Stabsschwarme was decided at Geschwader level. Not all Stab officers necessarily flew with the HQ Schwarm, and in these instances its numbers would be made up by appointing ordinary Staffel members of proven worth and experience to fill the gaps. Stabsschwarme could thus often be found with some aircraft bearing Stab symbols, and others sporting normal Staffel numerals. In some Jagdgeschwadern it became customary to indicate each machine's position within the Stabsschwarm formation by incorporating a small numeral within, or alongside, the chevron or other Stab symbol. For example, the Bf 109E of Oberstleutnant Gerd von Massow, Kommodore of JG 2 in 1939-40, not only displayed a full set of (1937-pattern) Geschwaderkommodore symbols, it also underlined its owner's position as leader of the Stabsschwarm by adding a '1' above the horizontal bar forward of the fuselage cross. By the same token, the more unlikely combination of a double chevron enclosing a small '5', as carried by a Bf 109G on the Eastern Front circa 1943-44, would seem to indicate that this particular Gruppenkommandeur – unless the '5' was a 'good-luck charm' carried over from a previous aircraft – only narrowly missed becoming the 'tail-end Charlie' of his own (six-strong) Stabsschwarm!

In fact, as the war progressed, nearly every aspect of the marking system produced its own crop of exceptions and anomalies. A number of Geschwaderkommodoren, the aforementioned von Massow of JG 2, Wilcke of JG 3, and Galland of JG 26, for example, continued to use the earlier form of Geschwader markings well into the war years. (In fact, the 1937-pattern chevron and bars were even to reappear in the closing months of the conflict on such unlikely types as the Me 262 and Ju 87!). Other Kommodoren devised their own styles: Mölders of JG 51 used a combination of new and old, double chevrons with horizontal bars; while JG 27's Gustav Rödel opted for an unusual triple chevron (combined with the positional number '4').

The various other Stab symbols also suffered at the hands of the individualists. Normally applied in black with white edging, these colours were sometimes reversed or, less commonly, replaced by grey or green. Not only the size, but also the angle and style of chevrons differed widely from the official pattern; extreme examples of the latter being provided by JGs 52 and 54. JG 52 also tended to display their

Stabsschwarm position numbers much larger than most other Geschwadern (possibly employing ordinary Staffel number stencils for the purpose); whereas JG 26, upon re-equipping with the Fw 190, elected for a time to do away with chevrons and positional numbers altogether, choosing instead to use the pilot's initials (e.g. 'S' for the Kommodore, Major Gerhard Schöpfel, and 'He' for the Geschwader Ia, Hauptmann Rolf Hermichen), in conjunction with the horizontal bars, to identify individual members of the Stabsschwarm. Some units designed their own symbols (such as that carried on at least two Bf 109Fs flown by Leutnant Jürgen Harder of Stab III./JG 53), whose meaning can now only be guessed at, but perhaps indicating a pilot's special duties – or dual role combining two functions – within the Stab organisation. Other markings – the three vertical bars displayed ahead of the fuselage cross by a bomb-carrying Fw 190 of JG 54, for example – have simply passed into photographic history; not even surviving Geschwader members can now recall what these represented.

Gruppe markings provided their fair share of anomalies too. Few liberties could be taken with the non-existent I. Gruppe symbol; although some units did choose to position their Gruppe badge in the vacant space aft of the fuselage cross. The II. Gruppe horizontal bar also remained constant, and fairly tamper-proof, from 1936 right through until the end of the war. Although, again, some units displayed a Gruppe badge on the rear fuselage in its stead; and at least one, II./JG 51, appears for a while to have placed the horizontal bar forward of both the fuselage cross and the individual aircraft number.

Like certain of the Geschwaderkommodore, however, a number of III. Gruppen showed a preference for the earlier style of markings, in their case the horizontal wavy bar, rather than for its 1937 vertical bar replacement. Several units continued to use the early style during the opening years of the war, but few could compete with III./JG 52 or III./JG 77 for size; their 'wavy bars' at times occupying almost the entire rear fuselage. Other Jagdgeschwadern dutifully adopted the vertical bar for their III. Gruppe, only to resurrect the horizontal wavy bar for their IV. Gruppe when these latter were formed in 1944. Some aircraft, the Bf 109Gs and Ks of IV./JG 53 for example, carried late-war wavy bars indistinguishable from those of the pre- and early war years. Others – such as the Fw 190D-9s of IV./JG 51 – sported examples bearing little more than a passing resemblance to the original design. Indeed, the whole area of IV. Gruppe symbols seems to have been based on personal choice on the part of the Geschwadern concerned. A number remained faithful to the solid disc introduced by JGs 132 and 134 back in 1938, but JG 1 opted for a variation on this theme by using a small circle instead; others displayed a miniature cross.

Discrepancies also occurred in the positioning of individual aircraft numbers. Although there was, inevitably, a wide range of styles of presentation – angular and rounded, narrow and broad, large and small – most Jagdgeschwadern did follow the basic rule by placing their numbers on the side of the fuselage between the cockpit and the Balkenkreuz. But, of course, there had to be an exception; or rather, two exceptions. When the East Prussian-based I./JG 130 exchanged its Arado Ar 68s for Bf 109Ds it decided, for some reason, to move the biplanes' front-fuselage numerals even further forward and now carry them on the engine cowling itself. Redesignated I./JG 1 shortly thereafter, the Gruppe was instrumental in establishing a second unit, also initially housed at Jesau. This latter, I./JG 21, although equipped with the Bf 109D from the outset, displayed its numerals in the old biplane position forward of the cockpit. Here, for the most part, they were to remain until the close of the French campaign in mid-1940, when the two Gruppen were redesignated III./JG 27 and III./JG 54 respectively. And although III./JG 54's markings gradually fell into line with established practice, III./JG 27 continued to carry its numerals – and its Stab symbols – on the engine cowling for many more months to come.

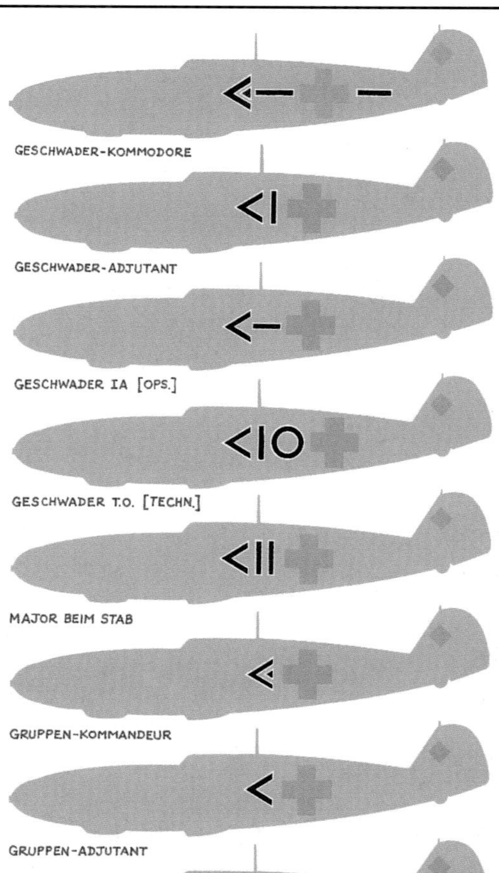

***Left:* Even ex-members of the Gruppe cannot remember what the 'three vertical bars' marking on this I./JG 54 Fw 190 fighter-bomber signified. Note the eastern front theatre band centred behind the cross – a JG 54 'trademark'.**

***Right:* Here is an early example of a Gruppe badge displayed behind the fuselage cross – in this instance, however, it is the badge of II./JG 51 who placed their badge here in place of the normal horizontal bar. (Bf 109E downed in the Battle of Britain.)**

***Below:* Ever the individualists, where II./JG 51 did carry a horizontal Gruppe band later in the war, they placed it ahead of the cross and individual aircraft number (and is believed to have been the only unit to have done so). Note the Geschwader badge on the cowling of this Bf 109G-6/Trop, Italy 1943.**

***Below:* This view of III./JG 52 Bf 109Es in the Balkans during the spring of 1941 shows not only the large 'wavy bar' III. Gruppe marking, but also Balkan theatre markings – yellow engine cowling and rudder, plus fuselage band.**

Luftwaffe Markings: Part 2

Representative and commanding officer's markings

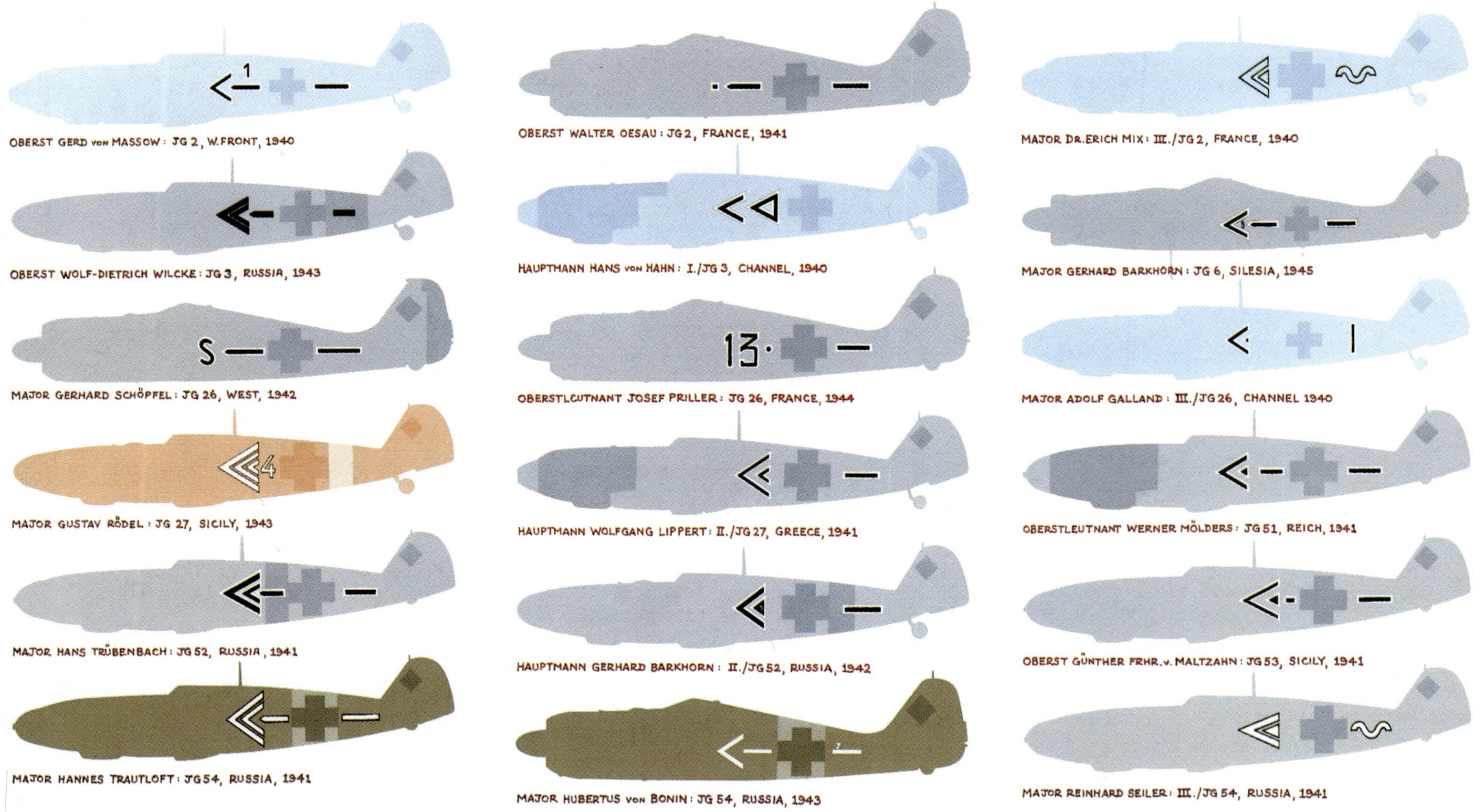

OBERST GERD von MASSOW: JG 2, W.FRONT, 1940

OBERST WOLF-DIETRICH WILCKE: JG 3, RUSSIA, 1943

MAJOR GERHARD SCHÖPFEL: JG 26, WEST, 1942

MAJOR GUSTAV RÖDEL: JG 27, SICILY, 1943

MAJOR HANS TRÜBENBACH: JG 52, RUSSIA, 1941

MAJOR HANNES TRAUTLOFT: JG 54, RUSSIA, 1941

OBERST WALTER OESAU: JG 2, FRANCE, 1941

HAUPTMANN HANS von HAHN: I./JG 3, CHANNEL, 1940

OBERSTLEUTNANT JOSEF PRILLER: JG 26, FRANCE, 1944

HAUPTMANN WOLFGANG LIPPERT: II./JG 27, GREECE, 1941

HAUPTMANN GERHARD BARKHORN: II./JG 52, RUSSIA, 1942

MAJOR HUBERTUS von BONIN: JG 54, RUSSIA, 1943

MAJOR DR.ERICH MIX: III./JG 2, FRANCE, 1940

MAJOR GERHARD BARKHORN: JG 6, SILESIA, 1945

MAJOR ADOLF GALLAND: III./JG 26, CHANNEL 1940

OBERSTLEUTNANT WERNER MÖLDERS: JG 51, REICH, 1941

OBERST GÜNTHER FRHR. v. MALTZAHN: JG 53, SICILY, 1941

MAJOR REINHARD SEILER: III./JG 54, RUSSIA, 1941

Stab anomalies and unidentified markings

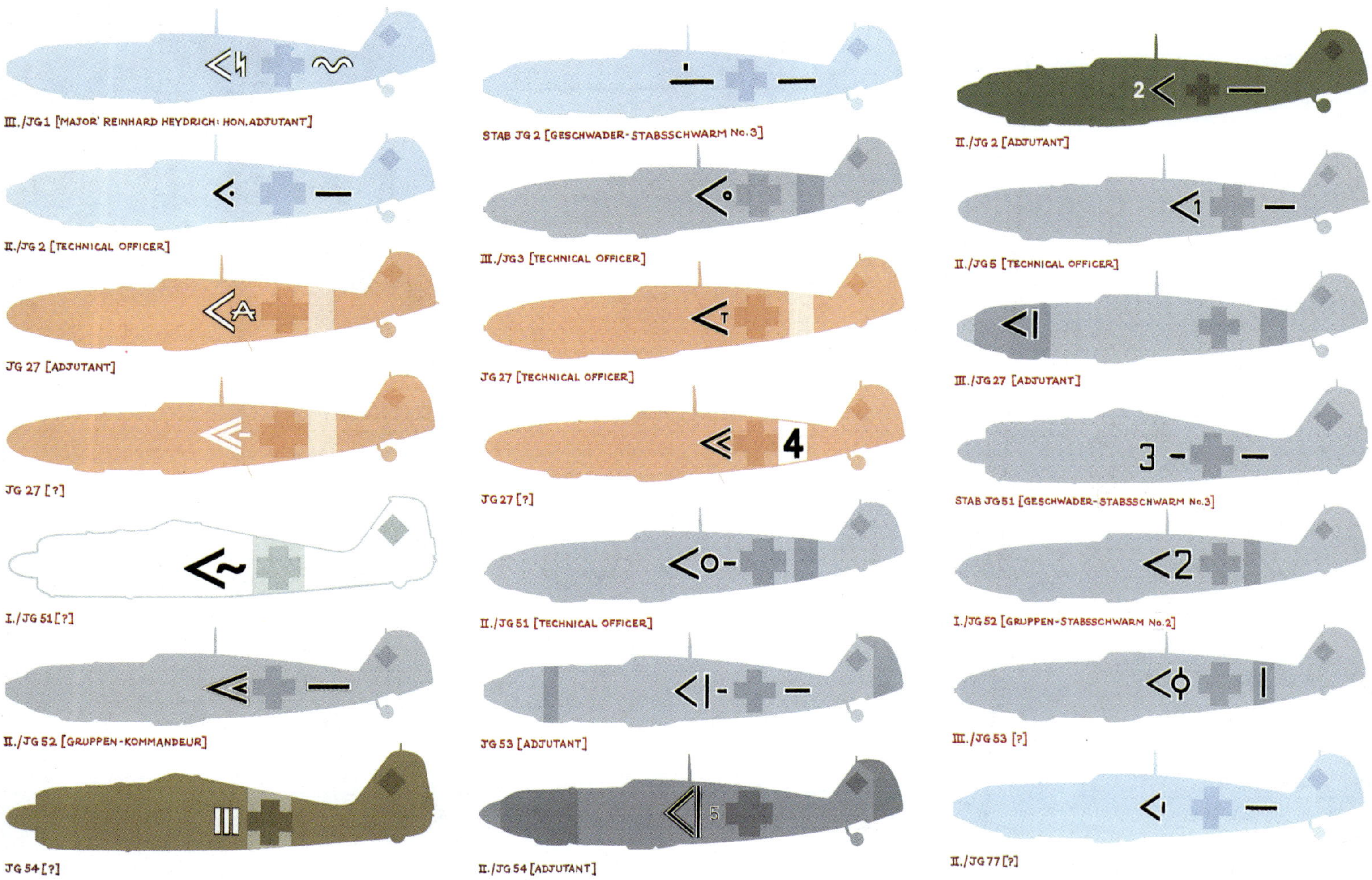

III./JG 1 [MAJOR' REINHARD HEYDRICH: HON. ADJUTANT]

II./JG 2 [TECHNICAL OFFICER]

JG 27 [ADJUTANT]

JG 27 [?]

I./JG 51 [?]

II./JG 52 [GRUPPEN-KOMMANDEUR]

JG 54 [?]

STAB JG 2 [GESCHWADER-STABSSCHWARM No.3]

III./JG 3 [TECHNICAL OFFICER]

JG 27 [TECHNICAL OFFICER]

JG 27 [?]

II./JG 51 [TECHNICAL OFFICER]

JG 53 [ADJUTANT]

II./JG 54 [ADJUTANT]

II./JG 2 [ADJUTANT]

II./JG 5 [TECHNICAL OFFICER]

III./JG 27 [ADJUTANT]

STAB JG 51 [GESCHWADER-STABSSCHWARM No.3]

I./JG 52 [GRUPPEN-STABSSCHWARM No.2]

III./JG 53 [?]

II./JG 77 [?]

Gruppe and individual markings

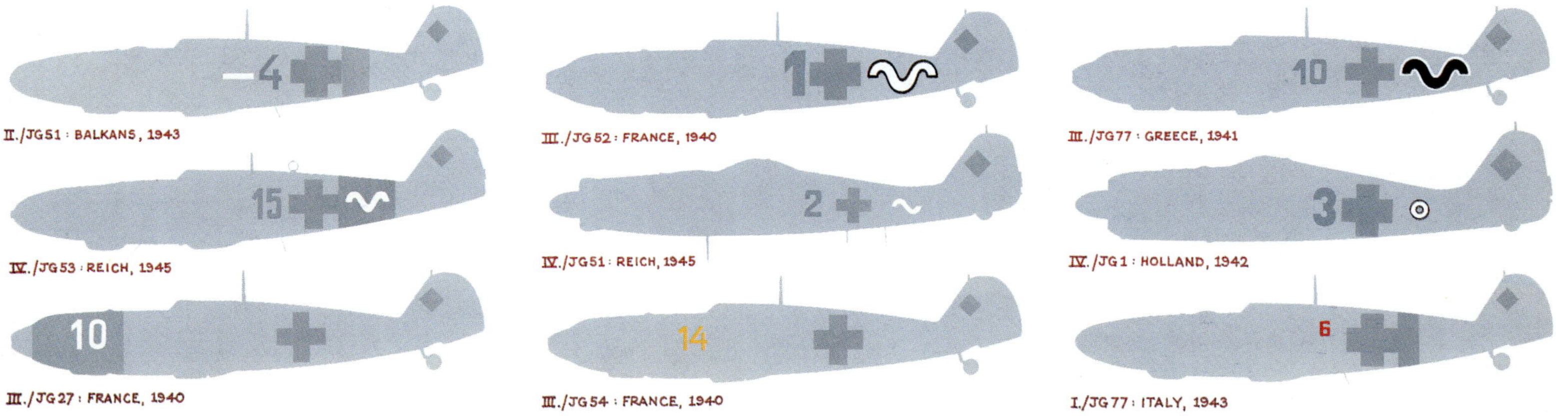

These photographs depict examples of III./JG 27 Bf 109Es on Sicily preparing for fighter-bomber attacks on Malta. Note the individual aircraft numbers carried on the engine cowling – a practice begun when the Gruppe was I./JG 1 pre-war – and the yellow 'Balkan' noses of the aircraft. Note that on aircraft '2' a darker background is used behind the white numeral applied over yellow.

Not unnaturally, the introduction of three separate systems of fighter markings in little more than as many years led to some confusion. This was further confounded after the outbreak of hostilities when operational front-line units, freed of the administrative shackles imposed by all peacetime home-base régimes, began to give full rein to personal interpretation of the basic rules.

But while the Luftwaffe's fighter arm was busily engaged proclaiming its individuality and nonconformity to all and sundry, a quiet revolution had been taking place in the other flying branches of the service. The reorganisation of the Luftwaffe into four Luftflotten (air fleets) early in 1939 had resulted in the scrapping of the original system of three-figure unit designations. On 1 May 1939 a much simplified 'block' system was introduced in its place: units within Luftflotte 1 being numbered 1-25; those within Luftflotte 2 commencing with block 26-50; Luftflotte 3 block 51-75; and Luftflotte 4 block 76-99.

These unit redesignations heralded the inevitable demise of the alphanumeric marking system still employed by all but the Jagdgeschwadern. Henceforth, all operational units other than single-engined fighters would display a standard four-part identity code which would remain in use until the end of the war.

Of course, there were the inevitable exceptions. Many of these were of an individual nature. Others were brought about by wartime developments; the entry into service of reconnaissance Bf 109s, for example, saw these latter discarding the four-part code in favour of single identifying letters or fighter-style numerals. But exceptions notwithstanding, these two systems – fighters and the rest – set the pattern for the whole of World War II.

The standard four-part code ... and its exceptions

An excellent example of a four-part code is shown here (albeit all in black, including the third – individual aircraft – letter 'X') applied to winter-camouflaged Ju 88 of KG 76 (specifically 4. Staffel; final letter 'M') on the Russian Front.

During the war the great majority of the Luftwaffe's operational units – other than the single-seat fighters – displayed a standard four-part fuselage code marking. The first half of this code – comprising a letter/number or number/letter combination to be carried to the left of the fuselage Balkenkreuz – indicated the parent unit (be it Geschwader, autonomous Gruppe or Staffel, special battle-group, etc). This code combination was allotted seemingly at random for reasons of security (see table on the following page).

To the right of the fuselage cross, two further letters indicated – respectively – the individual aircraft and the Staffel (or the Stab) to which it belonged (note that the superfluous Gruppe identification, other than for Stab machines, had now been done away with). And whereas, in most cases, the first pair (unit code) and the last (Stab or Staffel) letter of the fuselage markings would be in black, the third (individual aircraft identity) letter was normally in the Staffel colour of white, red or yellow (or Stab colour of blue or green); or it was black outlined in the appropriate Staffel/Stab colour.

Thus, for example, the two He 111 bombers, coded 'A1+EL' and 'A1+GL', which were among those reported missing over London on the afternoon of 15 September 1940, Battle of Britain Day, both came from the same Staffel. In fact, they were 'E'-Emil and

Luftwaffe Markings

Transport wing KGrzbV 9 (later I./TG3) used the code '9P' Ju 52/3m '9P+DD' is a III./KGrzbV 9 machine.

'G'-Gustav of the 3. Staffel (code letter 'L') of Kampfgeschwader 53 (code combination 'A1').

Like the RAF, the Luftwaffe used the phonetic alphabet as a means of identifying its aircraft (other than single-seat fighters). Within their own Staffel, the above pair would have been identified simply as 'Emil' and 'Gustav'. Within the wider context of the Geschwader as a whole, however – when the particular Staffel (and thus the Gruppe) to which they belonged would need to be specified – they would have been referred to phonetically by their 'last two' as 'Emil-Ludwig' and 'Gustav-Ludwig'.

Upon the outbreak of war a standard Geschwader comprised – or aspired to – three Gruppen, each of three Staffeln. Later a fourth, and sometimes even a fifth, Gruppe was added. This accounted for 21 of the 26 letters of the alphabet which were employed in the fourth-place Stab/Staffel code sequence (the letters I,J and G,O,Q were not used to avoid confusion between them). And thus the complete system was made up as follows:

Geschwader component	individual (third) letter colour	fourth letter code
Geschwaderstab	Blue	A
I. Gruppenstab	Green	B
1. Staffel	White	H
2. Staffel	Red	K
3. Staffel	Yellow	L
II. Gruppenstab	Green	C
4. Staffel	White	M
5. Staffel	Red	N
6. Staffel	Yellow	P
III. Gruppenstab	Green	D
7. Staffel	White	R
8. Staffel	Red	S
9. Staffel	Yellow	T
IV. Gruppenstab	Green	E
10. Staffel	White	U
11. Staffel	Red	V
12. Staffel	Yellow	W
V. Gruppenstab	Green	F
13. Staffel	White	X
14. Staffel	Red	Y
15. Staffel	Yellow	Z

Initially, a few units (notably KG 26) elected to repeat the four-part fuselage code across both upper and lower wing surfaces as had been the rule with the earlier alphanumeric system. But this practice soon fell by the wayside and wing markings, if carried at all, were usually confined to the individual aircraft letter's being displayed outboard of the wing Balkenkreuze on either both – or, more commonly, just the lower – surfaces.

(Incidentally, the component Gruppen of a Geschwader were also allotted a colour code sequence; white, red, yellow and blue indicating I.-IV. Gruppen respectively. This was not utilised as part of the official code marking system, however, but rather was employed as an additional means of identification within the Geschwader; in some units by fuselage bands (see below), but more frequently by the use of coloured spinners, or as different coloured backgrounds to a common Geschwader badge.)

Although employed by a whole range of various units, the four-part code system resulted in far fewer discrepancies and anomalies than were to be found in fighter markings. But, of course, there were exceptions. A number of Zerstörer, night-fighter, Stuka and Schlacht units affected Jagdgeschwader-style Stab chevrons in conjunction with their four-part codes; presumably in recognition of their fighter unit origins. Other autonomous Staffeln, having been allotted their own unit identity code, but not having to comply with the overall Geschwader colour coding rules, sometimes opted for their own colour combination of letters and/or numbers. But there were very few units that actually breached the basic rules. One exception – there always has to be at least one! – was a tactical reconnaissance Staffel based in northern Finland. 1.(H)/32's Fw 189s bore their allotted Gruppe code 'V7' to the left of the Balkenkreuz on the fuselage boom strictly according to the book but, for some reason of their own, each machine's 'last two' behind the cross comprised the number '1' (indicating the Staffel), followed by a white individual aircraft letter, e.g. 'V7+1A' being the Staffelkapitän's 'A'-Anton.

Later in the war the Geschwader code was reduced in size, as shown here on a Ju 52/3m of KGrzbV 800. The individual letter 'K' is the correct colour – white, for 1. Staffel; code letter 'H'. White is also used to outline the Geschwader code, seemingly defeating the object of size reduction – to make it harder for the enemy to read!

The Alphanumeric codes (known codes of major units only)

A1	KG 53 'Legion Condor'
A2	I./ZG 2 (later II./ZG 2)
A3	KG 200
A5	StG1
A6	AufklGr (F) 120
A8	KSG 2 (later KG 102)
B1	TrSt 'Don' (later StöKGr 1)
B3	KG 54 'Totenkopf'
B4	NJSt Finnland (later NJSt Norwegen)
B7	Wekusta 1
C2	AufklGr (H) 14
C3	TGr 5
C5	Wekusta 26
C6	KGrzbV 600
C8	KGzb 323 (later TG 5)
C9	NJG 5
D1	AufklGr (See) 126 (later SAGr 126)
D3	NSGr 2
D5	NJG 3
D9	NJG 7
E3	NAGr 8
E8	NSGr 9
F1	KG 76
F3	KGrzbV 23
F4	SeenotGr 80
F6	AufklGr (F) 122
F7	LLG 2 (later SchleppGr 1)
F8	KG 40
F9	NSGr 5
G1	KG 55 'Greif'
G2	AufklGr (F) 124
G6	TG 4
G9	NJG 1
H1	AufklGr (H) 12
H4	LLG 1 (later NSGr 10)
J2	NAGr 3
J3	NAGr 9
J4	LTSt 290
J6	KGrzbV 500 (later II./TG 4)
J8	NAGr 2
J9	I./StG 186 (later III./StG 1)
K3	SeenotSt 6
K4	Wekusta 4
K6	KüFlGr 306
L1	LG 1
L2	LG 2
L5	KGrzbV 5 (later TGr 10)
L8	NAGr 4
M1	SeenotSt 8
M2	KüFlGr 106
M4	AufklGr 32
M6	SeenotSt 3
M7	KüFlGr 806
M8	ZG 76 (first formation)
M9	NAGr 14
N3	KGzbV 172
N7	SeenotSt 2
P1	KG60
P2	AufklGr (H) 21
P7	SeenotSt 51
Q1	NAGr 1
Q5	Wekusta 27
Q9	I./StG 5
R4	NJG 2
S1	I./StG 3
S2	StG 77
S3	TGr 30
S4	KüFlGr 506
S7	StG 3
S9	ErpGr 210 (later SKG 210; ZG 1)
T1	AufklGr 10 'Tannenberg'
T3	BordFlGr 196
T5	AufklGr (F)/Ob.d.L.
T6	StG 2 'Immelmann'
T9	VersVb/Ob.d.L.
U2	NAGr 5
U5	KG 2
U8	I./ZG 26 (first formation)
U9	NSGr 3
V3	KSG 3
V4	KG 1 'Hindenburg'
V7	AufklGr (H) 32
V8	NSGr 1
W4	SeenotSt 1
W7	NJG 100
X4	LSTt(See) 222
X8	KGrzbV 900
X9	NAGr 11
Y9	NAGr 12
Z6	KG 66
1B	13.(Z) JG 5 (also Wekusta 5)
1G	KG 27 'Boelcke'
1H	KG 26
1K	KG 26
1L	NJGr 10
1M	SeenotSt 8
1T	KGr 126 (later I./KG 28; III./KG 26)
1Z	KGrzbV 1 (later TG 1)
2F	II./KG 28 (later II./KG 54; Stab StG 3)
2H	VersSt 210
2J	ZG 1 (third formation)
2N	ZG 1 (first and second formations)
2Q	NAGr 15
2S	ZG 2 (second formation)
2U	NAGr 13
2Z	NJG 6
3C	NJG 4
3E	KG 6
3K	MSGr 1
3M	ZG 2 (first formation)
3U	ZG 26
3W	NSGr 11
3Z	KG 77
4B	Wekusta 3
4D	KG 30
4E	AufklGr (H) 13
4F	KGrzbV 400 (later III./TG 4)
4M	ErgSchlGr
4N	AufklGr (F) 22
4R	NJG 2
4T	Wekusta 51
4U	AufklGr (F) 123
4V	KGrzbV 106 (later III./TG2; TG3)
4X	NSGr 7
5B	NSGr 10
5D	AufklGr 21
5F	AufklGr (H) 14
5H	NAGr 16
5J	KG4 'General Wever'
5K	KG3
5M	Wekusta 26
5T	KSG 1 (later KG 101)
5W	SeenotSt 10 (and SeenotSt 50)
5Z	Wekusta 76
6A	NSGr 12
6F	TrSt 40
6G	III./StG 51 (later II./StG 1)
6I	KüFlGr 706 (later SAGr 130)
6J	NSGr 8
6K	AufklGr (H) 23
6M	AufklGr (F) 11
6N	KGr 100 (later KG 100)
6R	AufklGr (See) 127 (later SAGr 127)
6W	5./BordFlGr 196 (later SAG r128)
6Z	KGrzbV 600 (also SchelppGr 1)
7A	AufklGr (F) 121
7J	NJG 102
7R	AufklGr (See) 125 (later SAGr 125)
7T	KüFlGr 606 (later KGr 606)
7U	KGrzbV 108 (Later TGR 20)
7V	KGrzbV 700 (later IV./TG5)
8A	LTSt (See) 1 and 2
8H	AufklGr (F) 33
8L	KüFlGr 906 (later 2./SAGr 131)
8M	SchleppGr 3
8Q	TGr 10
8T	KGrzbV 800 (later II./TG 2)
8V	NJG 200
9K	KG51
9P	KGrzbV 9 (later I./TG3)
9V	FAGr 5
9W	NJG 101

Glossary follows...

GLOSSARY

AufklGr	Aufklärungsgruppe – Reconnaissance Wing
AufklGr (F)	Aufklärungsgruppe (Fern) – Long Range Recce Wing
AufklGr (H)	Aufklärungsgruppe (Heer) – Tactical Reece Wing
AufklGr (See)	Aufklärungsgruppe (See) – Maritime Reece Wing
BordFlGr	Bordfliegergruppe – Shipboard Air Wing
ErgSchlGr	Ergänzungsschlachtgruppe – Ground Attack Training Wing
ErpGr	Erprobungsgruppe – Trials Wing
FAGr	Fernaufklärungsgruppe – Long Range/Strategic Recce Wing (replaced AufklGr (F))
KG	Kampfgeschwader – Bomber Group
KGzbV	Kampfgeschwader zur besondere Verwendung – Special Purposes Bomber Group (LIT.) i.e. Transport Group
KGr	Kampfgruppe – Bomber Wing
KGrzbV	Kampfgruppe zur besondere Verwendung – Special Purposes Bomber Wing (i.e. Transport Wing)
KSG	Kampfschulgeschwader – (Heavy) Bomber School
KüFlGr	Küstenfliegergruppe – Costal Air Wing
LG	Lehrgeschwader – Operational Evaluation Group
LLG	Luftlandegeschwader – Air Landing Group
LTSt	Lufttransportstaffel – Air Transport Squadron
LTSt (See)	Lufttransportstaffel (See) Maritime Air Transport Sq.
MSGr	Minensuchgruppe – Minesweeping Wing
NAGr	Nahaufklärungsgruppe – Short-range/Tactical Recce Wing (replaced AufklGr (H))
NJG	Nachtjagdgeschwader – Night-Fighter Group
NJSt	Nachtjagdstaffel – Night-Fighter Squadron
NSGr	Nachtschlachtgruppe – Night Ground Attack Wing
/Ob.d.L	Oberbefehlshaber der Luftwaffe – (attached to, or subordinated directly to, the) Luftwaffe High Command
SAGr	Seeaufklärungsgruppe – Maritime Recce Wing (replaced AufklGr (See))
SeenotGr	Seenotgruppe – Air-Sea Rescue Wing
SeenotSt	Seenotstaffel – Air-Sea Rescue-Wing
SchleppGR	Schleppgruppe – Glider Tug Wing
SKG	Schnellkampfgeschwader – Fast Bomber Group
StG	Stukageschwader – Dive-Bomber Group
StörKGr	Störkampfgruppe – (Night) Harassment Bomber Group
TG	Transportgeschwader – Transport Group (replaced KGzbV)
TGr	Transportgruppe – Transport Wing (replaced KGrzbV)
TrSt	Transportstaffel – Transport Squadron
VersVb	Versuchsverband – Experimental Unit
VersSt	Versuchsstaffel – Experimental Squadron
Wekusta	Wettererkundungsstaffel – Meteorological Sqn
ZG	Zerstörergeschwader – Heavy Fighter Group
(Z)/JG	(Zerstörer)/Jagdgeschwader – Zerstörer Sqn (attached to) Fighter Group

The standard four-part code

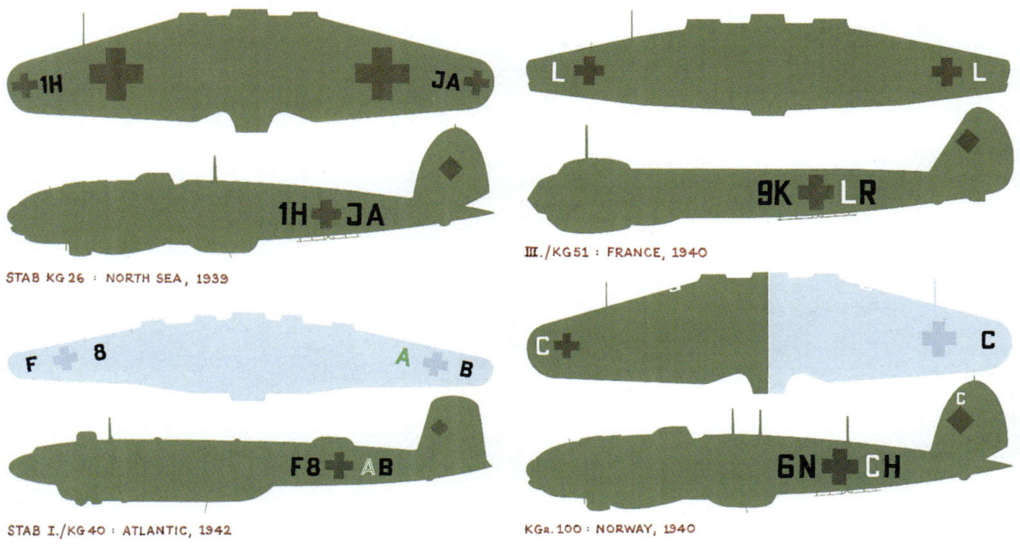

... and some exceptions

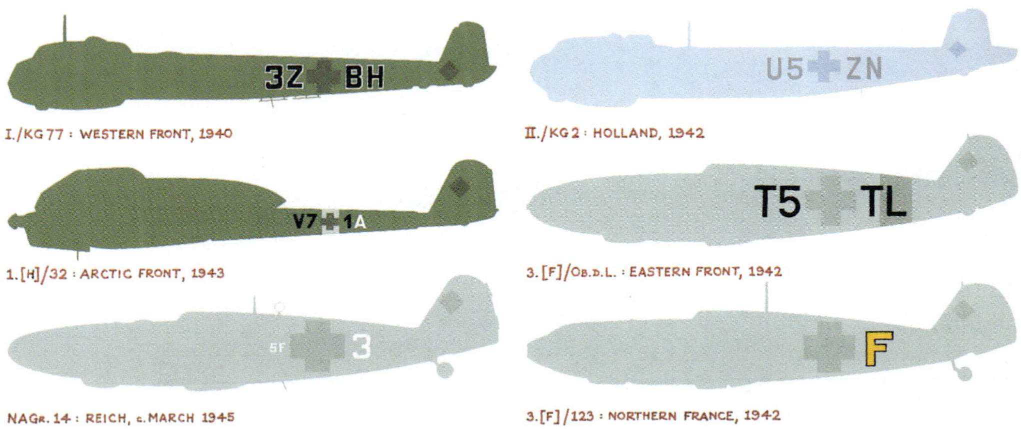

This Ar 196A (probably at Souda Bay, Crete in August 1943) displays a good example of a miniaturised Geschwader code – in this case '7R' of SAGr 125, applied over a white Mediterranean fuselage band. The remainder of the code ('AK') indicates an aircraft of 2. Staffel.

Despite the provision of identification markings, operational conditions soon led to the advent of purely tactical recognition markings. These served a number of purposes, but primarily denoted formation or section leaders, or, in the case of some bomber units, facilitated formating and station-keeping.

Early wartime tactical markings

During the campaign in Poland, Bf 109 and Bf 110 units could already be seen sporting narrow bands, single and double, around their rear fuselages. Introduced primarily at Gruppe level, these are thought to have identified Staffel and Schwarm leaders. At least one Stuka Gruppe displayed a similar band immediately aft of the gunner's position on each of its Stab machines. The double white bars applied to the nose and aft fuselage of some He 59 transport floatplanes operated by KGr.z.b.V. 108 during the invasion of Norway are less easily explained.

The concerted bombing raids mounted by the Luftwaffe against Poland and France also saw the introduction by some Geschwader – principally KGs 2, 55 and 76 – of coloured Gruppe bands which were intended to facilitate aerial formation and recognition. As the Battle of France spilled over into the Battle of Britain the use of such bands became less common. In their place, more Gruppen took to spraying large temporary white bars (single, double or triple) on their aircraft's upper wing and vertical tail surfaces to assist their formating and station-keeping.

The savage, swirling dogfights which have since become synonymous with the Battle of Britain also highlighted the inadequacy of the fighters' means of instantaneous air-to-air recognition; especially in head-on encounters or from directly astern. Consequently, increasing amounts of high-visibility yellow – and, to a lesser extent, white – paint began to be applied to nose and tail by the Bf 109 units on the Channel coast. The exact areas covered seem to have been a matter of personal choice; ranging from a small triangular segment atop the rudder (a practice revived on some late-war Bf 109Gs), to the whole rudder, and even – at times – the entire vertical tail surfaces. Likewise, part of the engine cowling, or all of it – including the spinner – or occasionally the complete forward fuselage, would be painted to match. Less common, but by no means rare, was the use of coloured wing and tailplane tip markings as well. Bf 110 units seemed to favour predominantly white as an aid to recognition, painting either the upper, or entire, nose section to correspond with the narrow rear fuselage bands first sported in Poland. But the long-held belief that red markings were applied during this period, and after, has never been properly substantiated; its origins perhaps arising from that same misleading propensity of certain orthochromatic films to make yellows seem that much darker in tone.

One fighter unit, however – JG 53 – did feature a broad red band around its engine cowlings. But this was not for tactical purposes. The 'official' reason for its introduction was that the Geschwader's badge – the famous Pik-As, or Ace-of-Spades – had become too well-known, and its sudden disappearance from the front line would throw British intelligence into confusion! In fact, it is now believed that the adoption of the red band – or, more accurately, the forced removal of the Pik-As – was a manifestation of Reichsmarschall Göring's displeasure with the then Geschwaderkommodore, Oberstleutnant Hans-Jürgen von Cramon-Taubadel. The validity of this latter explanation would seem to be corroborated both by the violent reaction on the part of the Geschwader members – III. Gruppe went so far as to paint out the swastikas on their tailfins and use the vacant space to display their victory bars – and by the fact that the treasured Pik-As was reinstated when Major Günther von Maltzahn took over from von Cramon in the autumn of 1940.

The first 10 months

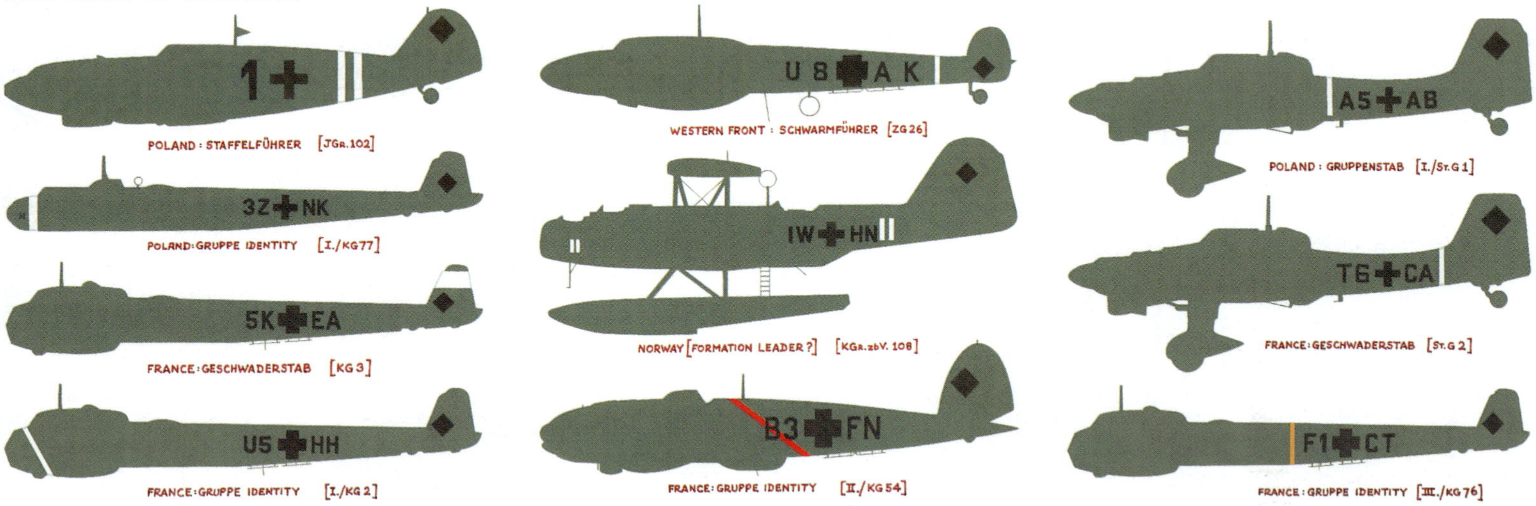

POLAND: STAFFELFÜHRER [JGr.102]
WESTERN FRONT: SCHWARMFÜHRER [ZG26]
POLAND: GRUPPENSTAB [I./St.G1]
POLAND: GRUPPE IDENTITY [I./KG77]
NORWAY [FORMATION LEADER?] [KGr.zbV. 108]
FRANCE: GESCHWADERSTAB [St.G2]
FRANCE: GESCHWADERSTAB [KG3]
FRANCE: GRUPPE IDENTITY [I./KG2]
FRANCE: GRUPPE IDENTITY [II./KG54]
FRANCE: GRUPPE IDENTITY [III./KG76]

The Battle of Britain

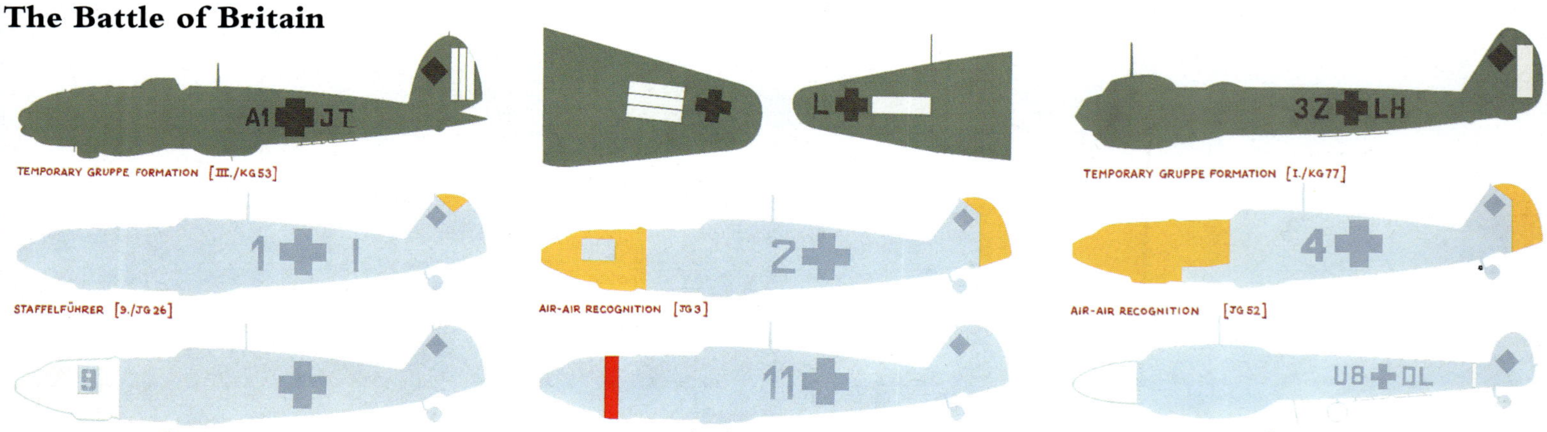

TEMPORARY GRUPPE FORMATION [III./KG53]
TEMPORARY GRUPPE FORMATION [I./KG77]
STAFFELFÜHRER [9./JG26]
AIR-AIR RECOGNITION [JG3]
AIR-AIR RECOGNITION [JG52]
AIR-AIR RECOGNITION [JG 27]
GESCHWADER IDENTITY [JG 53]
AIR-AIR RECOGNITION [SCHWARMFÜHRER ZG 26]

Left: ***These Dornier Do 17s of 1. Staffel/KG 2 carry the white nose bands of I./KG 2 (Geschwader code 'U5'), based at Tatoi, Greece during 1941. Note also the Gruppe badge on the nose of the aircraft and the white Mediterranean theatre fuselage band on the aircraft in the background.***

Right: ***I. and III./KG 76 were initially equipped with Do 17Zs and saw their first action over France and, later, southern England. Just visible behind the trailing edge of the mainplane of this example (downed during the Battle of Britain) is the white fuselage band indicating that the aircraft was allocated to III.Gruppe. Note that the aircraft's fourth letter appears to have been painted over, presumably as a result of a hasty reassignment.***

A different form of coloured trim was brought about by the opening up of new fronts. Three theatres of war – the Balkans, the Mediterranean and the Eastern Front – saw the Luftwaffe's introducing distinctive recognition markings intended to provide a quick and easy means of identifying friend from foe.

Theatre markings

After the brilliant yellow hues of the daylight Battle of Britain had given way to the matt black night finishes of the winter Blitz, the Luftwaffe next turned its attention south-eastwards, to the Balkans. Here, with every likelihood of encountering opposition from Yugoslavian-flown Bf 109s and Do 17s, the matter of aerial recognition was even more critical. Consequently, every aircraft engaged in Operation Marita, the invasion of the Balkans, was ordered to have its engine cowling(s) and rudder(s) painted bright yellow. This was one decree which seems to have been followed almost to the letter. Even the sole surviving four-engined Junkers G 38 airliner – its unmistakable semi-'flying wing' silhouette and biplane tail surfaces hardly constituting a recognition hazard of the first magnitude – received the obligatory yellow theatre trim when pressed into service ferrying mountain troops down to Greece for the forthcoming aerial invasion of Crete. Some Marita participants did go further than was strictly necessary, however, by adding yellow elevators and/or fuselage bands to the stipulated nose and tail markings.

Even before the Balkans campaign had been successfully concluded, the Luftwaffe had begun to 'lean' across the Mediterranean into North Africa. The first fighter arrivals in Libya were the Bf 109s of I./JG 27, each wearing a wide white band around the rear fuselage. This fuselage band, supplemented by white wingtips, subsequently became the accepted theatre marking for the entire North African and Eastern Mediterranean areas. The exact position and width of the fuselage band differed widely between unit and aircraft type, some Ju 87s applying it at mid-fuselage as a white background to emphasize the Balkenkreuz. Similarly, the wingtip markings also reflected personal preferences; being carried both above and below the wings, on the lower surfaces only, or simply dispensed with altogether.

For Operation Barbarossa, the invasion of the Soviet Union in June 1941, the Luftwaffe reverted to yellow recognition markings, carried – as in the Mediterranean – in the form of rear fuselage bands and on the wingtips. Again, wide variations occurred as individual choice became the order of the day. JG 54, for example, also electing to display the band in the mid-fuselage position as a background to the Balkenkreuz on almost all its fighters; Bf 109s and Fw 190s alike. Wing markings were more usually restricted to the undersurfaces only, but on some types – notably Ju 52 transports – they extended inboard far beyond just the tips themselves, sometimes to as much as a third of the span.

Meanwhile, in the west – although, strictly speaking, not theatre markings – the two Jagdgeschwadern retained on the Channel coast, JGs 2 and 26, continued at times to sport some areas of yellow on cowling undersides and rudders to distinguish themselves from the growing numbers of RAF, and later USAF, fighters opposing them.

The choice of white Mediterranean markings was made to conform with those of the Regia Aeronautica already in the theatre. Here a Luftwaffe Bf 110 reconnaissance aircraft of AufklGr(H) 14 is escorted by a Fiat G.50bis of 151ª Squadriglia RA.

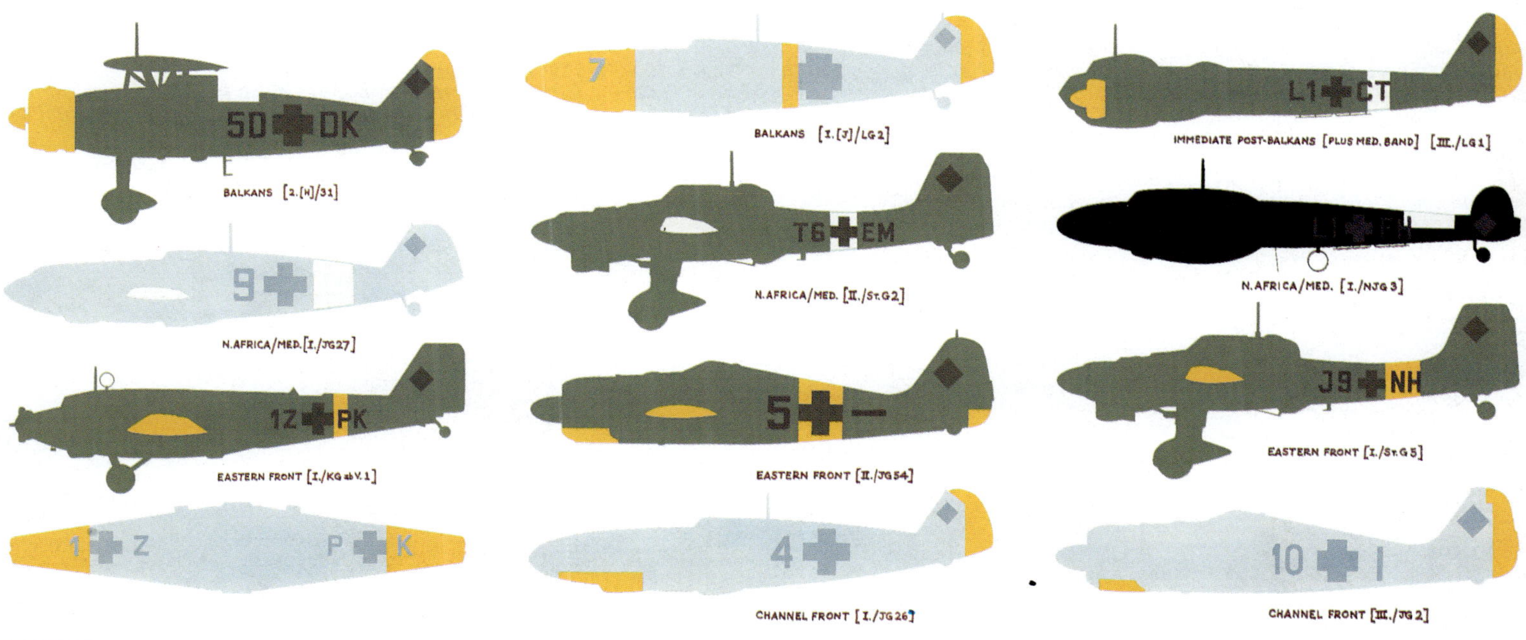

Above: This Bf 109F of II./JG 54 shows the Geschwader's positioning of the Russian front yellow theatre band, as a background to the fuselage cross. The Gruppe's horizontal bar is just visible, aft of the cross.

Left: II./JG 54 retained the yellow marking in the same position after converting to Fw 190s. The Bf 109 in the foreground has its yellow band positioned aft of the cross.

Theatre markings (cont'd)

II./KG 2: SOUTHERN FRANCE, 1942

II./KG 26: SICILY, 1941

I./KG 100: EAST, 1942

II./SKG 210: EAST, LATE 1941

I./ZG 1: EAST, EARLY 1942

Selected Stab and theatre markings

Above: This photograph of a II./JG 54 (note the Gruppe badge forward of the cockpit) Bf 109E was taken towards the end of the Balkan campaign, the aircraft's distinctive camouflage pattern beginning to show through the thin yellow wash of 'theatre colour' on its nose. It is flown by the Geschwader-Adjutant, as indicated by the 'chevron and vertical bar' marking. Of note is the small '5', possibly indicating the adjutant's position within the Staff flight formation.

Below: Here the plain black double chevron of a Gruppenkommandeur is shown on the Bf 109G-4 of Major Wolfgang Ewald, Kommandeur III./JG 3 'Udet', in the Crimea, spring 1943. A yellow theatre band is applied aft of the cross, with a III. Gruppe vertical bar superimposed. The aircraft in the background sports an unusual, and certainly non-standard, Stab marking.

Above: The two vertical bars in this marking indicate a 'Major beim Stab' (Major on the Geschwader staff) and are seen on an Fw 190D-9 brought down on 1 January 1945 during Operation Bodenplatte. The (possibly) red-white-red fuselage bands suggest that the aircraft belongs to JG 6.

Below: In spring 1943, somewhere in the Mediterranean theatre, Hauptmann Ernst Düllberg, Gruppenkommandeur of III./JG 27, favoured white-outlined Kommandeur's chevrons with an additional (non-standard) horizontal bar.

Heinkel He 115B-1
1./Küstenfliegergruppe 406
Sørreisa, Tromsø
1942

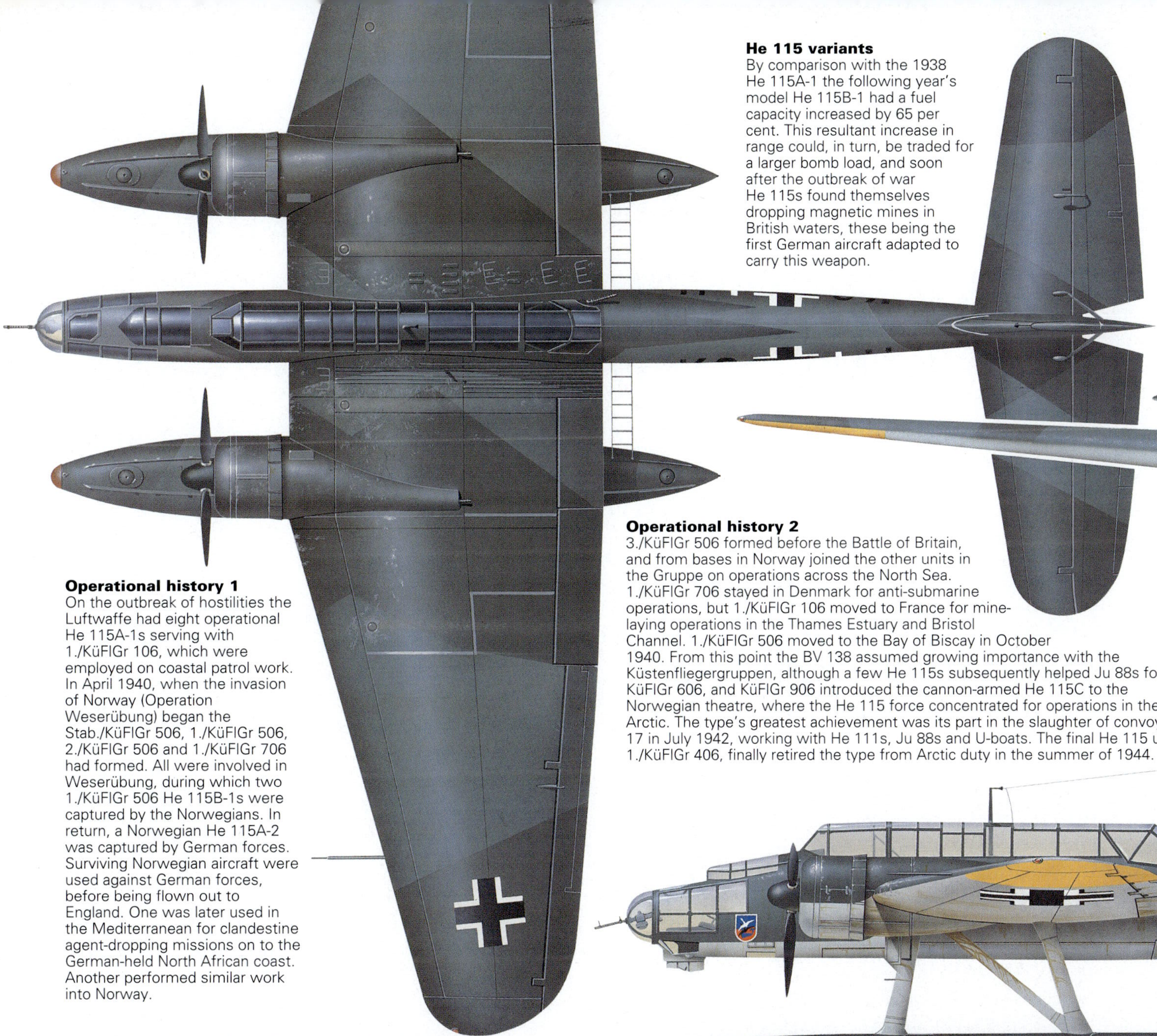

Operational history 1
On the outbreak of hostilities the Luftwaffe had eight operational He 115A-1s serving with 1./KüFlGr 106, which were employed on coastal patrol work. In April 1940, when the invasion of Norway (Operation Weserübung) began the Stab./KüFlGr 506, 1./KüFlGr 506, 2./KüFlGr 506 and 1./KüFlGr 706 had formed. All were involved in Weserübung, during which two 1./KüFlGr 506 He 115B-1s were captured by the Norwegians. In return, a Norwegian He 115A-2 was captured by German forces. Surviving Norwegian aircraft were used against German forces, before being flown out to England. One was later used in the Mediterranean for clandestine agent-dropping missions on to the German-held North African coast. Another performed similar work into Norway.

He 115 variants
By comparison with the 1938 He 115A-1 the following year's model He 115B-1 had a fuel capacity increased by 65 per cent. This resultant increase in range could, in turn, be traded for a larger bomb load, and soon after the outbreak of war He 115s found themselves dropping magnetic mines in British waters, these being the first German aircraft adapted to carry this weapon.

Operational history 2
3./KüFlGr 506 formed before the Battle of Britain, and from bases in Norway joined the other units in the Gruppe on operations across the North Sea. 1./KüFlGr 706 stayed in Denmark for anti-submarine operations, but 1./KüFlGr 106 moved to France for mine-laying operations in the Thames Estuary and Bristol Channel. 1./KüFlGr 506 moved to the Bay of Biscay in October 1940. From this point the BV 138 assumed growing importance with the Küstenfliegergruppen, although a few He 115s subsequently helped Ju 88s form KüFlGr 606, and KüFlGr 906 introduced the cannon-armed He 115C to the Norwegian theatre, where the He 115 force concentrated for operations in the Arctic. The type's greatest achievement was its part in the slaughter of convoy PQ 17 in July 1942, working with He 111s, Ju 88s and U-boats. The final He 115 unit, 1./KüFlGr 406, finally retired the type from Arctic duty in the summer of 1944.

Markings
Most He 115s wore a standard splinter pattern, although often a pale shade of grey was used for Arctic operations. The aircraft wears standard tactical codes 'K6' (for KüFlGr 406), 'L' (individual aircraft) in white (for first *Staffel* in the *Gruppe*) and H for the 1. Staffel. Yellow theatre bands are worn, as the war in Norway was loosely regarded as the Eastern front. This aircraft wears kill markings on the tail.

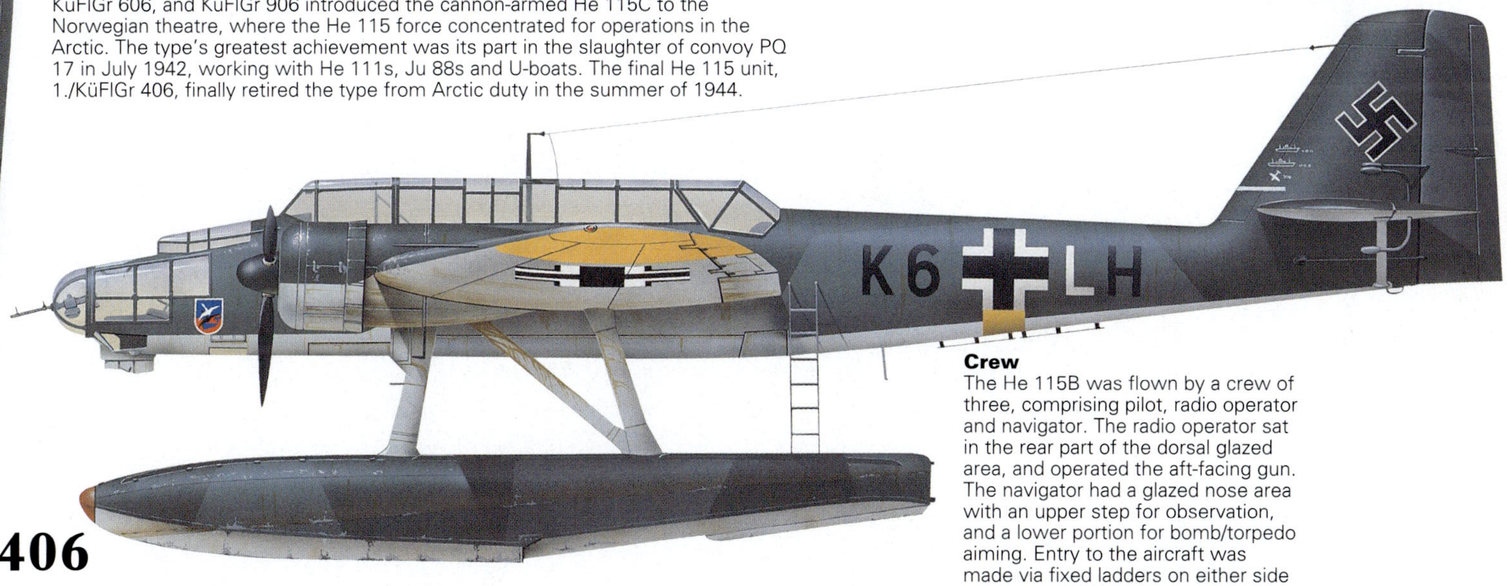

Crew
The He 115B was flown by a crew of three, comprising pilot, radio operator and navigator. The radio operator sat in the rear part of the dorsal glazed area, and operated the aft-facing gun. The navigator had a glazed nose area with an upper step for observation, and a lower portion for bomb/torpedo aiming. Entry to the aircraft was made via fixed ladders on either side of the rear fuselage, stretching between the floats and the fuselage just behind the trailing edge of the wing. The He 115D, of which one example was built, had a fourth crew member to fire a ventral gun.

INDEX

INDEX

Picture acknowledgments

Front cover: A. K. Smith via Marty Isham. **4:** Charles E. Brown/RAF Museum. **5:** Blackburn (three). **6:** Aerospace (two), Blackburn, Napier. **7:** Blackburn (three), Air Ministry. **8:** Blackburn, A&AEE, Hawker Siddeley Aviation (Blackburn Division). **9:** Charles E. Brown (two), Blackburn. **10:** via Simon Watson (two), Air Ministry, Aerospace. **11:** Charles E. Brown/RAF Museum. **12:** Blackburn. **13:** Aerospace. **14:** Charles E. Brown, Aerospace, Royal Navy, via Simon Watson (three). **15:** Blackburn (three). **16:** Shlomo Shapira collection via Shlomo Aloni (SA), Dan Sever via SA. **17:** Giora Epstein via SA (three). **18:** Shlomo Shapira via SA, Giora Epstein collection via SA. **19:** Giora Epstein collection via SA (two). **20:** Giora Epstein collection via SA (two), Shlomo Shapira collection via SA. **21:** Danny Shapira collection via SA, Amos Peleg collection via SA. **22:** Shlomo Shapira collection via SA (two), Amos Amir collection via SA, Giora Epstein via SA. **23:** IDF/AF via SA (two), GPO via SA. **24:** Amos Peleg collection via SA, Giora Epstein collection via SA, via Peter R. Mersky (three). **25:** Shlomo Shapira collection via SA (two), IDF Spokesman via SA. **26:** via Robert C. Mikesh (RCM) (two), USN via RCM. **27:** Aerospace (two), Imperial War Museum, USN via RCM. **28:** via RCM (two), John K. Davis via RCM. **29:** RCM (five). **30-31:** USAF via Marty Isham (MI), **32:** Convair, Convair via Terry Panopalis (TP). **33:** Bruce Chavis via Warren Thompson (WT), Convair, Aerospace. **34:** Aerospace, via Robert F. Dorr (RFD), Convair, AFFTC via TP. **35:** Convair, Harry Gann collection. **36:** AFFTC via TP, via RFD (three), Convair via RFD, Convair via TP. **37:** Convair (two), USAF, via RFD. **38:** Convair (three). **39:** Aerospace, AFFTC via TP, via RFD. **40:** Convair, Convair via TP, Aerospace. **41:** USAF, Convair, Convair via TP. **42:** Lockheed Martin via TP (two), Convair via TP, via Larry Davis (LD). **43:** Convair via Bruce Robertson (two), B. Butcher via MI, via LD, LD. **44:** Lockheed Martin via TP, Preciado via LD, USAF via LD, D. Henderson via MI. **45:** Convair via Bruce Robertson, Aerospace, Convair, NASA Johnson via TP. **46:** R. L. Lawson via MI, B. Maleba via MI. **47:** Convair (six), Hughes via TP, USAF. **48:** MI collection, J. Geer via MI, via Duncan Macintosh (two), via LD, Robert Mock via WT. **49:** Convair (two), Convair via TP (two). **50:** MI collection, Jack Morris via MI, USAF (three). **51:** USAF (three). **52:** via RFD, Budd Butcher via WT, R. Satterfield via MI, USAF, Bill McDonald via WT, Tom Hally via WT. **53:** via RFD, USAF, Bill McDonald via WT, Don Dickman via LD. **54:** via LD, Warren Bodie collection, via LD, Peter Mersky collection. **55:** E. John Raboin via WT, Clair Carling via WT, Charles Morden via WT, Bill Winkeler via WT, USAF. **56:** A. K. Smith via MI (two), Jim Monaco via WT, Don Spering, James Cobb via WT, MI collection. **58:** Aerospace, General Electric, via Chris Knott, via Bruce Robertson. **59:** Geoff Hughes via Chris Pocock, USAF via LD, USAF, MAP. **60:** USAF (two), Aerospace (two). **61:** S. Miller via LD, W. H. Strandberg Jr., via Bruce Robertson, B. Butcher via MI. **62:** Aerospace (four), KLu. **63:** via LD, Chris Ryan, USAF, Mike Hooks. **64:** A. R. Robinson, Chris Ryan. **66:** Aerospace (three), via RFD. **67:** Aerospace (two), René van Wouzik (two). **69:** Don Spering/AIR. **75:** Convair via Robert F. Dorr (two), R. E Kling. **76:** via Terry Panopalis (two), USAF, Don Spering, Convair. **77:** Hughes via Terry Panopalis (six), via Terry Panopalis, Terry Panopalis. **78:** MI, Warren Bodie collection, Don Spering, via Chris Knott, **79:** Bill Curry via RFD, TP collection. **80:** Sperry via TP, Peter R. Foster, USAF. **81:** via Duncan Macintosh, NASA Dryden via TP, Aerospace, NASA via Johnson (two), USAF via TP. **82:** via RFD, Aerospace, Chris Pocock, Robert E. Kling. **83:** Sperry (five), Mike Herring via Chris Pocock. **84:** T. Cuddy via MI, K. Minert via MI, D. Menard via MI, Bill Curry via MI, D. Higbeg via MI. **85:** G. Wildt via MI, MI, via LD, M. Olsted via MI, Major P. Bracci via MI. **86:** via LD, B. Burgess via MI, via LD, B. Malerba via MI. **87:** Taylor via MI, Freeburg, Aerospace, J. Wogstad via MI, MI collection, B. Yocum via MI. **88:** Kaston via MI, MI collection, Malerba via MI, W. M. Jefferies via MI, via Larry Davis. **89:** Barry Miller via LD, Don Spering/AIR, Aerospace, MI collection. **90:** LD collection, Jim Winchester collection, Aerospace/Dave Menard, Aerospace, LD collection. **91:** via RFD, Aerospace, D. Dickman via MI, Aerospace. **92:** F. Retter via MI, Aerospace, Jim Monaco via WT. **93:** Dave Willis collection, Don Spering/AIR (three), Geoff Rhodes via Chris Pocock. **94:** via TP, D. Larsen via MI, MI collection, Don Spering/AIR (two). **95:** Don Spering/AIR (three), via Duncan Macintosh, J. Morris via MI, G. Brown via MI. **96:** via Chris Knott, J. Morris via MI, B. Strandberg via MI, Don Spering via Chris Pocock. **97:** Harry Gann, Freeburger, Peter Greve via Chris Pocock, NASA Lewis via TP, FAA, Aerospace (two). **98:** Aerospace (two), US Navy (USN) via National Museum of Naval Aviation (NMNA)/M. Hill Goodspeed (MHG). **99:** USN via NMNA/MHG, Aerospace (two). **100:** Aerospace (two), via Harry Gann (two). **101:** Aerospace (two), USN via NMNA/MHG, via Harry Gann. **102:** Aerospace, USN via NMNA/MHG (three), USN. **103:** USN via NMNA/MHG (two), via Harry Gann (four), USN. **104:** via Harry Gann (three). **106:** via Alpine Fighter Collection, Yefim Gordon archive. **107:** Yefim Gordon archive (two). **108:** Yefim Gordon archive, via Alpine Fighter Collection. **109:** Yefim Gordon archive (two). **110-129:** Yefim Gordon archive. **130-135:** Jack Kerr via Warren Thompson. **136:** Juan Carlos Cicalesi. **137:** Juan Carlos Cicalesi, BAC. **138:** BAC via Santiago Rivas (two), BAC. **139:** Aerospace (two), via Orlando Piazza/Santiago Rivas (two). **140:** via Salvador Mafé Huertas (SMH) (three). **141:** via SMH (two). **142:** via Santiago Rivas, via SMH (two). **143:** via SMH (two), via Santiago Rivas. **144:** via SMH. **145:** Juan Carlos Cicalesi, Horacio J. Claria via Santiago Rivas (two), P. Steinemann. **146:** Horacio J. Claria via Santiago Rivas (two), Santiago Rivas, Juan Carlos Cicalesi (two). **147:** Santiago Rivas (two), Raul Penazola via Santiago Rivas. **148:** Aerospace. **149:** via John Weal (two), Bundesarchiv, Aerospace. **151:** Bundesarchiv (three). **152:** Aerospace (two). **153:** Bundesarchiv. **154:** Aerospace. **155:** RAF Museum, Bundesarchiv via John Weal. **156:** Bundesarchiv (two), Bundesarchiv via John Weal, Aerospace, via John Weal (two).